MEDIA& SOCIETY

SAGE was founded in 1965 by Sara Miller McCune to support the dissemination of usable knowledge by publishing innovative and high-quality research and teaching content. Today, we publish more than 750 journals, including those of more than 300 learned societies, more than 800 new books per year, and a growing range of library products including archives, data, case studies, reports, conference highlights, and video. SAGE remains majority-owned by our founder, and after Sara's lifetime will become owned by a charitable trust that secures our continued independence.

Los Angeles | London | Washington DC | New Delhi | Singapore

MEDIA & SOCIETY

PRODUCTION, CONTENT & PARTICIPATION

NICHOLAS CARAH & ERIC LOUW

Los Angeles | London | New Delhi
Singapore | Washington DC

Los Angeles | London | New Delhi
Singapore | Washington DC

SAGE Publications Ltd
1 Oliver's Yard
55 City Road
London EC1Y 1SP

SAGE Publications Inc.
2455 Teller Road
Thousand Oaks, California 91320

SAGE Publications India Pvt Ltd
B 1/I 1 Mohan Cooperative Industrial Area
Mathura Road
New Delhi 110 044

SAGE Publications Asia-Pacific Pte Ltd
3 Church Street
#10-04 Samsung Hub
Singapore 049483

Editor: Mila Steele
Assistant editor: James Piper
Production editor: Imogen Roome
Copyeditor: Gemma Marron
Marketing manager: Michael Ainsley
Cover design: Jen Crisp
Typeset by: C&M Digitals (P) Ltd, Chennai, India
Printed and bound by CPI Group (UK) Ltd,
Croydon, CR0 4YY

© Nicholas Carah and Eric Louw 2015

First published 2015

Library of Congress Control Number: 2014949571

British Library Cataloguing in Publication data

A catalogue record for this book is available from
the British Library

ISBN 978-1-4462-6768-4
ISBN 978-1-4462-6769-1 (pbk)

FSC MIX Paper from responsible sources FSC® C013604 www.fsc.org

At SAGE we take sustainability seriously. Most of our products are printed in the UK using FSC papers and boards.
When we print overseas we ensure sustainable papers are used as measured by the Egmont grading system.
We undertake an annual audit to monitor our sustainability.

CONTENTS

COMPANION WEBSITE

This book is supported by a brand new companion website (https://study.sagepub.com/carahandlouw). The website offers a wide range of free learning resources, including:

- **Additional Case Studies** with related activities/discussion points
- **Links** to key websites, articles and YouTube videos
- **Annotated Further Readings**
- **SAGE Journal Articles**: free access to selected further readings

INTRODUCTION

HOW IS MEANING MADE?

For a long time accounts of media and cultural production have used the encoding and decoding of meaning as a basic conceptual schema. This schema places the many moments in the process of mediated communication in relation to one another. Meanings are created or encoded in an institutional and social context, transferred by technical means, and received or decoded in another context. Each moment in the process has a bearing on the other moments, but no moment dominates the others completely. Media are social processes of transferring and circulating meaning. This process matters because it shapes how we understand the world and our relationships with others. How we understand the world organizes how we act in it. The process of sharing meaning is intrinsic to the exercise of power. Those who have the material and cultural resources to control, organize and regulate the sharing of meaning can shape how flows of resources and relationships between people are organized.

In the field of media and communication some accounts, and even some periods, have paid more attention to one moment or another. Political economy and production approaches have been charged with devoting too much attention to the process of encoding and determining that it shapes all the other moments in the process. Audience and reception approaches have been said to too easily equate the audience's active decoding of meaning with having power. For the most part though the media and communication field is interested in both how meanings are created, encoded and disseminated *and* how they are received, decoded and recirculated. In this book we build on this encoding and decoding heritage by taking as a starting point the proposition that we can only understand moments in this process when we consider how they are related to each other. To understand meaning and power we have to understand how relationships between people are shaped within flows of meaning organized by institutions, practices and technologies. The book examines the relationships between powerful groups, the means of communication and the flow of meaning.

This is a book about meaning, power and participation. We use meaning to recognize one another. By making and sharing meaning we acknowledge the existence of others, their lives, their desires and their claims for a place in the world. Meanings are created via the negotiation we undertake with each other to create social relationships, institutions and shared ways of life. The process of maintaining relationships with each other is embedded in relations of power. We relate with each other because we seek to realize our will, our desires, our ways of life, in conjunction or competition with others. The sharing of meaning facilitates both consensus and conflict. Groups aim to generate consensus for the social relationships and institutions they have established, and they generate conflicts and contests that might change social relationships or distribution of resources in ways that might benefit them.

HOW IS POWER MADE AND MAINTAINED?

Media and culture are central to generating consent and organizing participation. For much of the twentieth century, accounts of meaning and power focused on the industrialization of meaning making. One of the key institutions of the industrialized mass society is a culture industry. The culture industry is composed of the range of institutions that make meaning and use it to shape and manage mass populations. These institutions include schools, universities, government policy making, and importantly for this book, industries that produce media and popular culture. We trace the role of the culture industry in creating national identities and facilitating the management of industrial economies. The media and cultural industries that emerged in the twentieth century produced content for mass audiences. This was a result of a range of social, political, economic and technological factors. Mass media like radio, television and print could only produce one flow of content to a mass audience. Everyone in the audience watched the same television programme at the same time, or read the same newspaper. This system suited nation states and industries that demanded mass publics and markets. Nation states sought to fashion enormous populations into coherent collective identities; industrial factories could only produce a standardized set of products for a mass market.

The audience of the industrial-era culture industry was largely conceptualized as being on the receiving end of a standardized flow of meanings. There were a variety of accounts of the audience's role in this process. Some critical and dystopian accounts saw the audience as passive recipients of meaning who were manipulated by the powerful groups that controlled cultural production. The importance of radio, cinema and other kinds of mass media propaganda in the rise of authoritarian fascist and communist societies seemed to demonstrate the power of industrial cultural production to direct enormous populations. More nuanced accounts developed too; these views pointed to the way that the industrial production of meaning shaped the cultural world within which people lived their lives. The media couldn't tell people what to think, but it could tell them what to think about. Media industries played a critical role in creating the frame through which people viewed the world and providing the symbolic resources that people used to fashion their identities. While the audience actively decided what to do with the meanings and symbolic resources they had access to, they had little input into the broad cultural schema in which they lived. The culture industry was a key mechanism in establishing and maintaining this schema. It limited audience participation to a representational frame constructed and managed by powerful interests. These arguments were powerful because they articulated how the media controlled populations even as they were actively involved in decoding and circulating meaning.

Over the course of the twentieth century, arguments developed that accounted for the active participation of audiences in the reception and circulation of meaning. Some of these accounts were functionalist and instrumental. They sought to explain to states or corporations how the management of populations depended on more than just creating and disseminating meanings. They also had to work to fashion the social contexts within which individuals interpreted and decoded meanings. Other accounts have been much more celebratory: they saw the audience's capacity to interpret meanings as proof that the culture industry couldn't exert as much power over populations as critics claimed. Audiences were always free to decode and create meanings offered by the culture industry. These accounts focused on the creative capacity of audience members to resist, rearrange and reappropriate mass-produced meanings to their own identities, wills and worlds. With the rise of interactive media technologies from the 1990s onwards, these celebratory accounts took on a life of their own. If the 'problem' with the industrial culture industry was the way it thwarted participation and relegated audiences to the reception and interpretation of pre-made meanings, then interactive technologies offered a solution. The audience could actively participate in the creation of meaning. This book considers several important rejoinders to these claims.

CONCEPTUAL MAP

A series of key ideas form a map for the arguments in this book. We begin with two foundational concepts: **meaning** and **power**.

Meanings are the elementary building block of human communication. Humans use meanings to express their perceptions, intentions, feelings and actions. Meanings take shape in language, images, gestures and rituals. They indicate how we make sense of ourselves, each other and the world we live in. We use meaning to recognize one another. By making and sharing meaning we acknowledge the existence of others, their lives, their desires and their claims for a place in the world. Meanings are created via the negotiation we undertake with each other to create social relationships, institutions and shared ways of life.

Power is the ability to realize your will against the will of others. Relationships between people are characterized by struggles over material, economic, political, symbolic and cultural resources.

Making and maintaining **power** depends in part on the capacity to control **meaning**. In any human society, relationships can be observed between powerful groups, the means of communication and the flow of meaning.

Three concepts are useful in examining the relationship between meaning and power: **ideology**, **hegemony** and **discourse**.

(Continued)

3

(Continued)

Ideology is a framework of ideas upon which people make decisions and act. Critical studies of media and communication have often examined ideology in order to demonstrate how powerful groups construct frameworks of meaning that cohere with their interests.

Hegemony is a cultural condition where a particular way of life and its associated ideas, identities and meanings are accepted as common sense by a population. Groups are hegemonic when their ideas seem natural, inevitable and common sense. Groups have to work at achieving and maintaining their hegemonic status.

Discourse refers to a system of meanings and ideas that inform the rules, procedures and practices of a society and its institutions. Discourses affirm some people and their practices, and discourage others. They mark out some ways of life as acceptable and others as unacceptable.

Exercising **power** – by producing and managing ideologies, hegemonies and discourses – depends in part on the capacity to control the creation of **representations** and **identities**.

Representation is the social process of making and exchanging meaning. People use media to construct a view of reality. How people understand the world organizes how they act in the world.

Identity is produced by representations, and is the process of locating ourselves within the social world and its power relationships. We do this by drawing on the representations and discourses available to us.

During the twentieth century, the process of constructing **representations** and **identities** was organized in a mass **culture industry**.

The culture industry is composed of the range of institutions that make meaning and use it to shape and manage mass populations.

The culture industry employs a class of **professional communicators** whose job is to make and manage meaning.

Over the past generation parts of the culture industry have become **interactive**. In addition to making and disseminating meanings to mass **audiences**, the culture industry relies on the **participation** of audiences in the production and circulation of meaning. Audiences receive, decode, circulate and create meanings. Audiences are also subject to mass **surveillance**. The culture industry invests significant resources in watching and responding to audiences. The contemporary culture industry exercises **power** by relying on **interactive** technologies to watch, organize and control the **participation** of audiences.

WHAT DOES TODAY'S CULTURE INDUSTRY LOOK LIKE?

The mass culture industry of the twentieth century still exists. Every day people all over the world watch television, listen to the radio, read news, go to the movies and see advertising on billboards as they travel through the city. Arguments about the capacity of the culture industry to shape shared ways of life, and the role that audiences play as active participants in that process, still matter. The development of interactive technologies has dramatically extended the role the culture industry plays in organizing everyday life. The emergence of an interactive culture industry is embedded within the development of a global, networked and informational form of capitalism. Just as the mass societies of the twentieth century used mass media to fashion mass collective identities and mass markets, the networked and flexible economy of the twenty-first century seeks adaptable identities, niche markets, and fragmented and asymmetrical flows of content. A flexible economy based on the mass customization of goods, services and experiences is interconnected with a culture industry that can produce multiple identity-based audiences on-demand. If the industrial economy of the twentieth century created one kind of product for a mass market, the flexible economy of the twenty-first century can create many customized products for many niche markets at once. A mode of production that can cater to niche lifestyle groups is interconnected with the development of a media system that can simultaneously fashion, target and manage multiple identities.

The twentieth-century culture industry was criticized for its disciplinary forms of representational control, limiting the range of symbolic and cultural resources audiences had access to, and thereby containing the extent to which populations participated in the creation and circulation of meaning. The interactive culture industry appears to dramatically open up the space within which ordinary people can make and circulate meaning. Where the twentieth-century culture industry's mode of control could be explained in a representational sense – captured in Lasswell's (1948) formula 'who says what to whom in what channel with what effect' – the interactive culture industry of today adds participatory and reflexive modes of exercising power to the mix. In this media system, telling audiences what to think about is augmented with giving them constant opportunities to express themselves within spaces and processes where the culture industry can track, channel, harness and respond to those expressions. Where once the culture industry might have acted to thwart audience participation by limiting who can create and circulate meaning, today's culture industry works to stimulate audience participation in meaning making. What celebratory accounts of audience participation often miss is that the culture industry's method of making and managing populations has enlarged to include participatory and responsive techniques. These forms of control operate by getting audiences to interact within communicative enclosures where their meaning making can be monitored, channelled and harnessed. Today's culture industry is far more permissive and participatory, but is also more responsive and deeply embedded into everyday life.

HOW DO INTERACTIVE MEDIA UTILIZE AND STRUCTURE OUR PARTICIPATION?

Think of the differences between television and smartphones. Television is emblematic of the mass culture industry, the smartphone illustrative of the networked culture industry. Television beams one stream of images into the homes of a population. Those populations watch television each morning and evening. They make sense of the world via a flow of images created by professional communicators who control who gets to speak and how the world is represented. Television offers a representational mode of control; it uses a flow of images to shape the identities and practices of populations. With television everyone sees the same flow of meaning at the same time. Broadcast television watched by mass audiences fashions collective identities and ways of life. The smartphone also distributes a continuous flow of images to audiences. This flow of images though is dynamic. Each audience member sees a different flow of images depending on their identity and place in social networks. The flow constantly adapts to their preferences and practices. It is a mixture of content created by professional communicators, cultural intermediaries and peers. Nearly all of the content we see on our smartphone flows through networks made and maintained by the culture industry. Most of the content that flows through our smartphone is either produced by professional communicators or circulated within networks where professional communicators monitor us. Furthermore, we carry our smartphones with us all day. They passively monitor our movements through the city, our interactions with friends, and increasingly our expressions, moods and bodies. Television was confined to the home, was often switched off, and could only distribute meaning (it couldn't watch or listen to us). The smartphone is constantly attached to our body, always on, sends and receives meaning, and enables data collection. The smartphone offers a far more flexible, responsive and continuous way of communicating with, monitoring and managing populations. Where television was central to the fashioning of mass collective identity, the smartphone facilitates the production and positioning of identities within networks.

Interactive media have been celebrated for the way they afford new forms of participation, and critiqued for the way they dramatically extend the use of information and meaning in the management of populations. Audience participation is integral to this culture industry, but this doesn't mean that audiences have more power or control. The more audiences participate, the more they contribute to the development of networks, flows of meaning and collections of data that enable the more reflexive and real-time management of populations. We examine throughout the book how news, politics, brands and popular culture rely on the participation of audiences. We aim to develop an account of how the interactive culture industry's construction of opportunities for audiences to speak is interrelated with the enormous investment in technologies that enable it to watch everyday life.

WHAT IS THE ROLE OF PROFESSIONAL COMMUNICATORS IN THE EXERCISE OF POWER?

In this book we are particularly interested in the work of professional communicators in managing meaning and power. In an interactive culture industry the work of professional communicators extends beyond the production of meanings as content to include managing the participation of cultural intermediaries and audiences in the ongoing circulation of content. Professional communicators don't just create and disseminate meaning; they manage other meaning makers, and they watch and respond to populations in real time. Professional communicators are also involved in creating and managing social and urban spaces within which they organize audience participation. Rather than just create meanings and representations distributed to mass populations, professional communicators manage open-ended processes of meaning making in complex and diffused networks. Professional communicators need to be highly skilled at using their communicative, strategic and analytical abilities to create and maintain social relationships within structures controlled by the culture industry. The work of professional communication involves more than just the creation of persuasive or valuable content: it extends to managing space, populations and complex communication processes.

Many of the theoretical ideas in this book are critical ones. Critical theories are concerned with how the construction of social relationships is embedded in the exercise of power. Critical theories offer arguments about the role media play in shaping our social world. They account for individual, institutional, social, cultural, historical and technological dimensions of media and communication. These arguments are valuable to us as scholars, citizens and professional communicators. Understanding how uneven flows of symbolic resources shape the world we live in makes us more critically informed citizens. It helps us to reflect on how we might be heard in meaningful ways, how we might participate in communicative activities that materially shape the world we live in, and how we might create new kinds of social relationships. The best professional communicators have a nuanced understanding of the place of media in broader social, cultural and political processes. Being a leading professional communicator involves more than just having communicative skills to use technologies to produce compelling content or create interactive platforms that harness audience participation. Professional communicators also need the critical and analytical ability to determine how they contribute to the construction of social relationships and structures. Critical theories prompt us to think carefully about human experience and relationships. Even if you aren't especially interested in the consequences of using meaning to exercise power, critical theories offer ways of developing a detailed understanding of the relationship between meaning and power. This relationship is the business of professional communication. Understanding this relationship can inform a variety of strategic ends. Critical ideas aren't ones that think power is bad or the media are bad, or that attempt to unmask and reveal how things really are. Power is important; it governs how we get things done in the world. Critical theory doesn't attempt to imagine a world without power, but rather to examine how power is organized. Critical ideas are ones that pay attention to how power is exercised and how meaning shapes relationships between people. Power isn't a simple one-way application of brute force; power works through a combination of disciplinary and participatory mechanisms. Populations are easiest to manage when they consent to, and participate in, established power relationships. The best leaders – regardless of their political or personal views about media and power – understand the relationships between meaning and power.

ENGAGING WITH CRITICAL DEBATE ABOUT MEDIA PRODUCTION, CONTENT AND PARTICIPATION

The book is organized in three parts. The first part outlines key conceptual ideas in our study of meaning and power, including: hegemony, discourse, ideology, representation, rituals and the culture industry. We also examine the development of the culture industry in the twentieth century and its transition to a networked and interactive culture industry in the past generation. We conclude this section by examining the work of professional communicators in the contemporary culture industry. In the second part of the book we examine several modes of production within the culture industry – news, politics, identity, branding and popular culture. Throughout this section we examine the shift from the production of mass audiences and identities in the twentieth century to the management of a network of flexible identities and audiences in the contemporary culture industry. In the final part of the book we consider in detail the forms of participation and control central to the ongoing development of the interactive culture industry. In the conclusion we examine how the contemporary culture industry assembles a network of representational, participatory and responsive modes of control. Meaning is fundamental to the exercise of power, but not only because it tells us what to think about. By taking part in networks of meaning making we make ourselves a visible participant in the power relationships the culture industry manages.

ENGAGING WITH ACADEMIC DEBATE

Throughout the book we cite work by scholars in the field, and we encourage you to go and read their work to extend your thinking, consider our point of view, and come to a view of your own. This book, like all academic publication, is not a stand-alone work. It is situated in a broader academic debate. Understanding how academic publication works and how to read journal articles will help you make better sense of the ideas and arguments in this book.

Journal articles and academic publication

A journal article is a research study or essay where academics present their research findings and arguments to a scholarly field. To be published in a journal an article must be blind peer-reviewed. This process ensures that research is appropriately evaluated by experts in the field before it can be published. When an academic submits an article for publication in a journal the editor anonymizes the submission and sends it on to two or more experts in the field. Those experts read the submission and respond to the editor with their comments about the article and recommendation on whether or not it should be published. The reviewers make two judgements. The first judgement is about the rigour of the article's argument, method and findings. The article must conform to the scholarly norms and principles of the field. The second judgement is about the contribution of the article to debate. The article must offer some new ideas and insights and help to further important debates in the field. Journals are a forum for iterative and ongoing debate. Consider a journal article as being one part of a larger conversation. Whatever journal article you are reading will be responding to what scholars in the field have had to say in the past, and in time – if the article is a good one – future scholars will respond in turn. The purpose of academic journals is to animate a structured conversation between researchers where they share their research and arguments in a considered and rigorous way.

Journals are the bedrock of any academic field. They are the institution through which experts construct and manage the production of ideas that shape and define their fields. They are the forum where ideas and debates are mapped out, critiqued, presented and debated. Without journals there would be no shared mechanisms for academics to disagree with each other, challenge each other and support each other in a constructive way. Good journal articles are those that can articulate a problem that matters to the field, challenge current thinking in a productive way, and map out a rigorous method, findings and argument that suggest a way forward for those in the field. Journal articles that have been published recently give you an insight into the debates that matter right now in the field. But that doesn't mean that older articles aren't still relevant and important. If you find a debate or idea in an older article that is useful and relevant, then use it. The important thing with using older articles is that you consider how to contextualize it within contemporary debates. Look for who has cited, engaged with or extended the debate since the article was published.

HOW TO READ A JOURNAL ARTICLE

Not all journal articles are the same, but they do all tend to have some fundamental elements. If you understand what these elements are, how to find them and why they matter it will help you to understand articles, evaluate their quality, read more efficiently and incorporate their arguments into your own writing.

There are five elements you should aim to identify in any journal article you read:

- a significant question or claim
- a position in the academic debate
- an explanation of the research method or approach
- a presentation of the findings and argument
- a statement of the implications and contributions of the research study.

QUESTION OR CLAIM

The first element to look for when reading a journal article is the main question the author poses or the main claim they are making. This question or claim effectively sets the frame through which the author wants the reader to judge their writing. The editor of the journal, when agreeing to publish the article, would have decided that the question or claim is an important one and that the author clearly demonstrated it in their writing. You will usually find this claim in the first section of the article. Once you've found it, use that claim as the

(Continued)

(Continued)

foundation upon which the article is built. The author will also explain why their question or claim is significant and who or what it matters to. The significance might be presented in relation to the academic field, a policy or governance problem, or events that matter to politics, cultural life or an industry.

POSITION IN THE ACADEMIC DEBATE

The presentation of a question or claim is interrelated with a review of the relevant academic literature. In some articles this will be presented as a clear literature review section; in other articles the first few pages of the article will weave together the author's claim and question, with an analysis of relevant literature. This might not be titled 'literature review' but come under several themed subheadings.

The purpose of this section of a journal article is not just to summarize the debate, but to organize it and frame it. A good literature review will set out competing perspectives or clearly articulate shortcomings and limitations in the current scholarly debate. The purpose is to demonstrate how the author's question and claim will respond to significant debates in the literature. Sometimes the author will claim to fill a gap in the current debate by adding some now evidence; in other cases the author will claim to correct or refute a significant assumption or claim in the literature by providing confounding evidence or demonstrating how new developments change previous understandings.

The academic literature is always under construction: journal articles don't aim to end the debate with a final piece of definitive knowledge, but rather contribute to the ongoing effort to push debate forward. The engagement with the literature at the start of a journal article aims to position the article in relation to those debates. Sometimes the literature review will position the study's contribution as an 'applied' one, other times it will be 'conceptual'. An applied contribution is where existing ideas from the literature are taken and applied or tested in a new context. For example, if research has mainly been conducted with people in one setting (like a city), new research might test those ideas by examining people in a different setting (like a rural area). A conceptual contribution is where existing ideas from the literature are reformulated, or new ideas are proposed, as a way of contending with new developments in technology, society or culture.

At the end of this section of a journal article you should have a clear idea of the debate the author is engaging with, why that debate matters and how they intend to contribute to it. As a reader the literature not only familiarizes you with a debate but also offers you some reference points for your own research. Often, a good way to target your reading is to go out and engage with the authors that others are engaging with. If you find a journal article about a topic or issue that is relevant to you, then check out who the author is engaging with and follow their lead. If you read authors that are citing each other then you are more likely to find a coherent conversation to ground your own thinking and writing within.

EXPLANATION OF RESEARCH METHOD OR APPROACH

Once an author has explained their question and claim, and why it matters, and then situated it within current academic debate, they will then set out how they went about doing their research. This is where they explain how they will make an original contribution to the literature.

The media and communication field crosses a broad range of approaches. Some journals have a very systematic way of presenting research methodologies. These journals tend to come from more empirical disciplines that follow a scientific method like psychology or sociology. A journal article might label its methodology section clearly and offer a sustained and clear explanation of the methodological approach and often also an evaluation of its strengths and limitations.

Many journals also come from humanities traditions. In these articles the explanation and justification of the methodology may be more implicit, but it will always be there in some form or another. In its most basic form the author will provide a paragraph that explains how they did what they did and who has used similar methods to address similar questions.

A quantitative and scientific methodology might involve a descriptive or experimental survey for instance, where the author would clearly explain and evaluate the validity of the constructs used in the survey, the sample size and the analytic procedures. A discourse analysis might explain the range of texts selected for analysis and the analytic procedure used to make sense of them. An interview study might explain the sample of people interviewed, the range of questions asked, how the interviews were analysed and what claims were possible from them.

Sometimes a journal article will be making a critical and conceptual argument, and therefore won't necessarily have empirical evidence or methodology. In these articles though there is still a method in the sense that the author will explain clearly how the argument is structured and what material it will engage with: instead of empirical material like interview, textual or survey data, it might be a scholarly debate or conceptual framework that the author is framing, critiquing and contributing to.

In the media and communication field there are no right and wrong methods, or methods that are better than others. What matters is that the author clearly explains how they did their research and how that approach was appropriate for responding to the question they are posing or making the claim they are making. You need to understand the methodology in order to understand the basis on which the author will go on to make their arguments. You might also find the methodology useful for developing your own research projects and approaches.

PRESENTATION OF FINDINGS AND ARGUMENT

The first three elements – the problem, literature review and methodology – clearly set out what the article is about, why it matters and how the research was done. From there the author moves on to present the findings and argument from the research. This is where the author makes their contribution to the literature by presenting original material and arguments. These sections are sometimes called 'results' and 'discussion', other times they are organized under themed subheadings. In more empirical articles the results will be presented separately and then discussed. This is common in journal articles presenting survey research for instance. In other articles the results and analysis will be woven together; this is more common in qualitative and critical research articles. The structure of this section often offers a useful conceptual framework for your own writing. In the findings and argument, scholars usually present concepts that you can use to structure and inform your own arguments, analysis and research.

(Continued)

(Continued)

STATEMENT OF IMPLICATIONS AND CONTRIBUTIONS OF THE RESEARCH STUDY

A journal article will conclude with an explanation of the implications of the research, its limitations, and suggestions for further research. The author will explain what the consequences and significance of the research findings are to the scholarly debate. They will then map out what they think the next steps in research on this problem should be. You can use the conclusion as a launching point for your own arguments, taking up the questions and challenges authors arrive at in their journal articles as a starting point for your own thinking and writing. As academics read each other's journal articles they look to the implications and suggestions of previous publications and use them as the basis for formulating their next research projects and arguments.

PLACING A JOURNAL ARTICLE IN BROADER DEBATE

You should also aim to place a journal article within the broader academic debate. The first way to do this is to go to the journal article's reference list and locate other articles that extend ideas in the article which are of use to you. Do this in conjunction with reading the article. Where the author makes a claim that you find compelling or useful and then cites it in reference to another author, go to that author's work and read it too. The second way to place the journal article in the larger debate is to conduct a search to find out who else has cited the article since it was published. Citation is when an article is referenced in another article after it is published. Academics use citation to follow how articles get incorporated into ongoing academic debate after they have been published. Academic publishing is reasonably slow, so you may find that articles don't accumulate citations until two or three years after they have been published. Articles by prominent scholars or articles that are key to debates in the field will accumulate many citations.

The easiest way to find citations is to use Google Scholar. Search for the article you are reading in Google Scholar. When you find it you will see underneath the listing a link that says 'Cited by …' followed by a number. That number is the number of articles that have cited it since publication. Click on that link to go through to the list of articles and search in there for publications that are relevant to you. If there are many hundreds of citations for an article you can click the 'search within existing articles' box to search key terms within those articles citing the original article. If you pay attention to how an article is positioned in the broader academic debate it will help you select a collection of articles that are in conversation with one another. This will help to improve your writing because you will have identified and mapped out a shared conversation between scholars who are already mapping out and contributing to a debate that you can then engage with.

On the companion website of this book, we provide you with a selection of journal articles we've specifically chosen to help you with your study and research. They're free to download and we encourage you to use this 'reading a journal article' guide to help improve your essays and take your studies deeper. Go to study.sagepub.com/carahandlouw and read on!

MEANING, REPRESENTATION AND POWER

THE CREATION AND CONTROL OF MEANING MAKING IS CRITICAL TO THE EXERCISE OF POWER.

* How is meaning made and controlled?

* How does representation work as a social process?

* How is meaning used to exercise power?

In this chapter we:

- Define meaning and power
- Consider how meaning and power are related to one another
- Examine several fundamental accounts of the relationship between meaning and power: hegemony, ideology, discourse and representation
- Overview how media representations organize everyday life.

DEFINING MEANING

Communication is central to human experience. When we are born we are immediately situated in, and gradually socialized into, language and meaning. The language we learn to speak, the culture that informs our view of the world and the ideas we are taught precede our arrival in the world. As we grow up we embody history: clusters or pools of ideas, meanings and practices that have congealed over time. We identify these ideas and practices as societies and cultures.

Communication has an array of affective and material roles to play in how we relate to others, how we imagine our lives and how we get things done in the world. In his history of the idea of communication Durham-Peters (1999: 1) writes, 'Though humans were anciently dubbed the "speaking animal" by Aristotle, only since the late nineteenth century have we defined ourselves in terms of our ability to communicate with one another.' In this book, we are particularly interested in how communication has become central to the development of society, culture and politics since the early twentieth century. In western societies, like the United Kingdom, Ireland, United States, Canada and Australia, communication has become bound up with the production and circulation systems we call 'the media'. Before we get to the media though we must first consider meaning as an elementary building block of communication. And we must examine the role of communication in forming and maintaining social relationships.

By internalizing meanings, practices and ways of communicating we become members of various social groups and cultures. Meanings are resources that we use to generate our identities, negotiate with others and position ourselves within a social milieu. Meanings are never stable, static or fixed. As we use, circulate and share them, we also remake and reposition them. Our societies and cultures then are also not static. They are continually being reinvented and struggled over. Every individual makes some contribution to reshaping meaning as we engage in the everyday process of communicating with each other. As we grapple to make sense of, and shape, our world, we necessarily change the meaning structures and cultural practices we are born into. The meanings and practices that shape us, and that we use to shape our relationships with others and our world, shift throughout our lives. Numerous, often imperceptibly small, shifts result in the networks of meanings changing from generation to generation, place to place and group to group. Culture is a dynamic and living process. Meanings change and grow precisely because the process of communication – perceiving, receiving and decoding; imparting, disseminating and encoding – relies on innumerable small creative transactions between active human beings.

All individuals play a role in making, remaking and circulating meaning. Some individuals and groups, however, have more power than others within the communicative process. The networks of meaning making we live within are not arbitrary or random. People are positioned differently by the power relationships in which they are embedded. These positions impact on the access individuals have to media production and circulation systems. Some individuals have more symbolic, cultural and economic resources to control the production and circulation of meaning. This is by no means to suggest though that communication is a linear hierarchy. Each person who communicates is located in a network of social relationships at a particular place and time. They each have differing capacities to adopt, negotiate or resist the production and circulation of meanings that constitute their lives, identities and social worlds.

The making of meaning is embedded within human relationships. Human relationships are marked by an uneven allocation of symbolic and material resources. Those resources are the basis upon which some individuals are able to exert control over the shape of human societies, cultural practices and the shaping of the material world. In this book we refer to these processes as power relationships. One way individuals gain and maintain power is by using meaning to position themselves relative to others. To do this they create and control systems of meaning production and circulation. Just as meanings are never fixed, so too are power relationships always in a state of flux. Meaning is struggled over as people work at improving their position within networks of power relationships. Gaining access to the means of communication, and even particular meanings, is both derivative of power and a means of acquiring power. Those with power have a greater capacity to make and circulate meaning because they are able to control communication institutions and practices. Sites where meanings are made, and the channels through which meanings flow, are significant sites of struggle. Meaning-production spaces like newsrooms, film and television studios, parliaments, courts, universities and research institutions are sites of struggle where people compete for access and argue over ideas.

To understand why a particular set of meanings circulates at a certain time and place we must examine the power relationships between people. Mapping power and meaning is complex because each is constantly shifting in relation to the other. There is a continual struggle over power in all human groups and a constant realignment of winners and losers. Shifts in power are accompanied by changes in the production of meaning. Mapping the mechanics of meaning production, as with mapping meaning itself, requires careful consideration of the time, place and power relationships in which meanings are embedded.

THE POWER TO INFLUENCE MEANING MAKING

At the outset then we need to examine the relationship between power and meaning. Power does not have the tangibility of an object, yet as human beings we all intuitively recognize its presence. We implicitly know in our day-to-day lives how to act according to the power relationships that surround us. In our homes, classrooms, workplaces, and in public spaces we know that some people are able to exert control over how we act. That control is often subtle, and we willingly consent to power via our actions. Like communication, power is omnipresent, yet it can be overlooked because it seems to be just there. Power is though a crucial dimension of the production and circulation of meaning. When we examine power we pay attention to how ideas are made and circulated, by certain people, in particular settings and moments in time. Power is a slippery phenomenon with numerous definitions. For the purposes of this book, power will be seen as the capacity to get what you want when interacting with others. Max Weber (1978) expressed this best when saying that those with power are able to realize their own will even against the resistance of others. Power is also found in the more subtle capacity to stop conflicts from emerging by preventing oppositional agendas from even developing in the first place (Lukes 1974).

Proposing this definition of power raises three related issues.

- Firstly, what is the relationship between power and social elites?
- Secondly, where does power come from?
- And, thirdly, what is the relationship between being embedded within a power relationship and free agency?

What is the relation between power and social elites?

Discussions about the relationships between meaning making and the media can easily end up sounding like a conspiracy theory in which power elites are seen to manipulate media content to serve their own interests. Studies of media ownership and control, sometimes drawing on the political economy approach to communication, have posited conspiratorial interpretations of media control. These conspiracies more or less argue that powerful groups carefully control the messages and meanings made and circulated in the media. They see an all-powerful media being used to generate 'false consciousness'. While powerful groups might use media to create and circulate their preferred meanings, they can't guarantee that the meanings they make will do what they intend. The process of making and managing meaning is messy and opportunistic. There is no conspiracy of elites sitting in a closed room engineering social meanings. The control of meaning making is not always repressive; it can be reflexive and adaptable. That is, elites don't control meaning making by policing specific meanings, but often by watching and responding to meaning making in general: by steering, shaping and channelling. The control of meaning making can be nuanced and subtle. Media production is used by powerful groups to maintain power. But this does not mean they can simply use the media to exert direct manipulative control over people.

The debate about the power elite theory between the American political scientist Robert Dahl (1961) and the American sociologist C. Wright Mills (1959) is useful when considering the power elite argument. In his book *Who Governs?* Dahl put forward a pluralist position that argued there is no unified elite because power is diffused within a democracy. Whereas Mills argued in *The Power Elite* that ultimately power resided with a small group of people within a society. Dahl's pluralist model sees society as made up of multitudes of intersecting and cross-cutting interest groups without a clear elite. Mills' power elite model sees society as hierarchically structured, with a small unified elite commanding the rest of society. In this book we engage with a third approach, the hegemonic domination model. Hegemony refers to the establishment of a culture – a certain set of ideas, practices and values – as common sense. Hegemonic ideas are ones that people consent to. In western societies, for instance, liberalism, democracy and capitalism are dominant hegemonic ideas. Most people appear to consent to these ideas and the actions people take as a consequence of them. Hegemonic elites are formed out of alliances of interest groups. These hegemonic alliances become powerful, but their dominance is messy and tentative. It is less hierarchical than in Mills' conceptualization.

While at first Mills' and Dahl's positions may seem mutually exclusive, it is possible to see each as valid if power is seen to migrate and mutate. Sites of power constantly shift in the course of struggles taking place. Pluralist theory's denial that elites can (and do) emerge seems naive. But neither is the existence of power elites a necessary condition of human existence – contexts can exist where power is diffused in the way described by pluralist theorists like Dahl (1961). Similarly, the pluralist failure to address the fact that elites can and do intentionally work to manipulate and control non-elites also seems naive. But the notion that non-elites are necessarily powerless and perpetually manipulated seems equally dubious. It is more helpful to recognize the existence of elites and aspirant elites, as well as non-elite groups who are part of a complex pluralist competition for (material and cultural) resources and power. Within this framework the media are one of the many social sites struggled over as a means to acquire and build power.

The hegemonic dominance model is based on this mutable and shifting conceptualization of elites. At certain moments elites might well congeal and manage to become the dominant power brokers within a particular context; only to later have their power challenged and overthrown. This challenge might come from another emergent elite or it might come from a diffused and pluralist network or alliance of interests. One way to imagine Dahl's model is as society having no centre of power, but rather being composed of a series of fragmented and competing interests; this constellation or balance of interests is susceptible to change. If society is conceptualized as a fluid and continually mutating entity it becomes possible to view elite theory and pluralist theory as describing different moments of a shifting continuum. Gramsci's (1971) notion of hegemonic struggle is especially useful when conceptualizing the interaction between various competing interest groups. Hegemonic struggle is also helpful in conceptualizing existing, emergent and decaying power elites. Hegemonies have to be built and maintained. Becoming and remaining powerful is never completely accomplished, it requires continuous work: investing resources, managing relationships with other would-be elites, amassing material resources and creating and attaining consent for your ideas. Ruling elites are not conspiracies somehow manipulating society

Dahl's pluralist model

Mills' power elite model

Hegemonic dominance model

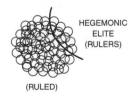

Figure 1.1   Pluralism, power elites and hegemonic dominance

behind the scenes: they are instead the outcome of continual hard hegemonic labour. In present day societies, creating and maintaining hegemonies involves managing the interests of millions of people.

Where does power come from?

There are three common explanations of the source of power.

- Firstly, access to material and cultural resources needed to get your way and attain the consent of others. This includes the use or threat of violence.
- Secondly, the occupation of social positions that enhance your capacity to get your way, have others comply with you and restrain the capacity of others to act.
- And thirdly, using and controlling language to structure social relations.

All three explanations are valuable. Power is derivative of access to economic and cultural resources, social positions and the ability to control language.

To acquire and maintain power, elites and would-be elites seek to control institutions that make and manage ideas. Various institutions are 'licensed' to manufacture and circulate meaning: education institutions, the media, parliaments and courts of law. These sites are cultural resources. Access to them is struggled over and controlled. In any given society, struggles around these sites can be observed. These struggles are most intense when power relations are fragile or contested. Powerful groups attempt to control and limit access by a variety of means.

A common means of control is via credentials. Credentials are criteria produced by institutions to govern access. For instance, to be a teacher in a school, or an academic in a university, or a lawyer admitted to the bar you must have acquired the appropriate qualifications. During the twentieth century universities became the key credentialing mechanism in western society. Not just anyone can gain access to a media institution and become a producer of meaning. Besides having the appropriate skills and qualifications, those who run media institutions also ensure the meaning makers they employ share the meanings of that institution. You will not remain employed at a mainstream western news organization if you produce stories that are anarchist, anti-capitalist, fascist or that encourage terrorism, for example.

The media became an important cultural resource during the twentieth century for positioning people: as good or bad, as powerful or weak, as important or unimportant, as credible or illegitimate. Media representations are necessarily battled over because such discourses serve to legitimate or de-legitimate particular hierarchies of social positions and the incumbents of those positions. Given the importance the media assumed in the process of making and circulating powerful ideas from the second half of the twentieth century, media institutions have become prized possessions for those seeking power. Owning or controlling a media institution empowers the owner to hire and fire the makers of meaning. Often, media empower particular people and ideas based simply on who and what they pay attention to. Media can disempower not only by saying a particular person or idea is bad, but by simply failing to acknowledge its existence. Whether the ownership and control of media sites does actually confer power will depend on the individuals concerned, the context they operate within and the wider struggles taking place within that context. Power is, however, not immutable and the institutions that produce meaning are dynamic sites. One observation we can make though is that already having material and symbolic power is an advantage in future power struggles.

What is the relationship between being embedded within a power relationship and free agency?

This is a question about the relationship between being controlled and being free. Essentially, there are two different conceptions of power.

- In the first, people are passive and have power exercised over them. They merely inhabit preordained structures and social roles. In this view people are conceptualized as imprisoned within power relationships and structures, whether these are economic, political or cultural.
- The second sees humans as active and part of a process in which power is struggled over. Here, people have agency. Our lifeworlds are seen as the outcome of mutable and creative human activity in which we make and remake our own structures.

For our examination of communication, this poses a question of whether we are seen to be free to make meaning, or whether we merely inhabit predetermined sets of meanings.

The question of predetermined structure versus human agency needs to be positioned within the shift in western philosophy from structuralism to post-structuralism that developed in the mid-twentieth century. This is a complex shift, involving several of the key figures of twentieth-century thought and philosophy.

Meaning is fixed

For Ferdinand de Saussure (1974), a founding theorist of linguistics, we are socialized in a prison-house of language. We are born into a world of subjective structures and we learn their pre-existing signs and codes. The Marxist theorist Louis Althusser (1971) took Saussure's notion of linguistic structures and used these to develop his idea of ideological state apparatuses. Ideological state apparatuses include family, religion, media and education. These structures position us within fixed ideologies or meanings. The way we understand the world and act is determined by those meanings. Within the Althusserian world-view, power derived from controlling these ideological state apparatuses. Human agency was given little scope within this structural and subjectivist view of human communication.

Meaning can be temporarily fixed

The shift into a post-structural interpretation of meaning came with the French philosopher Michel Foucault (1977, 1979). Foucault also saw humans as being constituted within linguistic structures. However, for Foucault, we are constituted within discursive practices, and these practices are created by human agency within institutions. This Foucaultian shift was highly significant because it opened a space for human agency and struggle that was tied to a notion of institutionalized communication.

Structures exist, but these structures, institutions and practices are mutable and changeable because they are the outcome of struggles between active human beings. Structures are something humans maintain through their discourses and practices. The Foucaultian notion of discursive practices represented a shift away from linguistic determinism, that is, away from the idea that we are born into a language or system of meanings and ideas that we cannot change. His notion of knowledge as being constituted by active human practices, within human-made institutions, placed Foucault's understanding of communication within the same terrain as that of Antonio Gramsci's (1971) notion of hegemonic struggle. For both Foucault and Gramsci, communication is the outcome of human practices that are struggled over. There may be communicative structures which set boundaries or parameters, but these do not predetermine human action.

Meaning is never fixed

The French philosopher Jacques Derrida (1976) took this Foucaultian notion one stage further, and explored the struggle over meaning as a process of trying to either fix meanings into place or uncouple meanings. For Derrida there is a constant shift in meaning structures as the process of fixing and uncoupling and re-fixing unfolds. The political theorists Ernesto Laclau and Chantal Mouffe (1985) took Derrida's notion one stage further by even questioning the possibility of ever fixing meanings into place. At most Laclau and Mouffe saw 'fixations' as partial. Within this account we shift into an understanding of communication as a pure semiosis, where meaning making is understood as purely about language games. The cultural studies academic Stuart Hall (1983) noted the limitations of

Table 1.1 Meaning from Saussure to Derrida

Saussure	Althusser	Foucault	Derrida
Linguistic structuralism	*Early French structuralism*	*Mature French structuralism*	*Post-structuralism*
Sign and code systems are a prison-house of language into which we are born	Sign systems are institutionalized within socio-political apparati (ISAs). ISAs socialize us into a prison-house of language	We are socialized into sets of discursive practices which structure meaning. But human agency struggles over these meanings. Hence they are not fixed structures (prison-houses)	Meanings are never fixed within structures, but are constantly shifting
Predetermination through linguistics	Predetermination through an ideological apparatus	Human agency moderates the impact of structures	Pure human agency operative

this extreme post-structuralist world-view. Essentially, extreme post-structuralism decontextualizes meaning making. It ignores power relationships embedded in identifiable political and economic contexts, and so loses the substance and complexity that a Foucaultian or Gramscian approach has. The Laclau and Mouffe position of 'pure semiosis' is ill-equipped to deal with how power relationships emerge between humans engaged in struggles over resources and positions. These struggles involve symbolism and cultural resources but they are not reducible exclusively to mere battles over meaning.

The Gramscian or Foucaultian positions have the advantage of allowing for both human agency and structural limitations. When making meaning we necessarily operate within pre-existing economic, political and linguistic structures, and hence within pre-existing power relations. But these existent structures and power relationships are not immutable or fixed. Rather they set parameters within which the next wave of struggle for power and influence takes place. These contextual parameters may advantage certain individuals and groups engaged in the process, but it does not imprison anyone into a predetermined outcome. Ultimately, both meaning and power relations emerge from a process of ongoing struggle. Within this process there will be those attempting to freeze certain meanings and structures if these advantage their position. And if they have sufficient power or influence they may even be successful for a while. But power is relational and messy, dependent upon the way humans interact in a particular location and time. There will always be gaps and contradictions in any system of control, and there will always be those who wish to circumvent, and will often succeed in circumventing, the mechanisms of control and meaning closure. Ultimately, relational shifts cannot be prevented, hence power shifts are inevitable. Power is always contextually bound, transitory and slipping away from those who try to wield it. Both meanings and power relations are constantly sliding around, migrating and mutating, sometimes in sync with one another and sometimes out of sync. This constant churn creates gaps for those who wish to challenge existent power relations and structures. It is this relational flux that constrains the powerful because the powerful can never permanently pin down relationships that benefit themselves: there will always be some other group pushing back. Power is consequently constrained by the propensity humans have for struggle, and their capacity to find gaps and contradictions in any social structure. No structure, whether it be economic, political or cultural, is ever a permanent prison. At most, structures channel human agency.

The same is true for meaning production. The processes of meaning making are bounded by a multiplicity of human-made power relationships and structures which may restrict human industry and creativity but which can never eliminate it. Even if power relationships and structures do not determine meanings, they are part of the contextual framework within which meaning is made and controlled.

THE STRUGGLE OVER MEANING: INTRODUCING HEGEMONY

An important dimension of human relationships is the struggle continuously taking place over power and dominance between competing individuals and groups. This competition impacts on both the circulation and production of meaning. All societies have dominant and dominated groups. Naturally, dominant groups prefer to remain dominant. Dominant groups have two mechanisms for creating and maintaining power:

- using or threatening violence against those challenging their interests
- creating legitimacy for the social arrangements which grant them a dominant position.

The more legitimacy dominant groups have, the less violence they need to employ

Ruling groups generally employ a mix of violence and legitimacy to maintain their dominance. Legitimacy is preferable to violence. Power relationships that are viewed as legitimate are easier to maintain. For this reason, the processes of meaning making and circulation are important instruments for making and maintaining power. As Gramsci argued, a key element in building and retaining dominance is manipulating meaning to gain the consent of the dominated. Professional communicators are central to the work of building hegemony, that is, building legitimate and common-sense meanings. Professional communicators are therefore implicated in power struggles.

Meanings are fluid because they are the outcome of a constant struggle between professional communicators. Professional communicators can work for either dominant or dominated groups. Generally speaking, dominant groups have an advantage because they have more resources to employ professional communicators and create or acquire the institutions in which they produce meaning. Think for example of the election process for the US President. Those with resources are disproportionately able to influence the meaning-making process with campaign donations, funding independent advertising campaigns, lobby groups and think tanks that make and circulate ideas. They use their resources to frame the parameters of the political debate, by making certain issues a legitimate, and others an illegitimate, part of the political and media agenda.

Those able to afford the best consultants, policy makers, public opinion researchers, campaigners and communicators increase their chances of success because they increase the likelihood of placing their ideas onto the agenda. This not only gives them access to law makers, but also frames the political and social parameters within which those law makers operate. Similarly, those who can afford the best legal teams are more likely to gain favourable court rulings, which also impacts on legal precedence. For instance, the 2010 US Supreme Court Citizens United *v.* Federal Election Committee ruling used the First Amendment right to free speech to prevent government from restricting corporations, unions and other groups from funding political campaigns.

Building hegemony requires a mix of professional communicators: lobbyists, policy makers, lawyers, researchers, journalists, advertisers, political strategists, data analysts, designers and so on. This mix of professional communicators is employed not only to make, but also to influence and control the social, cultural, legal and political structures that organize the circulation of meaning. The capacity to buy the most skilled professional communicators does not, however, predetermine the outcome of meaning making. At most, it skews meaning production in favour of those who are socially dominant or powerful at any point in time. Grappling with the nature and extent of this capacity is the task of any serious examination of meaning and power.

Defining hegemony

Professional communicators build hegemony. Hegemony is the creation and maintenance of the legitimacy of dominant and powerful groups. Legitimacy is granted when dominated groups consent to domination by more powerful groups. According to Gramsci this involves intellectuals or professional communicators engaging in three tasks:

- Firstly, professional communicators help to build consent and legitimacy for a society's dominant groups. They develop support for the interests and goals of powerful groups. They get other groups to accept as 'natural' the leadership, ideas and moral codes of the powerful groups. This legitimacy-making work is at its most obvious in our media and education systems.
- Secondly, professional communicators organize alliances and compromises. This work is most visible within parliaments, where bargains are struck between different interests, deals are done and compromises made.
- Thirdly, professional communicators strategically direct political or coercive force. For Gramsci, violence underpins all hegemonies. It may not be necessary to actually use violence against most citizens, but the threat of violence is omnipresent. The simplest example of this is the enforcement of a legal code by the police and judicial system. For most citizens, understanding the consequences of breaking the law is enough to deter them from doing so. Intellectuals and professional communicators organize and legitimate these deterrent forces.

At any particular place and time it is possible to identify the ideas that make powerful groups legitimate. Those ideas are produced and managed by professional communicators working in a variety of institutional settings. These dominant discourses are often opaque, but they establish the parameters within which meaning in any given time and place is made, circulated and contested.

Not everyone accepts the dominant discourse. At any moment there will be individuals and groups unconvinced by the ideas professional communicators circulate. Hall (1980) argues such 'oppositional' people negotiate or reject the meanings generated by professional communicators. There are always professional communicators working against the dominant ideas. In any given society we can find groups expressing oppositional ideas. Throughout state socialism in the Soviet Union and Eastern Europe those in power had to contend with anti-communist intellectuals and activists. The National Party in South Africa was challenged by anti-apartheid activists. European nationalists oppose migration and multiculturalism within most European countries. In many countries anti-globalization activists are readily identifiable. These activists might communicate via political parties, acts of violence, rallies, independent press, art or music. Some professional communicators consciously work to develop and circulate oppositional ideas designed to undermine hegemonic discourses and promote the interests of dominated or disempowered groups. Such intellectuals, cultural producers and professional communicators are engaged in counter-hegemonic work.

The struggle over ideas matters because meaning has material real-world consequences (Volosinov 1973). What people think informs how they act. And, vice versa, the world created out of the actions of people affects how we think and what we can say. The meanings we make and circulate have real-world consequences. By changing the nature of meaning one can also change human interactions, social organizations and the distribution of resources. Feminist successes in placing gender issues on the social agenda have, for example, altered human interactions, work practices and resource distribution in western societies. The converse is equally true: changing material relationships affects the way that meaning is made. For example, the significant transfer of wealth in post-apartheid South Africa created a new black elite, transforming many from socialist comrades into free enterprise businesspeople. The struggle to construct and reconstruct societies, cultures and economic systems, in part, involves battles to attach, detach and reattach meanings. These shifts affect more than just how we see and talk about the world, they change the way we live. Our lifeworld is altered. This in turn impacts on power relationships. As new power relationships emerge, so to do new hegemonic struggles of meaning, resources and power.

Hegemonic work is consequently complex. There are constant shifts between competing interests. People are always being positioned and repositioned within these shifting relationships. This produces an infinite number of positions from which people make sense of meaning. No possibility exists of ever producing a permanently stable set of dominant meanings. Instead, hegemonic work involves the never-ending task of dealing with challenges, oppositional decodings, power shifts and ever-changing alliances. Meanings are thus only hegemonic in a temporary sense. They are under challenge from the moment of their conception. Despite this, there will always be professional communicators trying to control and stabilize meaning. This brings us to an important question then: to what extent can meaning be controlled?

THE CONTROL OF MEANING: INTRODUCING IDEOLOGY AND DISCOURSE

Powerful groups attempt to control meaning. In some places and times those attempts will be successful. The meanings they produce and circulate will acquire a hegemonic dominance. That is, they will come to be seen as common sense or true. As we have already argued though, meaning is not entirely controllable, immutable or fixed. Humans will actively read, interpret and decode meanings. Despite the efforts of dominant groups, their efforts to control meaning will always be susceptible to resistance and the possibility that new meanings will emerge.

Efforts to control meaning are related to competition over material and cultural resources. Human society is characterized by scarce resources. Our life chances are set by the share of material and cultural resources we get access to. As long as there are insufficient resources to satisfy all, struggles will occur between groups and individuals. Central to the nature and outcomes of such struggles are the rules of engagement, that is, the acceptable terms on which competition over resources will be undertaken. In a liberal-democratic capitalist society, individuals cannot simply go and forcibly acquire the wealth of others. There are a myriad of laws and institutions that govern the ownership and production of wealth. From Gramscian and Foucaultian perspectives, these rules of engagement are set and maintained via battles over meaning. Powerful groups seek to use meanings to set rules that are favourable to them.

Ideology

The concept of ideology offers a framework for thinking about how the rules and parameters of social life are established and maintained. Ideology is a multi-layered concept that has evolved and grown over the past two centuries. We commonly use the term 'ideology' to refer to the beliefs of another person and the values or principles upon which they make decisions and act. It is often used with a negative connotation. When one politician calls another an 'ideologue' they insinuate that they are guided by certain beliefs which prevent them seeing how things really are. This everyday use captures some aspects of the idea. Implied here is the notion that there are right and true or wrong and distorted meanings or ways of seeing the world. And that, when the powerful attempt to control meanings, what they do is distort those meanings in order to create a view of an issue that suits their interests, rather than create meanings that represent how things actually are. This way of thinking assumes that someone has corrupted an ideal form of communication and prevented others from seeing the 'right' meanings. It posits that there is an actual and final truth that exists and that we can find it.

This problem brings us into rich, fruitful and tricky philosophical terrain. At its most elementary the critical understanding of ideology is captured in the formula: 'They know not what they do'. That is, people only act as they do because they don't understand how things really are. For instance, we might say that people only consent to the way our liberal democracy works because we don't fully appreciate that rather than empower us as citizens, as we are always told, it in fact protects an economic system that enables the rich to protect their wealth and resources. In this view, the empowering narratives of liberal democracy are a set of meanings that obscure the real nature of human relations in a society where a small number of people accumulate the majority of the wealth and resources. A basic ideology critique contends that these social contradictions – between how we are told society works and how it actually works – are hidden from view. For some, an ideal society would emerge if this distortion was revealed.

There are two important rejoinders to this basic ideology critique that we must consider. Firstly, this critique is based upon a belief that an ideal society can be identified and realized. Secondly, contemporary critics have drawn attention to the fact that contemporary citizens often appear to know how things are but nevertheless carry on as if they didn't know (Žižek 1989). This might be because they don't care, aren't too bothered by the social contradictions that affect their lives, or can't think of anything to do about it. For instance, contemporary citizens are often sceptical that politicians are telling them the truth or really acting in their best interests, but despite this knowledge they still carry on and act *as if* the politicians do have their best interests at heart. Very rarely do we see citizens in established liberal democracies protest against the way the political system is structured. Ideology does not work by sustaining the sincere belief of subjects. Our disposition towards media representations is often a cynical one; we profess not to believe them or to see through their constructed nature. Instead, ideology works by offering symbolic resources that make social reality functional and possible. To work, ideology requires our participation rather than our belief (Žižek 1989).

The important point here is that merely understanding how things are will not change power relations. Communication or knowledge alone will not solve social problems. We cannot change the world by talking about it. Ideology doesn't disguise contradictions; it is instead a way of living with them, a way of making life meaningful despite the contradictions. If we view it this way, then people aren't dupes for adhering to ideologies, but rather ideologies are a way for people to make social life workable despite its contradictions. Within this approach, ideology or distorted communication cannot disappear while social contradictions exist. And, because social contradictions cannot be resolved, ideology cannot disappear. Ideology doesn't mask social contradictions, it is produced out of them.

Discourse

Michel Foucault's (1972) notion of a 'discursive formation' offers an explanation of how meanings get made by people in specific contexts. According to Foucault, societies create institutions. He looked at prisons, clinics and asylums. Each institution develops its own set of practices and discourses. Those working within such institutions have to learn the interconnected practices and discourses appropriate to that institutional site. Practices are the acceptable way of doing things. Discourses are the acceptable 'language' within that site. A person is unlikely to be recruited into an institutional site unless they are able to demonstrate a compatibility with practices or discourses already operative within it. They are unlikely to remain employed unless they continue to conform to the institutions' practices and discourses.

Conformity is a key governing mechanism within Foucault's system. This implies recognizing negative consequences for failing to conform. Importantly, Foucault's system does not necessitate seeing us as prisoners of natural language structures. Instead, it allows space for active human choice regarding conformity to existing practices and discourses. But whether by choice, or not, adherence to a discourse limits what one is able to say and, over time, what one might think. According to Foucault, a discourse governs the knowledge and ideas that can appear. Foucault explored the way in which discourses constrained the emergence of knowledge and concluded that parameters were set by establishing linguistic boundaries and organizing fields that contained acceptable meanings and practices. These organizing fields not only make certain ideas impossible and others possible; they actually make certain ideas inevitable. Implicitly, the struggle to make new meanings is enmeshed within, and constrained by, sets of power relationships within the spaces where intellectuals work.

Both Foucault and Gramsci recognize the contradictory nature of human existence – in which although humans are free to act, it is a constrained freedom. Ultimately then, Gramsci's notion of 'hegemony' and Foucault's 'discourse' conceptually overlap. Both recognize structural conditions to meaning making. At the same time, they recognize that people have a choice to act either as change agents or as conservatives because, up to a point, intellectuals and professional communicators can choose between the institutional and discursive arrangements available within their context. Fluidity and struggle are central to both the Gramscian and Foucaultian world-views. In each conception intellectuals can choose how they relate to existing power relationships; those power relationships are not fixed, but mutate as struggles are won or lost.

What Foucault offers is a means for conceptualizing how discourse is a potentially powerful hegemonic tool for social control. Discursive formations have the power to exclude from discussion certain questions or issues. This forecloses debate and so predetermines what conclusions may be reached. There are many instances of discourses automatically excluding alternative perspectives. For example, free market discourses can block adherents from grappling with the notion that capitalism may disadvantage some people with merit and undermine their capacity for achievement. Similarly, socialist discourses can block adherents from confronting the view that competition may generate achievement and wealth, while state interventionism may promote dependence and undermine wealth making.

REPRESENTATION AND POWER

Representation is the social process of making and exchanging meaning (Hall 1997). Media do not simply reflect or mirror reality. Media are social processes. People interact with others to construct a view of reality. These social interactions unfold between people with different levels of access to economic, cultural and symbolic resources, institutions and rituals. By social construction of reality we mean that reality as we understand it is produced out of social relationships between people. There is a real world out there, with real material things in it and events that actually happen, but as humans we can only come to understand that world out of the social process of interacting with each other. For us then, there is no understanding of reality outside of our social interactions and cultural practices. The 're' prefix in representation is important. It is a process of *re*-presenting reality to others. Representations are social productions: their meaning depends on who creates and circulates them, the cultural schema within which that circulation takes place, and who receives them. Representation takes place within the context of power relations. Some people have more power to shape not only particular meanings, but also the contexts within which meanings are produced, distributed and received.

Media representations shape how people think about and act in the world. Representations also have significant affective dimensions. They anticipate, construct and amplify how we feel about things. They reinforce or challenge our attitudes. They arouse our emotions: fear, passion, anxieties. Representation is not simply a rational process of creating and circulating inert bits of information. The question is not always about whether or not representations are accurate, but how they subtly frame events in ways that position individuals in the social order. We are interested in how representations mediate relations between people. Relations between people are complex and messy, and are constituted as much by how we feel, and our relative level of power towards each other, as they are by empirical facts.

Representation is a process embedded in how we make sense of the world and in doing so it shapes the world. Representation does this subtly and over a long period of time. Images and narratives do not have meaning on their own. They only become meaningful in relation to other images and narratives that have preceded them or are produced in relation to. As groups of people attempt to 'fix' particular representations, other groups will attempt to create different ones. In doing so they are making claims on how we ought to make sense of, and act in, the world. An important philosophical question to consider is the extent to which representations accurately portray the world 'as it actually is'. We can distinguish two responses to this question:

- *A post-modern view that representations can never be finally fixed.* This view celebrates the possibilities opened up by a continuous game of making meaning. The capacity of humans to create new meanings, and new ways of seeing the world, opens up the possibility that power relationships can be continuously rearranged via meaning making. This position arguably creates a significant problem. By celebrating the constant play of meaning making it loses the capacity to distinguish one meaning as better or more plausible than another. The game of meaning making can become divorced from material reality and daily life.
- *A hegemonic view that powerful groups aim to fix meanings.* This is a complex process that unfolds over time. When groups have power they can fix meaning, as other groups acquire power though they may be able to unfix and create new meanings. This is not a teleological process. Each new set of meanings is not necessarily better than the last. Importantly, this position retains the view that we can distinguish between 'good' and 'bad' meanings by judging them against our engagement with and experiences in the world. This view is characterized by humans who make and defend judgements about the value and truth of their meanings.

Considering these two positions enables us to reflect upon our own position about the representations we create and use to make sense of the world.

Control over representation

While some people have more power to control the resources used to create meanings, and the structures and spaces where meanings circulate, no one has complete control over how meanings are encoded and decoded. Powerful groups have the capacity to control media institutions and technologies, and the resources to employ and direct professional communicators. That level of control only gets them so far, because representations work discursively. Once produced, messages have to be circulated. They become meaningful when incorporated into social practices and institutions. Institutions can't entirely control those social practices. The process of representation is contingent on the actors in each moment, and their relative power to influence or control others. The moments of 'encoding' and 'decoding' messages are 'relatively autonomous' (Hall 1980). A television programme is produced within the institutional structures, technical infrastructure and production practices of a television network.

The way television producers encode messages is shaped by the way they anticipate others will decode their messages. Few professional communicators want to be misunderstood by their audience, and most communicators need to pay attention to the power relations they are embedded within. For a professional communicator working on a television news programme for instance, they most likely anticipate how their messages will be perceived by political and corporate elites on one hand, and by their audience on the other. Their messages are discursively shaped by their sense of how it fits within a broader cultural hegemony that reflects both the interests of political elites and the desires of the audience. Professionals pay careful attention to wider cultural discourses and power structures: the interests of political elites, corporate sponsors and advertisers, and audience feedback through ratings and market research. The producer isn't an autonomous creator of a message, but rather working at one interval in an ongoing process of representation. We might argue though that they are working at a particularly influential interval. The messages they encode can be distributed to a mass audience, and individuals in that audience can decode the messages however they like, but they are probably unlikely to be able to encode and distribute messages. Even though our media system is increasingly interactive, this remains a crucial distinction.

Once a message is encoded and distributed though, it can only have an effect – influence, entertain, instruct or persuade – once it has been decoded. The meaning structure used to encode a message may not necessarily be the same as the meaning structures in which the message is decoded. Even though professional communicators might set the agenda and frame messages, they can't ever guarantee what their readers and audiences will do with those messages. The process of representation is always open-ended to some degree. We must then always pay attention to what audiences do with representations, in addition to examining the messages themselves.

Human communication is characterized by struggles over power and meaning. Hall (1980) suggests three possible positions within which messages might be decoded: dominant, negotiated and oppositional.

- When the message is decoded as the encoder intended, the process of representation operates within a *dominant* hegemonic code. The social exchange constructed here is one of consent or agreement between encoder and decoder. The message attempts to be hegemonic in the sense that it claims its own truth and legitimacy; it achieves this hegemony where the decoder consents to that claim. The work of professional communicators is to encode messages in such a way that their claims are legitimized by others.
- A *negotiated* process of representation takes place when the decoder understands quite well the claim to truth or legitimacy the encoder is making, but they resist consenting to the claim. The decoder acknowledges the legitimacy and power of the message at the same time they mark out their own position, adapting the message to their own local conditions and social relations. The capacity of the decoder to negotiate depends to some degree on their relative autonomy, power and cultural and economic resources. Negotiated processes of representation demonstrate the messy and contingent nature of power. The decoder simultaneously acknowledges the existence of the power and legitimate dominant code and at the same time they resist it with whatever local resources they have available. Much communication, and the ongoing work of hegemony and representation, is about these everyday negotiations.
- An *oppositional* exchange takes place where a decoder understands perfectly well the encoded message, but rejects it entirely. Oppositional decoding threatens to disrupt power relations. If a large group of people refuse to decode the intended message of the encoder, and that oppositional decoding is backed up by other economic, social and cultural resources, it may be the sign of a hegemony breaking apart, or losing its legitimacy.

Hall's model is useful for thinking about how in a society at any given time there is a complex process of meaning making and representation taking place. The process of encoding and decoding gives us a useful rubric for mapping out a variety of positions from which individuals and groups might have the capacity to encode, circulate, decode and recirculate messages.

Encoders with power are likely to have access to the means of communication from which they can create and distribute messages. Their messages are likely to be decoded as intended, and consented to, by those aligned to the ruling hegemony. They might also find other groups undertaking a negotiated decoding of the messages at local levels. This process of negotiation is part of managing hegemony, but doesn't fundamentally disrupt it. These other groups might not be happy with the meanings, but they understand that in practice they need to consent to them.

In addition to *encoders with power* are *encoders seeking to build power*. These individuals and groups also largely operate within the ruling or dominant hegemony, but are seeking to negotiate a different position within that structure, to acquire more economic and cultural power. They are often perceived within the process of representation as an accepted part of the debate. For instance, in the United States, a Democratic President might find conservative media disagreeing with much of what he or she has to say, but ultimately not disputing their shared liberal-democratic-capitalist hegemony. What is taking place here is a continuing negotiation *within* a hegemonic structure that the various encoders and decoders largely agree upon. This process of encoders and decoders, either aligned to the ruling hegemony, involved in a process of active negotiation within it, or ambivalent about it, characterizes the representation process that most of us are familiar with on a day-to-day basis. For those of us who live in societies like the United States, United Kingdom, Ireland, Australia, New Zealand and Western Europe, the media, cultural and political processes we are embedded within are part of a liberalized order where the fundamental power relationships are not in dispute, but within those frameworks groups are negotiating and jostling for resources.

Distinct from dominant and negotiated processes of representation are those societies characterized by *encoders and/or decoders opposed to the ruling hegemony*. Any society at any given time will have individuals and groups fundamentally opposed to the ruling hegemony. For the process of representation, though, this opposition is only of consequence if those groups are able to gain access to the means of communication through which to create and distribute messages, and if there are corresponding groups who will decode their messages as intended. That is, if they have the capacity to create, circulate and have their messages made meaningful by others.

#IFTHEYGUNNEDMEDOWN

The shooting of Mike Brown, an unarmed black teenager, by police in Ferguson, Missouri, in 2014 drew attention to how news organizations draw on social media profiles to depict victims or perpetrators of crime.

Some news organizations ran a photo of Brown in his graduation cap and gown, while many others used a photo of Brown wearing a basketball singlet and making a hand gesture that naïve viewers might interpret as a gang sign.

The use of an image that implied Brown was a member of a gang prompted many black Americans to post contrasting images from their social media accounts to Twitter using the hashtag #iftheygunnedmedown. Many featured young black men in formal dress for church, military or graduation in one image, while in the other image they wore street wear that could be used to suggest they are gang members.

Like the images used for Brown, people drew attention to the way that selective use of images from their social media profiles could be used to construct very different representations of their identities. By constructing their identity one way or another the media could invoke differing perceptions of the extent to which the use of force by police was legitimate.

Figure 1.2   Images circulating on Twitter using #iftheygunnedmedown

Consider these images. How do the two images of the same individual represent them in different ways? What symbols in the images convey different meanings that you associate with that individual? How do the images position the individuals differently in power relationships?

Examine images of yourself on your own social media profile. Find two contrasting images. Consider the way in which the images represent your identity differently. If the media were reporting, could they use the images to tell different stories about your character? Would characteristics like your gender, ethnicity or sexuality be at play in the interpretation of those images? If not, would the images suggest different aspects of your character that might affect your reputation?

You can find links to the images and stories about these images on the *Media and Society* website study.sagepub.com/carahandlouw

MEDIATIZATION AND MEDIA RITUALS

Media form a part of the rhythms, texture and background of everyday life. As much as we might be interested in the particular meanings media circulate, we also need to pay attention to how media play a foundational role in organizing our day-to-day lives (Couldry and Hepp 2013). Mediatization is the process by which media become more and more a part of how social, political and cultural processes operate. Mediatization unfolds in three ways. Firstly, media become increasingly important to understanding and organizing relationships with one another. We come to know and understand the world and our place in it via media representations and technologies. Secondly, social institutions and processes gradually adapt to the routines and practices of media institutions. Politics and government is now substantially organized around the production and management of media narratives. Professional sport is largely a performance for television broadcasts. Thirdly, our private and public spaces are organized around material media technologies. The television is an important object in the layout of our homes. Urban spaces are filled with mobile reception towers and WiFi coverage that enable us to remain connected to the web via our smartphones.

Couldry and Hepp (2013) suggest that we see human history as 'a process of intensifying mediatisation'. Over time the societies we live in become increasingly media-dense. They are filled in with media objects. Daily rhythms are organized around flows of media: from radio in the car on the way to work, to television in the evenings, to smartphones while lying in bed. More of our individual attention is paid to media, and more of our institutions address themselves to the way the media works.

Media frame and represent the social world in routine and organized ways. Couldry (2003: 1) suggests that we ought to pay attention to the 'media's role in ordering our lives, and organising social space'. In media-dense societies media are essential to how we imagine our 'lives together as social beings' via political institutions and shared national and cultural identities. Media are the primary site through which we come to know the larger social and political structures within which any meanings, practices and identities might make sense to us. Regardless of the specific messages the media convey, their primary claim is often simply that they reflect our world, way of life and values within power relationships. Media promote the idea that the social world has a 'centre' of power and legitimacy, and that they have a 'privileged relation to that "centre"' (Couldry 2003: 45). Media 'naturalize' the idea 'that there is a social centre to *be* re-presented to us' and that the media are the legitimate site for producing and managing that process of representation. Processes of representation are organized in media rituals which legitimate the idea that 'the media is our access to the social centre' (2003: 2).

Through media rituals we see how the media 'stand in' for the social world and position themselves as central to the 'holding together' of society (Couldry 2003: 4). Professional communicators don't just make meanings, they fashion the social relationships and processes that hold society together. Sometimes these rituals can appear spectacular and extraordinary: such as watching a royal marriage, or the Olympic Games, or the inauguration of a President, or during natural disasters. But importantly, media rituals are also just written into everyday life every time we watch the news at breakfast time, log on to Facebook on our smartphone, or talk with a colleague about something we saw on television the night before. Media rituals frame reality in the sense that they draw our attention in a variety of spectacular and ordinary ways to shared values and ideas.

Media rituals frame what is 'in' and 'out' of the picture. For example, what politics is, who does it and where it takes place. By 'going' to parliament each day to report on the events there, interacting with the politicians and advisors there to narrative events, media rituals frame where politics happens and who participates in it. Over time this representation of politics seems predictable, natural and legitimate. As ordinary citizens we come to assume that politics *is* how it is represented through media rituals. Some people are 'in' the frame and have access to the symbolic resources to influence representation, while others do not.

Access to meaning-making sites is uneven. Media present themselves as the legitimate sites through which we imagine society. While media *claim* to speak for us, those who *actually* speak are those with the economic, political and cultural resources to create, access, regulate and use media institutions, technologies and processes to manage representation. Media production is characterized by an uneven distribution of symbolic resources. In a media-dense society the media have the symbolic power to construct' and name reality (Couldry 2003). From this power flows the legitimacy of economic and political relationships and cultural identities and practices. Media power seems legitimate because it seems common sense to us that the media are the sites through which we imagine our lives and our relations to others. For all of us living in media-dense societies it is impossible to imagine day-to-day life, the political process, cultural practices, leisure and entertainment without the media. The myth of the mediated centre, that there is a centre to the social world and the media give us access to it, is the basis upon which we accept the media's centrality to our lives. Media empower and disempower because they are sites where symbolic power is concentrated, organized and regulated. Those with access to media institutions have the symbolic resources to make and distribute meanings.

While the powerful might use media to produce particular ideas, the efficacy of that activity depends in the first instance on the legitimacy of the media as representative of the social centre. The media themselves need to build and maintain everyday legitimacy in order to be sites where symbolic power is concentrated. Without the media being continuously incorporated into our everyday lives, without most of us switching on and tuning in everyday, they wouldn't be sites of power and legitimacy in the first place, through which particular messages and representations could flow. Media rituals then are the fundamental ground on which media power can be established and maintained.

REPRESENTATION AS A SOCIAL PROCESS

THE OCCUPY PROTESTS AND CASUALLY-PEPPER-SPRAY-EVERYTHING COP MEME

Representation is a social system involving the continuous production and circulation of meaning. People interact with each other to represent events. Media representations work intertextually. That is, meanings are transferred from one text to another. Texts make new

(Continued)

(Continued)

arrangements of meanings that often depend on the capacity of readers to decode them by understanding them in relation to other texts.

Internet memes demonstrate the intertextual and social process of representation in action. The first image below is an image from a protest at the University of California (Davis) in 2011. The protest was part of the global Occupy movement. When students refused to disband a campus police officer sprayed them with pepper spray. The cop's act was a violent one. As an authority figure he used physical force against people. The police are licensed to do that by the state and the university. The act though is also a symbolic one. When police use force against citizens they demonstrate to them what will happen if they do not obey the law.

The cop's act set off a chain of events where the student protestors, university management, news organizations and the public interacted with each other in an effort to represent the event in different ways.

The protest was videoed and uploaded to YouTube. In the video the crowd can be heard chanting 'the whole world is watching' as the cop sprays the protestors with pepper spray. The protestors captured the act on camera. The protestors understood that they could use videos to bear witness to the event. In doing so, they were able to 're-present' it. They take

Figure 1.3 A campus police officer pepper-spraying student protestors at UC Davis

the act from its original context and turn it into a media text. That text then circulated rapidly through social networks. The 're-presentation' of the act symbolizes the excessive use of force by the powerful. The Occupy protests aimed to represent the '99%' of ordinary people against the world's privileged '1%'. The representation of the cop pepper-spraying the protestors symbolizes – stands in for – the entrenched privilege and blatant use of power the Occupy movement as protesting against in its slogan 'We are the 99%'.

The protestors' videos of the incident became a news story. The university needed to respond to the way the video of the protest represented the institution and its relationship with students. The Chancellor of the university organized a media conference. This was an attempt to 'counter' the meanings and narratives circulating in conjunction with the pepper-spray video. The university attempted to control how the event was represented. They did that by inviting selected media organizations to the media conference, and excluding students from the venue. The students responded to being excluded by forming a silent protest outside. When the Chancellor eventually emerged they formed a silent guard all the way from the venue to her car. This silent protest was also filmed and the video circulated widely online. The protestors used silence to represent their exclusion. In doing so they drew attention to how the powerful maintain power by controlling who speaks where and when, by

Figure 1.4   An internet meme where the pepper-spray cop sprays Bambi

(Continued)

(Continued)

attempting to control who gets to represent events. When the Chancellor excluded students from the press conference, she attempted to work with the police and media organizations to control how the event was represented.

Following this event, images of the cop pepper-spraying students were widely reappropriated and recirculated. The pepper-spraying cop represented the use of excessive force, the attempt of the powerful to control who gets to speak, the disrespect for democratic values. The cop more broadly represented the use of force against ordinary people, the undermining of democratic rights and the policing of public space.

The powerful – like the Chancellor and the police – use strategies to attempt to control media representations. They use their relations with media and their resources to organize media events and control who gets access to those events. In contrast, ordinary people use tactics to resist those meanings.

One way this unfolded with the pepper-spray cop was by using the cop as a symbol of excessive power and 'remixing' his image into other popular culture texts. The image of the cop worked intertextually to create new representations. In the image above, the cop pepper-sprays Bambi. To make sense of this image we need to understand both texts it references: the pepper-spray cop and the film *Bambi*. In the image, the cop is crudely superimposed over a scene from Bambi. In doing so, the innocence of the scene from Bambi evident in the joyful expressions on the characters' faces and the colourful animation is juxtaposed with the dark, menacing and violent presence of the cop. The cop is larger than the characters from the animation, towering over them and his head is cropped out of the frame, as if to make him a faceless and distant figure. This image is one of many examples where the cop was super-imposed onto another scene – a movie like Bambi, an important historical moment like the Declaration of Independence, or a cultural icon like a Renaissance painting. The creators of these images were able to repeat this juxtaposition by 'photoshopping' the cop over images in this way. Meaning is created via the repeated gesture of imposing the cop in scenes that evoked the innocence of childhood memory or shared cultural history and values. We can see throughout this example how representation works both as a social process, constructing how we understand and act in the world, and as a process in which some people have more power than others.

Map out the array of actors involved in attempting to represent the student protest at UC Davis. What were their preferred representations of the event and why? What resources and techniques did they use to create their preferred representations? Who did they interact with to create their preferred representations?

Find other examples of the pepper-spray cop meme.
What texts are referenced in the memes?
How is meaning created in the interplay between the texts?
What do the texts represent?

For links to the images and videos in this case visit the *Media and Society* website study.sagepub.com/carahandlouw

CONCLUSION

In this chapter, we defined meaning and power. We introduced several significant theoretical concepts that offer an account of the relationship between meaning and power: hegemony, ideology and discourse.

- Hegemony draws our attention to the continual and ongoing struggle over meanings and the meaning-making process as groups work to make and maintain their legitimacy and power. This also encouraged us to consider how meaning making is embedded in real world relationships and material resources. Making and maintaining legitimacy is interrelated with access to economic, political and cultural resources.
- Ideology is useful for critically considering the meanings that are produced out of struggles and contradictions. Ideology offers us ways of seeing how we make everyday life meaningful despite its contradictions and antagonisms.
- Discourse enables us to consider how institutions produce frameworks of meaning that organize social practices. Meaning doesn't just govern what we think, but structures the social spaces and institutions in which we act. Individuals act within the coordinates of institutions. This is a permissive mode of control. Institutions reward some ideas, practices and identities while discouraging others. Individuals have the freedom to do or say what they like, but learn that resources are shifted towards preferred ideas and practices.

Each concept – hegemony, ideology and discourse – leads us to a conceptualization of meaning making as a continual process where, despite attempts to fix and control meaning by some groups, we always retain the agency to think and act in our own right, resisting the intended meanings and actions, and creating new meanings in their place.

Being able to make and circulate meaning requires material resources to organize and fund the creation of meaning. These material resources include tangible things like buildings, tools and machinery. Material resources enable individuals to acquire and control the time, knowledge, skills and social relationships required to make meaning, attract attention and manage populations. The creation and dissemination of representations of ways of life creates a cultural schema of ideas, values, practices and desires within which people live their lives and fashion their identities. While we can never guarantee what people will do with representations, the opportunity to structure, in the first instance, the flows of symbolic resources people use to make sense of the world affords power.

The power of meaning-making institutions is embedded in their capacity to construct and control not just meanings but the social spaces and frameworks within which we all make and circulate meaning. In the next chapter we examine how cultural production was institutionalized in the twentieth century. We chart the emergence of a networked, interactive and participatory culture industry towards the century's end. The development of flexible, networked and informational modes of production has enabled forms of control based on continuously monitoring and responding to an open-ended circulation of meaning. In the rest of this book we consider how meaning and power work in today's systems of media and cultural production. The critical debates extending from hegemony, ideology and discourse enable us to develop a reflective account of the place of media in facilitating social life and power relationships.

FURTHER READING

The work of Stuart Hall and Nick Couldry is instructive in developing an account of media representation. Stuart Hall's 'Encoding/decoding' essay (1980), originally published in 1973, provides a seminal account of the process by which meanings are inscribed into texts and deciphered by audiences. Hall's book *Representation,* published with several colleagues in 1997 (and in an updated edition in 2013), provides a clear and accessible explanation of the cultural and media processes of representation. In the past decade Nick Couldry's work on mediatization, media power and rituals has further advanced our understanding of media representations within a media-dense society. Couldry draws our attention to how practices of media representation are embedded in everyday cultural practices, social spaces and power relationships. In this chapter we also referred to Foucault's notion of discourse. For more advanced readers his book *Discipline and Punish* (1977) is a good place to start. In that book he defines the relationship between power, knowledge and representation.

Couldry, N. (2002) *The Place of Media Power: Pilgrims and Witnesses of the Media Age.* London: Routledge.

Couldry, N. (2003) *Media Rituals: A Critical Approach.* London: Routledge.

Couldry, N. and Hepp, A. (2013) 'Conceptualizing mediatization: contexts, traditions, arguments', *Communication Theory*, 23 (3): 191–202.

Foucault, M. (1977) *Discipline and Punish.* London: Penguin.

Hall, S. (1980) 'Encoding/decoding', in S. Hall, D. Hobson, A. Lowe and P. Willis (eds), *Culture, Media, Language.* London: Hutchinson, pp. 129–138.

Hall, S., Evans, J. and Nixon, S. (eds) (2013) *Representation: Cultural Representations and Signifying Practices.* London: Sage.

THE INDUSTRIAL PRODUCTION OF MEANING

DURING THE TWENTIETH CENTURY THE PRODUCTION OF MEANING BECAME INDUSTRIALIZED.

* How did the organization and production of meaning change during the twentieth century?

* How have interactive technologies changed the production of culture?

* What are the differences between various media and cultural institutions?

In this chapter we:

- Examine the industrialization of communication in the twentieth century
- Propose that the culture industry is central to controlling the production and circulation of meaning in society, and therefore has material consequences for the kind of society we live in, the way we live and the way we relate to each other
- Explore the role professionalized and industrialized communication plays in forming and maintaining power relationships.

CONTROLLING WHO MAKES MEANING AND WHERE MEANING IS MADE

The roots of today's cultural industry lie in the institutions created by Western European bourgeoisie between the seventeenth and nineteenth centuries. The bourgeoisie were the newly emergent middle-class traders, merchants and early industrial capitalists who coalesced in the free cities of Europe. During its first stage, mediated communication was located in small organizations. Until well into the nineteenth century bourgeois media took the form of small owner-operated firms. In part this was because, until the arrival of steam-powered printing presses, media technology only allowed for the limited mass production of messages. Consequently, early mediated communication remained a relatively small-scale affair, staffed by multi-skilled individuals. A typical newspaper owner, for example, wrote, edited and printed the copy as well as running the business. This was not communication made within hierarchical 'meaning factories' for dissemination to a mass audience. Early bourgeois mediated communication was generally targeted to relatively small groups of literate people. These publications circulated in particular among middle-class activists agitating to end feudal and aristocratic privilege which blocked the growth of bourgeois power. The publications also served a commercial purpose by circulating information among traders; Von Klarwill (1924) provides examples of these trader newsletters.

The nineteenth century brought with it a number of developments which, when combined, generated the conditions for the creation of a new type of communication. The invention of ways to produce cheap paper and ink, the rotary printing press and typesetting machines generated the necessary technology for mass-produced newspapers. The industrial revolution also led to the creation of large cities, growing literacy rates and improved road and rail transport, which provided expanding markets for mass newspapers. Technological developments made it possible to produce ever larger quantities of identical products at a diminishing cost. Industrial production began to develop economies of scale. Industrial factories began to develop on the basis that the more units they produced the more the cost of each unit declined. With the development of industrialized cities came the rise of a consumer society. Merchants sought to advertise their goods to the newly literate market living in these rapidly growing cities. Advertising made it possible to sell newspapers cheaply. The mass circulation press was born.

Towards the end of the nineteenth century, Americans invented the corporation as an institution for organizing the production of large infrastructure projects like railways and transport. This form of organization came to underpin the production of culture as well. From this confluence of variables grew the mass media: an industrialized production and distribution of meaning. The set of practices and discourses about meaning making that emerged at this time underpinned the development of newspapers, magazines, film, radio and television throughout the twentieth century. Each of these technologies was developed and applied as part of the industrial production of meaning. During this time, other modes of cultural production like education were similarly institutionalized. Only with the arrival of digital electronic networking during the 1990s did these practices undergo significant modification.

The twentieth century was characterized by many different attempts to industrialize the production of culture. Different powerful groups attempted to create institutions that established and maintained ideologies or discourses. These institutions aimed to control meaning in ways that they thought would help develop desirable societies. Each mode of cultural production emerges in a specific place and context. In this chapter we focus our attention on the development of the liberal-democratic culture industry from newspapers to the internet.

DEFINING DIFFERENT TYPES OF CULTURE INDUSTRY

During the twentieth century culture was industrialized in the following ways:

- privately-owned media
- state-licensed media
- public service broadcasting
- state-subsidized media
- communist media
- development media.

Since the beginning of this century we have also seen the emergence of social or interactive media.

Since the beginning of the twentieth century culture industries have taken many institutional forms. Below we define several key formations.

Privately-owned media

The media institution we are most familiar with in our day-to-day lives is most likely privately-owned media. Most of the media we consume on a daily basis is produced by an organization that intends to make a profit from us as an audience. This has some important consequences that we will consider as the book progresses. These media have their roots in the small presses developed by the emergent middles classes of north-west Europe during the seventeenth and eighteenth centuries (Smith 1979). The distinctive feature of these organizations is that they primarily produce and sell audience attention to advertisers. The content they produce is driven by a commercial imperative to attract audiences that advertisers want to reach. Throughout the twentieth century these businesses became more adept at constructing and packaging audiences for advertisers (Smythe 1981).

State-licensed media

Some forms of public sector involvement in the culture industry have not entailed direct ownership or control of the media. The oldest of these are state-licensing of newspapers, stamp duties and government censorship. Licensing or censorship involves governments closely regulating who can produce media. This form of control was widely used by European governments well into the nineteenth century (Smith 1979). The history of press licensing is a fascinating one and the battles fought over it forged our idea of a 'free press'. As the emerging middle class in Europe used new technologies like the printing press to make their case for greater political representation, the old elites like monarchs, aristocrats, feudal lords and the church imposed licenses to regulate the production of this material. For the monarchs of Europe these printing presses represented sites from which potentially destabilizing discourses could emerge. On the other hand, European rulers found the economies and trading networks developed by these emergent middle classes valuable. Their solution was to allow middle-class printing presses to exist, but circumscribed what they could disseminate. A state-run licensing and censorship system was the result. The American Revolution, French Revolution and the Revolutions of 1848 all contributed to the process of challenging these restrictions. From the 1820s to 1870s such restrictions were gradually overthrown in Europe and its colonies as the ever-expanding middle classes came to successfully challenge the power of the European monarchies and assert their own liberal hegemony.

Public service broadcasting

Public service broadcasting originated with the British Broadcasting Corporation developed by Lord Reith in Britain (Briggs 1961: 229–249). The model was replicated throughout the former British Empire. Reith saw broadcasting as a vehicle for educating people. His view was informed by a middle-class paternalism that drew upon Mathew Arnold's (1957 [1869]) vision of using schools to 'civilize' the lower classes. Although these corporations are state-owned and funded, they are not directly government-run (as they are in the communist model). Governments appoint a board that is accountable to a charter set by parliamentary legislation. The boards offer independence from direct political interference. The degree to which these corporations were actually autonomous of governments, however, varied from country to country. At one extreme, the BBC retained a fair degree of autonomy, while at the other extreme, broadcasting corporations in Africa effectively became government mouthpieces (see Louw and Milton 2012). Irrespective of the extent of actual government control, all the public corporations drew upon productive practices based on hierarchical managerialism and specialist division of labour practices. All produced industrialized top-down communication. This served the hegemonic needs of state bureaucrats trying to create administrative-economic units – such as 'Australia', 'Canada' or 'South Africa' – during the first half of the twentieth century. It also suited the top-down nation-building hegemonic needs of development bureaucrats in places like India and Zimbabwe in the wake of decolonization because it provided the ruling elites with a means for uni-directional communication with those they were trying to organize into nation states. At its best, public service broadcasting can provide quality programming unencumbered by the direct ideological control of the state or the commercial imperatives of the private sector.

State-subsidized media

The state-subsidy model is common to social-democrat states in the Netherlands, Belgium and Scandinavia. These states decided market-driven media systems skewed meaning making by only creating and serving commercially viable audiences. Their response is to use state subsidies to ensure that all demographics, classes, regions and political viewpoints are adequately represented in the media. Parliaments allocate funds to media subsidy boards. Board members are appointed by Parliament. These boards allocate the funds available. Like public service broadcasting, these boards operate within the dominant norms and values of the state. Another form of state subsidization operated in Latin America in the 1960s and 1970s. The state funded the development of media infrastructure like telecommunications and broadcast networks that it then licensed to commercial media. These state-subsidized private media companies produced meanings compatible with the interests of the governments subsidizing them (Fox 1988).

Communist media

Although it is no longer the case, the most extensive system of direct government-controlled mass media to emerge was that created by twentieth-century communist states. This media system was built upon Lenin's (1929) interpretation of Marxism. In Lenin's model, the Communist Party represented workers. Leninists believed this Party needed to capture the state in order to advance worker interests in the face of capitalist exploitation and repression of workers. According to communists, a media system owned by capitalists would necessarily portray a minority capitalist world-view. Leninists argued that the state should establish state-run media systems. In terms of this logic, a communist government-run media would be more democratic than a capitalist-operated media system because communists claimed to represent the exploited majority. This communist system produced an explicit government intervention into the meaning-making process, with Leninist logic ultimately leading to the creation of enormous state-run media systems in the Soviet Union, Eastern Europe and China. Instead of representing a working-class majority, this system came to represent only the minority apparatchik ruling class of communist state functionaries, who used repression and ideology to remain in power (Bahro 1981).

Development elites and media

The institutionalization of media in post-colonial states is often opaque to western citizens. As the colonial powers withdrew from Africa, Asia and the Middle East many new countries were created and handed over to local, but westernized, elites. Their states were economically underdeveloped; often riven with ethnic, racial and religious differences; and there was usually a deficit of skilled and experienced people to run them. Furthermore, the elites struggled to establish their legitimacy where they were a visibly privileged minority granted enormous power by the departing colonial rulers. The consequence was that a high proportion of these new elites established authoritarian control to stabilize their fragmented and precarious new countries. While from the outside the new post-colonial leaders looked legitimate, within their own countries they were viewed as a westernized minority whose power and interests were tethered to maintaining their economic and political links with the former colonial powers. This authoritarianism extended to taking control of the media, using it explicitly to promote a unified national identity. This led to the formulation of the New World Information Order (NWIO) which justified 'development journalism' as necessary in the 'developing world' (Masmoudi 1979). Within the NWIO formulation, it was justified for the media to be used by the state to control, manipulate, educate, manage and develop their populations. There was some overlap between the communist and NWIO understandings of the culture industry – both saw the media as tools to be used in a top-down way to bring about hegemonic ends deemed desirable by the state. But by the start of the twenty-first century a number of developing countries, especially those in Africa, had become failed or fragile states. Manipulation and control of their culture industries and 'sunshine journalism' had not helped them to maintain their hegemonies or develop their countries.

In each of these models of institutionalizing media production we can discern control mechanisms. Decisions in privately-owned media institutions are controlled by the commercial imperative to create and sell audiences. Communist, development and state-licensed media systems are distinct for their direct ideological control of media content. In these systems the state explicitly intervenes to ensure that content conforms to particular ideas and values. In state-subsidized and public service broadcasting models the mode of control is more indirect. The boards that manage the distribution of subsidies or a public service broadcaster operating under a charter ensure they conform to a mainstream discursive consensus.

THE INDUSTRIAL PRODUCTION OF MEANING

To produce meaning on an industrial scale, institutions needed to be created that employed professional communicators and organized them in managerial hierarchies and mechanistic work routines. These institutions reflected the dominant mode of production at the time. Factories began to use standardized assembly lines to produce material products like cars. Media institutions also followed these principles, developing routines and processes for producing meaning. This process of institutionalization structured the way meaning was made and the kind of meanings that could be made.

The diagrams in Figure 2.1 represent a distinctive aspect of industrialized communication. In the first diagram, communication involves a process of sharing. Meaning flows back and forth between the communicator and recipient. The roles of communicators and recipients are interchangeable. Meaning emerges out of the interchange. The medium merely facilitates the process of exchange. Some might argue that this model represents an ideal mode of human communication. Both sender and receiver are able to impart and receive meaning. The model might even suggest that the exchange is marked by equality, freedom and rationality. While it is tempting to say that this model of communication is pre-industrial, this risks romanticizing the forms of communication in pre-industrial societies. In pre-industrial society we can identify people who had more power in communication exchanges like royalty, clergy or other elites. Perhaps though we can say that in pre-industrial society the production and circulation was more haphazard and less organized. There wasn't a whole class of professionals who managed the production of meaning. In the second diagram then, the communicator works within a communication institution. The organizational form of the medium becomes a central part of the communication process. The communicator becomes a professional functionary within a highly routinized and rationalized process of cultural production. Importantly, the professional communicator and the medium are 'collapsed' into one another.

From the point of view of the audience or recipient, distinctions between the communicator and medium become increasingly unimportant. For instance, when we watch television the person appearing on the screen, the technical medium of television and the institution are interdependent. We can't have television as we know it without all three. Professional communicators and technologies become part of an organizational entity: the media. In a sense, the professional communicators and their meaning become increasingly depersonalized. Their individually held ideas have become much less important than in the first model of communication, where the exchange between individuals is the foundational idea. In the second diagram, recipients consume meaning that is the product of the collective labour of professionals working within the organization. While they might see a newsreader on the television screen talking to them, this newsreader is reading a script written by others, presenting images collected and edited by others and being distributed by technologies being managed by others. The final communicative product is the outcome of the work of many employees in the organization. This makes it very difficult to identify the opinions or work of a single author. The meaning exchange then is not mediated by an individual author as another human being, but by an institution made up of the interaction between many humans operating in their defined institutional roles.

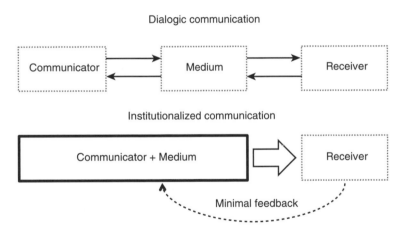

Figure 2.1   Institutionalized communication

MASS COMMUNICATION

By the end of the twentieth century the mass media's reach had become ubiquitous across the globe. It is now difficult to find a society, culture or set of human relations that are outside of the reach of media. The few places where media don't reach are economically, politically and socially marginal.

The mass media simultaneously increased the reach of professional communicators, while dramatically narrowing the role of recipients. Recipients became increasingly passive receivers and circulators of meanings made by others. For those working within the culture industry, audiences became conceptualized as abstract objects: publics, target markets, niche groups. Communicators depersonalize the meaning-making process; instead of addressing other human beings, they construct techniques for assembling and addressing abstract groups in instrumental ways: to grow audience share, influence public opinion or disseminate promotional messages.

The industrialization of communication led to *mass* communication. This process began with newspapers but reached its zenith with television. Mass communication is inherently top-down. By 'top-down' we mean that only a select group of professionals, working under frameworks set by managers, owners or other political elites, are able to make and distribute meaning on a large scale. Industrialization reduced the spaces for non-professional communicators to engage in meaning making as anything other than audiences. This form of communication is uni-directional: one group speaks, the other group listens. To the extent that the industry listens to the public or audience, it is in strategic forms like market research, public opinion research or other kinds of surveillance. Where the industry listens, it does so in order to more efficiently structure and rationalize the way it manages the audience. The audience's capacity to either speak or monitor the industry is set almost entirely on the industry's terms.

A professional communicator makes meaning according to the norms, rules and power relationships of the institution they work in. The space for individual creativity is curtailed by daily organizational needs, routines and hierarchies. Further, industrialized communication constructs the recipient as an audience. The flow of messages becomes one-way. There is little scope for input, adaptation or feedback in industrialized communication. Simultaneously, the capacity to deliver messages is greatly enhanced. Rather than facilitating dialogic communication, industrialization dramatically increases the capacity of one group to speak while neutering the ability of the other group to speak back. Similarly, as media technologies have developed, organizations have developed the capacity to watch and monitor their audiences, at the same time as they speak to them. The organization develops the capacity to speak to and watch over the audience, while the audience is relegated to listening to the organization, or at best, participating in circulating content within networks managed by those organizations.

THE CULTURE INDUSTRY

An early and foundational critique of the industrial production of meaning came from a group of German intellectuals, including Theodor Adorno, Max Horkheimer and Herbert Marcuse, collectively known as the Frankfurt School. The Frankfurt School observed the development of mass societies organized around different political ideologies: fascism in Germany, communism in the Soviet Union and liberal democracy in America. They observed that each of these societies relied on the industrial production of culture to organize and manage enormous populations. Film, television and radio in particular were being rapidly developed and used in each society. Much of the Frankfurt

School's concern about the culture industry was due to their recognition that mass communication lent itself to top-down rhetoric, manipulation and control. For the Frankfurt School, industrializing communication created two interrelated negative effects. It increased opportunities for manipulating and controlling communication while reducing the spaces for dialogical communication. The Frankfurt School saw this as producing a mass society in which they believed the majority of people passively consumed, and were effectively manipulated by, mass-produced meanings. The passivity induced by mass media created a 'one-dimensional society'. They saw this one-dimensionality as the inevitable outcome of a meaning-making process that significantly narrowed the range of voices and opinions that were distributed widely and loudly by the mass media. In their view, industrialized communication tended to silence or ignore those voices that the mass media did not deem fit to distribute. While at one level it might make sense for elites to create systems that curtail opportunities for oppositional meaning making, for the Frankfurt School this kind of one-dimensional society could go dramatically wrong. In their view, it was through debate and conflict that new and better ideas emerge. Human society would be better served if elites didn't seek to close and control meaning making. To them, the culture industry stifled this process.

Narrowing what we think about

Seen from another angle, Bernard Cohen (1963) argued that the mass media had become 'agenda setters'. He famously argued that the media, 'may not be successful much of the time in telling people what to think, but it is stunningly successful in telling its readers what to think about' (1963: 13). This argument was further developed by the mass communication researchers Maxwell McCombs and Donald Shaw (1972) in their 'Chapel Hill study' of the 1968 US Presidential election. They carefully examined the media that voters in an American community consumed and the political issues they felt were important. They found that the issues people felt were important, like the economy or healthcare, were those issues that were prominently covered by the news media they consumed. It has been argued that in industrial societies the mass media have come to set the agenda for the bulk of the population. Most people tend to think about things that the media place on the agenda.

Narrowing what can be said

The German political scientist Elisabeth Noelle-Neumann (1973) developed an interpretation of the 'narrowing process' that complements the arguments made by the Frankfurt School and Cohen, but goes beyond it. Noelle-Neumann's idea of the narrowing process goes beyond merely the pressures of industry discourses and practices. She also looked at the wider pressures of social conformity. According to Noelle-Neumann there is a tendency towards an ever-narrowing range of opinions due to the interaction of culture industry practices and public opinion. She argued that when an issue first arises there will be many opinions about the topic. However, over time media practices produce a narrowing of opinions heard. This happens because media workers choose to advantage some opinions over others, in accordance with their own preferred discourses, institutional norms and other power relationships into which they are embedded. Pressures towards social conformity mean that members of the public who disagree with the dominant media interpretation progressively fall silent. As a result, counter-opinions or antitheses disappear. This, in turn, leads media workers to conclude that there are no opposition views to report. A 'spiral of silence' develops in which fewer and fewer of the full range of opinions are heard. If Noelle-Neumann's theory is correct, the culture industry is centrally implicated in the process of discursive closure. This raises two interrelated questions: can one identify those exercising power within and over the culture industry so as to close social discourse? And, how do discourses themselves acquire the power to structurally lock alternative views out of the culture industry?

Thinking dialectically: arguing for a contest of meanings

The Frankfurt School argued that society was at its most healthy when no perspective, idea or thesis could go unchallenged. This argument was informed by a philosophical idea called the 'dialectic'. A dialectical analysis begins with the premise that a system or idea always already contains contradictions and antagonisms. History unfolds as it does because our ideas and the societies we create with them always contain struggles between winners and losers. Power relationships are dynamic, no one gains immutable power, for every winner there is a loser who tries to push back. This way of conceptualizing power is dialectical in the sense that we strive in this book to avoid conspiracy theory approaches that would argue some powerful groups control media and use it to dominate and control society. Counter to this we argue that while there are powerful groups, the kinds of social relationships they create always contain antagonisms, anxieties and competitions that constantly threaten to undermine and destabilize them. The dialectic is a useful way of conceptualizing these power relationships.

Where the Frankfurt School make a compelling argument is that for them the dialectic is not a problem to be overcome: it is instead core to our humanity and something to be encouraged. For them, the dialectic is a kind of motor or engine that drives society. Without it we would stagnate. The Frankfurt School argued that the dialectic would not cease and that it was dangerous to act as if it could. For them, society was at its healthiest and most vibrant when counter-arguments, radically different ideas and antithetical arguments were encouraged (see Jay 1973). This involves not only accepting the inevitability of conflict between different positions, but going further and seeing this conflict as a social good because it generates new ideas and social relationships. The current state of social relationships is always the product not of one perspective obliterating the other, but of the conflicts and oppositions of the past. There can be no permanent and absolute winner. Those in power are shaped by the conflicts, compromises and challenges they faced along the way. Their power is channelled and restrained by others whose ideas and resources press back on them. Creative ideas emerge out of these struggles.

Even though ideas assert themselves as absolute, they also rely on marking themselves out against other ideas. A dialectic way of thinking encourages us not to ignore how ideas rely on their opposites and recognize this as central to the production of ideas. That is, we recognize an idea as independent of, and interdependent with, other ideas at the same time. A simple way of thinking about this is in terms of our identity. We think of ourselves as independent people with distinctive characteristics: gender, ethnicity, cultural interests or political views. While at one level each of those things is distinctive, they are also all dependent on other different ideas other people might have. They only become meaningful when we position ourselves relative to others. It is only meaningful to have a particular political viewpoint because we have to set it out against someone else with a different point of view. If everyone had *exactly the same* political viewpoint, then politics would necessarily disappear because there would be no need for a process of contesting ideas and power relationships. That is unlikely to happen. And in any case, if we create social relations that filter out different points of view we risk weakening our own ideas and identities. We risk misrecognizing how our own ideas are dependent on others.

THE LIBERAL-DEMOCRATIC CULTURE INDUSTRY

The Frankfurt School became concerned that the twentieth-century industrialization of cultural production thwarted the dialectic process. They argued that when intellectuals were industrialized they were locked into institutional arrangements and power relationships which had the effect of stifling and neutering antithetical views. In some cases the culture industry makes and distributes ideas that confirm the interests of those with power to control the media while views that are fundamentally contradictory are simply ignored. Another even more troubling form of production was the capacity of the culture industry, particularly in the liberal-democratic west, to stage a pseudo-dialectic, where apparently opposing views are presented. Consider for example the two-party system in the UK, Australia or America. The culture industry stages a continuous debate between two positions that are fundamentally the same. Despite their differences, all the major parties in these countries believe in the same core ideas: capitalism, economic growth, liberal democracy, secularism, human rights and so on. The capacity of the culture industry to neuter or fake the dialectic troubled Adorno and Horkheimer greatly. As German Jewish intellectuals they emigrated to America after Hitler's rise to power. In America, they discovered a culture industry which fascinated them because they came to see it as far more sophisticated and adaptable than the authoritarian and fascist manifestations of cultural production they had observed with Hitler and Stalin. In America they observed a process of cultural production that didn't need to overtly censor antithetical ideas. It either ignored them, or even worse, co-opted and repurposed them into its own world-view.

A later Frankfurt School figure, Herbert Marcuse (1964), expressed this capacity most clearly when he observed how the American culture industry could commodify and sell the 'counter-culture' back to itself. When young Americans rebelled against the system in the 1960s with alternative lifestyles, music and fashion, the culture industry rapidly began to produce those ideas, the music industry rapidly commercialized anti-establishment folk and rock music, and the fashion industry mass-produced formerly working-class clothes like Levi's jeans as symbols of youthful freedom, and printed t-shirts featuring the Marxist guerrilla Che Guevara. While on the surface level American popular culture appeared vibrant and free, this masked a canny ability to ensure that alternative ideas had no meaningful impact. Where Hitler and Stalin controlled cultural production by ruthlessly oppressing alternative ideas, the American mode of control tamed ideas by celebrating and commodifying them. The flexibility of this culture industry to curtail and co-opt alternative perspectives was of great interest to Adorno and Horkheimer. This culture industry relied on our avid participation, but that participation was limited in ways that made it almost disempowering. For instance, we choose between ten brands of soap powder, or two political parties, or every week there is a new Hollywood blockbuster or a new reality TV pop star to vote on. These things appear different on the surface, but are really all the same. The freedom of the culture industry is the freedom to choose what is really the same. Their critique is reflected in arguments today about pseudo-participation in interactive media. Yes, we can click, like, comment, post a blog, but does any of this participation amount to much? In the Frankfurt School's account, instead of the media facilitating consideration and conflict over substantive alternatives, it instead presents narrowed options that aren't really different. What they observed was industrialized culture stifling and replacing the social dialectic with 'one-dimensionality', where conventionally dominant ideas were continuously circulated, and never seriously challenged. Foucault's notion that discourses organize and limit communication has an interesting complementarity to the Frankfurt School's view of the culture industry as a site for discursive closure in the twentieth century.

In addition to their work on undialectical communication as discursive closure, the Frankfurt School were also concerned that the culture industry focused on trivia rather than substance. Presenting trivia makes it possible to avoid issues that might lead to real debate and conflict. Examples of this trivialization are found in the continual cycle of celebrity culture, reality TV and lifestyle media. The media frenzies surrounding events like the death of Princess Diana, the titillation of political scandals like the Monica Lewinski affair, or the banal trivia of Paris Hilton's driving conviction, or Britney Spears' shaved head, or Miley Cyrus' performance at the VMA music awards, are all examples of the culture industry as a system of advanced distraction. While some of these events might be meaningless to you, they all dominated media attention for a time, just as some event is probably dominating media coverage as you read this book. Even when the culture industry does draw attention to significant political issues, it can be content to uncritically recycle dominant discourses. Complex conflicts in places like Bosnia, Kosovo, Iraq, Afghanistan, South Africa, Syria and the Arab Spring are presented in simplistic terms. Although it is often argued that Adorno and Horkheimer were overly pessimistic, wherever we look we can find examples of the culture industry they described in 1947 developing far beyond even some their most pessimistic predictions.

THE CULTURE INDUSTRY IN THE INTERACTIVE ERA

For contemporary readers some of this description of a top-down media might feel jarring. From the 1990s onwards, interactive digital media technologies created possibilities for challenging the mass media model of meaning making in three ways.

- Firstly, interactive media created the potential for new forms of audience participation.
- Secondly, interactive media made it easier for new voices to create and distribute their ideas and stories to large audiences via the internet.
- Thirdly, interactive media made it possible and economically viable to reach niche audiences. This meant commercialized media no longer had to conform to mass production logics in order to be profitable.

While at first inspection this development might please social critics like the Frankfurt School, we should also be cautious in our approach to these changes. While the development of interactive media has been accompanied by new opportunities for participation and meaning production, they have also been accompanied by sophisticated modes of control. The forms of participation and control characteristic of interactive media are a central narrative of this book. The advent of interactive media has seen:

- the proliferation of niche media
- large organizations attempting to cultivate audience participation
- a proliferation of platforms not organized solely around the production of content by professionals
- growth in new media voices.

These changes led to much hype about the demise of the old culture industry and the empowerment of participatory bottom-up communication which would render critiques of mass society and communication like the Frankfurt School's obsolete. However, even in the interactive media environment, a small number of media organizations have remained, or become, dominant.

Although the interactive media revolution has generated a rich new flow of meanings via the internet from a much widened pool of meaning makers, a few large powerful media organizations, some old and some new, have remained key influential sources of meaning. At the outset, there are at least two important observations to make about the enduring power of large media organizations. The first is that culture industry organizations are still the dominant source of news and opinion. While audiences might use new platforms like social media and new devices like smartphones and tablets to access and circulate content, that content is largely produced by mainstream organizations, and the opinions individuals circulate are largely about stories and agendas set by those organizations. The second observation is that while ordinary people may be circulating their opinions to larger audiences using social media, this isn't necessarily prompting debate that changes power relationships. Instead, people appear to get most of their ideas from mainstream media, and circulate their views within small niche groups online, mostly made up of people who are similar to them.

To date, the digital revolution has not fundamentally changed the industrial logic of media production, or diminished the capacity of the institutions to manage and control communication. While industries might appear in some cases to have less control over the production of particular meanings, they do appear to have expanding control over communication in general. New technologies might make it technically possible to say whatever we like; it appears though that most people either circulate ideas already produced by the industry or they circulate ideas within platforms owned by the industry. Neither case disrupts the power relationships of media production. The most profound change is that the industry must invest resources not just in creating and disseminating content, but in managing the circulation of that content on interactive platforms. Watching and managing audiences is critical to the process of making and distributing content. This presents the industry with both challenges and opportunities: challenges in the sense that the meaning-making process is much more diffused and fragmented, but opportunities in the sense that interactive platforms afford the ability to watch and respond to audiences in real time. As the mass audience has fragmented into numerous, constantly changing niche audiences, communication professionals have had to become specialists in targeting and managing those audiences. Rather than dilute the control of professionals, interactive technologies increase the scope for them to manage audiences more effectively.

Interactive media technologies have the capability to facilitate dialogical communication, at the same time they afford the culture industry significantly more control to manage audiences. We are moving into an era where the binary between 'top-down' manipulative communication and 'bottom-up' participatory or dialogical communication has collapsed. They are no longer distinct opposites; instead participatory and dialogical communication is becoming the key mode of communicative control in today's culture industry. This poses exciting and interesting questions and debates for us to consider in this book.

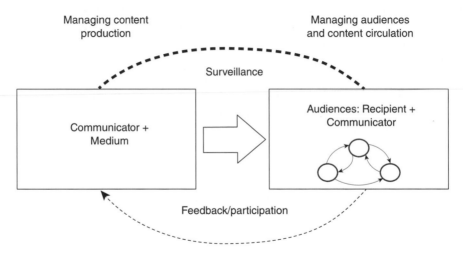

Figure 2.2   Institutionalized communication in the interactive era

In Figure 2.2 we map out how the production and circulation of meaning is managed in the interactive era. In the twentieth century, meaning making was institutionalized. These institutions made and disseminated meaning to mass audiences. While the Frankfurt School claimed that everyday life was organized by the culture industry, audiences were not fully incorporated within the institutions of meaning making. The audience was largely 'outside' of the institution.

With the emergence of the interactive era, the public and audience became much more directly incorporated into the production and circulation of meaning. The audience becomes institutionalized. In the mass era, audiences' meaning-making activities were not fully incorporated into the institutionalized production and circulation of meaning. In the mass era, audiences:

- were monitored using public opinion, market and audience research – this monitoring informed the production of meaning to some degree
- consumed institutionalized meaning but actively decoded it within their private social lives and peer networks.

In the interactive era, these activities have been much more directly institutionalized and rationalized. There are now two types of institutionalized processes for making and managing meaning:

- producing meaning
- managing the circulation of meaning.

Some institutions do one or the other, some institutions do both. Many institutions are linked together in the joint effort to produce and manage meaning. Institutions that produce meaning like the news, television, film and music industries remain powerful. They are now interdependent with organizations that manage the circulation of that meaning like social media and social networking sites, content aggregators, database companies and search engines.

Where in the twentieth century the culture industry was organized around institutions that produced meaning and disseminated it to audiences, institutions that manage audiences are now central to the meaning-making process. These institutions don't produce meanings of their own. They manage audiences by offering them the means to make and circulate their own meanings and interact with meaning produced by other institutions. These institutions are organized around developing techniques for watching and responding to their audiences. The more active the audience is in participating in the circulation of meaning, the greater the capacity of these institutions to manage them. If in the mass culture industry of the twentieth century, audiences' active meaning making took place largely outside the watch of cultural institutions, in the interactive era audience activity is extensively monitored. Institutions that produce meaning and those that manage and watch meaning making are interdependent. Institutions that manage audience interactivity generate data they can provide to the content-producing industries about those audiences; the content-producing industries in turn provide the content that is often circulating within interactive platforms.

The relationship is symbiotic and competitive. Each institution occupies different moments in the production and circulation of meaning. While audiences' capacity to 'speak' is greatly amplified in the interactive era, this speaking is more institutionalized within the process of cultural production. This enables institutions to shape and manage audiences more effectively. Institutions that produce meaning are able to make and target content at niche audiences. Institutions that manage audience interactivity shape the networks, connections and flows of content to niche audiences. As these institutions interact they adapt to the interests and preferences of many different audience niches. Audiences have little control over how this system watches and responds to them. And this mode of cultural production reaches into their everyday life in ways that the twentieth-century culture industry did not.

TRACING OUR ENGAGEMENT WITH INDUSTRIALIZED COMMUNICATION

Starting with the left-hand box in Figure 2.2, trace the relationships between each component and ask the following questions.

What industrially produced content do you consume? Make a list.
Where and how do you consume industrially produced content?
Who do you consume it with?
How often do you consume industrially produced content?
How do you respond to and circulate industrially produced content?

Now consider the content that you create and circulate on the web.

What do you make?
Where do you upload it?
How do you and your friends interact with it?
List and define practices where you consume, circulate and create content. What institutionalized technologies, networks and devices do you use to circulate content?
What kinds of information does your creation and circulation of content online create?
What are the values and uses of that information?
What are the ways in which you as an audience member contribute directly to the production of industrially produced content that you then consume?
List the range of institutions you engage with, and categorize their control over the way you create and circulate meaning.

As a simple illustration imagine television as the key institution of the twentieth-century culture industry. Television had extensive reach into the homes and lives of ordinary people. Powerful groups could use television to disseminate messages that were in their political and economic interests. Television organized everyday lives in many households. Once broadcast into homes, however, television producers had limited access to what audiences did with the meanings. It was a one-way flow of content and meaning. Only market research and public opinion research could offer some understanding of what effect television had on the ideas and meanings in the public mind. With the emergence of interactive media ordinary home life has changed considerably: we don't just consume media, we also make and circulate it. Think about how many of us now still watch television, but at the same time are accessing the web on a smartphone, tablet or laptop. We might be private-messaging friends, circulating photos of our own lives, or commenting on a television show. While we are very active and busy, this activity is more institutionalized. Each of these communicative acts is positioned within an institutionalized network of cultural production.

PRIVACY POLICIES

We can examine the relationships established by the interactive culture industries by carefully reading through the privacy policies we agree to when we sign up.

How often do you read the privacy policies you agree to?

Why don't you read them?

What conditions in a privacy policy would concern you?

If a privacy policy of a platform all your friends used concerned you what would you do?

These policies are a contract between you and the platform about how the data and content you generate can be used. Through these policies you agree to a certain role within a system of cultural production.

Read the privacy policies of platforms like Instagram, Facebook, Google and Twitter. For links visit the *Media and Society* website study.sagepub.com/carahandlouw

INSTAGRAM'S 'INFORMATION WE COLLECT'

From Instagram's privacy policy, here is a list of information it collects about you. Consider what this information might be used for.

Your username
Your password
Your email address
Your name
Your profile picture
Your phone number
Images you upload
Videos you upload
Comments you make
List of images you like
List of people you follow
Web pages you visit
Your movements
Times of day and locations when you use the service
When you view images
What images you view
How many images you view
How you scroll through the image feed
What accounts you visit
Which filters you use
How often you upload images
Who you tag in images

(Continued)

(Continued)

What your images depict
What hashtags you use or view
Your IP address
Web pages you visit
Browsers you use
What devices you access Instagram from
What your use habits are between different devices
Words you use in your comments
Where images are uploaded
Geo-tags you add to images.

The privacy policy explains that this information has many uses. Some of which include enabling Instagram to:

- Tailor or target 'personalized content and information to you and others, which could include online ads or other forms of marketing'. The information it collects about you and people like you is used to shape flows of content on the platform.
- Monitor how users engage with the service. This includes monitoring 'visitors, traffic, and demographic patterns'. This data is useful for Instagram in packaging and selling its audience to advertisers and investors.
- Conduct continuous experiments to 'test' and 'improve' the service. Instagram might use the information it collects to trial new features on certain parts of its audience. For instance, some users will see targeted advertising in their home feed before others.

FACEBOOK'S 'HOW WE USE YOUR INFORMATION'

Facebook also lists an extensive array of information it collects about users. It explains that it uses the information to customize content which is 'more relevant to you'.

In addition to most of the information Instagram collects, Facebook explains that it also collects information that it can 'infer from your use of Facebook'. This broad statement suggests a constantly evolving array of data it collects about the daily habits of users.

Facebook explains that the information you provide is used to 'target relevant ads'. For instance, 'If you like a page about gluten-free food, you may receive ads about relevant food products' or if you check in to a sci-fi movie at a theatre they may infer you are a sci-fi fan for future ad targeting. Facebook suggests we use this tool to understand how its advertising model works: www. facebook.com/ads/create/

Log in to the tool and undertake an experiment. Imagine you are a brand targeting someone like yourself and your peers. Experiment with different categories and information to see how Facebook can define and deliver an audience to you based on information individuals have uploaded to the platform.

Considering these privacy policies, identify the relationships between users and the platform, and the uses of information, which the privacy policies institutionalize. How do these privacy policies value and protect the information generated by users for both users and the platforms?

CONCLUSION

The development of networked telecommunications and digital technologies reshaped the global economy, and has had a particularly profound impact on the production and circulation of culture. This will be a core theme in this book. The transition from mass to interactive and networked production entails a number of profound shifts. These include:

- a shift from hierarchical linear production, to flexible and networked ways of organizing production
- a shift from tightly controlled national markets, to open international trade-flows and global markets
- a fragmentation of mass consumer markets and audiences into a series of globally dispersed niche markets and audiences.

Communication and information became central to the facilitation of these global, networked and flexible forms of production. While professional communicators and the culture industry grew in this phase, it also reformed into a more fragmented and flexible industry. These developments are the subject of the next two chapters.

The interactive culture industry that has emerged out of the development of the internet and web is caught in the same contradictions as the forms of cultural production that are remaking themselves (print, radio and television). We have a culture industry that is largely commercial and therefore must make a profit while at the same time we expect it to serve the public. This has been a paradox that concerned critics like the Frankfurt School and political economists of television, newspapers and radio. In response to these public values and hopes, the internet's decentralized structure, as a cultural industry with no centre of power, has been mythologized. Early digital optimists equated 'nobody' ultimately being in charge, with potentially 'everybody' or 'anybody' being in charge. For some digital optimists the internet, and the web in its commercial form, empowered ordinary people. Some of these influential people and sites include public intellectuals like Nicholas Negroponte, Howard Rheingold, Henry Jenkins, technology industry publications like *Wired* magazine and research centres like MIT Media Labs and Microsoft Research. In their view of the internet and web, technologies that enabled ordinary users to create and circulate content were inherently empowering. These claims were built on the binary that the 'old' culture industry was top-down: it simply distributed content to audiences whose only choice was to consume it. If the 'new' culture industry enabled them to participate in creating and circulating the meaning then it must be empowering. In this book, we'll argue that this binary is a false one: participation and control can work very well together. They are not binary opposites, rather they are interdependent.

FURTHER READING

The founding reading on the culture industry is Adorno and Horkheimer's essay 'The culture industry: enlightenment as mass deception' in their book *Dialectic of Enlightenment* (2008). This essay was originally published in 1944 in German and translated into English in 1972. You can also find it easily online. In this essay Adorno and Horkheimer conceptualize the culture industry, connect it to wider developments in the mass society, and critique how it organizes everyday life. Adorno reflected on his original argument about the culture industry in the essay 'The culture industry reconsidered' (in Adorno 2001). This chapter offers a relatively accessible reflection on Adorno's main arguments about the development of the culture industry. Thompson (1995) offers a historical account of how the media emerged as part of wider processes of modernization and industrialization. Where Adorno and Horkheimer's account of the culture industry is philosophical and critical, Thompson provides a rich descriptive explanation of media processes and institutions. Hesmondhalgh (2013) offers an account of the contemporary organization of the cultural industries. Steemers (2014) examines the dynamics of the global television industry. Taylor (2007) explores the changing nature of the music industry. Napoli (2014) and Wilken (2014) each offer accounts of the development of social media industries and platforms.

Adorno, T. W. (2001) *The Culture Industry: Selected Essays on Mass Culture.* New York: Routledge.

Adorno, T. and Horkheimer, M. (2008) *Dialectic of Enlightenment.* London: Verso.

Hesmondhalgh, D. (2013) *The Cultural Industries*, 2nd edn. London: Sage.

Napoli, P. (2014) 'On automation in media industries: integrating algorithmic media production into media industries scholarship', *Media Industries,* 1 (1): 33–38

Steemers, J. (2014) 'Selling television: addressing transformations in the international distribution of television content', *Media Industries,* 1 (1): 44–49.

Taylor, T. D. (2007) 'The changing shape of the culture industry; or, how did electronica music get into television commercials?', *Television & New Media*, 8 (3): 235–258.

Thompson, J. B. (1995) *The Media and Modernity: A Social Theory of the Media.* Redwood City, CA: Stanford University Press.

Wilken, R. (2014) 'Places nearby: Facebook as a location-based social media platform', *New Media & Society*, 1–17.

Any article marked with is available to download at the website **study.sagepub.com/ carahandlouw**

POWER AND MEDIA PRODUCTION

POWERFUL GROUPS USE PROFESSIONAL COMMUNICATORS AND MEDIA INSTITUTIONS TO MAKE AND MANAGE MEANING.

* How do groups become hegemonic?

* What institutions are used to maintaining hegemony?

* What role do professional communicators play in making and maintaining hegemony?

In this chapter we examine:

- How groups and meanings become hegemonic
- The flexible and responsive hegemonies that have taken shape in the networked era by using new communication technologies and channels to make and manage niche markets and publics
- The work of managing hegemonies using communicative sites, communication professionals and meanings
- The dynamics of resistance and change that characterize any hegemony.

MEANING AND POWER

Meaning is not some free-floating abstract entity, detached from the grubby realities of human struggles for influence and power. Rather, the meaning-making process is always embedded in power relationships. Power – the ability to have one's interests prevail over others – is derivative of access to economic and cultural resources, social position and linguistic factors. Institutionalized communication is implicated in organizing each of these. Power relations get encoded into meaning via the various sites that have effectively been 'licensed' to manufacture, circulate and manage discourse. One of these is the media, because they have become important for defining social position and status and for positioning people.

Importantly, power is not automatic. It is the outcome of labour and struggle. One of the sites of struggle is the battle over media discourses. To understand the process of meaning making we need to examine how communicative flows involve an ongoing struggle between different groups of players. On the one hand we find those who wish to restrict, narrow, close and manipulate flows of communication – those who want to bring about discursive closures. On the other hand we find those who have a vested interest in resisting such discursive closures and manipulations. There is no need to privilege one of these as better than the other. Rather, both those who are striving for closure and those resisting can simply be viewed as the necessary and inevitable outcomes of humans organizing themselves. If one adopts the 'trying for closure' versus 'resisting closure' approach to analysing communication, a series of six questions emerges as a systematic way of unravelling the nature of media and cultural production:

- What is the nature of the context within which the communication is taking place?
- Which group or groups are socially and politically dominant?
- How did they get to be dominant and powerful?
- How do they stay dominant and powerful?
- How do they manage the discourses within their society?
- Who is resisting these discourses?

Together, these six questions provide a basic route map for unravelling the struggle for hegemony.

BECOMING HEGEMONIC

Becoming hegemonic means becoming the dominant or leading group – or, more likely, alliance of groups – in a society. This entails becoming the ruling group or elite whose concept or definition of reality sets the tone. Hegemonic groups are effectively able to set the overarching intellectual agenda in a given society and manipulate dominant discourses. Becoming the ruling group appears to require being simultaneously successful in three spheres:

- Building and maintaining a working set of political alliances. That is, constructing a ruling group.
- Successfully generating consent among the ruled. That is, developing the legitimacy of the ruling group.
- Building coercive capacity to generate authority through police, courts, prisons and possibly a military.

The more legitimacy rulers have, the less coercion they need to employ. However, even the most legitimate systems rely on some coercive underpinning, even if it is only the *threat* that the police and legal machine *can* be used if individuals break the law. Each of these three hegemonic functions relies on communication and intellectual organization. The legitimacy and consent function is entirely communicative, and is also the sphere most obviously associated with media production. Becoming politically and socially dominant requires ruling groups to successfully learn, mobilize and organize two key skills: the art of coercion and the art of communication and negotiation.

A key contextual variable is power. For anyone concerned with exploring the relationships between power, communication and context, Gramsci's notion of hegemony becomes invaluable. Gwyn Williams explains that:

> By 'hegemony' Gramsci seems to mean a sociopolitical situation, in his terminology a 'moment', in which the philosophy and practice of a society fuse or are in equilibrium; an order in which a certain way of life and thought is dominant, in which one concept of reality is diffused throughout society in all its institutional and private manifestations, informing with its spirit all taste, morality, customs, religious and political principles, and all social relations, particularly in their intellectual and moral connotation. An element of direction and control, not necessarily conscious, is implied. (Williams 1960: 587)

Seeing social communication as embedded in a struggle over power draws attention away from ideals and contextually specific morality, and locates attention instead on the impact that 'lived battles' over hegemony have on communication. The notion of hegemony helps remove moralism and idealism from the picture because hegemonic analysis recognizes that, for those in power, striving to close discourse whether conscious or unconscious is sensible, just as for those not in power it is often, but not always, sensible to resist such closures.

Hegemonic communicative labour became increasingly mediatized over the course of the twentieth century. By the start of the twenty-first century, becoming socially and politically dominant required an ability to play a media game across print, radio, television and the web. Not surprisingly communicators like public relations (PR) professionals, media and communication advisors, and 'spin doctors' are now key features of the political machinery that ruling groups must build. In some senses the very art of ruling became dependent upon successful impression and discourse management using media. This has necessarily impacted on the nature of those staffing hegemonic groups. To join the ranks of the socially dominant it has become increasingly important to be able to play mediatized politics, or at least to know how to get others to play it for you.

How do groups become hegemonic?

If sketching out the broader social context is a good starting point for analysing media production, then it leads us to the following two questions:

- What is the nature of the socially dominant group(s) within the context under examination?
- How did they get to be dominant or hegemonic?

Industrial, and post-industrial, societies are highly complex entities, involving the interactions of millions of individuals and multiple interest groups. Taking the lead and becoming hegemonic in such complex entities requires constructing alliances that draw together players from a range of social sectors – like business, legal, media, health, security, education, labour and so on – and demographic or belief groupings. Becoming a ruling elite is hard and continuous work.

A political elite – whose job it becomes to coordinate the various sectoral interests of the wider ruling elite – has to be constructed and then held together through a process of negotiating and bargaining. This political negotiating task has become professionalized and institutionalized within a range of sites, including parliaments, boards, bureaus and more recently multinational organizations such as the World Trade Organization (WTO). Politics is an intensely communicative occupation. Building and maintaining hegemony requires the capacity to alternate between consensus and conflict-driven communication. In part, alliance construction involves producing and circulating successful internally directed discourses, that is, discourses which hold teams together and keep such teams focused on a particular vision of governance and collaboration. The birth of a successful hegemonic group needs to be understood as a contextually unique creation emergent from effective leadership and communication skills. Hegemonies also emerge from contextually unique sets of synchronic and diachronic interactions with other groups; and often, from sheer good luck. Once formed, hegemonies constantly change because the leading group must continually adjust and make new compromises to survive. This makes hegemonies highly contextual organisms tied to a particular location and moment. The actual composition of a hegemonic alliance is seldom the same for very long, because the membership and patterns of influence are ever mutating. But, in addition to small ongoing shifts through which hegemonic groups continually renew themselves, huge cataclysmic hegemonic shifts also occur. At those moments the hegemonic 'rules of the game' are fundamentally altered. Such revolutionary changes usually transpire when dominant groups have failed to sufficiently renew their composition and their discourses, and so lose their ability to lead and organize a changed society. The collapse of the Soviet system in 1989 represents such a revolutionary hegemonic shift. At such moments the organizing discourses of a society are rendered transparent. The collapsing hegemonic discourse no longer has the capacity to normalise the old order's way of life and world-view, but the new hegemonic order will not yet be in a position to normalize its preferred vision. It takes a new order some time to fully dislodge old hegemonic discourses and practices and entrench, and close, its own preferred discourses and practices.

Feudalism and early capitalism

The processes of 'becoming hegemonic' have altered over time. Such processes first emerged in the post-feudal world. Under feudalism, power was located in hereditary families who did not have to become dominant, because they were born dominant. The bourgeoisie that became powerful with the collapse of feudalism had to find new mechanisms for creating and organizing their power, regulating differences between themselves and taking decisions. The result was the creation of bourgeois public forums such as parliaments. Within these sites bourgeois individuals and factions learned the communicative art of becoming dominant and hegemonic by forming alliances, discursively promoting their interests and negotiating. After bourgeois parliaments were widened to also include non-middle-class representation the hegemonic arts of becoming dominant became necessarily more complex. However, to some extent widening representation was rendered less significant by the emergence of managerialism, which saw the locus of power shift away from public forums. The managerialists used boards, bureaus and government executives such as cabinets as their key decision-making sites. The role of parliaments as the true seat of power declined.

Managerial to global network capitalism

As parliaments became less important to the negotiation of ideas under managerialism, the differences between parliamentary groupings – for instance, labour parties and conservative parties – have greatly narrowed over time, so that eventually elections in liberal democracies seemingly only produce intra-elite rotation rather than fundamental policy changes. This is partly because the key centrist parties are all committed to the same pragmatism and maintenance of the same managerialist hegemony. Further, all parliamentarians rely on the same bureaucratic managers for advice on decisions and policies. Managerial elites created one-dimensional hegemonies in which only pseudo-choices were available (Marcuse 1964). In the liberal democracies, managerialist rulers increasingly lost legitimacy as the twentieth century progressed, leading to declining voter turnouts, growing voter cynicism and a generalized distrust of politicians. A parallel East European legitimacy crisis saw Soviet managerialists overthrown in 1989 and 1990.

Significantly, the managerial era was also the era of mass communication, with the culture industry disseminating and legitimating mass discourses, appropriate to the needs of managerialist hegemonies. The Frankfurt School noted the interesting parallels between the mass discourses of liberal and social-democrat managerialism, Soviet managerialism and Nazi managerialism. In the 1950s managerialist discourses generally resonated with mass audiences, and managerialists gained widespread legitimacy in societies like the United States, Canada and Australia as they delivered new material prosperity in the form of mass suburban housing, affordable electricity and household appliances, automobiles, and popular culture like television and rock records. Product delivery also helped make science into something of a new secular religion helped along by the excitement of rocket launches and the space age. Among Anglo-intellectuals, managerialist discourses like functionalist behaviourism, structural functionalism and systems theory gained widespread currency. Each of these discourses assumed an onwards-and-upwards story of human progress by adhering to rational scientific processes of discovery and innovation.

However, this legitimacy progressively unravelled when managerialists and scientists were seen as responsible for creating the threat of nuclear warfare, and were unable to find solutions to the Vietnam ordeal, crime, inflation and unemployment. Creating a hegemony requires both inwardly directed discourses to hold the hegemonic team together and externally directed discourses that make the hegemonic team credible in the eyes of other groups. The latter involves mediatized impression management for the consumption of the ruled, and is geared to legitimating the rulers. Managerialist legitimation problems arose once they began to lose touch with the external audiences and created discourses resonating with fellow managerialists (that is, the socially dominant) but which sounded elitist to the ruled. Managerialists responded to growing 'steering problems' of unemployment and crime by building bigger bureaucracies to administer top-down planning. These managerial solutions made ordinary people feel manipulated by experts who appeared unable to solve social problems. One outcome was the emergence of conservative-populism in societies like the United States, United Kingdom and Australia that railed against elite and managerialist interventions associated with welfare targeting sectional interests. By the time global networkers emerged and began challenging the discourses and practices of managerialism, the managerialists already found themselves hegemonically vulnerable.

HEGEMONY AND THE ART OF MANAGING DISCOURSES

It is not enough to simply *become* hegemonic. Hegemonic groups, as Gramsci noted, have to work at staying dominant. In part, this involves operating a discourse that keeps the ruling alliance together. However, another hegemonic task is maintaining a leading position in society relative to all other groups such that the dominated accept the position of dominance held by the leading group. This involves generating consent among the ruled. That is, ensuring the discourses, practices and authority or coercive capacity of the ruling group are seen as legitimate, and ideally as natural and universal, by the ruled. For hegemonic groups, the more naturalized and obfuscated such discourses and practices are, the better. A naturalized set of hegemonic discourses and practices effectively positions the dominated within a set of hidden power relationships. The discourses that are embedded in, and govern, institutions (as described by Foucault) produce an especially obfuscated and opaque form of power.

Although dominant groups strive for it, a fully naturalized hegemony is unlikely. Rather, hegemonies have to continually be remade as dominant groups struggle to maintain their leadership through a process of negotiating with subordinate groups and a related process of discursive management. Those in power have three discursive goals:

- Produce discourses that advance and confirm their interests.
- Create as much discursive closure as possible. Use the power already possessed by ruling groups to try to influence, or nudge, discourse-making processes in the direction of closures favouring perspectives and practices advantageous to themselves and their allies.
- Regulate discursive shifts such that discursive change favours the interests of the already dominant.

Groups that are already hegemonic have an advantage over newcomers because they have the resources to employ and offer patronage to intellectuals, and even to offer some intellectuals derivative power in the form of positions on boards, commissions and advisory committees. During the era of social-welfare Keynesian intervention many social-democrat intellectuals acquired real power.

They effectively became part of managerialist capitalist hegemonic alliances by helping to create appropriate discourses and practices to manage the welfare state. These intellectuals made themselves valuable within the capitalist hegemonic order. The already-hegemonic are also in a position to direct, or at least strongly influence, the discourses promoted within schooling systems. This is significant because children are formed as subjects within ruling discourses. Their world-view is constructed within established parameters. After several generations this education system creates citizens that effectively police or manage themselves because they have internalized discourses appropriate for the needs of the ruling hegemony. This remains stable for as long as the ideas, including dreams and aspirations, taught in school continue to largely correspond with the lived experience and life chances of those people. One explanation for the Arab Spring revolutions was the creation of a young educated population who had been taught to aspire to a life that the state was unable or unwilling to provide. A serious political problem in the wake of the Euro-zone crisis has been the large educated but unemployed youth populations in countries like Spain and Greece. The crisis means their aspirations cannot be fulfilled. People raised in an education system are 'inducted' into a system of meaning (Althusser 1971). The hegemonic closure facilitated by the education system is undermined because of the dissonance between the common sense taught to this generation of people and their real life experience.

In addition, already-hegemonic groups have an advantage over newcomers with regard to their ability for developing symbiotic relationships with the media. This is useful for facilitating discursive closures. However, relationships between various sections of the media and different factions of ruling hegemonies are subject to ongoing flux and negotiation. This means symbiotic relationships are contextually bound rather than ongoing and automatic. Further, media-related discursive closure is complicated by the fact that intra-hegemonic factional struggles are often fought out in the media, which generates the impression of discursive turmoil and non-closure. The Frankfurt School would argue that such discursive battles in the media do not mean that truly antithetical ideas are allowed to surface. Rather, they would argue such oppositional ideas merely constitute superficial 'huffery and puffery', that is the 'freedom to choose what is always the same' (Adorno and Horkheimer 2008: 167). Contemporary philosophers too make similar arguments. Žižek (1989) suggests for instance that when we participate in circulating oppositional discourses in media and popular culture we strengthen the ruling order, rather than disrupt it, because we give the appearance of debate that legitimates it as a freely chosen state of affairs. This can be seen in the way the United States' Democrats and Republicans, United Kingdom's Labour and Conservatives and Australia's Labour and Liberals have engaged in a struggle to win the same middle ground. The more important point is that media battles, even when not involving substantive issues, help construct liberal democracy as a tolerant and legitimate system. The debates produce the idea that liberal democracy allows for multiple oppositional ideas to be seriously considered; this conceals the real limits of what is and isn't acceptable in liberal-democratic societies. This is helpful for constructing liberal hegemonies because it reduces the danger of ideas surfacing that fundamentally challenge the system's core underpinnings. Habermas (1976) argued that this was the real weak point of managerialist systems because if the public ever demanded democracy be practised, it would constitute a threat to administrative rationality and lead to the disintegration of the system. The Frankfurt School's argument is that those ideas which are fundamentally contradictory to ruling hegemonic interests will be marginalized, repressed and belittled. In liberal hegemonies they are deemed radical or crazy. Although this notion may exaggerate the capacity of ruling hegemonies to achieve closure, it should not be dismissed out of hand. Clearly, all ruling hegemonies would like to achieve closures if they could. The question is: to what extent are they able to achieve such closures? Ultimately the success each ruling group has in this regard will depend upon its skills at managing discourses by making them both dominant and taken for granted or obfuscated and opaque.

Ruling hegemonic groups necessarily intervene to try to influence the production, circulation, and reception of communication. No ruling groups can afford to adopt a laissez-faire approach to communication given the centrality of communication in building and maintaining hegemonic influence. At the very least, discourse management requires ruling groups to pay some attention to five communicative variables. We discuss each below. In the era of early capitalism many communicative functions would have been carried out by middle-class leaders themselves. But progressively the number of communicative functions has increased, and during the managerialist era, hegemonic communication emerged as a set of specialist functions. By the start of the twenty-first century, communication was not only a set of specialist functions, but a set of institutionalized practices, with hegemonic groups employing a range of professional communicators like spin doctors, PRs, journalists, educators, policy makers and so on to practise the arts of hegemonic communication. These communication professionals concerned themselves with the following sorts of communicative hegemonic issues.

Managing the structures of meaning making

Ruling groups and some aspiring ruling groups employ communication professionals possessing an understanding of the structures of meaning making. These professionals develop strategies and tactics for using whatever discursive possibilities such structures may offer. The twentieth century saw discourse making progressively institutionalized, largely in accordance with industrial managerialist logic, within schools, universities, research institutions, the media and even charismatic churches. These institutionalized sites provide platforms for the production and dissemination of discourses. Already-hegemonic groups are in a position to influence the discourses in circulation within their area of jurisdiction by intervening to either facilitate or undermine the functioning of such discursive spaces. The extreme end of hegemonic action against such sites would involve censorship or disallowing such discourse-making machinery. For example, we have seen a number of hegemonies, like the United States, China and Japan, take action to crush institutionalized religious cults. Sometimes this even involves the use of violence such as the Waco siege in Texas, or persecution of Falun Gong in China. But, more commonly, ruling groups regulate the structures for meaning making through intervening in ways that impact on the resources flowing into such structures.

Institutions producing discourses that the hegemonic bloc approves of may receive direct funding from factions of the ruling alliance, or the state, or receive tax breaks. They can also be favoured by regulatory decisions like licensing or spectrum allocation. Institutions receiving such funding, tax breaks or regulatory favours will often provide hegemonic groups with discursive space in return. Alternatively, structures producing discourses not approved of by ruling hegemonies can be actively discouraged through taxation and regulatory obstacles. Such hegemonic interventions, which are often so low key as to go unnoticed, are responsible for steering social discursive flows in one or other direction by allowing some structures to grow, while encouraging others to decline or die. Much discursive steering is subtle and hidden, and only becomes transparent at moments of a hegemonic shift. For example, the end of the Cold War saw clearly discernible interventions to steer meaning-making machineries into new directions during the 1990s such as South Africa and the old Soviet bloc. These non-opaque interventions included a mix of funding shifts, regulatory shifts, direct political pressure for transformation and the creation of an industry involved in policy transfer and the dispatch of reconstruction missions to promote liberalization and democratization. Of the plethora of meaning-making structures in existence, the media probably now receive the most attention, from both hegemonic and counter-hegemonic groups, because from the mid-twentieth century onwards they became the key instruments for circulating discourses.

Managing the meaning makers

Communication professionals employed by ruling groups need to pay attention to the personnel involved in meaning making. Structures may provide the fulcrums for discourse manufacture and circulation, but ultimately it is those staffing these structures who are the creative heart of the machinery. Discourse management must involve a concern with meaning makers or intellectuals. Managing discourse making involves attracting the 'right' sort of people to do the job. Discourse managers need to establish what an appropriate candidate would be. This sets the parameters for what meanings are likely to be produced. Deciding what is appropriate need not necessarily involve conscious decisions about world-views and ideological positions. Instead, decisions may, in the educational sector for example, be set according to knowledge of certain research topics or methodologies. This can constitute a disguised and even unconscious form of discourse steering. Similarly, setting salary levels can be a decision about what sort of person will be recruited, as are decisions about recruitment procedures.

Recruitment is a central function of discourse management. From a hegemonic point of view only the 'right' people are empowered to take recruitment decisions. That is, those taking such decisions, like editors, should hold appropriate views themselves. Discourses can be managed by promoting appropriate people into those positions selecting the next generation of meaning makers. A process of 'cloning' by recruitment can be established. Naturally, recruitment mistakes can be made, and people may be appointed who produce meanings deemed inappropriate. Such persons will not be promoted. Some will be tolerated but marginalized, while others will be driven out. In long-standing hegemonies such personnel management can be so naturalized that it becomes an unconscious form of discourse management and censorship. Only in rare circumstances will such personnel management cease being opaque and become a set of conscious acts designed to change a society's dominant discourses by removing intellectuals like journalists, academics and policy makers from their jobs. Such deliberate interventions were implemented in post-Second World War militarily occupied Germany and Japan (Louw 2010a), in East Germany following reunification and in post-apartheid South Africa (Louw and Milton 2012).

Regulating meaning-making practices

Communication professionals employed by ruling groups pay attention to meaning-making practices. Such practices are learned both through education and training programmes and on-the-job socialization. Detaching training from meaning-making sites is not a problem in some sectors. For instance, training teachers in colleges and universities mostly away from schools is a long-accepted practice which does not appear to have caused undue tension between practitioners and trainers, in part because teachers appear to feel some ownership of the training processes, and school placements create a space for socialization to occur. However, the same cannot be said of media training, where tensions have emerged between practitioners and some media and journalism schools. This tension emerged when practitioners felt they were losing control of media training processes when in-house journalism cadetships were replaced by university programmes. Practitioners became concerned that university programmes involved too much critique and theory and not enough practical skills. These programmes are seen to teach a set of inappropriate practices and values. On-the-job training and cadetships created the ideal conditions for cloning, ensuring journalists were socialized into existing appropriate sets of meanings and practices. Tensions will presumably continue until media practitioners feel they have regained some degree of control over media training. The question of who controls training is a significant issue for hegemonic managers.

Adapting and repurposing meanings

Communication professionals employed by ruling groups pay attention to the issue of appropriating, recycling and reworking discourses from the past and from other contexts. Discourses and practices from the past are omnipresent in the form of residues underlying, intermeshing and interpenetrating contemporary discourses and practices. The British Empire left such residues in South Asia and East and Southern Africa, as did the Ottoman Empire in the Balkans and Middle East. Further, discourses are continually migrating from their original context, and mutating and hybridizing with other discourses in new contexts. The spread of Christianity, Islam and Marxism are examples of this. Globalization processes are likely to intensify the migration and hybridization of liberal discourses. Discursive migration, mutation and hybridization and residues can have unrecognized influences. Discursive management requires sensitivity to the contextual roots of any discourse or practice and its migrations and mutations. Such knowledge enhances opportunities for appropriating or reworking discourses for use in new contexts, and offers both hegemonic and counter-hegemonic players a set of tools for discursive intervention and manipulation. For those who are the targets of such manipulation, knowledge of how discourses are created, travel and mutate can provide at least some inoculation.

Monitoring and responding to shifting meanings

Communication professionals employed by ruling groups need to monitor the actual flows of meaning. The way meanings flow through social networks is a good indication of the arrangement of power relationships between individuals and groups. Constructing hegemony involves, in part, cobbling together sets of relationships between people: sectors of the dominant, the dominated, plus the relationships between these. Constructing hegemonic relationships therefore requires communicative interventions to regulate information exchanges and power relationships, such that the dominant orchestrate, as much as possible, what is communicated to whom. There will be occasions when hegemonic players wish to retain and stabilize existing communicative patterns. On other occasions they may wish to alter communication flows to create new groupings or alliances, or to undermine existing groupings that are no longer deemed hegemonically useful.

During the managerial era, hegemonies became consciously managed. The move towards global network capitalism is generating shifts from hierarchical bureaucratic managerialism to control through networking. However, these shifts are not resulting in a diminishment of the wide array of institutionalized communicative functions established under managerial hegemony. What is changing is the style of control. Building hegemony in the global networking era appears to involve developing new communicative practices by rejigging and mutating existing communicative infrastructures and routines, rather than building a completely new infrastructure. At its core, the art of building hegemony remains unaltered: it involves becoming and staying dominant and powerful by using communications to organize ways of life. Hegemony is built and organized by managing discourses, institutions and practices. Intellectuals, as specialists in setting communicative parameters, are necessarily implicated in all three functions. Becoming dominant simply requires being successful in getting one's definitions of reality accepted as correct; and thereafter closing, or at least narrowing, discursive flows in favour of the dominant perspective.

At the dawn of the twenty-first century, managerialists had seemingly lost the battle to maintain discursive closure, although managerialist discourses and the intelligentsia serving the old managerialist hegemony were still far from dislodged. Now, the global networker hegemony is solidly embedded within dominant discourses and practices. The discursive battles between the managerialists and networkers are not over. It is not even clear that the global networkers are assured of hegemonic dominance, although some managerialist forms appear to have been completely defeated, like Soviet managerialism; resistance from other managerialists, especially Keynesian managerialists in western welfare sectors, is not yet exhausted. In addition, the role of luck should not be underestimated in establishing hegemony. During the last part of the twentieth century global networkers had a run of good luck; but it is possible the turmoil generated by the post-2007 global financial crisis may be the end of this lucky streak.

DISCURSIVE RESISTANCE AND WEAKENING HEGEMONIES

All hegemonic groups wish to remain dominant. They will necessarily attempt to stabilize those discourses and practices through which they secured hegemonic dominance. Stabilization strategies can range from attempts to freeze discourses and practices, through to permitting reform, but on terms set by the hegemony. The 'freezing' approach is unlikely to be a successful strategy because there are always going to be contextual shifts which demand mutability. Also there will always be those resisting the dominant hegemony. Oppositional individuals and groups will be constantly looking for, and finding, communicative gaps. The bourgeoisie found their gaps in the public sphere, that is, in spaces the feudal elites could no longer police. The managerialists colonized the gaps flowing from capitalism's socio-economic 'steering crises', such as the First World War, Great Depression and Second World War.

For the managerialists, the 1970s and 1980s brought a series of steering problems. Problems within civil society became especially intense during the 1980s. The 1989 Leipzig uprising against East German Soviet managerialists illustrates how an activated civil society can pose a crisis for managerialists; effectively the demands and resistances could simply not be managed away. Consent collapsed because the gap between the discursive promises and the lived reality of citizens became too great. The problems got too big. A similar pattern was seen in South Africa where apartheid managerialists lost the capacity to manage multiple steering problems arising in the 1980s. In the face of massive problems and resistances both the Soviet and apartheid managerialists engaged in attempts at reform mixed with repression. But they were minimalist reforms, framed within the same sort of managerialist logic that gave rise to the systemic crises in the first place. Hence, the steering problems simply got more intense. As a result, the Soviet and apartheid hegemonic elites simply gave up. The Soviet decision to allow the Berlin Wall to come down in November 1989 and the announcement that apartheid was over in February 1990 were both deeply symbolic of the fate of managerialist elites who reformed too little and too late. Effectively both systems became ungovernable and unmanageable and the old managerialist frameworks simply collapsed under the weight of multiple problems. The anarchy ensuing from these collapses was still in evidence as post-apartheid and post-Soviet societies entered the twenty-first century.

The response of capitalist managerialism to its steering problems and discursive resistance has been quite different. The western managerialists retreated and reformed more successfully than Soviet or apartheid managerialists. Liberal capitalism allowed alternative sets of practices and discourses to emerge. Out of this emerged the global networkers, whose practices appear to constitute a successfully reformed capitalism. In addition, when it became clear that social welfare managerialism was no longer sustainable, liberal capitalism began winding back the managed welfare system. This wind-back reform began when managerial solutions were found to no longer be working, that is, when managerialist interventions created bigger systemic problems and sustainability became an issue. Another complicating factor was that the costs of this managerialist system were blowing out. Multiple demands outstripped the capacity of managerialists to deliver. Similarly, national economic management and managed protectionisms were wound back when steering problems began to outstrip managerial solutions. Naturally, in the process of reforming the system, there were intra-elite conflicts between managerialists who opted for reform and began attaching themselves to the emergent new networker elite, and conservative managerialists who put up resistance to change. A clear sign that the networkers were winning the struggle was the spate of deregulation across the OECD, because this deregulation clearly undermined many of the props that sustained the managerialist order. Interestingly, once the networkers became hegemonic they initiated a process of re-regulation. But, of course, the new regulations now suited networker rather than managerialist interests.

REGULATING AND DEREGULATING THE CIRCULATION OF CULTURAL CONTENT

We can observe the process of deregulation and re-regulation by examining the attempts to control the circulation of information and culture by corporations, citizens and governments over the past two decades. The web has afforded citizens and new cultural organizations the capacity to create, access and circulate cultural content outside of the content channels created and controlled by the traditional culture industry. Once television content was regulated by television networks, who secured exclusive contractual access to television programmes and were granted spectrum licences to distribute that content. Now television content can be rapidly copied and circulated through the web. The flexibility and scale of these technologies has rendered copyright difficult to enforce.

The traditional mass music, movie and television industries have responded by attempting to enforce the old regulations that protected their content and its circulation. Below we examine some of their responses.

Generating consent for the regulation of the circulation of cultural content

The culture industries have undertaken the following activities:

- constructing peer-to-peer downloading and other forms of content sharing as illegal piracy
- running public information campaigns explaining illegal downloading as theft
- attempting to convince the public that illegal downloading could lead to less content being made because it wouldn't be profitable to make music, movies or television if no one paid
- arguing that not paying for content ultimately harms cultural producers and artists who won't get paid or will lose their jobs.

Using the legal system to prosecute pirates and criminals

In the United States the recording industry instigated lawsuits against predominantly young music fans who had downloaded copyrighted music illegally. Some young music fans were selected out and sued for large sums of money in order to make examples of the consequences of illegal downloading.

Since the Napster case in the late 1990s the music, film and television industries have attempted to shut down and prosecute pirates and websites that facilitate illegal downloading. Some of these cases have included Napster, Kazaa, Pirate Bay and Megaupload. The people behind these sites have had their wealth and assets taken off them, spent time in prison or lived in a legal limbo under house arrest or unable to travel. Several of these lawsuits have involved cooperation between corporations and government authorities to track, identify and prosecute pirates.

A series of lawsuits against internet and technology companies that attempt to make them responsible for enforcing the old copyright rules. In these cases the 'old' content industries attack the 'new' ones. Music, television and film companies have sued social media platforms, file sharing providers and internet service providers in an attempt to make them responsible for policing the flow of content. In a dispute that has gone on for over five years Viacom has sued Google for billions of dollars for copyrighted videos on YouTube. Google argues that the Digital Millennium Copyright Act's 'safe harbour' provisions protects them from prosecution as long as they quickly delete any content that infringes copyright. In Australia, an industry group called the Australian Federation Against Copyright Theft (AFACT) attempted to set a precedent by taking iinet, an internet service provider, to court to make it responsible for authorizing its customers' copyright infringements. The High Court found in favour of the internet service provider. The case was seen as an attempt by the content industries to set a legal precedent with potentially global implications.

Each of these strategies can be seen as attempts to both generate consent for, and enforce, the old rules surrounding the value and circulation of content.

Using the political system to adapt the old rules or create new rules

Throughout the twentieth century the music, television and film industries developed powerful lobby groups such as the Recording Industry Association of America and the Motion Picture Association of America. The traditional culture industry has used these lobby groups to influence politicians to enact legislation that protects the value of their content. Most recently, in the United States the Stop Online Piracy Act (SOPA) and the PROTECT IP Act (PIPA) were proposed. These pieces of legislation attempted to strengthen the regulation of content circulation. They proposed changes such as:

- five years in prison for streaming copyrighted content
- closing websites involved in distributing copyrighted content without permission
- requiring internet service providers to block access to sites that enable access to unauthorized copyrighted content.

The legislation dramatically expanded the responsibility of internet-based firms for protecting the copyright of the music, film and television industries. SOPA and PIPA became a hallmark moment in the political contest between the old culture industry and the emerging information and network enterprises. The acts were both withdrawn after intense lobbying from the internet industries and supporters of open and public internet and copyright reform. This was the first time the mass culture industries' lobby groups had been substantially and publicly defeated by the internet-based culture industries. The contest goes on, as these groups continue to build legitimacy and consent for their interests. The prosecution of Megaupload founder Kim Dotcom in 2012 indicates that United States government is prepared to invest significant resources in finding and prosecuting pirates. And, in late 2012, the Republican Party sacked a staffer who wrote a memo urging copyright reform. Each of these events indicates that they still have much lobbying power in Washington. Reporting this case, the technology publication *Ars Technica* noted that 'copyright reform enjoys broad popularity among internet-savvy young people' (Lee 2012). The inference is that at some point a major political party will sense there is more to gain in taking up the cause of copyright reform than there is in protecting the old mass culture industries' interests.

Negotiations with the new organizations to craft a new consensus

At the very same time the old mass content industries and new internet industries are competing with each other to establish their own interests as the consensus, they are also collaborating with each other. YouTube has solved many disagreements with the music and television industries that own copyright to music clips and television programmes or segments by instigating complex rights and royalties deals. In these deals the old content industries effectively agree that YouTube has acquired enough power that they cannot be defeated and instead have to be negotiated with. In the process, new alliances and formations are created. The old and the new industries create agreements to realize their mutual interests. In the case of the music industry, new players like Apple's iTunes store or streaming services like Spotify and Rdio have also signed rights and royalties deals to enable them to sell and stream content. No longer able to protect their content in their own channels and technologies like CDs and record stores, the music industry enters into alliances with internet-based enterprises they consider to be legitimate. In some cases, the internet-based players have become so powerful that the old content industries are coerced into negotiating on their terms. New organizations like Apple, Google and Spotify have the power to shift the debate about copyright away from attempting to protect and enforce the old rules, and towards establishing new rules and new legitimate channels. Pressing all the while on the formation of these alliances are new groups such as legal activists for copyright reform, and political activists like the Pirate Party, who are seeking out even more radical rewriting of the rules.

The emergence of global network capitalism has empowered new organizations who have sought to create new rules and frameworks within which to operate. Where the old culture industry profited from owning and selling content, the new culture industry profits from circulating content in order to capture attention and information. These two different sets of interests employ different frameworks of meaning, and use commercial, legal and political structures to attempt to protect or promote their ideas and interests. They lobby government to create laws that reflect their view of the world. They sue each other to try to weaken the other position. They attempt to take over each other. They negotiate compromises. What is going on here is a 'sorting out' of the new rules of the game in terms of creating and circulating cultural content. This is partly a hegemonic process of crafting consent around ideas of copyright, ownership, culture, theft and piracy.

EXAMINING LEGITIMATE POSITIONS ON COPYRIGHT

Above we proposed a number of ways that different groups are attempting to regulate, deregulate and re-regulate the flow of cultural content through the internet by:

- generating consent for the regulation of the circulation of cultural content
- using the legal system to prosecute pirates and criminals
- using the political system to adapt the old rules or create new rules
- negotiating with the new organizations to craft a new consensus.

There are many examples of this debate playing out over the past decade or more.

Key industry organizations like the Motion Picture Association of America (MPAA) have put forward their case. You can read their position on copyright, together with their policy statements and research at their website: www.mpaa.org/why-copyright-matters.

The industry argues that copyright protects the creative process by ensuring cultural industries remain profitable. Critics dispute many of the industry's claims and the influence of the industry's lobbyists on the political process.

Read some of the claims made in reports on the MPAA website. For instance, they claimed in November 2013 that the copyright industries employ nearly 5.4 million US workers, account for 5 per cent of private sector employment and contribute $142 billion in foreign sales and exports. On this basis, they argue that the US government should reform legislation to provide greater protection for copyright online.

Watch Rob Reid's TED talk on 'copyright math' for an insightful and amusing critique of the copyright industry's claims about the economic cost of online piracy. You can find a link on the *Media and Society* website study.sagepub.com/carahandlouw

During 2011 and 2012 a major struggle played out in the US around the SOPA (Stop Online Piracy Act) and PIPA (PROTECT IP Act). The major copyright industries like the MPAA wanted to greatly increase penalties for sharing copyright content and make internet companies responsible for blocking access to copyright content.

The internet industries argued that the proposed legislation ran counter to the technical infrastructure and cultural practices of the internet. To block access to particular sites or restrict flows of specific content is technically and practically difficult. Furthermore, the digital culture of the internet is based on endless copies and remixes of cultural content. To attempt to regulate what information could be copied would undermine the innovative and open nature of online culture. Internet industries and activists came together to mobilize public protest against SOPA and PIPA. This culminated in a blackout of many websites on 17 January 2012. Instead of access to Wikipedia or Google, users saw a STOP SOPA banner and an invitation to contact their member of Congress. The action resulted in millions of messages of protest being sent to Congress. The bills were consequently withdrawn.

The defeat of SOPA and PIPA represented a key moment in the struggle over the regulation of cultural content. For much of the twentieth century the major copyright industries controlled the technologies and regulatory frameworks. With the emergence of the internet they have lost much of that control. While major copyright and internet organizations, lobbyists and activists continue to struggle over how the circulation of content online should be regulated, with SOPA and PIPA the internet was able to defeat the copyright industries. Many argue this was the first time that organizations like Google asserted themselves as major players in the policy process.

DecodeDC's podcast 'The future was now' explains the history of struggles between copyright and technology industries over the regulation of cultural content. The podcast offers a detailed analysis of the battle over the SOPA and PIPA bills. You can find a link to the podcast on the *Media and Society* website study.sagepub.com/carahandlouw

A major figure in the push against SOPA the internet activist and co-founder of Reddit – Aaron Swartz. You can find a link to his talk 'How we stopped SOPA' on the *Media and Society* website. We have also included there a link to Yochai Benkler's analysis of the social networks formed around the SOPA and PIPA debate.

Consider the activities and positions of groups involved in each process and what communicative sites, professionals and meanings they use to manage their position and present it as legitimate:

Who is making the case for regulating the flow of content online?
On what grounds do they make the case?
Who is calling who a pirate or a criminal?
How do they justify and pursue these accusations?
Who has tried to use the political system to shape policy around copyright and ownership?
What have they done?
How have they been successful or not?
Who has made agreements with each other about managing content online? What kinds of power did each party bring to the negotiation?
How were they able to influence the other and get what they want?
Consider how hegemonies are changing: Who is gaining and losing power? What rules are changing?

SHIFTING HEGEMONIES

Hegemonies are never permanent fixtures. Dominance is always subject to being challenged. However, resistance in some contexts is pointless. When hegemonies are very strong, alternative discourses and practices can at best cling to life in marginal spaces. But all hegemonies have life cycles – they grow old and weak – which is when those advocating alternatives are presented with momentary opportunities for asserting their hegemonic dominance. Hegemonies are at their most fragile just after being born, before they have naturalized their discourses and practices and before they have consolidated their grip on the steering mechanisms of society, and then again when they grow old and weak. When dominant groups lose the capacity to set the intellectual agenda, negotiate new deals and alliances, and police all the 'spaces' in society, opposition groups sense the weakness because the old hegemony communicates its fragility and insecurity. Alternative visions are empowered by the growing availability of communicative 'spaces' and 'gaps' as dominance slips away. And the more that alternative visions are able to colonize communicative spaces, and thereby become empowered, the greater become the crises facing the existing hegemonic group. Holding a hegemony together, once the crises born of weakness begin, becomes a little like trying to plug an already leaking dyke. Weak hegemonies ultimately crumble, and one of, or an alliance of many, formerly resistant groups learns to become the new hegemonic group. These processes of hegemonic weakening, death and birth have occurred again and again in history. The end of the British Empire and the Soviet collapse are among the most spectacular of recent hegemonic upheavals. Not surprisingly, hegemonic crumbling is usually associated with wars breaking out, as aspirant hegemonic groups try to grab space from a retreating hegemonic order. Hence, the decline of the British Empire produced the two World Wars and a series of smaller ones such as Israeli–Arab and Indian–Pakistani conflicts, while the end of Soviet hegemony has already produced wars in the Balkans and Caucasia.

Trying to remain hegemonically dominant always involves dealing with those attempting to challenge one's hegemony. There will always be resistance. However, resistance and alternative discourses and practices are usually only a problem – that is, can only seriously challenge a hegemonic group – during vulnerable moments. Hegemonies are vulnerable when they are still establishing themselves or no longer able to renew themselves. Another way hegemonies are overthrown is when more powerful external groups chose to intervene to overthrow hegemonies using warfare, economic sanctions or other measures. Of course, counter-hegemonic groups will always be on the lookout for external players willing to intervene on their behalf when resistance groups are too weak to seriously challenge their own hegemonic rulers.

Ruling hegemonies will always strive to keep themselves informed of all potential challengers. They endeavour to keep abreast of emerging and declining oppositional discourses and alliances. Their growth and strength is a central function of maintaining a position of dominance. Challengers can emerge from a number of different sources: from break-away former members of one's own hegemonic alliance, from new players inside one's society, from foreign players seeking to intervene, or from alliances between these. Essentially, maintaining hegemonic dominance involves more than maintaining and promoting one's own discourses and practices. It also involves meeting constant challenges from counter-hegemonic challengers. The management of discourse consequently involves constantly renewing one's own discourses to keep one's own ruling alliance and dominant profile intact, plus working to prevent potential counter-hegemonic discourses from ever becoming serious challengers. Communicative struggle lies at the heart of being hegemonic.

A NEW HEGEMONIC ORDER

In the past generation, social relationships have been altered in three ways that impact on the mechanics and processes of hegemony building.

New communication technologies

Firstly, the new communication technologies emerging in the 1970s evolved into a series of global communicative channels. A new breed of entrepreneurial networkers learned to exploit these to accumulate wealth. These entrepreneurs found ways to generate wealth from exploiting rapid information and data sharing. A new capitalist elite was born from learning, in an ad-hoc way, to exploit new communication technologies. Some of these new entrepreneurs appear to have created long-term wealth generation enterprises – like News Corporation, Apple, Microsoft and Google – whereas other contributions have only involved rejigging older discourses and practices rather than building new business empires. The post-2007 global financial crisis for instance exposed a complex web of speculative trading of 'junk' bonds, derivatives and financial products. Corporations were using a complex networked system of financial trading to invent and trade high risk and potentially high yield products, but with no or little underlying material value. This system was only possible in the 'spaces' opened up by the development of global capitalism and information technologies. But there have also been corporations that reinvented themselves by learning to exploit the new communication technologies and, in the process, reworked their structures and practices. Many Japanese corporations during the 1980s reinvented themselves as dynamic, information-driven enterprises. Toyota invented *kanban* principles. This system of just-in-time inventory management radically changed manufacturing innovation and management. It enabled corporations to quickly develop new technologies, and deliver them to changing markets, using lean and flexible organizational structures. Many Japanese manufacturers out-paced the inflexible and hierarchical mass manufacturers in the United States and Europe in this period. Entrepreneurs driving this emergent global network capitalism necessarily shook up the old managerial hegemony by introducing new practices and new rival sets of players. As these entrepreneurs emerged they pragmatically allied themselves to whichever ruling hegemonic faction or individual would promote their interests. For example, Rupert Murdoch at News Corporation pragmatically worked with both Bush's conservative Republican Party in the United States and Blair's social-democratic Labour Party in the United Kingdom since both were prepared to create policy frameworks advantaging his global information enterprises and interests.

As the twenty-first century dawned, the struggle between managerialists and global networkers was far from resolved. But, in general, the networkers gained the upper hand in the struggle for dominance in OECD countries, and OECD dominated transnational forums, with deregulatory, laissez-faire and globalization discourses sounding confident and ascendant; while managerial interventionist and national-protectionist discourses sounded increasingly defensive. Even setbacks – such as the rise of anti-globalization political parties like Australia's One Nation, the British National Party and the 1999 anti-WTO demonstrations in Seattle – did not substantively undercut the overall international success of those promoting the merits of globalization and an information economy. Global networkers have, in fact, shown themselves to be highly proficient in the legitimating arts of externally directed impression and discourse management. Their promotion of the information super highway and e-commerce are excellent examples of successful information age rhetoric.

New communication channels undermined mass production and communication

Secondly, new communication channels actually undermined some of the requirements for hierarchical bureaucratic practices in both private and state corporations and within the state bureaucracies and government departments. New communication technologies made it possible to bypass old hierarchical chains of command. Old managerialist pecking orders were undermined because it was possible to share information instantaneously with anyone linked to the communications network. Hierarchical chains of command relying on middle managers became too slow and cumbersome when competing with fluid networked teams. Consequently, managerialist organizational structures faced increasing deconstructive pressures during the 1990s. Both business and government sectors experienced changes to their organizational practices and staffing structures, a process associated with the rise of neoliberal discourses advocating 'winding back the nanny state' and fixed managerial structures via deregulation and creating flexible organizations with outsourcing and downsizing. There is no guarantee, however, that the networked, participatory and consultative forms of decision making that replaced managerialism are better or more efficient. These organizational shifts necessarily impacted upon the construction of hegemonic alliances as the players learned to use the new communication channels and manipulate data flows. Communication professionals were no longer limited to using mass media for message delivery, although the mass media were and are still extensively used.

The emergence of niche markets and publics

Thirdly, global network capitalism and digital media facilitates the creation of a plethora of new market niches, which led to the emergence of new lifestyle identities. The new communication networks made disaggregating the mass market possible because micro consumer demands could not only be rapidly communicated to producers, but the productive process could also be relatively easily rejigged and retooled thanks to computer-integrated manufacturing. The result was a shift from economies of scale required for Fordist mass production to economies of scope reflective of post-Fordist production of the widest possible range of commodities (Crook et al. 1992: 179). This generated new social groupings and identities organized around niche consumption-based lifestyles. The new identities supplemented older identities, like ethnic and religious groupings, which were also reinvigorated by the de-massification and de-managerialization of society. The result was the emergence of 'identity politics' served by growing niche-based media. The new politics leaned towards socio-cultural issues related to lifestyle and *consumption* rather than socio-economic *production* issues (Crook et al. 1992: 146). This made the task of building hegemonies infinitely more difficult. Mass publics fragmented into a plethora of subcultures based upon localism, ethnicity, new and revivalist 'belief formations' like religion and ecology, and lifestyles based around sexuality and other values. Consequently, hegemony builders now need to communicate to a plethora of new groups. Becoming hegemonic has become extremely complex given the need to master multiple discourses appropriate to a patchwork of, often shifting, identities, and develop strategies for building coalitions out of diversity. This also involves learning to use both niche media formats and remnant mass media forms, the latter generally employed to target non-elite groups. This process of communication is arguably more complex, slower and cumbersome to manage than more top-down managerial forms of communication.

POLITICAL LEADERS AND NEW COALITIONS

Building dominance now requires developing a highly complex patchwork of media strategies. Centre-left political parties have become especially adept at building such coalitions. In part this occurred because globalization led to a deindustrialization of OECD countries as factories were relocated to places were labour was cheaper, such as China (we address this in more detail in Chapter 4). This shrank OECD working-class populations, which was disastrous for traditional labour parties like the Democrats in the United States, British Labour Party and Australian Labor Party. To save themselves these parties under the leaderships of Clinton, Blair and Keating reinvented themselves into rainbow coalitions of workers, environmentalists, identity groups organized around sexuality and gender, urban cultural and communication professionals, and multiculturalists who they spoke to using a plethora of niche communication platforms.

When Bill Clinton was sworn in as President of the United States in 1993 he ended a generation of conservative power. His campaign creatively solved a problem that had beset progressive parties in the west throughout the 1970s and 1980s. The emergence of global network capitalism had rapidly changed the structure of the economy in countries like the United States, United Kingdom and Australia. This created new winners and losers in society. On the losing side was the collapsing working class that had been the traditional base of social-democrat labour parties like the Democrats, British Labour Party and Australian Labor Party. The large scale outsourcing of industrial manufacturing to developing countries meant that traditional labour heartlands fragmented. The working-class base had shrunk so dramatically that social democrats could no longer rely on it to win elections. Some in the working class fell into an unemployed or underemployed underclass, where many were attracted to populist conservative values-based politics. On the winning side, a new middle class began to emerge. This new middle class included many people who had come from working-class backgrounds. Through mass education many children of the working class had managed to enter a growing middle class of cultural and information-based professionals. Social-democrat parties had to respond to this fracturing of their base by fashioning a new consensus or coalition of interests, rather than rely on a uniform base or bloc of voters. They found themselves battling with conservatives for an increasingly contested middle ground. The hegemonic contest here was to name, define and then own that middle ground. Politicians from both social-democrat and conservative parties spoke to 'ordinary' citizens, 'battlers', 'working families', 'small business owners', 'mom and pop', the 'high street' or 'main street', 'middle America', those 'outside the beltway' and so on. In developing these terms they were aiming to construct, identify and speak to an aspirational and newly emerging middle class.

Political parties were trying to construct a consensual identity or narrative under which they could organize many competing interests. As there was no longer a stable middle ground, mainstream parties developed coalitions of interests which have taken many shapes. In some cases social-democrat parties have aligned with green politics, in others conservative parties have reached out for the disenfranchised working class and the vulnerable lower-middle class. This has created unique alliances. On the social-democrat side politics has become articulated with green, feminist and multicultural discourses under the broad rubrics of state intervention and social justice. Social democrats claim to engage in reforms that give capitalism a human face. On the conservative side, free market politics and traditional cultural values have come together under narratives of small government and tradition. In each case these are often uneasy alliances of competing interests. The political professionals who hold them together work to suture over their paradoxes and fractures.

BILL CLINTON'S LEGITIMACY

FROM THE 1992 PRESIDENTIAL CAMPAIGN TO THE 2012 DEMOCRATIC NATIONAL CONVENTION

D. A. Pennebaker's 1993 documentary film *The War Room* followed political strategists James Carville and George Stephanopoulos throughout Bill Clinton's 1992 Presidential campaign. The film offers a rare fly-on-the-wall examination of hegemonic communicative labour as Carville and Stephanopoulos go about crafting a new consensus around Clinton and the Democrats. Pennebaker followed the campaigners as they constructed and managed Clinton's political image.

Clinton and his campaign strategists successfully invented a new covenant or consensus under which they organized progressive politics. They used a collection of narratives to explain and construct this consensus in the minds of American voters. The mantras of his campaign included:

- 'It's the economy, stupid': the binding idea that without a strong and growing economy there could be no middle class.
- 'The forgotten middle class': the idea that demarcated the Democrats from the Republicans. It signalled that the conservatives had omitted ordinary middle Americans from their political consensus.
- 'The gap between the rich and the poor': an idea that articulated the social justice values of progressive politics.
- 'Don't forget healthcare': an idea that emerged from the broader narrative of the 'forgotten middle class' and the 'gap between the rich and the poor'. Healthcare is one way ordinary Americans could materially envisage a better middle-class life.
- 'Change versus more of the same': a mantra of modern campaigning. Barack Obama went with 'Change' and 'Hope' in 2008 and 'Forward' in 2012.

In Clinton's campaign slogans we can see some ideas that have become well-established in mainstream politics over the past generation. In particular, 'change' becomes a mantra for politics in a globally networked world where constant flexibility and adaptation are a fact of life. Progressive parties have focused on finding a consensus between economic growth, social welfare and progressive cultural values as a way of maintaining power. Conservative parties for their part have aimed to build a consensus between economic growth, individual freedoms and traditional cultural values.

Towards the end of *The War Room* Carville gives a famous speech on the eve of the election. In that speech he explains that they 'changed the way campaigns were run' by using grassroots networks of campaigners. You can find a link to the speech on the *Media and Society* website study.sagepub.com/carahandlouw

Watch *The War Room* and consider the variety of ways Carville and Stephanopoulos make Bill Clinton a legitimate political leader. How do they manage Clinton's image? What meanings do they create? What resistance do they face?

Consider the way they constructed a highly organized campaign that drew on the grassroots participation of volunteers. How does this compare with today's political campaigns? For instance, how did Obama's 2008 and 2012 campaigns extend and develop the use of grassroots participation to make him a legitimate candidate?

While *The War Room* offers a portrait of Clinton at the beginning of his political career, he was largely credited during the 2012 Presidential campaign with helping to make Barack Obama a legitimate candidate in the eyes of middle-class Americans.

You can find a link to Clinton's speech at the 2012 Democratic National Convention on the *Media and Society* website study.sagepub.com/carahandlouw

In that speech Clinton makes a series of statements about the beliefs and values of Democrats:

- 'I want a man who believes with no doubt that he can build a new American Dream economy, driven by information and creativity.'
- 'We Democrats think the country works better with a strong middle class, with real opportunities for poor folks to work their way into it – with a relentless focus on the future, with business and government actually working together to promote growth and broadly share prosperity. You see, we believe that "We're all in this together" is a far better philosophy than "You're on your own".'
- 'It turns out that advancing equal opportunity and economic empowerment is both morally right and good economics. Why? Because poverty, discrimination, and ignorance restrict growth. When you stifle human potential, when you don't invest in new ideas, it doesn't just cut off the people who are affected; it hurts us all'.

What ideas, meanings and stories does Clinton invoke? How does Clinton present himself, and Obama, as legitimate?

Compare Clinton's ideas to other ideas in contemporary American political life: progressive or conservative, mainstream or radical. How is Clinton similar to and different from the Republican narrative? How is Clinton different to more radical political perspectives in America?

CONCLUSION

In this chapter we have argued that power is the outcome of struggles between different groups in society. Those struggles are partly over meaning, as groups aim to make their preferred social relationships hegemonic. Meaning is central to producing legitimacy and consent. Hegemonies are never fixed. Even though a powerful group might establish its dominance as legitimate, the work of maintaining that legitimacy is continuous. Professional communicators are centrally important in producing and managing legitimacy. To understand these processes we have to understand the context within which struggles over power and meaning take place. This involves examining who is dominant and how they make and maintain their dominance. To do this we need to consider:

- the meanings that dominant groups produce
- the sites and institutions where those meanings are made
- the people who are employed to make meaning.

A thorough analysis also needs to pay attention to groups attempting to resist and disrupt the hegemonic dominance of some groups over these meanings, sites and professional communicators.

A new hegemonic order was formed in the past generation. New communication technologies and channels undermined mass production, consumption and control. This led to the emergence of fragmented niche publics and markets. This requires responsive and flexible modes of control. Meaning and information management becomes intrinsic to managing legitimacy and dominance within this system. Hegemony gives us a way of understanding power relations as always 'under construction'. The construction of hegemonies draws on both material and symbolic resources like media and culture. Our study of meaning and power needs to track efforts to create, maintain and resist hegemonies.

FURTHER READING

Each of the readings below examines how institutions like corporations, governments and think tanks attempt to organize and control the production and circulation of culture and ideas using economic resources, market dynamics, policies and laws. McKnight and Hobbs (2011) examine how book deals made by HarperCollins promote conservative intellectual and political ideas. The authors argue that agenda aligns with the conservative politics of its owner Rupert Murdoch. Athique (2008) explores the structure of Indian media industries, paying attention to their interconnectedness with informal economies and piracy. This article draws attention to the role that players outside of formal institutions play in organizing and influencing the circulation of cultural content like music and film. Bar and Sandvig (2008) consider how communication policy responds to and regulates new media technologies. Schlesinger (2009) examines how experts and power plays shaped UK Labour government policies that developed the creative industries as a new way of configuring and controlling cultural production. Zhang (2006) offers an account of how Chinese policy makers conceptualize and implement their control of the internet.

Athique, A. (2008) 'The global dynamics of Indian media piracy: export markets, playback media and the informal economy', *Media, Culture & Society*, 30: 699–717.

Bar, F. and Sandvig, C. (2008) 'US communication policy after convergence', *Media, Culture & Society*, 30: 531–550.

McKnight, D. and Hobbs, M. (2011) '"You're all a bunch of pinkos": Rupert Murdoch and the politics of HarperCollins', *Media, Culture & Society*, 33: 835–850.

Schlesinger, P. (2009) 'Creativity and the experts: New Labour, think tanks, and the policy process', *International Journal of Press/Politics*, 14: 3–20.

Zhang, L. (2006) 'Behind the "Great Firewall": decoding China's internet media policies from the inside', *Convergence*, 12: 271–291.

Any article marked with ⊗ is available to download at the website **study.sagepub.com/ carahandlouw**

THE GLOBAL INFORMATION ECONOMY

A NEW FORM OF ECONOMIC ORGANIZATION BEGAN EMERGING IN THE LAST PART OF THE TWENTIETH CENTURY.

* What role do information and communication play in the management of global capitalism?

* What are the distinctive characteristics of information and communicative capitalism?

* What is networked and flexible production?

In this chapter we:

- Examine the emergence of the global information economy over the past generation
- Outline how the emergence of information communication technologies, the end of the Cold War and emergence of America as the dominant superpower form the critical context for understanding meaning and power in today's world
- Introduce the network as the key organizational form of the global information economy; the flexible and fragmented modes of production, culture and power enabled by networks and communication technologies have created a new geography of power
- Identify some of the winners and losers from the emergence of the global information economy; we consider how power is made and maintained in networks.

THE EMERGENCE OF A GLOBAL INFORMATION ECONOMY

Global network capitalism took shape over the last two decades of the twentieth century (Harvey 1989, Hall and Jacques 1990, Lash 1990, Lash and Urry 1994, Castells 1996). During this period a new way of organizing wealth making and people developed. This process congealed during the 1990s when conditions emerged that created the space for a new capitalist elite to invent itself. This new elite reformed and mutated the practices and discourses of industrial capitalism by learning, in an ad-hoc way, to take advantage of two sets of opportunities that emerged:

- the emergence of information communication technology
- the collapse of the Soviet empire, the end of the Cold War and rise of America as a lone super-power.

The information communication technology revolution

The first opportunity was the information revolution that unfolded during the 1970s and 1980s. The key innovations that took shape during this time were satellites, fibre-optics and co-axial cables, microwave telecommunications, networked computers and digitization. These innovations created the means for building global communication networks that in turn enabled the rapid collection, transmission and sharing of data and ideas. For capitalism this information revolution presented an opportunity for rebirth and reinvention of capitalist wealth generation because it provided new spaces for investment. These opportunities for reinvention were particularly fortuitous because they coincided with a looming crisis for top-down managerial social, political and economic systems. Managerial capitalism was becoming less dynamic and efficient, leading to the political economic problem of stagflation during the 1970s. Stagflation is a situation where incomes are falling but cost of living is rising. For Keynesian economists such conditions were theoretically impossible and as such they didn't know how to fix them. New economic ideas and policies were required.

The end of the Cold War

The second opportunity that presented itself was the collapse of the Soviet empire. One reason for capitalism's crisis was that new areas of investment had become difficult to find, and this generated problems because it restricted capitalist growth. The collapse of state socialism created conditions for a new global order, in which the United States became globally hegemonic. This hegemony is a 'Pax Americana' (Louw 2010a), a kind of global agreement by which the United States and its allies control the political, economic and cultural agenda globally. Not only did the Soviet collapse open up Eastern Europe for capitalist colonization and investment, it also led to the integration of China into a global economy, and paved the way for third world states to be 'recolonized' by foreign capital because their status was no longer contested by a bi-polar Cold War system of international governance.

These two opportunities – new areas to invest in plus the communication technology to coordinate a system of global investment – coincided fully during the 1990s. The result was the birth of a new global networker elite who built a new way of doing business globally. The global networkers' style of building overseas hegemony does not involve adopting the formal empire model used by the British Empire. The British Empire established and maintained its power by annexing land, dispatching occupation armies and police forces and planting new settlements. The American model for building hegemony works differently.

The emergence of the Pax Americana as an informal empire

In contrast to the formal empire of the British, the American empire is informal. It establishes and maintains power without building the same material infrastructure of the British. Instead the Pax Americana uses a comprador approach in which partner allies are relied upon to run their independent states in accordance with the needs of the United States' trading empire (Louw 2010a: Chapter 1). This American-run system grew out of the termination of Europe's formal empires. In each administrative entity created by European imperialism, a small westernized middle class emerged. The United States saw these westernized middle classes as natural allies of the Pax Americana and pushed for power to be transferred to them through the process of decolonization. Where European colonial possessions did not have native middle-class populations large enough to run independent states, America encouraged the colonial powers to actively build such middle-class populations. Successfully rolling out the American model meant promoting decolonization and then transferring power to local westernized elites, who stepped into the shoes of the departing colonials. These comprador elites became administrators of new independent states that served America's economic interests. The bulk of these westernized elites were quite happy to retain the socio-economic system built by colonials and serve as comprador partners in America's trading empire. Most were prepared to administer the client state and its economy on terms dictated by the multilateral system created by America as long as they received a share of the profits. It was a symbiotic relationship from which both sides benefited, as long as these compradors proved able to maintain the economic and political viability of their states. The comprador model is built on symbiotic relationships: America relies on their local partners to run client states in its far-flung informal empire, while these comprador partners rely on America to underpin their rule. The Pax Americana is characterized by comprador partnerships based on mutual need, with America ruling indirectly and informally through comprador allies. America prefers people who are culturally proximate and who have a vested interest in maintaining or expanding the old colonial economy.

The comprador elite create a local set of laws, institutions and practices that accord with the needs for their allies in the global nodes of power. This informal empire is a much cheaper way of organizing foreign populations than the formal empire model. Actual occupations of territory are now reserved only for those populations proving difficult to organize. In the recent times these have included Bosnia, Kosovo, Iraq and Afghanistan. The emergent global network capitalist model only dispatches small numbers of the networker elite to the peripheries for tours of duty. They go and set up branch offices and production facilities, assist the comprador allies to strengthen local hegemonies, and teach appropriate discourses and practices to foreign allies. Increasingly, relocations and long-term tours of duty are not required because air travel and information technology mean members of the networker elite no longer have to relocate their homes away from the core global cities. They can now pay short-term visits to the margins. Inspection, education and control can now be administered from a distance.

A globally networked elite

Significantly, Anglos or those comfortable using English and western discourses and practices dominate the emergent global network elite. The United States' global hegemony is beginning to take on the characteristics of a western alliance. This hegemonic alliance was first manifest in the first Gulf War of the early 1990s, and seen again in the Iraq, Kosovo and Afghanistan Wars of the 2000s. This alliance appears to be based on a set of special affinities between the USA and its junior partners of Britain, Canada and Australia. The other key player in global network capitalism is the European Union. Within the European Union Germany is emerging as a dominant power. These are places where western practices and discourses have been implemented since the Second World War. Another key player in the emergence of global network capitalism was Japan, also a nation rebuilt by America after the Second World War. To a considerable extent, globalization appears to be a phenomenon primarily involving the coordination and networking of a western elite that has been dispersed around the globe firstly by the British Empire and then via the Pax Americana. Globalization increasingly involves implanting western discourses and cultural practices, and global network capitalism, into non-western contexts. This is a fragmented and incomplete process. It is still unclear whether western discourses will replace, hybridize or exist alongside non-western ones. Each of these scenarios is discernible in different contexts. What is apparent is that the hegemonic dominance of the United States makes it possible in most parts of the world to transpose: western values and morality into a universal notion of human rights; western capitalism into a universal notion of the free market; and western liberal democracy into a universal notion of politics. American hegemonic dominance enables them, for the time being, to largely ignore or dismiss non-western complaints about western arrogance because they've made their own discourses natural and opaque. This is never a complete or closed process of course; we can see for instance the way that Chinese, Russian and Islamic discourses press on this hegemony in various parts of the world.

One of the key features of global network capitalism is that post-Fordist production is now spread across the globe. Capital is increasingly mobile. Products and services no longer tend to be manufactured in one location. They are designed in places with skilled and educated workforces; components are manufactured wherever it is cheapest to do so based on labour power, electricity, manufacturing infrastructure and resources, then transported to assembly sites, and then marketed and distributed through global networks. The production of a product might involve sites in multiple continents: design in America, resources from Africa, component production in Latin America or South-East Asia, assembly in Southern China, distribution throughout Europe and North America, and marketing to local markets in nations around the world. This requires a significant process of coordination and planning. Information about markets, resources and labour has to be collected and analysed. Financing, production and marketing decisions need to be made. This process is often undertaken by teams of people who are themselves scattered across the globe at various nodes in the network of global capitalism. The production processes need to be negotiated, set up and coordinated. This sometimes involves alliances or cooperative partnerships, which can be short-term and flexible arrangements. This system has become, as Castells (1996) says, an informational economy. The people who succeed are those who can best find, organize and exploit information rapidly. Production is increasingly premised on mass customization. Computer-integrated manufacturing (Crook et al. 1992: 181–184) enables flexible short production runs. Products can be adapted to multiple niche markets based on constantly changing patterns of demand. Consumers can be offered choice as long as the communication system exists to collect their demands, channel them into production systems and deliver them via distribution networks. A corporation like Amazon gained market dominance by developing the capacity to use information technology to manage the global distribution of books. They created a system that responds to myriad customer demands in real time.

Figure 4.1   Rows of bookshelves occupy the distribution warehouse of online retailer Amazon.com

© Macduff Everton/Corbis

Communicative capitalism

Communication is central to global network capitalism (Dean 2010). The system is reliant both on a material network of telecommunications and computers and the communicative capacities and coordination skills of immaterial labourers. In short, the practices of this new form of capitalism are centrally dependent on discursive creativity and communicative networking. As Lash and Urry (1994: 61) argue, the economy has become reflexive. The capacity to process information, reflect and respond is critical to the accumulation of capital and the acquisition of power. Cultural capital, knowledge and access to the network itself have become as important as capital. Good ideas are materialized in the analytic capacity of computer programs, well conceptualized production processes, and effective use of space, energy and other resources. The interface between communication and material production, mobilized in a reflexive and timely way, is fundamental to wealth making. Building communication networks, and regulating meaning flows through them, have become central components of global network capitalism's wealth-making machinery. Communication and media networks are now elements of the productive process. Consequently, the infrastructure and processes of communication and media have become central to developing and maintaining power relationships. Naturally, as global network capitalism emerged and managerialism has been wound back, power relationships have been altered. Shifts have consequently occurred in the processes of governance and hegemony, and the flows of meaning.

REORGANIZING CAPITALISM

Building global network capitalism effectively constituted a massive reformation of the capitalist system. In the initial stages of this process, managerial capitalism became 'disorganized' and 'de-managed' (Urry 1990). From the 1980s onwards, the discursive formations of managerial capitalism were deconstructed and deregulated as the old managerial elite lost the capacity to manage growing systemic crises. The unravelling of the old managerialist discourses, practices and institutions generated a growing sense of unease in the first world or core countries of managerial capitalism.

During the 1990s, the period of deregulation and deconstruction began to be replaced by new regulations, practices and institutions. A new networker elite took shape and set about generating a discernible set of global networking discourse and practices. They developed the hegemonic skills required to begin making those discourses dominant. By the beginning of the twenty-first century the, still emergent, networker elite had made significant progress towards building their hegemonic order. The discourses and practices of a reorganizing capitalism had become naturalized in key global cities where those that ran the informational economy resided: the heartlands of global network capitalism of North America, the European Union and Japan. As important, the new elite appeared to have moved a long way down the road of de-legitimizing many managerialist discourses characteristic of the western social welfare state, the centrally planned Soviet state and third world development states. Large constituencies of people and intellectuals were still supportive of these managerialist discourses. However, their growing defensiveness, and in some cases even a reticence to openly advocate such discourses, revealed their weakness in the face of the confident expansionist globalization discourses.

In the struggle for hegemony, the emergent global networker elite possessed an important advantage – their highly developed informational, cultural and discursive skills. After all, the growing informational economy was precisely built by those who first learned to use and exploit the possibilities of new communication technologies, which they then used to restructure social, economic and cultural relationships. The emergent elite built new global communication networks and they colonized and modified old communication infrastructures. By the turn of the century they appeared largely able to dominate the communication infrastructures operating in the heartlands of global network capitalism.

From the point of view of hegemony building, the global networkers are communication players par excellence. Together with the professional communicators they employ, they are highly skilled manipulators of symbols and communicative infrastructures. When this aspirant elite first began promoting their discourses, practices and institutional needs their hegemonic dominance was far from inevitable. When Vice-President Al Gore first began talking about the information super highway many other elites saw it as a vague futuristic dream. Or, when Bill Gates described his vision for a home filled with interactive screens connected to a global communication network many thought he was describing something in the far-off future. When he said he had the technology to build it now if only the market was ready for it many couldn't fathom what he meant. Or, when Steve Jobs proposed that practically everybody should own a personal computer many couldn't see why they would ever need one. All of these visions have now largely come to pass. At the time though, it was hard for the incumbent elite to see how such interconnectedness would materialize; how it would change discourses and institutions and generate new power networks and economies. As the 1990s progressed, however, these new elites incrementally and iteratively built on success after success. The aspiring elite of the 1980s – people like Al Gore, Bill Gates and Steve Jobs – began to look ever more capable of building a twenty-first-century global hegemony. While industry leaders like Gates and Jobs saw massive commercial opportunities, political leaders like Gore recognized the political need to build a global communication infrastructure.

A key feature of global network capitalism is that large transnational firms are the organizing hearts of the networkers' hegemony. The organizational principle of these transnational firms is a dispersed, flexible network. Just as the global networkers' hegemony is never complete and totally stabilized, so too is this networked mode of production always a work in progress. We can observe several inflections of the network idea as this economy has developed. The logic or dream of the network has driven the development of communication systems, corporations and media technologies. Below we examine three networks from different periods of this process: the network design of Paul Baran from the first days of the internet in the 1950s, the early 1990s management model of the 'pepperoni pizza' and the recent 'grouped' model of Facebook researchers and designers.

CONCEPTUALIZING NETWORKS

The ubiquitous network of the global era is the internet. The internet wasn't initially a media invention. It wasn't created by media organizations or with media in mind. The internet was devised as a solution to a military and political problem. In the Cold War era the United States invested in information and communication technology research as part of a broader industrial and technological competition with the Soviet Union. Within this broader research and development effort, the internet emerged as part of the search for a solution to a military and geopolitical problem. The United States wanted to build a communications network that could be used for global surveillance and command networking, and would survive an attack on any of its parts. All previous electronic communication networks had relied on a central node through which all communication passed. The risk of such a network was that if an enemy could destroy the central node the whole network would go down. The solution was to develop a network with no central node, so that it could continue to function if any part of it was destroyed. This meant envisaging and creating a communication system devised of distributed nodes with multiple lateral connections (Seel 2012).

The internet as a distributed network

Paul Baran was an engineer working on the development of computer networks in the 1960s. In a famous article he offered a visualization of centralized, decentralized and distributed communication networks.

Baran was interested in building a network that would survive in the event of a nuclear attack. This was one of the key strategic problems of the Cold War. A centralized network is vulnerable because an attack on its central node incapacitates it. All information is processed through that central node: without it the network does not function. A decentralized network is less vulnerable, though attacks on several key nodes would greatly reduce its capacity. A distributed network, however,

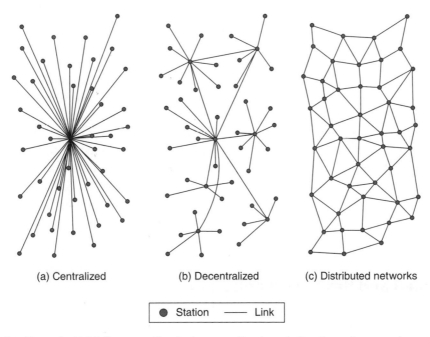

(a) Centralized   (b) Decentralized   (c) Distributed networks

● Station   —— Link

Figure 4.2   Baran's (1964) centralized, decentralized and distributed networks

would be far less vulnerable to attack because there is no central node. Information is distributed throughout the network. The proposal of a distributed network was a technical way of responding to a strategic problem. Baran (1964: 1) demonstrated that a distributed communication network could 'rapidly respond to changes in network status'. If you 'killed' a node, link or combination of nodes the network would figure out a new way to distribute information via the available links and nodes. This network was flexible and responsive. It was not dependent on a central vulnerable control point.

Networked modes of communication are productive structures. The responsive, flexible and autonomous nature of networks has underpinned the development of global network capitalism. Baran's simple illustrations of decentralized and distributed networks are useful for thinking about the organizing principles of networked economies, enterprises, cultural production and workplaces. Baran (1964) makes an important technical observation about this network that serves as a useful metaphor for the political shape of networks. He argued that designers need to build 'very reliable systems out of the described set of unreliable elements' (1964: 4). While nodes and links are flexible and adaptive, the network itself is resilient. Even in 1964 Baran was well aware that 'one day we will require more capacity for data transmission than needed for analogue voice transmission' (1964: 1) and, as such, societies needed to make sure they didn't box themselves into inflexible networks.

The internet is a social construction. The development of the internet is also a story of diverse groups of people, with varying degrees of power and different interests negotiating with each other. Negotiation and conflict between groups is central to internet history. The military saw it as a matter of national security. Governments saw it as a national asset. Computer scientists saw it as a matter of pure science and research or as a libertarian project that enshrined particular political values. Technologists and philosophers saw it as a public good and an empowering and democratizing technology. Technology corporations, and eventually media corporations, saw it as a path to expanding markets, or a threat to current business models. Each of these groups struggled with each other to realize their ideal version of the internet, or to shape the internet with their own values and political or commercial interests. These struggles were unfolding too in a particular historical context, at first the Cold War, and then as a key part of the development of neoliberal and global economies. While there is no centre of the network, and perhaps no centre of power, there are complex networks of power that manage how it works. At critical points in the history of the network those with power have had to negotiate and agree with each other on common protocols for its technical and political development. In a technical sense they had to agree on a common protocol or language for the internet: TCP/IP and HTML. Governments, corporations and designers had to agree on how to manage the physical architecture of the internet, the telecommunications networks that support it and network principles like 'net neutrality'. These struggles go on as governments, civil society and corporations attempt to realize internet structures that serve their interests.

Networked and flexible organizations and workplaces

The network idea spread rapidly in the late twentieth century, changing not only the technical design of communication systems but also organizational communication theories about the design of workplaces and management of labour forces. Network management gurus Jessica Lipnack and Jeffrey

Stamps (1994) argued that the network is the fourth human organizational style to emerge after the small group, hierarchy and bureaucracy. Similar to Harvey's (1989) argument that flexible accumulation incorporates prior modes of production, they argued that the networked organization adds a new layer around the older forms of organization. Networkers reorganize old organizational forms and practices. They network them into a complex hybridized amalgam. What transpires is a mutation rather than a radical break with the past. Lipnack and Stamps (1994) described the emerging organizational style as a 'pepperoni pizza organization'. This organizational style combines teams, hierarchy, bureaucracy and networks (1994: 13–14).

Lipnack and Stamps (1994: xvi) argue that 'life has become too complicated for hierarchy and bureaucracy'. Networks foster the shared responsibility, creativity and flexibility needed to respond to complex modes of production. Networks don't replace former organizational styles like small groups, hierarchies and bureaucracies; instead they find new ways to knit them together, adapt them and arrange them. Networks employ other organizational styles within their structures as required for particular tasks, problems and modes of production. This organizational style is characterized by

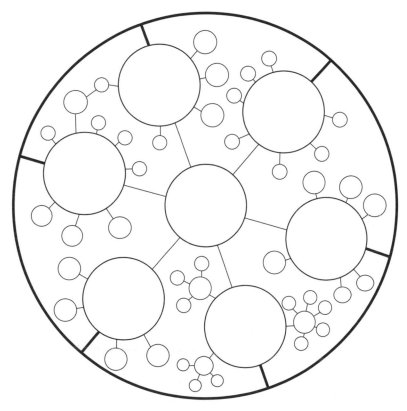

Figure 4.3 Lipnack and Stamps' (1994: 13) 'pepperoni pizza'

'systems within systems' and 'networks within networks' (Lipnack and Stamps 1994: 61). Within these organizations individuals form teams, become leaders and create processes. Of course, within these flexible structures, leadership and power still matter. Organizations are characterized by nodes or networks of power rather than a clear hierarchy. Employees may find themselves reporting to multiple managers and working in several processes at once.

Networked organizations run on social capital and trust, as much as the authority of strong leadership. Employees need to trust each other to work in teams, allow autonomy and encourage creativity. Networked production seeks to balance both trust and competition. Individuals within organizations, and organizations within larger production processes, need to trust each other at the same time they are in competition with each other. Lipnack and Stamps (1994: 191) suggest that Silicon Valley is a 'regional-networked-based industrial system that ... promotes collective learning and flexible adjustment among companies'. Those companies are also in competition with each other for the best labour, ideas, technologies and market share. Trust and flexibility work dialectically. At one level networks rapidly assemble links, teams and processes that bring people together, but those links and networks are always porous, temporary and flexible. They are rapidly dissolved as power and resources shift. Networked organizations can also paradoxically demand that everyone both lead and participate. While they might celebrate the facilitation of teams and collaboration, those structures are often underpinned by differing levels of power among participants. Trust and collaboration are always undergirded by competition and power struggles (we will examine the effect this has on workers in Chapter 5). The tension of the networked organization is that it demands both collaboration and competition simultaneously. Too much collaboration can create groupthink that stifles creative solutions. Too much competition can dissolve the trust required to innovate and achieve complex goals.

While some networks are incredibly flexible and distributed (as in Baran's distributed model above); most ultimately have discernible centres of power (as in Baran's decentralized model, and Lipnack and Stamps' pepperoni pizza model). This is an important distinction to consider. Most production systems ultimately congeal around clear nodes of power; in the case of a large media corporation, the CEO or senior management executive are the ultimate centre of power. As networked modes of production develop, though, we are perhaps seeing the emergence of messier, more decentred and distributed networks.

Networks in networks: the social web and everyday life

Facebook provides a way of thinking about networks in networks, and the power relations that structure networks.

At an organizational level we can see Facebook as an organizational network with a clear centre of power. Mark Zuckerberg and his management team are a central node guiding innovation and development within the company. They set the parameters and objectives within which the rest of the nodes and teams act.

We can also place Facebook within a larger and messier network of organizations competing and collaborating with each other to innovate and create value. Think about the way that Facebook is interdependent with YouTube, Twitter, Tumblr, Pinterest and Instagram (which they have now purchased).

While all these platforms compete with each other for audiences they also rely on each other in many ways. Much of what Facebook users do on the site is share content they make or get from other platforms (YouTube videos, news stories, Instagram photos and so on). There is no definite centre to this network, rather all of these organizations are interdependent nodes. Facebook also has to network with developers, advertisers and corporate brands who want to use the platform to track and interact with their audiences. Facebook's value depends on its capacity to be a responsive node within a larger network of cultural production. Its value rests to some degree on the desire of other cultural producers to create links with it and embed it within their networks of production.

In addition to being embedded in networks, Facebook can also be thought of as an organization that produces and exploits networks. Facebook's business model rests on creating a network where people create and circulate content between each other. This activity creates a dense network of links between people. Social media organizations are flexible providers of niche content in the sense that when you log on what you see in your news feed is a unique set of content based on your preferences and peer network. Facebook serves you as a singular node within a network of over 1 billion users. The way that you are connected to other nodes in the Facebook network – both sending and receiving content – is entirely unique to you. Think of how radically different this is to television, where audiences of hundreds of millions were served exactly the same content at exactly the same time. Facebook is a network of networks, or a network that produces and sells an infinite number of networks. Each user logs on to, and only interacts with, an infinitesimally small part of the network, especially assembled for them.

There is an asymmetry built into this network. While users can only see that small part of the network they interact with, Facebook's managers, programmers and designers can see the entire network. In this sense they are a node that sits 'above' the network – watching over it, collecting information about it and responding to it in real time. To do this, algorithms use big data sets and predictive analytics (ideas we will examine in the final section of this book). At this point though what is important for us to consider is the power relationships at work in this asymmetrical network. Some nodes can see and manage the whole network; other nodes can only see a small part of the network, and their interactions with other nodes are controlled and managed 'from above'.

Paul Adams (2012), a researcher who has worked with Facebook, argues that when examining networks we should pay careful attention not only to the nodes, but also to the links between nodes. Adams argues that the web is being 'rebuilt around people'. The distinction he is trying to mark out is that where the first generations of the internet have been built around content, the next generation will be built around social networks. He illustrates the point acutely by describing a connection between Etsy and Facebook. Etsy is a site where 'very, very small businesses' sell often handmade goods direct to consumers. Popular products on Etsy include jewellery, fashion and bespoke homewares. Etsy offer an application where a customer can 'connect' their Facebook network to the Etsy store. They can identify one of their Facebook friends, and ask Etsy to examine that friend's profile, friends and interests, and then generate a page of goods in the Etsy store that this friend would like. Think of a shop where the shopkeeper can immediately reassemble and restock the store based on one of your friend's tastes. Rather than this being a one-off and novel gimmick, this is in fact the forerunner of the connections between our everyday life and identity, our media use and the economy that are rapidly developing around us. What networks know about us will automatically shape the information we are served, and the way we are positioned within the network. The web is not a static set of links that we can choose to navigate how we like; the web constantly adapts to us, managing our experience, based on judgements it makes about us. Adams (2012: 12) argues that the connections between people are the organizing principle of the network and that this 'will move us away from the dominant form of marketing for the last 50 years: interrupting people to grab their attention'. Instead, media will manage their audiences as a network of many nodes that circulate information. Networks are organized within coordinates that are set and managed by organizations like Facebook. Facebook is a 'walled garden'. While users can participate in the network as they like, they do so on terms set by Facebook.

THE VISIONS OF GLOBAL NETWORKERS

Figures like Bill Gates, Steve Jobs, Sergey Brin, Larry Page and Mark Zuckerberg together with their teams of designers at Microsoft, Apple, Google and Facebook are examples of innovators who developed the infrastructure and ideas that underpin the networked information society. In their public appearances these Silicon Valley innovators explain and promote the iterative and experimental development of networked media technologies. Search online for their appearances at Silicon Valley events, like Mark Zuckerberg's appearances at Start-up School, or their product launches, like Steve Jobs' iPod and iPhone launches and Sergey Brin's announcement of Google Glass at TED.

As much as these events are promotional exercises for their companies, they are also historically important accounts of the continuous development of information networks.

MARK ZUCKERBERG AND FACEBOOK

Speaking at Startup School in 2013 Mark Zuckerberg explained to the audience of designers and developers how Facebook emerged from a range of open-ended experiments he undertook with software during his time as a student at Harvard.

He told them that at Harvard he learnt that his aim was to build software that is 'more human' and to build networks that 'connect everybody'. Connecting everybody enabled 'communities of people' to 'channel their energy' and to 'do great things'. Together with his team at Facebook he aimed to build the infrastructure for connecting people. Zuckerberg embodies the ideals and values of the networked society. The network elite don't see themselves as trying to control populations 'from above', but rather as building infrastructure that harness and channel the productive participation of large networks of people.

He explained that the first time he learnt this lesson was while he was a student at Harvard. He had an exam on art history but hadn't attended classes or done the study. He realized he was 'screwed' so he went to the course website, downloaded the material and made a program that showed all the images of art work and let students contribute their notes. He sent the website 'to the class and said, "Hey guys, I built a study tool" and within an hour the whole thing was populated with all the information that was needed to take the final'.

[handwritten: how is it doing?]

The lesson he learnt was that you needed to design software that brought real people together in useful ways as part of their real life experiences, needs and interests. While search engines could find information on the web, there was not yet a platform that enabled people to perform their real relationships in a seamless and ongoing way. Facebook didn't start out as a business or with a business model: it started as an effort to build a network that people would find useful in living their lives. From there, Zuckerberg imagined, this network could become a platform for all kinds of unexpected innovations and developments. Facebook's primary initial task was to create dense connections between people. The more connected people were in the network, the more opportunities there would be to leverage those connections.

Facebook continues to employ many experts who work together in varied teams to produce a more productive network. Those teams include data scientists, sociologists, psychologists, user experience designers and so on. Their job is to get connections and information flowing through Facebook's network in more seamless ways to increase user engagement with the network. They collect and analyse all the data that our participation in the network generates. As Facebook collects enormous amounts of data it has had to develop new hardware and infrastructure to store and process it. These innovations have led to the development of more productive networks and cloud computing services in other parts of the technology sector. The networked economy is characterized by these open-ended processes of innovation.

STEVE JOBS AND APPLE PRODUCT LAUNCHES

Steve Jobs was famous for his Apple product launches. He would gather together technology industry journalists and influencers for tightly scripted performances of new Apple technologies. The 2007 launch of the iPhone is a historically significant event. Search for Apple's iPod (2001), iPhone (2007) and iPad (2010) product launches online.

Jobs began the launch by telling the audience that Apple had invented several revolutionary products: the personal computer in 1984 which changed everything, the iPod in 2001 which changed the music industry, and that in 2007 they would launch 'three revolutionary products' in one device. As he showed an image of the iPhone for the first time, the industry audience broke into rapturous applause.

Over the course of an hour and a half Jobs demonstrated the features of the iPhone and explained how it revolutionized our day-to-day experience of mobile devices and information networks. The iPhone was a device upon which many apps could be developed. For instance, Apple could partner with networks like Google to provide services like email, search and maps. Eric Schmidt, the CEO of Google, joined Jobs on stage to explain that 'Internet architectures allow you now to take the enormous brain trust that is represented by the Apple development team and combine that with the open protocols and data services that

(Continued)

(Continued)

companies like Google [offer].' Working together these companies could bring a previously unimaginable range of services 'together in one place'. This was possible because of the 'cultures of innovation' in companies like Apple and Google.

Figures like Zuckerberg, Jobs and Schmidt present themselves as solving problems in the creation, consumption and circulation of information. They aim to build platforms and devices that create, manage and leverage networks.

Who are today's pioneering global networkers?

What is their vision for the future?

What are some of the forms of media they are developing, testing and experimenting with?

You can find links to talks and presentations by Mark Zuckerberg and Steve Jobs on the *Media and Society* website study.sagepub.com/carahandlouw

FLEXIBLE AND NETWORKED CAPITALISM

Networkers prefer federal arrangements which allow individual components autonomy. This is different to a hierarchical organization with top-down command structures. The networkers allow each unit to organize itself appropriate to its set task. Networkers deconstruct the huge bureaucratic structures built by managerialists and weaken top-down command chains of communication. Such organizational deconstruction became a feature of the late twentieth century as global networkers began challenging managerialist assumptions and practices.

At an organizational level workers find themselves in open plan offices, working in teams and communicating with co-workers via information technologies. At a global level the material infrastructure of the internet spans the globe via cables, route servers, server farms, and satellites located at key strategic points. Global network capitalism involves an untidy and constantly morphing set of practices and discourses. This is a mode of production that continually reorganizes itself. Reorganizing capitalism has involved moving away from a neatly structured world of uniformly hierarchical organizations, and of populations organized into neat blocs of mass audiences, mass markets and nations. Global networking capitalists are learning the arts of controlling multiple, overlapping territories and jurisdictions in ways that replicate many of the practices of pre-capitalist feudal lords. In this mode of production, power is far more dispersed and contingent:

- Where the managerialist sets up hierarchies, issued commands, disseminated ideas and information, the global networker processes, networks, coordinates and controls flows of ideas and data.
- Where the managerialist directs and commands, the networker facilitates and steers.

- Where the managerialist controlled particular activities, the networker sets parameters or boundaries within which they encourage and exploit innovation and creativity.
- Where the managerialist told people what to think, the networker monitors and modulates what people think about.

Harvey (1989: 147) argues that this mode of production is highly flexible and marked by rapid uneven development. By this he means that some countries, regions and even parts of cities have developed rapidly, while other parts have not. Flexible accumulation is also marked by the compression of time and space as a result of communication technologies, and flexible organization structures enable communication to flow quicker over large distances. This connects spaces, processes and people in new ways. Wealthy urban areas across the globe are interconnected. They often share more in common than poor urban or regional areas within their own national borders. The effects of time–space compression are seen in the rise of just-in-time and demand-driven production (Harvey 1989: 177). Flexible production responds to market demand. Rather than produce stockpiles of goods that are then sold to a mass market, this system uses information technologies and processes to continually assess market demand and adapt production. Just-in-time production enables organizations to create and serve a myriad of fragmented niche audiences and markets. To run a just-in-time production process organizations need diverse and flexible networks of labour. They need to be able to change the size, location and make-up of their workforces rapidly to respond to demand. This has led to the emergence of more flexible, precarious and competitive labour conditions. Corporations also require deregulation to enable them to have more flexible investment and production structures.

Harvey explains that flexible accumulation reorganizes rather than ends industrial modes of production. Industrial factories, with their low-paid workforces, are shifted to the periphery of the network (Harvey 1989: 186), where they can be managed from afar by highly skilled managers in global cities. Harvey notes that these skilled managers are 'a highly privileged, and to some degree empowered, stratum within the labour force'. They become powerful because 'capitalism depends more and more on mobilizing the powers of intellectual labour' (1989: 186). Global network capitalism is flexible enough to manage many alternative forms of labour. When Harvey argues that production is shifted to the periphery of the network, he is talking about the shift of industrial factories from developed countries to developing countries, but he is also talking about the emergence of flexible and exploitative forms of work within developed countries themselves like casual labour, subcontractors and other informal labour practices that are part of industries like media, fashion and cultural production.

As well as incorporating and reorganizing industrial production, the global networking era shares characteristics with the feudal era. Much decision making is privatized, personalized and located in nodes of power. The new style of organizing people is less defined and messier. It is somewhat analogous to a feudal 'patchwork' of overlapping powers. We find multiple and proliferating styles of control and decision making being tolerated in different parts of the network, so long as those in nodes of power can gain some benefit from allowing particular practices or organizational arrangements to exist in a part of their networked empire. In addition, the various empires are not discrete: they simultaneously overlap, intersect, cooperate and even conflict with each other in an ever-shifting feudal-like melange of networked power relationships. Table 4.1 attempts to map out the shifting nature of relationships between elite, organizational structures and communication patterns across historical eras. Global network capitalism doesn't completely replace all the previous eras; it instead incorporates, adapts and reorganizes them.

Table 4.1 Historical era, power elites and modes of communication

Era	Feudal era	Capitalist era/ early capitalism	Managerial era: managerial capitalism and Soviet managerialism	Global networking era
Who are the ruling elite?	Hereditary lords	Bourgeoisie	Professional managers	Networkers
Where is power located?	Family networks	Parliaments	Boards and bureaus	Information networks
	Decisions taken in private	Decisions taken in public forums: externalized debate where factions bargain in public sphere	Decisions taken in public and private domains: parliaments, cabinet rooms and board rooms	Growing privatization of decision making: especially in private companies
	Pre-state patchwork of principalities and overlapping jurisdictions	Limited state	State and private corporations	Re-feudalization of jurisdictions
How is power structured?	Loyalty	Control of capital	Bureaucratic hierarchy	Cultural capital
	Birth: rank and land-tenure linked			Access to information
	Theology			Networked teams
What is the dominant form of communication?	Ritualized communication: pageantry and ceremony	Elite communication: produced by small owner-operated media	Mass communication: produced by a culture industry	Fragmented niche communication: produced in a multiplicity of networked sites

BUILDING DOMINATION

Ruling elites are the product of successful hegemony building. Building hegemony involves making practices and discourses which serve the interests of powerful groups. Power that is achieved by naturalizing 'appropriate' discourses is most effective because, once naturalized, the rules police themselves and so less coercion needs to be employed by the powerful. At the turn of the century a capitalist networker elite had visibly emerged, and the process of naturalizing the practices and discourses of network capitalism was far-advanced in the global cities of the developed world. Few in these cities now question the inevitability of an information age capitalist future.

Resistance, however, is still felt from those living in high unemployment areas where the industrial economy of the twentieth century has collapsed, but the information economy has not emerged to replace it. In the post-socialist states this resistance can take the form of nostalgia for a return to state socialism. In capitalist societies the former working class and their allies seek a return to the big government and labour politics of the post-war era. Resistance has also emerged from anti-globalization and green movements that challenge the very assumptions underpinning global network capitalism. They see global network capitalism as fundamentally exploitative of people and the natural world. In the United States, United Kingdom and Australia right-wing resistance has emerged from groups opposed to multiculturalism, refugees and migration. In Europe this is becoming aligned with the re-emergence of far-right groups. In the developing world the discourses of global network capitalism are generally less securely embedded. Their acceptance resides with small groups of the information rich in these countries who presume they stand to benefit from integrating their societies as a node of global network capitalism.

NETWORKED PRODUCTION

Take yourself as the beginning point and think of the different networks you connect with on a day-to-day basis as you interact with the web, use mobile devices, consume media and popular culture.

Take an organization (like Apple, Amazon, Sony or News Corporation) and conceptualize the network required to produce, distribute and consume their devices or products. Where are they designed, produced and consumed? How is each part of the network managed?

Take a device like a smartphone or tablet and examine the variety of networks required to produce and distribute it, and the networks the device connects its users to.

There are a variety of forms of labour associated with the production, use and disposal of mobile devices. You can find links to stories about e-waste, Foxconn factories in China, and Facebook's content moderators on the *Media and Society* website study.sagepub.com/carahandlouw. Consider these forms of informal or below-the-line work in the information economy. Can you think of others?

(Continued)

(Continued)

Take a media technology or device that you use. Map out its entire life cycle.

> Who produces it?
> Where is it produced?
> How is it used?
> What relationships does its use facilitate?
> How is it disposed of?
> What power relationships are implicated in making, using and disposing of these devices?

CONCLUSION

In global network capitalism:

- A system of mass consumption that catered to homogenous cultural identities is replaced by consumption organized around a multiplicity of niche identities. We are each inculcated in the everyday labour of fashioning ourselves as individuals who fit into the entrepreneurial and flexible culture of global capitalism.
- Mass centralized forms of production are replaced by responsive, just-in-time and networked modes of production. Enterprises are organized around responding to the multiple and rapidly changing markets.
- Disciplinary and repressive modes of control are augmented with responsive and reflexive modes of control. Global network capitalism has created a far more diverse, flexible and controlling culture industry.

In this system, constructing and holding together hegemonic alliances has become much more complex, and communicating with increasingly fragmented constituencies now involves mastering a multiplicity of niche media discourses. It has also involved mastering new communication practices. Managerialism relied on top-down rhetorical communication. This is no longer the case. A wider repertoire of practices is now required to communicate with a multiplicity of niche identities. Additional to top-down methods, professional communicators now also need to mobilize a range of dialogical, participatory and consultative methods. They also need to know how to manipulate information in databases in order to manage, respond to and control more diffuse and interactive communication practices.

In this chapter we have examined the emergence of a global information economy. This is a complex and networked arrangement of power relationships that emerged from a series of technological developments and political events. The information technology revolution made it possible to manage populations and production at increasing distance, reflexivity and speed. The end of the Cold War opened up economic and political opportunities for stagnating western economies. The new markets enabled global corporations to expand. America was able to establish itself as a lone superpower, realizing throughout the 1990s the Pax Americana as a political, cultural and economic project. The Pax Americana is an informal empire which uses a network of political and economic alliances across the globe.

The global information economy is characterized by new modes of production, consumption and control. In global network capitalism, culture is central to making and maintaining power relationships. This is a complex process. It is not a linear process of authentic or exotic cultures being co-opted or obliterated by a mass homogenizing culture industry. The global networked culture industry relies on our avid participation, and it produces spaces for many niche and local identities and meanings. There is, however, an important distinction between 'speaking and being heard' (Hindman 2009). Part of the reason global network capitalism allows space for participation and niche identities is because information technologies enable it to efficiently manage and respond to multiple sites of meaning making simultaneously. The culture industry is now reflexive enough not to have to develop mass homogenous audiences and identities.

We might have shifted from the mass production and consumption of culture critiqued by the Frankfurt School and others throughout the twentieth century. Today's flexible and networked culture industry appears to offer a more durable, flexible and responsive mode of control. While some of the original critiques of mass homogenous culture no longer seem right, the arguments made about the immense power of a culture industry (which organizes everyday life and relies on the avid participation of ordinary people) seems more important than ever.

FURTHER READING

Harvey (1989) provides an authoritative account of the emergence of flexible accumulation as a political, economic, cultural and spatial phenomenon. He introduces key ideas like post-Fordism, flexible accumulation, time–space compression and uneven geographical development. O'Connor and Xin (2006) provide an account of the emergence of the creative industries as part of China being incorporated into the global information economy. They examine the tensions this creates within China. Tremblay (2011) critically considers how government policies construct and use evidence to promote the idea of creative economies in order to position the UK in the global information economy. Hassan (2003) examines the Massachusetts Institute of Technology's Media Lab as a key site for producing technologies and discourses that promote networked information technologies. Each of these readings critically examines an aspect of the development of creative industries and related government policies. Each addresses debates and tensions around the development of a flexible global cultural economy that relies on creative and communicative forms of labour.

Harvey, D. (1989) *The Condition of Postmodernity.* Oxford: Blackwell.

Hassan, R. (2003) 'The MIT Media Lab: techno dream factory or alienation as a way of life?', *Media, Culture & Society*, 25: 87–106.

O'Connor, J. and Xin, G. (2006) 'A new modernity? The arrival of "creative industries" in China', *International Journal of Cultural Studies*, 9 (September): 271–283.

Tremblay, G. (2011) 'Creative statistics to support creative economy politics', *Media, Culture & Society*, 33: 289–298.

Any article marked with ⊗ is available to download at the website **study.sagepub.com/ carahandlouw**

5 MEDIA AND COMMUNICATION PROFESSIONALS

COMMUNICATION PROFESSIONALS MAKE MEANING AND MANAGE MEANING-MAKING PROCESSES.

* How is access to communication professions controlled?

* What are the distinctive characteristics of communication work?

* What makes communication work 'good' or 'bad'?

In this chapter we:

- Examine how those who make meaning are controlled
- Define communication work and immaterial labour
- Consider the professional ideologies of professional communicators
- Examine some contemporary features of below-the-line work in the culture industry.

PROFESSIONAL COMMUNICATORS

We often think of media as things: a newspaper, a television programme, images on a computer screen. Media aren't just an inert set of texts though; media are the product of humans interacting with each other. Politicians and journalists interact with each other to mediate the political process. Within news organizations editors, journalists, producers and programmers interact to make news content. Our understanding of media then needs to be grounded in thinking about the social relationships that produce media. When those interactions happen in an industrial setting we think of the activity as work. Communication professionals make more than just texts. They produce and mediate relationships between people and the world we live in. Communication work is distinctive because its products are immaterial. Professional communicators produce ideas, meanings and social relationships. Immaterial labour requires not only material and mechanical skills like operating a machine. It also requires skills and abilities connected with our intellect, identity, imagination and values. This makes it a complex and nuanced form of work, grounded as much in who we are as in what we can do.

Controlling who can make meaning

If meaning is produced by humans interacting with each other, and those interactions are organized by power relationships, then we need to examine who gets to make meaning and where they make meaning. Many of the meanings we individually process on a daily basis are produced and circulated by professional meaning makers. All humans make meaning. For some people though, meaning production and circulation is their occupation. These professional communicators are able to exercise an influence in society because they become gatekeepers and regulators of meaning making. In western civilization there is a long-standing tradition of people being designated to make and produce meaning. This reaches as far back as the rhetoricians of ancient Greece. But, the communication professions we know today took shape and expanded rapidly during the twentieth century (see Chapter 2). They have taken on several new dimensions in the past generation with the emergence of global networked capitalism and information technologies (see Chapters 3 and 4). The development of communication professions took place as part of the transition towards mass societies with their systems of mass education, media and bureaucracy. Mass societies required a class of people that would manage the creation and circulation of meaning.

The twentieth century saw the widespread diffusion of mass education, print media, radio, film, television and later the internet. As these cultural and media institutions became more central to the functioning of society and the economy, the class of professional communicators who run these institutions also became more numerous and important to the exercise of power. The number and variety of workers whose job is to create, process and circulate information and meaning proliferated through the second half of the twentieth century. At least some of the professions to grow in this period include: academics, researchers, teachers, journalists, publishers, film makers, television producers, software programmers, digital media workers, architects, artists and designers, politicians, policy advisors and regulators, economists, lawyers and judges, psychologists and counsellors, celebrities, popular musicians and actors, and those working in fields like advertising, marketing, public relations and community development. All of these people are part of the process of making, circulating and regulating the flow of meanings within which we live our lives, interact with others and make sense of the world.

The industrialization of meaning making shifted the nature of intellectual work. Once, intellectuals were elites whose work was largely confined to other elite audiences and cloistered from the general public. Rhetoricians, clergy, writers, philosophers and political thinkers, and early scientists were confined to royal courts, universities or the homes and businesses of wealthy patrons. The industrial production of meaning meant that intellectuals both were drawn from the general public and interacted with and produced meaning for them. They were no longer 'ivory tower' intellectual elites. A more suitable image of an early twenty-first-century intellectual worker is an employee at a news network who works as part of a team creating, packaging and distributing ideas through a global electronic information network. Intellectual work is increasingly concentrated within organizational sites where creative people are employed to generate the ideas and relationships that hold society together. They circulate these ideas to multiple elite, niche and mass public audiences.

Professional communicators and power relationships

Professional communicators are significantly implicated in the creation of social power relationships through the way in which political and economic power elites form symbiotic relationships with them. The relationships between the powerful and intellectuals are central to creating the meanings and rituals that organize and control the lives of others (Berger 1977). The Frankfurt School saw these relationships between the powerful and intellectuals as ones of 'patronage'. In their view, professional communicators needed to work for one or other branch of the culture industry. To keep their jobs they need to produce content that serves the interests of the patrons who pay their wages. While intellectuals in the culture industry are free to think whatever they like, they are confined to producing meanings that serve the interests of the institution. This sometimes directly shapes the ideas in their content, but more routinely, it means being steered towards producing content that produces mass audiences.

As we will consider in this chapter, these relationships of patronage make for complex professional ideologies and identities. Professional communicators often find themselves balancing out their own views, desires, creative impulses and political viewpoints with the demands and objectives of the institution they work for. Patronage subtly, but dramatically, narrows the range of discourses and practices available to professional communicators. If you live in a large western city and want a job at a media corporation as a journalist, advertiser or researcher for example, you will find that most of the jobs in most of the institutions are much the same when it comes to the level of freedom and creativity in the ideas you will produce. Very few cultural workers can truly go to work every day and do whatever they like. Even those who appear to do so at first glance – like advertising creatives, fashion designers or film makers – work within coordinates set by their institutions, financiers or bosses. No advertising creative can produce campaigns that don't achieve the instrumental needs of their clients regardless of how creative the idea is. No film maker survives if their films don't acquire the audiences their financial backers seek. No fashion designer remains relevant and employed if their fashion range doesn't attract attention and sell.

Producing professional communicators

There is status attached to many professional communication roles because of their capacity to make and manage the parameters of social meaning. The status of media and cultural work has also grown as the culture industry has become adept at glamorizing and promoting the status, values and creativity of professional communicators. Think about the way that journalists, fashion magazine editors or hipsters who work as designers, columnists or advertisers are celebrated in Hollywood films and lifestyle magazines. There is significant competition for cultural jobs because they are perceived as influential, creative and powerful. Access to these jobs is managed via professional standards, qualifications and even professional rituals like auditions, portfolios and conferences. In tandem with the development of communication professions, universities and other education institutions created communication disciplines and programmes to supply industry with professional communicators who have the skills and ideas that industries want. The success of communication disciplines at universities has always relied on their ability to articulate themselves with industry needs and values. The development of journalism schools or business schools that taught disciplines like public relations or advertising emerged in the early twentieth century alongside the development of these industries. These fields were created as academic disciplines because of a demand from these emerging industries for employees with particular kinds of skills. Throughout the twentieth century the culture industry has played a significant role in shaping university disciplines and curriculums. The result is that professional communicators not only work in institutions; they are also trained to think and act in curriculums designed specifically for the needs of those institutions.

The mass production of professional communicators to staff the proliferating communicative machinery can become a repetitive and banal process. Rather than teaching students to think laterally, curriculums can lean towards teaching them the professional values, routines and skills of their chosen industry. Students are taught the basic skills and dominant ideas and discourses that will make them employable in professions like journalism, public relations and politics. The repetition of these skills and ideas can lead to a standardized 'cloning' of generations of professional communicators. As communication institutions and their training programmes have spread across the globe, critics warn that these industries have become populated by intellectual 'copy-cats' who follow the trends of a global communication network. This has consequences for individuals, industries and society. For individuals, it means that education turns you into a functionary rather than a thinker. Education is central to shaping the richness and quality of our lives and relations with others. Individuals who are only taught routines and skills miss out on the capacity to think and reflect. If institutions encounter crises and discover that their employees only know the skills and routines that have always existed then they may struggle to adapt. Journalism is an industry in crisis; the more journalists simply hark on about the skills and values of the past the less the industry appears capable of conceptualizing a way forward. The consequence for society is that the institutions we rely on to mediate our relations with others lose the reflective capacity to think through their role in shaping the lives we lead. They become factories that produce content and audiences, rather than organizations that reflectively and thoughtfully mediate our lives together.

IMMATERIAL AND CREATIVE LABOUR

Labour, like communication, is a distinctive aspect of the human condition. While we might commonly think of labour as producing objects (like cars, televisions, computers), labour is first and foremost about relations between people. Labour always involves working with and for others.

Labour produces human relationships. At its most elementary, work is purposive endeavour and activity that we undertake with our body and our brains. You can work in the garden, or on a piece of music, or on writing a poem. Under certain conditions these purposive and creative activities become labour. For most of us we think of labour as working for a wage. We do it because someone will pay us. We need to do it to have money to live. We can trade our labour because it produces value for someone. For a professional communicator that value is the capacity to create and circulate meanings that facilitate social relationships. The institutions that employ professional communicators valorize the social relationships labourers create. For instance, they sell to advertisers the audience's attention that labourers capture with the content they make.

While media organizations need to invest in material resources and technologies like buildings and machinery, it is the labourers who make value with their creative ability to attract attention, affect audiences and manage social relationships. Professional communicators produce, circulate and manage ideas, representations, identities, audiences and social relationships. Each of these is immaterial in the sense that they are not physical, durable products we can discretely identify, touch or hold. They are products that exist only in our minds and the minds of others. The labour of creating and circulating ideas relies not only on what we can do but also very much on who we are and our capacity to affect others. Immaterial labour is central to the relations of the networked information economy.

Professional communicators' products are immaterial – symbols, relationships, attention, audiences and populations. Immaterial labour has symbolic and affective facets (Hardt 1999). Symbolic labour refers to the production of communicative artefacts like news reports, videos, designs and text. Affective labour refers to the ideas, emotions and communicative capacities that people deploy to create communities, collective subjectivities and social relationships (Hardt 1999). Professional communicators are affective labourers who they channel the living attention of others (Brennan 2004). Where professional communicators employ their social network, creative practices and identity to create content and audiences, and facilitate social relationships and spaces, they are immaterial labourers. Immaterial labourers draw on their own identity and capacities to communicate and affect others to create meanings and social relationships.

Hierarchies of communicative labour

The terms and conditions of media and cultural work depend on the place of professional communicators within the production networks of global media. Communication strategists who devise and manage communication processes command high wages and good conditions, as might creative workers who produce high-quality content that attracts large or valuable audiences. Content makers working under the direction of strategists and creatives, though, often find themselves working in more flexible and precarious circumstances. Communications work is characterized by a divergence of power and resources. Top-level communication strategists are often powerful and important figures within organizations, whereas at the other end the proliferation of communication workers makes them interchangeable parts of organizational structures and production processes. Many professional communicators work in flexible and transient jobs, organizations and production processes.

At the end of the day, if a worker can get a better deal somewhere else they will. A balance is struck between the workers' access to other kinds of work, and industries' access to other kinds of workers. Creative communication and media workers in a city like New York will have different demands from factory workers in southern China. The workers in New York will also have the capacity to have their demands met because they have opportunities to work elsewhere and they produce a value that can't be acquired more cheaply anywhere else. While the popular Fox animation series *The Simpsons* is written and largely animated by well-paid writers and animators in the United States who demand particular pay and conditions, much of the more basic animation tasks are completed by workers in South Korea, who will work for less. Throughout the world particular aspects of the media production process are outsourced to emerging economies where there is a capable labour force that produces the same value for less money. In 2010 the street artist Banksy helped animate an opening sequence for *The Simpsons* which parodied these labour arrangements. Asian children were depicted working in a dirty sweatshop factory colouring in *The Simpsons'* film reels and manufacturing Bart Simpson dolls. *Time* magazine reported that the South Korean animators who have worked on *The Simpsons* since it began in 1989 were upset at being depicted as sweatshop workers. They work in 'high-tech workshops in downtown Seoul'. This is true: they aren't sweatshop workers. But part of the reason animation is outsourced to other countries is because the cost of their labour power is cheaper. *Time* reported that, 'Even though South Korea's wealth keeps wages high by regional standards, the country's animators still make one-third the salaries of their American counterparts – earning the South Korean industry a reputation for pumping out episodes on tight deadlines at reasonable prices' (Cain 2010). The South Korean workers are 'free' and 'happy' to work for one-third the wage of their American co-labourers in the production of the show. They perform creative tasks for less, lowering the cost to Fox in attracting human attention. They offer the cheapest and most efficient workforce for undertaking specific creative tasks in the production process. *The Simpsons'* workforce is organized globally based on where the cheapest labour power can be sourced. Labourers in each part of the production network negotiate the best conditions they can and often defend with pride the creativity and identity invested in their work.

Freedom and autonomy

Questions of freedom, choice and power are fundamental to our understanding of work. Our conceptualization of labour is entwined with how we think about our lives, identities and values. Freedom is more complex than it first appears because it is always constrained by power relations. It is always something negotiated within social relationships. Individual freedom often has a double character: we are both free to sell our labour and free of any direct access or control over the means of production within which we work. While media and cultural workers are free to sell their creativity, ideas and capacity to make meaning, this is a forced choice: if they don't sell their creativity they will have no money to live. Their creative capacities are appropriated by institutions or production processes over which they have no control. It is especially important to think about the relationships between professional communicators and the culture industries because often at first glance this kind of work appears free and unconstrained. In comparison to workers in factories, call centres or building sites, media and cultural workers appear to work in more flexible and creative settings. They seem to have greater autonomy to choose what they do and how they do it. Their sense of autonomy and creativity is a source of value for the organization they work for, rather than a thing to be controlled and disciplined; it is something to be amplified, channelled and harnessed. Often organizations that can engender the greatest feelings of creativity and autonomy among their media and cultural workers stand to extract the most value from them. For example, technology workplaces like Google's 'Googleplex' are open and playful environments featuring comfortable workspaces, gourmet food and relaxation spaces. The company invests in designing these workplaces in order to attract and sustain the creativity of the best designers, analysts and programmers.

Media and cultural industries rely on the creativity of their workers. The more creative and autonomous that communication workers feel the more likely they are to create value for the organizations they work for. Feelings of autonomy and creativity are both a rewarding and desirable part of cultural work (Hesmondhalgh and Baker 2011) and the means by which the culture industry organizes and manages the productivity of workers (Banks 2010). Government policies, economists and urban planners all produce discourses about flexible work, creative cities and entrepreneurial labourers. Workers also participate in creating and circulating these discourses about their autonomy. In fact, 'posing' as autonomous is a key way professional communicators make value for the culture industry (Banks 2010). Think about how the credibility of journalism rests on journalists presenting themselves as fearless and independent, or how the authenticity of a rock musician depends on them presenting themselves as ordinary working-class artists. The more these poses are accepted by the audience, the more value they produce for the modes of cultural production they work for. The more the public accepts the journalist as credible or the rock musicians as authentic the more newspapers or records that are sold.

'Good' and 'bad' work

Ideas of creativity and autonomy are often present in accounts of what makes communication and cultural work desirable. Our ideas about 'good' and 'bad' work are grounded in the norms and values of our society and shaped by our relative level of power. Hesmondhalgh and Baker (2011: 29) offer a schema for thinking about 'good' and 'bad' forms of communication, cultural and creative work:

- *Good* work is characterized by good wages, hours and safety, autonomy, interest, involvement, sociality, self-esteem, self-realization, work–life balance and security. Good work produces excellent products that contribute to the common good.
- *Bad* work involves poor wages, working hours and safety, powerlessness, boredom, isolation, low self-esteem and shame, frustrated development, overwork and risk. Bad work produces low-quality products that fail to contribute to the wellbeing of others.

This schema contends that autonomy and self-realization are central to 'good' forms of work. That is, because cultural work requires something of ourselves – our own values, identity and creativity – to be good, it has to be reflective of our own sense of the 'common good'. Hesmondhalgh and Baker (2011) suggest that professional communicators seek out forms of work that enable them to reflect their own identity and values. Of course, not all professional communicators are idealistic: many are also pragmatic, cynical or even Machiavellian about the meaning and value of their work.

While professional communicators are capable of thinking critical, oppositional and autonomous ideas, the culture industry demonstrates the ability to recuperate or incorporate these ideas even where in the first instance they appear to be truly radical or oppositional. The culture industry ultimately sets the coordinates within which the autonomy of professional communicators functions. At the very least, however, communication workers retain the capacity to 'think the unthinkable' (Banks 2010: 262). Even as the culture industry exerts control over its workers, it relies on their creativity and therefore will necessarily contain an element of unpredictability. It can't entirely discipline how its workforce thinks; if it did it would neuter the creative and relational work they undertake and that is the basis of the value they create. Instead, the culture industry works to set the coordinates and procedures that govern and harness this creativity. Professional communicators negotiate the extent of their freedom, creativity and autonomy depending on their place in the power relationships of cultural production. Communication and cultural workers are largely reluctant to see themselves as cloned, disciplined or tamed. Journalists are proud of their independence and ability to speak truth to power; advertisers celebrate their creativity and ability to think outside the box; web developers see themselves as constantly pushing the boundaries of human connectivity. We need to tread carefully, though, by sorting out compelling explanations of the autonomy, freedom and creativity of media, communication and cultural work from the narratives the culture industry produces to make this work appear desirable. Whenever we consider the creativity of communication work we need to examine the institutions and social context within which that creativity is appropriated.

PROFESSIONAL IDEOLOGY AND THE MEANING OF LABOUR

Labour is something given of ourselves. When it comes to professional communication it is not just that labourers choose to go to work and do the given tasks; they also choose how much of their own creativity and identity they will invest in the work. Professionals often construct narratives about the social value and purpose of their work. When we examine media and communication professionals we find values, narratives and practices they use to make their work meaningful to themselves as individuals, give them a collective identity as professionals, and position the value of their work for a broader public. The professional identity of media and communication workers is often embedded in their everyday practices and discourses. To understand them we have to do more than simply ask communication workers to explain the value of their work. We have to carefully observe how they give it meaning in their everyday interactions, the private and public places where they discuss their work, and the cultural artefacts that they produce (Caldwell 2008).

Professional communicators construct stories that explain how and why they do what they do. These practices are evident in representations or explanations of cultural work that producers create for their peers and the public. Media and communication workers use their skills and access to media infrastructure to publicize the meaning and value of their work. Professional communicators construct 'stories' or 'theories' that explain how and why they do what they do. While other professions like surgeons, social workers, teachers or military all care deeply about their work, they don't have the same access to communication infrastructure to tell the public about it on a continuous basis. In the trade press, online forums and blogs, industry events and showcases, and promotional activities, we can see media and cultural workers crafting both their professional identities and an account of the role their work plays in society. By carefully observing and analysing the texts and trade rituals that media and communication workers produce about their industrial practices we can understand how they account for their role in the power relationships of cultural production.

IDENTITY AND COMMUNICATION WORK: FLEXIBILITY, NETWORKING, ENTREPRENEURIALISM

Professional communicators draw on their identity to do their work and produce their identity through their work. The identity of professional communicators develops in relation to the cultural products they produce, the organizations and networks they work within and the people they work with. Cultural labourers adapt their identities and the way they make their work meaningful to the more flexible and networked nature of communication work.

In her study of the changing nature of television production in the United Kingdom Gillian Ursell (2000) argues that since the 1980s television networks have shed large numbers of permanent and unionized staff and brought in more flexible labour arrangements involving multiskilled and multi-tasking contractors and freelancers. The changes she describes for UK television reflect the changes we discussed in relation to global network capitalism in Chapters 3 and 4. Over-staffed and bureaucratic media industries sought more flexible relationships with their suppliers and labour force; this involved dramatic change to employment conditions as the power relationships of media production were reconfigured. Beneficiaries of mass unionized work had their power eroded, while those who could adapt to the flexible and contractual work conditions benefited. Ursell (2000: 807) argues that workers participate in 'organising their own labour markets' and create professional identities that normalize flexible, contingent and highly competitive labour arrangements.

The identity of professional communicators incorporated the values and norms created as part of the development of global network capitalism. Workers who were once employed by a large organization now work in freelance networks. In these settings they are required to create and manage their own outputs or work in collaborative teams. A professional communicator's reputation is shaped by their portfolio of work and their relationships with other producers. Their reputation is often interdependent with others they work with. In this form of cultural production a professional communicator needs to invest considerable energy and resources into the construction and maintenance of their reputation within their industry. Workers are 'collegial but in competition with one another' (Ursell 2000: 812).

Flexible work practices rely on the active participation of workers. The most successful professional communicators expertly promote themselves as particularly valuable kinds of labour. In doing so they promote the industry to an underpaid and aspirational 'underclass' by incorporating narratives about creativity and autonomy (provided by communicative and cultural work) into their identities. Professional communicators produce not only content but also the narratives about their work which enable cultural industries to use flexible, precarious and sometimes exploitative labour relationships. Cultural industries capitalize on the excess demand and desire for creative work. This demand is stimulated by cultural workers presenting their work as autonomous, creative and publicly esteemed (Ursell 2000). Media and communication workers aren't 'dupes' in this process: they often understand that by crafting identities to match these forms of labour they work against their own best interests in the long term and create exploitative relationships for younger and aspiring producers. Their love for the work, the attention and rewards it brings, and immediate need to get paid, though, can outweigh this sense of concern.

Self-promotion

Angela McRobbie (2002) sounds a critical note against the popular 'celebration' of creative, communication and cultural work as cool, autonomous and fun. She observes that flexible modes of cultural production create a 'workplace without politics' because there is no time and no place for critical reflection and discussion to develop. Reflexivity is not only a source of creativity; it also becomes a form of 'self-disciplining' (McRobbie 2002: 522). Workers 'inspect themselves and their practices' rather than the larger social, cultural or political context of their work. Networking in the flexible culture industry is reflexive, continuous and fast, but it is not reflective. As McRobbie (2002: 523) illustrates, 'After-hours, in the dedicated club/networking space, with free vodka on tap all night thanks to the sponsorship of the big drinks companies, who dares to ask "uncool" questions ... about the downside of the "talent-led" economy? ... It's not cool to be difficult.' Flexibility also works as a control strategy: those who aren't prepared to produce more for less, work long days or at short notice won't get the work. Ursell (2000: 816) suggests that this operates discursively too: 'What it was possible to think and express before is now marginalised.' That is, the new flexible workers are unable to express their disquiet about labour arrangements in the flexible networked economy. The workers who resist are just left out of the new labour arrangements and the social networks which govern access to work. To 'say' you have a problem with it is simply to be shifted out of the social milieu. These much less certain relationships lead workers to invest in themselves as creative and talented 'brands' competing against each other in the economy.

Professional communication involves producing, branding and promoting ourselves as flexible and entrepreneurial workers. Alison Hearn (2008) argues that self-branding 'developed against the backdrop' of global network capitalism. If the economy at large is based on permanent innovation, flexibility and communication, then individual workers also need to adopt these practices.

They need to be constantly engaged in creating a reputation and positioning it within changing professional and cultural networks in order to win attention. The work of the branded self is:

- embodied in the sense of how we look and dress – our gender, ethnicity, physique and clothing all communicate 'who' we are
- affective and interpersonal in the sense of how we maintain relationships with others, the tone of our speech, the qualities of our ideas, and our disposition towards others and the way others engage with us; an individual's brand is related to the reputation of those who will speak for them or recommend them
- mediatized in the sense of the way we present ourselves in business cards, portfolios, emails, online profiles, social networking sites and content we produce as part of our jobs.

All of these elements go together as part of a package of branded self-promotion. Professional communicators intuitively understand that to be competitive in the cultural industries we need to craft a self, a narrative, an image, a way of relating to others, and a social network that will make us credible and valuable. While professional communicators might work for organizations that seek to be enterprising, this disposition feeds into our culture, everyday lives and the way we think about ourselves. We become 'enterprising' in the way we self-consciously construct and display our own selves.

The forms of managerial control in the culture industry involve a combination of hierarchy, discipline and participation. Being successful involves knowing intuitively what the parameters and requirements of work in the industry are. Discipline, control and management are the responsibility of each entrepreneurial and self-directed individual. The work of self-branding is demanding. There is no option but participation: 'One *has* to express oneself, one *has* to speak, communicate, cooperate' (Lazzarato 1996: 135, in Hearn 2008: 204). Our labour power then is not just about what we can create, a cultural product like a TV programme or a news article, but about who we are and the dispositions we embody. The culture industry acquires us as creative workers who create and maintain particular kinds of social relations and organizations. The autonomy of workers is confined within the procedures, networks and objectives of cultural production. Our own resistance, creativity and autonomy become a source of value, rather than something to be disciplined and contained. The branded self is 'one of the more cynical products of the era of the flexible personality: a form of self-presentation singularly focussed on attracting attention and acquiring cultural and monetary value' (Hearn 2008: 213). For a critical scholar like Alison Hearn the problem with the competitive games of self-promotion is that as we 'recognise work is a game and its rules do not require respect, but only adaptation' we recede from investing in collective identities and cultural values. We lose common political projects and public spaces in which to envision collective practices. We retreat into the endless, and tiresome, creative labour of crafting, mobilizing and exploiting ourselves.

THE MEANING AND VALUE OF MEDIA WORK

When we examine media and communication professionals we find values, narratives and practices they use to make their work meaningful to themselves, give them a collective identity as professionals, and position the value of their work for a broader public.

The professional identity of media and cultural workers is often embedded in their everyday practices and discourses. To understand them we have to do more than simply ask cultural workers to explain the value of their work; we also have to carefully observe how they give it meaning in their everyday interactions, the private and public places where they discuss their work, and the cultural artefacts that they produce (Caldwell 2008).

Media and communication professionals are unique because they can use their own media and cultural production techniques and infrastructure to produce and publicize a narrative about the meaningfulness of their work. We see these narratives everywhere.

John Caldwell (2008: 346) identifies a range of 'registers' through which we can see and understand how professional communicators make sense of their work. These include:

- The range of texts that communicators produce in doing their work. For example: demo tapes, pitch sessions, equipment iconography, how-to manuals, trade and craft narratives and anecdotes, on-the-set work practices, association newsletters, corporate retreats.
- Texts and rituals where professional communicators explain their work and industry to *each other*. For example: trade shows, trade publications, internship programmes, technical reveals, panels on how to make it in the industry.
- Texts and rituals where professional communicators explain their work to *the public*. For example: making-of documentaries, DVD commentaries, docu-stunts during 'sweeps' weeks, online website, studio and network-supported fan conventions, screening Q&As, televised show business reports, viral videos.

TAVI GEVINSON ON ROOKIE AND CREATIVITY

Tavi Gevinson is an American writer and editor of the fashion blog Style Rookie. She rose to prominence in her early teens as a creative and critical observer of popular culture. Tavi is a unique cultural producer because her work creatively engages with popular culture, art and her fans' ideas and experiences in an open-ended way. The media she produces are often mixes and mash-ups of popular culture that draw on fan and internet culture.

Watch Tavi's presentation 'Tavi's Big Big World (At 17)' in Sydney's Ideas at the House. You can find a link on the *Media and Society* website study.sagepub.com/carahandlouw. This presentation is an example of a professional communicator explaining her work to the public. Tavi reflects on and makes sense of her own identity in relation to her creative process and work as a media producers.

(Continued)

(Continued)

> Is Tavi a fan or a professional? What's the difference? What is a professional fan?
>
> How is Tavi's engagement with popular culture, literature, art and her own audience part of her identity as a cultural producer?
>
> How does Tavi convert her identity and creativity practices – like scrapbooking – into valuable media content?
>
> How does Tavi perform a narrative about herself that gives meaning to her work?
>
> With Tavi or other professional communicators you are interested in, examine how they explain their work.
>
> What arguments are they making about its meaning and value?
>
> How do they make cultural work appear creative and desirable?
>
> Who is the audience for the text and what does the professional want to tell that audience about their work?

BELOW-THE-LINE WORK

Cultural production involves a complex network of 'above-the-line' and 'below-the-line' workers. Workers are employed in permanent, contractual, casual and unpaid roles. Traditionally, above-the-line workers are those who are publicly visible such as TV presenters, press gallery journalists and celebrity directors. These above-the-line workers are often the visible face of TV programmes, news reports or films. The cultural texts though are produced socially, by a large network of labour, much of which is not visible to the public. These cultural workers who are not visible to the public are below-the-line workers. They include many well-paid and established professions that typically work behind the scenes like media relations, advertising creatives, editors and scriptwriters. Their work is often highly skilled and creative.

The category of below-the-line workers made up of semi-professional, casual, freelance and unpaid work is rapidly proliferating. In recent times, the distinction between above-the-line and below-the-line workers can also refer to the difference between those in permanent or formal employment and those who work in more flexible and informal arrangements. As we discussed above, the growth in flexible and precarious forms of work is a feature of global network capitalism. These precarious forms of below-the-line work include freelance videographers, social media monitors, casting scouts and promotional photographers. As we discussed above in relation to *The Simpsons*, below-the-line networks of labour can spread across the globe. For instance, the website Gawker reported in 2012 that Facebook outsources work to developing countries in monitoring content on the social networking site (Chen 2012). Workers had complained about the poor wages and conditions for doing the work. Facebook provides a 'cheat sheet' to the monitors who trawl through reported content, assessing it against Facebook's community standards. These below-the-line workers are those often not visible within the formal production structure of the media and cultural industries. Below-the-line workers were once those who worked under the control of managers, while above-the-line workers were those who managed themselves and used their creative capacities (Mayer 2011a: 17). In the current flexible cultural economy, however, below-the-line workers must also be entrepreneurial, self-managing and creative. Above-the-line and below-the-line forms of work are interrelated with each other in the production and circulation of culture and maintenance of power relations.

Below-the-line labourers can work in flexible and precarious circumstances. In her study of reality TV scouts Vicky Mayer (2011a: 124) notes that scouts 'transformed their social relations with people they met into a productive means for making cast commodities'. Mayer explains how scouts go out into clubs and shopping malls to locate and meet potential reality TV contestants. They use their identity and social skills to strike up conversations and recruit people for auditions. In our research with nightlife photographers who work in entertainment precincts photographing patrons for club- and alcohol-brand Facebook pages, we found that nightlife photographers exploit their own identities, their appearance, fashion and ability to interact with patrons, to get them to pose for their camera and tag themselves in the images on Facebook. The cooler a nightlife photographer is, the more likely people will want to be photographed and tagged by them (Carah 2014a). This below-the-line work is affective in the sense that workers rely on their identity, appearance and ability to animate social relations and capture attention. Many of these below-the-line workers do not recognize their own value, and labour at low cost or unpaid for the love of the job or the hope that they will break into more formal forms of work (Mayer 2011a).

Internships

One prominent form of below-the-line work is internships. Focusing his analysis predominantly on the United States, Ross Perlin argues that the current internship system doesn't reward young people's labour with remuneration, experience or skills. The internship system gives insight into the increasingly precarious and networked nature of communication and cultural work and the demand for workers to acquire cultural and communicative capacities in order to secure that work. Internships are an increasingly important part of acquiring the necessary cultural capital, capacities and networks to begin a career in media and cultural industries. Echoing Hearn's (2008) notion of the 'branded self' and Ursell's (2000) argument about the way cultural workers create competitive and exploitative labour relationships, Perlin notes that the main value of an internship for many young people is the fact that they can 'spin' them on their CV. Simply having an internship, particularly if it is with a credible firm, is valuable regardless of any real remuneration, experience or skills. The problem though, Perlin argues (2012: xv), is that 'once you start "spinning" your work, it's hard to stop': you begin to develop a professional identity based on 'spin'. The production of a professional 'branded self' often begins in earnest with our first internship. Like the 'branded self' and flexible forms of labour already discussed, internships are a product of global network capitalism. Internships have become a principal point of entry into the workforce for many young educated people. Perlin argues that the internship system presents many questions and problems.

Firstly, the growth in internships reduces entry-level, graduate and unskilled positions. While the individual with the internship might (and this '*might*' is emphasized in many cases) develop skills, experience and networks that may lead towards better paid work, the work they do as an intern undercuts others who would otherwise do that work for fair pay. It makes industries tougher for those at the bottom. Organizations use interns to avoid new hires, replace departing workers, handle busy periods or undertake special projects.

Secondly, access to internships is often dictated by class. The best internships are often secured by family and professional connections. And, even if you can secure one, you need the financial means to support long periods of time working the internship for no pay. Each of these factors precludes those from lower socio-economic groups from accessing internships. This means they are less likely to break into industries that require internships as a point of entry. This is a particularly acute problem for the media and cultural industries because there is a strong argument to say that diversity in these industries has social, cultural and political consequences. In Perlin's (2012: 164) view these class issues matter because:

> many of the professions' internships unlock matter deeply to the broader society. Film and television shape our hopes and dreams, our stereotypes, our views of history and the future; journalists are opinion-makers, wielding access to vital information day-in and day-out; politicians are at the helm of our economic and social infrastructure, often responsible for matters of life and death.

Perlin (2012: 164) argues that it is easier for a 'working-class kid to enter the business or military elite, than to penetrate the cultural elite heavily concentrated in the internship crazed professions'. While internships may be exploitative, being denied one because of class circumstances is perhaps even more oppressive in both individual and social terms. To Perlin (2012: xi), 'Internships quietly embody and promote inequalities of opportunities that we have been striving to diligently reduce.' They provide the 'already privileged with a significant head start that pays professional and financial dividends over time' (2012: 161). Internships here operate hegemonically. They enable an elite to naturally dominate certain positions in society.

Thirdly, universities are implicated in an exploitative internships system where they charge students tuition fees to manage their internship as an academic course. In this situation students effectively pay tuition fees to work for free (Perlin 2012: 85). For some universities the internship programme is a significant source of tuition fee revenue for minimal cost. Universities have a responsibility to ensure that they add significant academic value on top of the internship experience.

In the United States, United Kingdom and Australia internships are generally only legal if they provide legitimate training and the intern is not doing activity that would otherwise have been paid work.

INTERNSHIPS AND THE LAW

In this chapter we've examined internships as a form of informal and low-paid or unpaid work. Internships are an increasingly mandatory part of studying and preparing for work in the media, communication and cultural industries.

What are your best and worst experiences with internships or work experience?

What would make an internship good or bad?

What do you think will be the good and bad aspects of work in the media and cultural industries?

What would be the advantages and disadvantages if unpaid internships were not a part of getting into the culture industries?

As part of responding to these questions you might also consider the legal status of internships. Below we've provided information on the legal status of internships in the United States, United Kingdom and Australia.

How has your experience with internships corresponded with these legal requirements?

Were you aware of these legal requirements before undertaking internships?

ARE INTERNSHIPS LEGAL?

In the United States an internship is only legal if it meets a six point test (Perlin 2012: 66–67). Those six points are:

- The training, even though it includes actual operation of the facilities of the employer, is similar to that which would be given in a vocational school.
- The training is for the benefit of the trainee.
- The trainers do not displace regular employees, but work under close observation.
- The employer that provides the training derives no immediate advantage from the activities of the trainees and on occasion the employer's operations may actually be impeded.
- The trainees are not necessarily entitled to a job at the completion of the training period.
- The employer and the trainee understand that trainees are not entitled to wages for the time spent in training.

The test clearly aims to encourage employers to provide training and protect employees.

In the United Kingdom Alan Milburn's report 'Unleashing Aspiration: The Final Report of the Panel on Fair Access to the Professions' in 2009 recommended changes to internships

(Continued)

119

(Continued)

after finding that they are only accessible to some, which mean employers miss out on talented people, and talented people miss out on ways to get ahead (Perlin 2012: 163). Milburn's report has been part of a wider debate in the United Kingdom about internships. Activist groups such as Interns Anonymous, Graduate Fog, Interns Aware and the National Union of Journalist's scheme Cashback for Interns have campaigned for fair internships and pay for internships and graduates. Much of their efforts have focused on lobbying HM Revenue and Customs to properly monitor and prosecute unpaid or underpaid forms of work. Graduate Fog ran the campaign Pay Your Interns to 'name and shame' those running unfair and unpaid internships. Interns Anonymous acts as a forum to promote discussion of the politics and ethics of internships. Part of their aim is to document the scope and nature of unpaid internships.

In the United Kingdom the term 'internship' has no legal status. Even if you agree to work for no pay, it is still illegal not to pay you. If an intern does regular paid work they may qualify for employee benefits. An intern can only do unpaid work in two circumstances:

- If the internship is less than one year and is a required part of a student's studies.
- If an internship only involves shadowing an employee, and no work is carried out by the intern.

If these conditions aren't met an intern may be entitled to the national minimum wage, even if they agreed not to be paid. The only exception would be people working for a 'charity, voluntary organization, associated fund raising body or a statutory body' who are voluntary workers who 'don't get paid, except for limited benefits' like travel and lunch expenses. This means that graduates who take up advertised unpaid internships for commercial enterprises are entitled to the national minimum wage, even if they agree to work for free. They cannot give away their right to fair pay.

In Australia the Fair Work Act covers work placements and internships. Like the United Kingdom, Australian legislation recognizes 'formal work experience arrangements that are a mandatory part of an education or training course'. To be an acceptable unpaid internship the arrangement must meet all these criteria:

- The internship is undertaken as a requirement of an Australian-based educational or training course.
- The internship is authorized under a law or an administrative arrangement of the Commonwealth, a state or territory.
- The internship is undertaken with an employer for which a person is not entitled to be paid any remuneration.
- Unpaid work experience can be lawful in circumstances outside of these arrangements only if the person doesn't meet the definition of an employee.

Fair Work Australia advises that the key considerations are:

Is the person assisting with business outputs and productivity?

Is the person in the role for an extended period of time?

Are there any expectations about the person's productivity?

Who benefits from the arrangement?

Was the placement part of a vocational or university programme?

If an intern is doing productive work over an extended period of time which benefits the organization, then the arrangement may come under the Fair Work Act, and the person may legally be considered an employee.

The principles governing unpaid internships in the United States, United Kingdom and Australia are broadly similar, as are the contemporary debates about their ethics. While many young people willingly choose to undertake unpaid internships outside of their educational programmes, the fact remains that these arrangements are often legally questionable. And the young people who choose to participate in these programmes also bear some responsibility to changing the culture of unpaid internships.

In response to the questionable moral, ethical and legal status of internships and to the detrimental social and cultural effects they have, Perlin refers to the Internship Institute's Intern Bill of Rights.

THE INTERN BILL OF RIGHTS

Given that the word 'intern' has no strict definition and covers a broad range of roles,

Given that most interns are workers, performing work of operational and economic importance,

Given that the laws and regulations pertaining to internships are often unclear, vary by jurisdiction, and rarely reference interns specifically,

Given that internships are of increasing, global importance, and have broad social implications,

Given that some internships are legal, just, and beneficial, while others are illegal, unethical and even exploitative,

Given that it is inequitable to require people to work for free to enter the workforce,

We proclaim this Intern Bill of Rights as a common standard by which to evaluate and improve internships for the benefit of interns, employers, and society as a whole.

Article 1: All interns deserve fair compensation for their work, usually in the form of wages and sometimes in the form of dedicated training.

Article 2: Interns are entitled to the same legal protections as all other workers, and should not be subject to discrimination, harassment, or arbitrary dismissal. Under these circumstances, interns should have the same standing in court and the same recourse to the law as all other workers.

(Continued)

(Continued)

Article 3: Interns should enjoy the same basic workplace benefits guaranteed to all other workers, including sick days, vacation time, worker's compensation and extra pay for overtime.

Article 4: The hiring of interns should be as transparent and nondiscriminatory as the hiring of full-time employees.

Article 5: No one should be forced to take an unpaid internship or required to pay in order to work.

Article 6: Any internships subsidized with public funds should meet exemplary legal and ethical standards.

Article 7: Internships are a category of work that should be defined, recognized by policy makers and officials, studied, monitored, and improved.

Article 8: Interns must be treated with dignity and respect by coworkers and supervisors.

Article 9: The word 'intern' should be applied ethically and transparently to opportunities that involve substantial training, mentoring, and getting to know a line of work.

Use the Intern Bill of Rights to prompt discussion with peers about the politics and culture of internships.

How do your experiences with internships correlate with the legal requirements and this bill of rights?

Is this bill of rights adequate for creating an internship system that is valuable to both industries and aspiring professionals?

You can find links to resources about internships on the *Media and Society* website study.sagepub.com/carahandlouw

CONCLUSION

In this chapter we have examined the nature and experience of work within a flexible and networked culture industry. We have examined how cultural workers use their identity in their work and present their work as meaningful to themselves, their colleagues and the public. The chapter makes three claims that are important as we go on to examine processes of representation and participation:

- Professional communicators produce and manage meaning within the power relationships of global information capitalism. Most professional communicators labour within organizations that channel and constrain their creativity towards the strategic goals of their patrons, investors or leaders.
- The culture industry both relies on and exploits the feelings of autonomy and creativity of professional communicators.

- Professional communicators work in increasingly flexible organizations and industries. They need to construct identities that position themselves within networks that will give them access to cultural capital and professional opportunities.

A flexible, interactive and participatory media system relies fundamentally on skilled professional communicators. These communicators don't just produce content; they produce social relationships and manage complex communication processes. The arguments we go on to develop about the management of meaning and participation in this book are grounded in a critical examination of how organizations and industries seek to enable, channel and control the creativity of professional communicators. The production and management of communication involves a dynamic and reflexive interaction between organizations and highly skilled creative professionals.

FURTHER READING

The readings listed here each address different aspects of the experiences of media, communication and cultural work. The readings by Banks (2010), Hearn (2008) and Hesmondhalgh and Baker (2011) each address the subjective experience of work and the way that professional communicators use their identity and creativity in their work. In each article questions about autonomy, creativity and freedom are addressed. The readings by Hearn (2008) and McRobbie (2002) each pay attention to the way professional communicators are called on to produce themselves as a valuable brand within flexible media and communication workplaces. They are each concerned about the effects that competitive relationships have on the identities, social relationships and products of professional communicators. Hesmondhalgh and Baker (2011) and Ursell (2000) each address the range of professional, casual, flexible and below-the-line employment relationships that exist in media and cultural industries.

Banks, M. (2010) 'Autonomy guaranteed? Cultural work and the "art–commerce relation"', *Journal for Cultural Research*, 14 (3): 251–269.

Hearn, A. (2008) 'Meat, mask, burden: probing the contours of the branded self', *Journal of Consumer Culture*, 8 (2): 197–217.

Hesmondhalgh, D. and Baker, S. (2008) 'Creative work and emotional labour in the television industry', *Theory, Culture & Society*, 25 (7–8): 97–118.

McRobbie, A. (2002) 'Clubs to companies: notes on the decline of political culture in speeded up creative worlds', *Cultural Studies*, 16 (4): 516–531.

Ursell, G. (2000) 'Television production: issues of exploitation, commodification and subjectivity in UK television labour markets', *Media, Culture & Society*, 22 (6): 805–825.

Any article marked with ⊗ is available to download at the website **study.sagepub.com/ carahandlouw**

MAKING NEWS

NEWS MAKING IS A KEY SITE FOR MAKING AND MAINTAINING POWER.

* What are the sites and routines used to manage the production of news?

* What are some of the power relationships that characterize news making?

* How has access to large troves of data changed journalism?

* How have mobile devices like smartphones changed journalism?

In this chapter we:

- Examine the sites and routines of news making
- Account for the relationships between journalists and powerful groups in the production of news
- Explore how news making has changed in the information era
- Examine how interactive mobile devices have changed news making.

THE EMERGENCE OF PROFESSIONAL JOURNALISM

The emergence of commercial, professional and objective journalism can be traced back to Lord Northcliffe's 'mass journalism' in the British press and Joseph Pulitzer's 'popular journalism' in the United States press (Smith 1979: 154–160). Pulitzer in the US and Stead in the United Kingdom developed 'new journalism' practices designed to attract the widest possible audience for sale to advertisers (Emery 1972: Chapter 17, Smith 1979: Chapter 6). The sites of these innovations were Stead's *Pall Mall Gazette* in London and Pulitzer's New York *World*. Large amounts of capital were required to buy the latest print technologies. The ventures required economies of scale to realize a return on the investment. This involved producing a product that would attract a large middle-class audience considered valuable by advertisers. The cost of producing the content of a newspaper, and owning and maintaining the cost of the factory that produces it, is more or less fixed. The investment in this content and infrastructure is realized when it is used to attract an audience that can be on-sold to advertisers. The bigger the audience the more advertisers will pay to have their advertisement printed in the newspaper.

The imperative to build mass audiences that could be sold to advertisers changed the nature of meanings produced, for a variety of reasons. Content was required that appealed to the largest possible audience, rather than to specialized niche groups of opinion makers. To produce content regularly and cheaply, industrialized work routines were required. This meant employing journalists who had specific rounds or topic areas and quantities of stories that needed to be produced on a daily basis. Journalists learned to produce content in a routine and systematic fashion. Within these institutions the routines and values of professional journalism emerged. Over time these practices were adapted to other mass media systems like television (see Audley 1983, Guimaraes and Amaral 1988, Abercrombie 1996: Chapter 1, Cunningham and Turner 1997).

Building hegemonic dominance involves, among other things, circulating appropriate discourses. Hegemonic labour requires making, distributing and naturalizing meanings that serve the interests of the dominant groups. School and university curricula, advertising, popular culture and news are key discursive fields for building dominance. More recently information databases have also emerged as a discursive resource. Each of the above discursive fields has its own sites and practices. This chapter will focus on news production and professional journalists.

Are journalists merely agents of the hegemonically powerful or are they autonomous? The chapter will seek to answer this question by exploring news as it emerges from the intersection of three variables:

- the sites where production takes place
- the dominant practices with these sites
- the discourses privileged by those working in these sites.

We will suggest that it is possible for journalists to be simultaneously agents and autonomous. They are not simply servants of the powerful, but are ensnared in webs of discourse and practice which set parameters upon autonomy. Essentially, each news-making site has its own set of preferred practices and discourses which guide the work of the journalists working at that site.

THE SITES OF NEWS MAKING

Newsrooms are the productive fulcrums for news making. But newsrooms are part of larger organizations. They are locked into a wider chain of organizational influence, and therefore necessarily conform to the practices and culture of their organization. This includes being influenced by pressures emanating from owners, although this influence is often indirect and opaque. Such sites also conform to the organizational practices of the wider society hosting them. Further, news-making sites are not autonomous of wider organizational and hegemonic pressures. But such pressures are usually not the result of authoritarian control by an owner or manager issuing directives, or conspiracy by a small group working to take control of key social sites. Rather, news making is constrained in a more indirect manner. Hegemonic dominance is created through the staffing practices of recruitment, promotion and dismissal of employees; and by decision making concerning rules, procedures and the configuration of technology within these sites. The hegemonically dominant are at their most successful when meaning-making decision makers police themselves and their staff in ways which confirm the needs of the ruling hegemony. In these instances, day-to-day operational decision making and longer-term policy setting in newsrooms complement hegemonic needs.

A key decision in meaning-making sites is choosing who gets promoted to positions where staffing decisions are made. Decision making over staffing is perhaps the core mechanism for moving meaning making in a preferred direction. Newsroom staffing profiles necessarily determine which discourses are promoted. Owners exercise control over staffing profiles indirectly by appointing the boards overseeing organizations. Owners and board members are overwhelmingly members of ruling hegemonic elites. Boards in turn appoint Chief Executive Officers (CEOs). It is unlikely a CEO would be appointed whose world-view was incompatible with that of the owner and board. The CEO in turn appoints and promotes managers into key decision-making roles. Those managers in turn hire and fire, train and socialize the rest of the staff. In the case of a newsroom these staff are the gatekeepers of news flows. Staffing decisions are indirectly gatekeeping decisions. Importantly, influence over staffing can be exercised by common sense. CEOs generally work out the preferred discourses of their owners and boards, and managers can sense the preferences of their CEO. Consequently, there is no need for directives concerning which discourses should be favoured because good staffing decisions (from CEOs down) can be relied on to shape a staff profile that is inclined to produce the desired discourses. Discourses serving the hegemonically dominant will be adhered to because staff will 'reproduce' themselves through hiring, training and socializing. When hegemonies are normal and stable this gatekeeping via staffing is opaque. Only when hegemonies undergo fundamental ruptures do staffing mechanisms (as discursive control measures) become visible. For example, the post-apartheid South African Broadcasting Corporation purged the bulk of its white staff and replaced them with staff holding views 'appropriate' to the gatekeeping needs of the new regime (Louw and Milton 2012: Chapter 4). By 1998 the new hegemony could rely on a normalized and opaque staff 'cloning' process at SABC to deliver stable and predictable discourses.

At first sight it might appear that the emergence of interactive and niche media will make discourse closures through staff selection less likely. However, under global network capitalism, positioning 'appropriate' gatekeepers is still an important hegemonic mechanism. The media system is now composed of many more niche production sites, but these sites are networked into large global corporations so that appropriate common-sense staffing decisions still deliver gatekeepers with apposite world-views. Global corporations have a variety of control mechanisms based on setting goals and objectives that managers must meet. Internet technologies have not dissolved the role of information gatekeepers. The sheer quantity of information that now circulates through the global media network means that professional communicators who can sort, aggregate and make sense of the growing volumes of information are critical to the construction of discourses. Newsrooms and journalists are critical gatekeepers in this process as they have the capacity to search, sort, aggregate and guide the public through this information. New information-processing and management occupations simply become new gatekeepers within media and information corporations. This means employment practices still play a key role in building hegemonic dominance. And, although newsroom practices have been modified by internet technologies, the basic principle of creating gatekeepers through staffing practices has not altered.

Decisions about funding also set parameters within meaning-making sites. Funding and staffing issues are often related. Managers decide which teams will get funding and opportunities. Those viewed favourably by boards and CEOs get resources to employ staff, deploy new technologies and pursue innovative projects. In doing so, they are granted the organizational capacity to influence meaning making. People who produce valuable discourses are granted further resources and opportunities. Within media organizations, flows of funding shape the direction of discursive production by rewarding over others the people and teams that produce certain discourses.

News making is also constrained by work practices, routines and rules. Some practices are the result of conscious local-level decision making; others are inherited from wider organizational practices and policies or even from the broader profession or industry. Related to these practices are questions of how technology is employed. Decisions over funding and deploying technology influence how meaning is made. This, in turn, impacts on the sorts of meanings that can be made. It is not only newsroom practices that impact on meanings made. The practices of the wider organization are just as important when it comes to setting parameters. For example, within commercial news organizations, newsroom practices are necessarily entangled with the needs of the advertising department – not because of direct advertiser pressure upon editors and journalists, although such pressure may occur. At heart, commercial media have to collect, package and deliver audiences to advertisers. The task of any editor in a commercial medium is to generate and package the sort of material that will appeal to the audience that advertisers are interested in. One of the easiest ways to achieve this is to appoint staff whose world-views correspond to those of the intended audience, but editorial intervention is also sometimes required. Effectively what transpires is a form of 'market censorship'. Discourses that may alienate the desirable target audience are avoided. Over time, newsroom practices will naturalize the collection of certain genres of information appropriate for the target audience. Newsrooms reproduce themselves through staff recruitment and training into these accepted practices and genres. Once naturalized, the constraints on news making will no longer be noticed; within that production site a certain set of discourses and practices will simply be routinized as 'the way things are done'.

ROUTINIZING NEWS MAKING

News is the product of a set of institutionalized work practices. These practices are enmeshed with discourses about the profession of journalism, journalists' discourses about themselves, and discourses about the audience. Journalists learn to work, and to understand themselves and their work, in a certain way. It is possible to identify a generic Anglo-pattern of news-making practices and newsroom structures – a pattern that has been carried across the globe during the periods of British and American dominance. This Anglo-pattern ultimately has its roots in the 'new journalism' of the nineteenth-century commercial newspapers developed by Pulitzer, Stead and Northcliffe. This pattern subsequently spread to radio, television and online newsrooms.

Mark Deuze (2005) identifies five claims that journalists make about the meaning and value of their work:

- Journalists see themselves as providing a public service as watchdogs and disseminators of information. They play a vital democratic role of informing the public.
- Journalists present themselves as credible because they are objective, impartial, neutral and fair.
- Journalists think of themselves as autonomous, free and independent.
- Journalists see their work as immediate, presenting reality 'as it happens'.
- Journalists 'have a sense of ethics, validity and legitimacy'.

Each of these elements fits together to create a narrative journalists tell themselves and the public about their work. While we might think that the news conveys the day's events, it also presents journalism as a socially meaningful and important practice. Professional ideologies often conceal their own constructed-ness. While journalists invoke a simple idea of objectivity, this conceals that events in the world are often complex and messy; they are often deeply and intimately embedded in people's perspectives and experiences. While journalists might value autonomy they also understand how it is limited by the practices of the organization they work for. Journalists apply these values and adapt them to specific audiences and circumstances (Muller and Gawenda 2010). Journalists' narratives about their objectivity and credibility create value for news organizations by legitimizing the quality of the content they produce.

Journalists are confronted by huge volumes of information and an enormous array of phenomena that could qualify as news. Creating news therefore involves sorting through these and selecting which will actually be allowed to reach audiences. News making is a process of selection, emphasis and de-emphasis. Journalists refer to this process as knowing what is 'newsworthy'. Effectively journalists are gatekeepers (White 1950) who allow some information through the gate and block other information. For anyone concerned with creating hegemonic dominance, the blocking process is of vital concern. Creating discursive dominance has as much, and possibly more, to do with what information is left out, as what is disseminated. As Cohen (1963: 13) said, the media 'may not be successful much of the time in telling people what to think, but it is stunningly successful in telling its readers what to think about'. As gatekeepers, journalists effectively decide what information is left out, and hence determine 'what is thought about'. So journalists become agenda setters – creating the agenda and setting the parameters for what is discussed within a society. As Noelle-Neumann (1991) has pointed out, these gatekeeping and agenda setting roles have the capacity to set in motion a 'spiral of silence' where social discourse is progressively closed because people fall silent if their views do not coincide with what the media portray as majority opinion. The role of gatekeeper or agenda setter then holds great social significance.

Gatekeeping has been institutionalized in newsrooms, where the process of selection, emphasis and de-emphasis has been turned into a set of systematized routines. Significantly, it is the very routinization of the process that has tended to render it opaque to journalists themselves. Anglo-journalists, in particular, work within an essentially empiricist world-view. They believe news is out there and that they simply find it. They apparently find it because they know what is newsworthy. Constructivists such as Tuchman (1978), however, argue that journalists 'construct reality' rather than find it.

News is a window on the world

News, as Tuchman (1978) says, is a 'window on the world'. Journalists, through their work practices, effectively break a window-opening through the wall, and so create a partial view of the overall panorama. That is, only one portion of reality is available through the window opening. The rest, outside the frame, is hidden behind the wall. News is consequently always skewed by the size, shape and position of the window frame. But this skewing is not usually the outcome of conscious decision making aimed at deliberately creating partial representations of reality. Rather, the window's position is the outcome of whatever set of practices, work routines and discourses journalists have been socialized into accepting as 'the way things are done'. The partiality, and hence distortion, of news derives from the news frame built by journalists applying their particular conception of newsworthiness. It is possible to identify a broad Anglo-conception of newsworthiness with its roots in what can loosely be termed the 'Fleet Street' tradition. This Anglo-conception of newsworthiness has been reproduced in journalism training programmes throughout the Anglo-world. These training programmes, plus on-the-job socialization, have effectively cloned the Fleet Street model from Los Angeles to New Delhi, and Sydney to Johannesburg. And so, despite minor regional mutations, a remarkably similar news frame exists across the Anglo-world. Training has been fundamental in spreading this 'Anglo-window'. The British Empire approach favoured sending Fleet Street and BBC staffers to the colonies as colonial migrants, or on secondments to train locals. The Americans have preferred routing overseas students through US journalism schools. Once a journalist has internalized the appropriate vision of newsworthiness and the work routines accompanying this vision, the model becomes naturalized and self-policing and the framing process is rendered opaque. Thereafter, journalists need not confront the fact that they are constructing a partial 'window on the world'.

Making news is about newsworthiness. But to become a useful analytical tool, the obfuscated and mythologized notion of newsworthiness, as used by journalists, needs to be given substance.

Essentially, newsworthiness is a learned perceptual mechanism for routinely guiding journalistic decision making when journalists are engaged in the reporting process. Newsworthiness is found in both journalists' practices and discourses: that is, both *how* they do their job and what they *believe* themselves to be doing. Effectively, a process of selection, emphasis and de-emphasis has been organized in a set of routines comprising formulas and frames, contacts, newsroom procedures, and presentation formats.

Formulas and frames

Journalists are trained to work according to a set of formulas. Consequently, they repeatedly look for the same things and routinely ask the same questions. The formulas effectively narrow the options for what can emerge as news by guiding the information-gathering process. There are two key formulas journalists use:

- *The 'who' does 'what' and 'when', 'where', 'why' and 'how' they do it (WWWWWH) question formula.* Journalistic training privileges the writing of 'hard factual news' that the five-Ws-and-an-H formula delivers. These questions are an excellent short-hand method for getting to the essence of immediate events-based stories like motor accidents or fires; but the formula becomes a great hindrance when trying to report on complex issues embedded in convoluted contexts like the reasons for the outbreak of warfare. The hard factual news formula does not equip journalists to report on complex situations, but it does serve to confirm the professional discourse of objectivity. The idea that one is objective because only 'the facts' (WWWWWH) are reported is a powerful self-image and value system central to Anglo-journalistic practice. In essence, because hard concrete facts are privileged, the stories acquire a tangibility that makes them appear factual rather than constructed. Tuchman describes this as 'facticity' (1978: 82). It allows journalists to hide from themselves the constructed and partial nature of their stories. Further, just as the hard news formula directs journalists to look at the world in a certain way, so too has television journalism developed a standardized matrix of action images that are sought out. Television news has developed a visual formula that drives journalists to produce a certain genre of news that seeks out action and the visually spectacular. Television news, combining the objectiveness of the WWWWWH formula with the visually spectacular, produces radically simplified news that eschews complexity.
- *The inverted pyramid.* This directs journalists to grab audience attention at the start of the story. The heart of the story is packed into the first one or two paragraphs. Journalists do not construct an argument by building towards a conclusion (a pyramid). Instead, they put the conclusion at the beginning of the study (an inverted pyramid). In part, this inverted pyramid formula emerged in response to the practice of newspaper 'stone-subs' in the era of hot-metal printing, who cut stories from the bottom to make them fit the page. Journalists learned that important material at the end of a story stood a good chance of being edited out; while material placed in the first few paragraphs was generally the least likely to be cut. The inverted pyramid is now

an entrenched and immovable practice not only in newspapers, but also in radio and television journalism. This focus on 'the intro' mutated within television news into the 'sound bite'. Television journalists seek out spokespersons able to provide 'snappy one-liners'. This makes television news even less able to report on complex situations than newspapers. Public relations personnel use their knowledge of journalistic formulas and the demand for sound bites to maximize their chances of placing media releases that promote their employer's interests.

On any given day there are a relatively small number of institutions, social sites and individuals who interact to make the news. A news frame is a way of thinking about how journalists present events to us, a way of defining their practices of representation. Robert Entman (1993) defines framing as:

- defining problems in terms of common cultural values
- diagnosing causes of those problems
- making moral judgements
- proposing solutions.

Frames 'call to attention some aspects of reality while obscuring other elements' (Entman 1993: 55). The problems, judgements and solutions journalists report and propose are nearly always well-established ideas. It is very difficult to tell people things they don't already know or think. News framing organizes common sense (Gamson et al. 1992) by reflecting commonly held cultural narratives in ways that privilege elite voices (Markens and Conrad 2001, Blood and Holland 2004).

Journalists, professional communicators, professionals from other fields and citizens feel compelled to act or position themselves with reference to accepted media frames (Kitzinger 2000). Meaning makers face real and perceived obstacles for veering outside of these enduring frames and templates because they tend to monopolize common sense and draw strong inferences between their common-sense view and the problem definitions, judgements and actions they propose. Where news reporting might appear substantial, balanced and thoughtful by raising competing frames, it may actually be framing debate within a closed socio-cultural space. Competing frames, because they are generated from a shared cultural context, often have more salient fundamental similarities than significant differences. The competition between frames obscures the maintenance of power relationships. The real impact of framing is felt at the cultural level where over time it incrementally creates ways of seeing the world that are opaque, and that reduce complex and messy realities into forceful intuitive narratives that become naturalized. Professional communicators often seek not only to frame their own point of view, but also to construct the perspectives and available positions of the competitors. Enduring frames and media templates close down the space within which real alternative views can be put forward. They make it difficult for alternative positions to appear credible because they solidify accepted ways of defining, judging and acting. Strategic use of frames by interest groups is most successful when it aims to shape the enduring frames or media templates, rather than just aim to frame the issue their way.

Contacts

Contacts are central to the news-gathering process. Contacts are people journalists regularly consult when wanting information or quotes. Each newsroom tends to develop a pool of contacts who are constantly consulted. News is effectively made through the symbiotic relationship emerging between journalists and this pool of contacts. Journalists need contacts to provide quotes and information, while the contacts need journalists to develop their profile or to promote particular ideas, products or organizations. For many, becoming a regularly consulted contact is vital for their career. For example, politicians need publicity, and ultimately the media are the dispensers of this publicity. Any aspiring politician has to develop relationships with journalists, both directly and through the ever-expanding teams of public relations officers, spin doctors and media consultants that manage interactions between journalists and talent. Just as journalists develop contacts, public relations officers and media consultants cultivate journalists. The need to cultivate journalists saw the growth, throughout the second half of the twentieth century, of the phenomenon of the 'professionalized contacts' practices of the public relations industry. By the turn of this century no large organization – corporation or government – was without a PR machinery, staffed by communication spin doctors and professionalized contacts. Often these PRs are ex-journalists who understand the routines and formulas of news organizations, and know many of the journalists in the local industry.

The pool of contacts used by any newsroom constitutes a very small minority of the overall population. Ultimately, the choice of contacts reflects how that newsroom sees the community it reports on. The choice of contacts is fundamental in defining the shape and position of the window or news frame that journalists construct (Tuchman 1978).

A key mechanism for creating this window is on-the-job socialization of journalists, which involves news editors or senior staffers passing on appropriate contacts to junior journalists as they are inducted into the newsroom. Learning whom news editors and editors consider to be 'appropriate' contacts constitutes an important part of the staff-cloning process in any newsroom. Journalists learn what types of contacts are appropriate by having contacts passed on and by encountering disapproval when 'inappropriate' contacts are used.

Using contacts narrows the window frame in two ways. Firstly, there is a tendency to favour quoting the hegemonic elite in part because they are already deemed to be important people and hence newsworthy; and secondly, because members of the already-existent social, political and economic elite tend to have the resources to staff publicity machines. The ability to run PR machines has become increasingly important in order to become a reliable contact. Reliability involves always being contactable and delivering appropriate quotes in a timely fashion. Good contacts understand journalistic deadlines and their need for quotes to fit their organization's in-house style and editorial policies. This is the second way in which using contacts narrows the window frame. Journalists stop phoning their contacts when the first one tells them what they want to hear. When constructing a story, journalists will work through their contact list, starting with the person deemed the most appropriate contact. Consequently, news construction has come to favour, and hence promote, certain kinds of people: those with the resources to maintain publicity machines and to be able to deliver quotes and an image concurrent with media requirements.

To some extent these requirements have altered the nature of hegemony building as television became ever more central to circulating discourses. Building dominance now drives hegemonic groups to recruit so-called video or image politicians. Ronald Reagan, Tony Blair, Barack Obama and Kevin Rudd all have or had images and demeanours that suit visual media. Furthermore, there is now a need to gain access to enormous financial resources in order to pay for the professionalized publicity machines required for promoting hegemonic discourses. In the USA this led to the emergence of political action committees (PACs) and Super PACs to raise money to pay for these machines. Contributors to PACs effectively buy influence in Washington. This introduced a new dimension into hegemonic alliance building. Developing a 'professionalized contacts' machinery has had the effect of modifying how power relationships are made and maintained (Smith 1989: Chapter 2).

Induction into newsroom procedures

Journalists induct new staffers into newsroom procedures. Each newsroom will have a set of procedures and related organizational culture. Some of the routinized procedures for collecting, writing and submitting will only be found in a particular newsroom, perhaps tied to a senior staffer's idiosyncrasies. Other procedures will be found across whole media groups when all the newsrooms in the group share a set of procedures and organizational culture. All procedures set parameters on news production, and so socializing journalists into an organization's procedures helps to steer their production into conformity with the genre associated with that organization. Similarly, journalists are socialized into accepting the newsroom bureaucracy, hierarchical pecking orders and the particular style of office politics operative in their newsroom. There is a relationship between the hierarchical chains of command and the bureaucratized procedures of the newsroom. It has been suggested that this is a defining characteristic of news production. News is the ultimate bureaucratized meaning making. News is simply the outcome of a highly routinized process of collecting and processing information, where the process is guided by formal rules. Hence news takes on the characteristics of an 'eternal recurrence' (Rock 1981); it is meaning that looks repetitive, precisely because it is meaning emergent from a repetitive set of bureaucratized procedures. For those building hegemonies this is the useful thing about news – it is a form of meaning making that is highly susceptible to manipulation for two reasons. Firstly, the existence of hierarchical bureaucracies in media organizations means that it is possible for hegemonic elites to diffuse their discursive needs downward from the CEOs. This can be achieved through normal bureaucratic control over procedures, routines and staffing profiles. Secondly, the existence of predictable journalistic routines and procedures means that ex-journalists working as PRs and communication spin doctors can employ their knowledge of these procedures to plant stories at the right time and with the right person. The predictability of news production enables them to maximize the chances of these stories being used and serving their purposes.

The presentation of news

Another aspect of journalistic practice to be routinized is the presentation of the news. Procedures have been developed for designing newspapers to give some stories prominence. Newspaper subeditors have a whole range of techniques at their disposal to emphasize some news and de-emphasize other stories in accordance with editorial policy. This includes decisions about which page a story is placed on, where on the page it is placed, the size of the headline, whether a photograph will accompany the story and what sort of photograph will be used (see Hall 1981). Similar mechanisms for emphasizing some news stories, and de-emphasizing others, exist within television and radio production practices. Such presentation decisions crucially influence the overall narrative being constructed and so impact on the interpretation of the news. These design and presentation decisions have also been routinized, with those taking these decisions having internalized a whole series of professional discourses which guide their work practices.

REPRESENTATION AND ETHICAL CODES

The ethical codes of journalists' professional associations point to the values that journalists aspire to in their representation of social life.

You can find links to the ethical codes of journalists in the US Society of Professional Journalists, UK National Union of Journalists and Australian Media, Entertainment and Arts Alliance on the *Media and Society* website study.sagepub.com/carahandlouw

REPORTING ON CRISIS EVENTS IN AUSTRALIA

Muller and Gawenda (2010) interviewed journalists who reported on the 2009 Black Saturday bushfires in Australia. The wildfires, common to Australia during the summer, swept through regional areas burning out whole towns and killing 177 people. Following the fires police and emergency services established blockades around towns because the hundreds of burned out homes and buildings needed to be searched and assessed. This restriction of access to the fire zone conflicted with journalists' impulse to report from the scene and inform the public about events. Journalists positioned themselves at the centre of events, seeing themselves as responsible for providing information to the public and the many people who had fled their communities and were anxious to find loved ones or to know what happened to their homes.

Muller and Gawenda found that many media practitioners responded to the roadblocks in a variety of ways. While journalists wouldn't deliberately 'run a roadblock', because it was illegal, they would justify other ways of circumventing them. For many journalists, 'Finding a way in that was not blocked was considered not only ethically justifiable but positively required by the countervailing ethical consideration of doing one's duty to the public' (Muller and Gawenda 2010: 75). This might involve being 'fortuitously mistaken' as an emergency worker or resident, or for some even deliberately misrepresenting their identity. While journalists had a range of positions on the lengths they would go to bypass roadblocks, what underlay their justifications was a sense that as journalists they had a responsibility to the public to access these closed areas in order to represent them. That is, their belief in the importance of the media rituals they facilitated guided their justification of their actions. This belief, though, also fitted with the commercial imperatives of their media organizations: 'Media people tended to place a higher value on successfully meeting the competitive pressures under which they worked, and on carrying out what they saw as their duty to inform the public, than on the countervailing ethical duty to respect the law' (Muller and Gawenda 2010). Here we can see how representations of events are constructed through rituals and actions in the world, and those rituals are undertaken by people who make and justify decisions based on a variety of factors: their sense of the value and meaning of their work, power relationships between media and other actors like politicians and emergency services, and commercial pressures.

Examine how significant crisis events are represented in your country. Who do journalists interact with to represent the event and tell stories? Consider their coverage in relation to the ethical codes of their professional association.

In Australia, or elsewhere, when journalists are reporting on crisis events:

  Do they use fair, responsible and honest means to obtain material?
  Do they exploit people's vulnerability or ignorance of media practices?
  Do they respect private grief and personal privacy?

SYMBIOTIC RELATIONSHIPS IN NEWS MAKING

News making revolves around journalists, their practices and the organizational sites – like newsrooms – into which they are embedded. However, journalists and news editors are also enmeshed in sets of symbiotic relationships with other professional communicators who are complicit in making the news.

The routinization of news making effectively directs journalists to privilege certain news-making sites over others. Some news is random and accidental, such as aircraft crashes and motor accidents. But even the reporting of this random news has been considerably de-randomized by the journalistic practice of using police, ambulance and hospital spokespersons as sources for locating and reporting such events. But in general it is non-random news that has become the staple fare of contemporary news production. Most news now comes from four institutionalized sets of news-making sites: the political and legal system, the sports industry, the entertainment industry and the business sector. Each of these sites has a highly developed PR machinery that provides media-trained contacts and media-ready content to journalists. Each site has 'news shapers' (Soley 1992) or pundits. Pundits are those promoted as experts by the news media who are consequently called on to comment upon and discuss events with journalists. The development of sound bite television reporting greatly enhanced the use of such news shapers. These news shapers are people who researchers at broadcast organizations have deemed to be appropriate experts, and who can be relied on to deliver comment that is both editorially suitable and which conforms to the sound bite needs of the broadcast media. The news-shaper pundits are seen as specialists in one of the above four news fields – political and legal system, sport, entertainment or business – and so will be routinely called upon to comment upon and frame the news. On-air discussions between these news-shaper pundits and journalists often become a form of editorializing, serving to set agendas in accordance with the editorial policy of the news organization concerned.

News and public relations

Each of the four news-making sites have professionalized their relationships with the news media. All major organizations in society have developed publicity machines. Some of these publicity machines are now heavily accented towards marketing communicators (like the sports sector); others are geared towards spin doctoring (like the PR and 'damage control' machines of politicians); while others are concerned with image building or public lobbying (for instance, many business sector PR departments). These publicity machines are now integral to the making of news. News has been substantively 'public relations-ized' as journalists have developed a symbiotic relationship with those staffing publicity machines. For news organizations it is simply much cheaper to use professionally produced material made available by these publicity machines than to produce it themselves. Publicity and PR machines have effectively evolved into a form of journalistic outsourcing. In the process, co-dependence has emerged between journalists and publicity machine staffers, as both have developed routines that intermesh with each other. Contemporary journalistic routines for news-gathering would simply collapse without the publicity machines journalists now connect to. Politicians, sports stars and business leaders would have no one to perform to if journalists did not provide the media conduits through which they reach their publics. A neatly harmonized and professionalized set of team practices has emerged which symbiotically meshes journalists with a whole range of people whose careers revolve around professional image making: PRs, spin doctors, marketers, politicians, sportspeople, entertainers and business leaders. Journalists need image makers and image makers need journalists and so each has necessarily developed routines and practices for using the other. Out of their routinized co-dependence emerges news.

The second half of the twentieth century saw meaning making, including news making, progressively public relations-ized. The culture industry produced a particular form of intellectual practice involving professional communicators working to skew meaning production in favour of their employer's interests. These professional 'skewers' – PRs and spin doctors – are at their most successful when journalists become dependent upon them to supply information. As newsrooms have become leaner, because of cost-cutting measures, the pressure on a smaller number of journalists to fill the 'news holes' has necessarily grown. This has tended to shift news-making practices into ever greater dependency on PRs, hence the growing public relations-izing of news. Consequently, for those who can afford to employ PRs and spin doctors, it has become easier to manipulate news.

NEWS AND POWER RELATIONSHIPS

Clearly news production is a complex process involving multitudes of communication professionals. The relationship between these professionals and hegemonic elites does not look like a simple transmission belt with professional communicators simply uncritically producing messages at the bidding of hegemonic elites. However, a complex set of, sometimes obfuscated, relationships exists between ruling elites and professional communicators, which generally ensures that these professionals overwhelmingly produce and circulate messages that service the needs of hegemonically dominant groups. These relationships seem to fall into three broad categories.

Firstly, those who succeed in establishing their discourses as dominant win the struggle for hegemony. This necessarily involves finding ways to exercise influence over the institutions of the culture industry. Such influence may entail direct ownership or membership of media boards. But influence need not be that direct. Hegemonic elites by definition constitute the membership of influential social networks. Media, cultural, government and business elites hang out together at alumni, industry, social, cultural and sporting events and clubs. Hegemonic elites transact a lot of their business informally within these networks, business that ranges from brokering deals to swapping favours at social events. Membership of these networks is restricted, but it is not static: as hegemonic elites mutate so too does the membership of these influential informal networks. Very few members of these networks will have any form of direct control over news-making processes. But their capacity to mobilize such networks to influence news production should not be underestimated.

Secondly, those with command over resources, which does not have to be one's own property, are necessarily in a position to buy influence, including influence over meaning-making processes. This may entail buying favours or bribery. Or it may mean funding organizations and people whose ideas one approves of, and training such people to become effective communicators. An example of this is the Alliance of Youth Movements (AYM) established by the US State Department in 2008. The State Department partnered with Google, Facebook, YouTube, MTV, Howcast, CNN, NBC, MTV and the Columbia Law School to bring together youth leaders from around the world and show them how to use social media to build political organizations, mobilize crowds and build insurgent movements. One of the offshoots of AYM was an online 'how-to' hub which hosted a series of 'how to' videos such as 'How to Create Grassroots Movement Using Social Networking Sites', 'How to Smart Mob' and 'How to Circumvent an Internet Proxy' (Bratich 2011: 627). Importantly, AYM also teaches its youthful activists how to make videos geared to stirring western publics into a state of indignation – in effect to produce video material that global news media like CNN and the BBC can use to help build a mood for action against those America deems to be tyrants. But, of course buying influence may simply involve being in a position to employ appropriate people. For example, those who can afford to employ skilled PRs and spin doctors are more likely to influence news production in ways beneficial to their interests. PRs and spin doctors are hired for their knowledge of journalistic gatekeeping. Their job is to deploy their knowledge of newsroom routines and practices so as to find ways to try to set the agenda for the agenda setters. If successful, the stakes are high for those involved in the struggle for hegemony. The end game for the builders of hegemony is to set in motion a 'spiral of silence' which closes discourse and so secures hegemonic dominance.

Lastly, ruling elites are necessarily at their most secure, and so can employ less coercion, when they succeed in naturalizing their preferred discourses and practices with three key groups of people: the gatekeepers of the culture industry; those who manage, hire and fire these gatekeepers; and those who train and educate these gatekeepers. Ultimately, when journalists see existing political and economic relationships as 'natural', the mechanics of existing political decision making as legitimate, and existing coercive arrangements like justice, policing and military systems as legitimate, they can be relied upon to 'ask the right questions', and produce reports and images that confirm the existing hegemonic arrangements. Successful hegemonic dominance involves achieving a naturalized and routinized system for staffing the culture industries, and perhaps especially newsrooms, with intellectuals who broadly accept the discourses and practices of the ruling hegemony. Hegemonic closure of discourse will be most effective when those involved in media-training programmes, media-staffing decisions and establishing media work practices routinely take decisions that confirm the discursive needs of the existing hegemonic order – and set up mechanisms to clone themselves. When hegemonically 'appropriate' decision making is routinized, ruling elites need not intervene to secure their discursive needs, and discourse closure becomes naturalized and opaque.

NEWS MAKING IN THE INTERACTIVE ERA

The emergence of interactive, mobile and networked media technologies have changed journalistic routines in at least two significant ways:

- The acquisition and use of large databases of information is an increasingly common part of the production of journalism.
- The use of content generated by ordinary people using smartphones is a common feature of news reporting, especially on crisis events.

In this chapter we have described the routine interaction between journalists and established institutions like government, business, entertainment and sports industries. This final section examines how data and eyewitness content generated on smartphones have changed journalistic routines and relationships.

THE CHANGING NEWS BUSINESS

The emergence of interactive media has fundamentally changed the revenue streams and structure of commercial news organizations.

Go through the Nieman Lab's multimedia essay 'Riptide' for a chronological examination of how industrial and technological change has changed journalism's business model. You can find a link to the essay on the *Media and Society* website study.sagepub.com/carahandlouw

The essay charts how interactive technologies, search and content aggregation, online classifieds, blogging and social media have impacted the news business model.

Draw up a timeline that maps the changes chronicled in the essay. Identify the key moments and consider their specific implications.

What does this timeline suggest about the future of journalism?

Consider how journalists' values are impacted by a changing news business.

Data and journalism

Data has become another source of information that journalists use to tell stories. Data is brokered as part of relationships journalists build with PRs in government, business or universities and sometimes political activists, leakers or whistleblowers. The term 'data journalism' is sometimes used to refer to a form of journalism where journalists produce stories by assembling, accessing and organizing large sets of data. Data journalism appeals to both established journalistic ideologies and the commercial pressures of news organizations. Journalists use large sets of data to amplify their claims to legitimacy and credibility by presenting the data as objective evidence or truth. Journalistic ideology is grounded in exposing and demonstrating the truth to the public. Large sets of data can be presented as compelling illustrations in the form of statistics, interactive models and infographics. Journalists play the role of interpreting the information, making sense of it and selecting elements to present to the public. These forms of data-driven journalism often dovetail with efforts of news organizations to create more interactive and engaging forms of content. For example, during the post-2007 global financial crisis many news organizations presented interactive models and infographics like 'balance the budget' tools where readers where invited to attempt to balance national budgets.

Data has become a valuable resource used by individuals and organizations wishing to build relationships of influence with journalists. PR increasingly involves not only issuing press releases, images and sound bite quotes, but also building relationships with journalists where they provide data, help them interpret it and assist in producing content. Businesses and governments can choose to provide large sets of data to journalists and news organizations together with experts to help interpret and explain the data. These activities are often a sophisticated form of public relations. The journalist is most often not the collector of data, or even the analyst, but rather a narrator or conduit for explaining complex innovations, policies or population trends. In the interactive era the assembly and management of enormous databases of information has become central to making and maintaining power. Journalists with specialist knowledge in policy, science, programming and design can play a role as intermediaries between the public and government, business, and research or policy organizations in organizing and explaining data.

In addition to using databases of information that are deliberately publicly disclosed by government, business or universities, some journalists also find themselves interacting with individuals or organizations leaking enormous amounts of data. Sometimes these leakers and whistleblowers are committed activists who believe in openness and transparency, other times they are motivated by specific violations of rights or misuses of power they wish to expose to the public. The cases of WikiLeaks, Julian Assange and Chelsea Manning – formerly Bradley Manning – and Edward Snowden, Glenn Greenwald and Laura Poitras are two prominent examples, although it is important to note that these practices of leaking sets of data to journalists is increasingly common. These events pose challenges for journalists and news organizations. On the one hand, collaborating with radical activists and leakers can disrupt the mutual and stable relationships news organizations and particular journalists have cultivated with power elites in government and business. On the other hand, the activity of leaking often embodies journalistic ideologies of exposing the truth, speaking truth to power and resisting relationships of power.

These activities establish new, highly flexible and networked relationships, between activists or leakers (who are often highly skilled data and IT experts), investigative journalists and mainstream news organizations. The data leaker is often not a whistleblower in the traditional sense of providing a small amount of 'smoking gun' insider knowledge to a journalist based on their access to government or corporate processes. Rather, the leaker provides journalists with vast troves of data collected from within government or corporations which need to be organized and interpreted. The data provided often doesn't detail one specific incident, but rather information about the ongoing and systemic operations of power.

The leaker, journalist and news organizations then form temporary relationships to share, make sense of and package the data as news. In part the leaker and investigative journalist may share a common ideology of speaking truth to power. The journalist may work within a news organization that then weighs up the commercial and political consequences of publishing leaked material. In practice these relationships are often fraught. The journalist is often protected by their news organization and laws relating to free speech and the public interest, whereas leakers have committed criminal offences. Journalists are also wary not to be used by leakers, and careful to ensure their stories don't have unintended consequences. Often the journalist isn't a gatekeeper in the traditional sense. For example, WikiLeaks publish most of their content online for any member of the public to access. The role that journalists play is in organizing, making sense of and publicizing leaked material. McNair argues that leakers like WikiLeaks depend on the 'traditional journalistic functions of sifting and sense making, of narrativising and interpreting' data (McNair 2012: 83). The question for journalists is the extent to which they provide this publicity and status to leakers. In the case of the leaks of Chelsea Manning and Edward Snowden, the public only came to understand the material because of the organizing and explanatory work of highly skilled investigative journalists, often working with data and policy experts. Journalists bring an infrastructure to organize and publicize the material.

Journalists find themselves having to decide who gets access to their infrastructure of publicity. They are a node in a network of power relationships that attempt to control the flow of information between governments, corporations and the public. Power elites and activists all try to access journalists for the legitimacy and publicity they can provide. Journalists then are a node in the use of data to maintain, acquire or disrupt power. Managing data has become part of the journalistic gatekeeping function. While journalists use data to make their news stories legitimate and objective, using data inevitably involves selection and emphasis. Data is framed just like any other source of information journalists use. The difference is that traditional journalism was based on information scarcity. The journalist had to manufacture, prise out and unearth information. Now, the journalist is a gatekeeper in a society of information abundance or overflow. A famous adage is that 'Journalism is printing what someone else doesn't want printed; everything else is public relations.' Rather than trying to find scarce information that powerful groups don't want public, they are a node through which enormous amounts of information flow, and their job is to shape it. Some of that information is threatening to power elites, but mostly it is flows of information that come from business and government and serve their interests. Data is good PR in a society centred on sociological and empirical representations of reality.

Organizations like WikiLeaks may demonstrate 'the capacity of digital communication networks to subvert the control of official information once enjoyed by political and other elites, and to shape the news agenda in ways that have the potential to seriously disrupt the exercise of power' (McNair 2012: 77). While it may be true that the leaking of information is more commonplace, it doesn't necessarily follow that it disrupts power. Governments and corporations are at the same time using massive flows of data and information as a strategy for control. We ought to consider how journalism's use of data to explain complex processes to the public and perhaps to reveal secrets alters the exercise of power. Does transparency and exposure make the powerful more accountable? Or, do governments require secrecy in order to be able to function effectively? Does revealing secrets or assembling large sets of data enable better debate or empower the public? Or is the public increasingly disempowered by a glut of information they cannot understand or act upon? And is the presentation of data simply part of the way powerful interests use media to frame reality? At the very least we should not assume that data and information are the answer to better kinds of journalism or democracy.

JOURNALISTS AND LEAKERS

A key representative, legal and ethical dilemma journalism has had to contend with in recent years has been the interaction of established journalism organizations with internet-based organizations and individual leakers like WikiLeaks, Julian Assange, Chelsea (formerly Bradley) Manning and Edward Snowden. These interactions have embedded journalists and news organizations in new networks through which information and news is created and disseminated. These engagements have led to a vibrant debate about the role of journalists in publicizing secrets.

Below are a number of quotes from the editors of news organizations defending the publication of leaks. These endorsements were published by the *Guardian* newspaper in October 2013 after the *Daily Mail* accused the paper of helping 'Britain's enemies'. You can find a link to the endorsements on the *Media and Society* website study.sagepub.com/carahandlouw

The story, we believe, is an important one. It shows that the expectations of millions of Internet users regarding the privacy of their electronic communications are mistaken. These expectations guide the practices of private individuals and businesses, most of them innocent of any wrongdoing. The potential for abuse of such extraordinary capabilities for surveillance, including for political purposes, is considerable. The government insists it has put in place checks and balances to limit misuses of this technology. But the question of whether they are effective is far from resolved and is an issue that can only be debated by the people and their

(Continued)

(Continued)

elected representatives if the basic facts are revealed. There are those who, in good faith, believe that we should leave the balance between civil liberty and security entirely to our elected leaders, and to those they place in positions of executive responsibility. Again, we do not agree. The American system, as we understand it, is premised on the idea – championed by such men as Thomas Jefferson and James Madison – that government run amok poses the greatest potential threat to the people's liberty, and that an informed citizenry is the necessary check on this threat. The sort of work ProPublica does – watchdog journalism – is a key element in helping the public play this role. (ProPublica)

In a democracy, the press plays a vital role in informing the public and holding those in power accountable. The NSA has vast intelligence-gathering powers and capabilities and its role in society is an important subject for responsible news-gathering organizations such as the *New York Times* and the *Guardian*. A public debate about the proper perimeters for eavesdropping by intelligence agencies is healthy for the public and necessary. The accurate and in-depth news articles published by the *New York Times* and the *Guardian* help inform the public in framing its thinking about these issues and deciding how to balance the need to protect against terrorism and to protect individual privacy. Vigorous news coverage and spirited public debate are both in the public interest. The journalists at the *New York Times* and the *Guardian* care deeply about the wellbeing and safety of their fellow citizens in carrying out their role in keeping the public informed. (Jill Abramson, *New York Times*)

The utmost duty of a journalist is to expose abuses and the abuse of power. The global surveillance of digital communication by the NSA and GCHQ is no less than an abuse on a massive scale with consequences that at this point seem completely unpredictable. (Wolfgang Beuchner, *Der Spiegel*)

Journalists have only one responsibility: to keep their readers informed and educated about whatever their government is doing on their behalf – and first and foremost on security and intelligence organizations, which by their nature infringe on civil liberties. The Snowden revelations, and their publication by the *Guardian*, have been a prime example of fearlessly exercising this journalistic responsibility. (Aluf Benn, *Haaretz*)

The *Guardian*'s work in the Snowden case is an example of great journalism, the kind that changes history and the kind that citizens need more every day, in a world where the powerful are increasingly trying to hide information from their societies. The real danger is not in the so-called 'aid to the enemy' denounced by the hypocrites, but in the actions of governments and state agencies that citizens cannot control. To fight it we need newspapers willing to do their job, rather than those ready to cheer on the self-interested deceptions of the powerful. (Javier Moreno, *El Pais*)

Consider how journalists and their news organizations explain and justify their relationships with leakers and leaking organizations.

What arguments do they employ?

How do other powerful actors (like governments) attempt to constrain relationships between journalists and leakers?

How do journalists' engagements with leakers reinforce and challenge their professional ethics, codes and values?

You can find links to a variety of articles and statements from news organizations and journalists about their decision to publish material from leakers, on the *Media and Society* website study.sagepub.com/carahandlouw

Witnesses with smartphones

News is informed by the participation of ordinary people using mobile devices to provide images, first-hand accounts and real-time information to journalists. These activities have expanded and fragmented the way journalists interact with others to create news. These new routines co-exist with established practices of sourcing information, framing events and setting agendas. Journalists mediate between new sources of information about events coming from ordinary participants and their established routine interactions with power elites.

While journalists cultivate large networks of professional contacts in government, business and cultural industries as dependable sources, they also need to be resourceful at interacting with social media networks where ordinary people circulate content. This is most evident during events where eyewitnesses with smartphones capture and circulate footage (Andén-Papadopoulos 2013).

Significantly, journalists play the important role of granting this content authority and legitimacy by framing it within their news formulas and representations. Footage of political protests, revolutions and assassinations is made meaningful when journalists incorporate it into their narrative about those events. The footage on its own is cultural raw material; the journalist is critical to framing it and giving it meaning. As eyewitness content has become a specifically authentic type of media content, PRs and activists have grown adept at using new media technologies to generate raw footage that can be provided to journalists. Journalists in crisis events don't necessarily collect but instead collate material provided by eyewitnesses. The content they use depends on both their ability to source it from fast-moving and chaotic social networks like Twitter and YouTube, and the ability of activists to create and get the content directly to journalists. As social networks become a source of content it can have problematic consequences. Journalists, used to trusting their sources, find fact-checking increasingly difficult. For example, in the days following the 2013 Boston bombing, people on social networking sites like Reddit trawled through user-generated videos and images of the event looking for likely suspects. The online 'mob' incorrectly identified individuals who were then falsely reported as suspects by journalists relying on social networking sites' interpretation of eyewitness footage.

As journalists use content generated by the networked public their claims to legitimacy shifts from objective truth to the authenticity of live, unedited, eyewitness accounts (Andén-Papadopoulos 2013: 344). The journalist's claim isn't to present an objective account of events but to enable us to bear witness to events as they unfold as if we are there. The journalist mediates the feeling of being present at the event. The subjective first-person content produced by eyewitnesses is affective and partisan. Its authenticity is grounded in the raw, non-narrative and hypermobile nature of the footage (Andén-Papadopoulos 2013: 347). The footage mobilizes emotions and feelings as it frames events for the viewer from the perspective of a live, engaged participant. Rather than offer an objective account of events, journalists are a conduit or channel to an authentic first-hand perspective. Just as we have argued that journalistic formulas over-simplify complex realities, we can argue that the formula emerging around use of eyewitness footage is a similarly simplified way of representing complex events like political protest, crises and violence. We see these events in their raw and visceral chaos without necessary careful explanation. Journalists use the footage as part of attention-grabbing live coverage, but don't necessarily verify or contextualize the material because their claim isn't to truth but to a direct authentic subjective experience. As journalists become conduits for content that ordinary people generate by circulating and thereby legitimizing it, they need to consider how they explain, verify and contextualize the material.

CONCLUSION

Professional journalists have always been embedded within power relationships. The content they produce needs to serve the commercial and political interests of the institutions that employ them. Journalists are a key node in a constant flow of data and content through the networks of the information society. As much as journalism might help us make sense of the deluge of data that goes with living in the information age, we must also recognize that journalists are central to enabling the smooth functioning of power relationships in this society. They remain central gatekeepers, framers and agenda setters.

FURTHER READING

The readings below examine how journalists give meaning to their work (Deuze 2005, North 2009), how journalistic norms and routines frame representations of events (Kitzinger 2000, McKnight 2010), and how technologies change the way conflicts are represented (Alper 2013, Andén-Papadopoulos 2013). Deuze (2005) examines how the professional ideologies of journalists inform their practice. North (2009) examines the role that gender plays in the production of news. Kitzinger (2000) describes the role journalism plays in representing and managing crisis events. McKnight (2010) examines how News Corporation represents climate change. Alper (2013) and Andén-Papadopoulos (2013) each examine the role that mobile media technologies play in representing conflict.

Alper, M. (2013) 'War on Instagram: framing conflict photojournalism with mobile photography apps', *New Media & Society*, 1–16.

Andén-Papadopoulos, K. (2013) 'Media witnessing and the "crowd-sourced video revolution"', *Visual Communication*, 12 (3): 341–357.

Deuze, M. (2005) 'What is journalism? Professional identity and ideology of journalists reconsidered', *Journalism*, 6 (4): 442–464.

Kitzinger, J. (2000) 'Media templates: patterns of association and the (re)construction of meaning over time', *Media, Culture & Society*, 22 (1): 61–84.

McKnight, D. (2010) 'A change in the climate? The journalism of opinion at News Corporation', *Journalism*, 11 (6): 693–706.

North, L. (2009) 'Rejecting the "F-word": how "feminism" and "feminists" are understood in the newsroom', *Journalism*, 10 (6): 739–757.

Any article marked with is available to download at the website **study.sagepub.com/ carahandlouw**

POLITICS AND COMMUNICATION STRATEGISTS

PROFESSIONAL COMMUNICATORS ARE CRITICAL ACTORS IN THE MANAGEMENT OF THE POLITICAL PROCESS.

* What is strategic political communication?

* How has professional communication changed the political process?

* How do contemporary political campaigns engage with popular culture, use data and manage the participation of ordinary people?

In this chapter we:

- Chart the rise of professional political communicators
- Define strategic political communication
- Examine the relationship between journalism and strategic political communication
- Explore the changes that strategic communication has made to the political process
- Analyse Barack Obama's publicity machinery.

THE RISE OF COMMUNICATION STRATEGISTS AS POLITICAL PLAYERS

In the 1920s, Walter Lippmann (1965) described the emergence of a new professional class of publicists and press agents standing between US politicians and the media (McNair 1999: xi). While Sabato (1981: 11) traces the first consultants engaging in today's genre of political communication strategy back to 1930s Californian politics, communication strategy became central to politics in the USA during the 1950s (Sabato 1981: 12). Jamieson (1984: 59) argues that the Democrat candidate Stevenson's defeat at the hands of Eisenhower in 1952 and Nixon in 1956 occurred because Stevenson, as the last of the old pre-television politicians, could not adjust to the requirements of televisualized politics. Eisenhower, on the other hand, was 'made over' by his media consultants, who televisualized his style (Jamieson 1984: 60). His media consultants had a candidate who understood the importance of managing images, messages and impressions. During the Second World War General Eisenhower had learned to use propaganda as an adjunct to warfare. He successfully mobilized media and public relations to promote himself as a war hero. The Stevenson and Eisenhower campaigns were the turning point. After the 1950s, communication strategists specializing in scripting televisual performances became a key feature of US politics – proliferating numerically, honing new tools and becoming ever more influential. This phenomenon subsequently spread beyond the USA.

Strategic political communication involves five sets of players:

- politicians who act as media performers
- the spin industry who manage impressions
- media workers like journalists, presenters, hosts and researchers
- media audiences
- policy makers who remain deliberately backstage, shielded from as much scrutiny as possible by the smoke-and-mirrors show.

Political consultants have emerged as public actors in their own right. Professional communicators are more than just behind-the-scenes advisors. The spin industry that undergirds the political process of mass democracies is readily visible. Spin doctors, minders, image specialists, opinion researchers and advertisers are key actors in the political process. In fact, to be taken seriously, politicians must now possess communication campaign machines. Consultants have become status symbols and media stars, performing alongside politicians-as-performers and celebrity journalists (see Sabato 1981: 19–20). As Boorstin said in the 1970s, 'Most true celebrities have press agents. And these press agents sometimes themselves become celebrities. The hat, the rabbit, and the magician are all equally news' (1971: 75).

Why did a class of political communication professionals arise?

Liberal democracy is grounded upon the notion of legitimate governance. Legitimacy requires the consent of the governed. But as McNair says, 'consent can be manufactured' (McNair 1999: 26). Ultimately, policy makers within liberal democracies have two (possibly contradictory) needs:

- To try to prevent the masses from disrupting and convoluting the policy process by keeping them at arm's length from the actual decision-making process.
- To try to make the masses believe they are actually participating in governance as a way of building consent.

Part of the solution for generating consent, while simultaneously keeping the masses disengaged from the real process of governance, is to pursue 'calculated strategies of distraction' (Jamieson 1992: 205). This is where the spin industry comes in.

A second reason for the rise of political consultants was the arrival of television. The pioneer political consultants in 1950s America were technical advisors about television (Jamieson 1984: 35). The media advisors and highly influential campaign strategists of today evolved from these not-very-powerful technical advisory positions (1984: 36). Television made the difficult process of mobilizing and steering citizenries much easier, because television delivers low-involvement viewers to political players who understand how to use television's manipulative powers (see Jamieson 1992: 52–53). Effectively television can splice together, speedily and seamlessly, images and ideas that are in reality unrelated. Furthermore, television creates such linkages in ways defying scrutiny and logic. These can have enormous political impacts because of the emotions generated by montage (Jamieson 1992: 54–56). It is not surprising that televisual politics first emerged in the USA given its very visual culture. Political communication strategists use filmic optical illusions to arouse, assemble and magnify viewer emotions (Ewen 1996). This 'optic-power' has become a central tool for steering public opinion. As televisual politics spread from the USA to other liberal democracies, so spin industry techniques followed.

Undermining the establishment media

A further impetus for the rise of US political consultants was the capacity of the 'eastern establishment' media in New York and Washington to influence political agendas (Maltese 1994: 42). If these journalists disliked a particular politician they could negatively impact upon his or her political career through their agenda setting role. Journalists do not have power, but in certain locations they have influence derivative of being authoritative. They can authorize certain versions of reality. This gives journalists opportunities to:

- disrupt the agendas policy makers wish to pursue by raising issues that undermine policy planning
- intimidate policy makers
- trivialize some issues and hype or exaggerate others
- direct attention one way or another.

To control the policy agenda, politicians need to limit journalists' capacities to disrupt, intimidate, trivialize and direct attention. Politicians employ communication professionals who deploy their knowledge of media practices to side-step the establishment media and facilitate unmediated communication with voters.

Richard Nixon regarded 'eastern establishment' journalists as hostile. Not surprisingly, President Nixon was a central facilitator of the revolution that saw campaign strategists emerge as powerful players within US politics. He stood for President three times – losing to Kennedy in 1960, but beating

Humphrey in 1968 and McGovern in 1972. His loss in 1960 because of a poor television profile taught Nixon to take the media seriously. Consequently Nixon's Republican administration sought ways to use strategic communication to both tame the media and develop mechanisms to communicate directly with voters over the heads of 'hostile' journalists in the elite Washington and New York presses. Nixon's presidency (1969–1974) was important for the evolution of spin doctors, who ultimately became political players in their own right due to their skill at using media, especially visual media, to build consent and steer public opinion. By the 1990s there was a large US spin industry, skilled in using the media as partners or side-stepping hostile journalists and communicating directly with voters when necessary. Serious political players need media teams. Bill Clinton's Democrat media team adopted and masterfully deployed a range of media and popular cultural forms to successfully reach 'ordinary people' (Newman 1994: 5–7). These US techniques were introduced to Britain by Tony Blair's Labour media team. Australia's adoption of these techniques has been fed by influences from both the US and UK versions. It has become commonplace for British, American and Australian spin doctors to migrate back and forth between campaign and political teams (Louw 2010b: 80).

Effectively, Nixon's belief that the media were hostile led to a range of media management and 'spinning' techniques that eventually became commonplace political practice in many Anglo-countries, although the US remains the pace-setter for developing new techniques. What has emerged is a political process investing considerable energy into producing stage-managed and largely televisual 'faces'. These stage-managed faces are ultimately the outcome of an often symbiotic relationship between two sets of communication professionals: those working for the media (journalists) and those working for the political machines (spin doctors and communication strategists). Politicians are the third party to the 'face manufacturing' process. There is a constant struggle for dominance within the relationship between journalists, politicians and spin doctors. Depending on the contextual conditions, spin doctors sometimes have the upper hand. On other occasions journalists are dominant, while at other times, politicians assume control. Sometimes power is shared. Who dominates at any moment depends upon the following variables:

- The resources available to the players: generally, the player with the most resources has an advantage over the others.
- How skilled the spin doctors are at dealing with the media: the more skilled, the more they are able to dominate relationships.
- The level of political agitation among the mass public: an agitated and unhappy public generates challenges for politicians and spin machines, which often increases the bargaining position of journalists.
- How skilled spin doctors are at steering mass public opinion: the more successful they are, the more power they accumulate.
- The nature and intensity of the struggles between politicians: the more intense the struggle, the more politicians need their spin doctors and journalists. This diminishes the bargaining position of politicians.

In general terms, although journalists have not been rendered completely powerless, the capacity of journalists to frame and interpret the news has been declining (Graber 2001: 440) for several reasons:

- New media forms have provided alternative sources of information.
- The political communication strategy and spin industry has been growing at the expense of journalists as news production is increasingly outsourced. For instance, the US Department of Labor said there were 320,000 strategic communication professionals and 59,000 journalists in America in 2010. A decade earlier it was 150,000 strategic communicators and 130,000 journalists.
- Spin doctors have grown increasingly skilled at using both old and new media forms to bypass 'problem' journalists.

WHAT IS STRATEGIC POLITICAL COMMUNICATION?

The strategic communication and spin industry aims to plant stories in the media by using journalists to disseminate stories serving the spin doctors' agenda. Both strategic political communicators and journalists attempt to play an agenda setting function. Good journalists resist being used, and do their best to turn the tables on spin doctors by using political communication machines as resources that can serve the journalists' agendas. For example, journalists can use the fact that all serious politicians now have strategic communication machines that are in competition with each other. Good journalists can potentially use this competition to play the various communication machineries off against each other in their search for stories. This is one reason why the strategic communication and spin industry is not always successful: it has a particular problem when ruling elites are deeply divided over policy options. Not surprisingly, during periods when elite consensus breaks down, journalists are more likely to unearth damaging stories. For example, the USA's torturing of Iraqi prisoners became a story during the consensus breakdown around the Iraq war. On issues where there is broad consensus among policy elites, journalists are unlikely to find exploitable cracks in the spin machine because the line being spun will be uniform and the consensus difficult to crack. Perhaps more troubling is the fact that there are some issues where policy elites and journalists build up a joint consensus. In these instances the symbiotic relationship between journalists, politicians and communication strategists generates a total closure of discourse. The process of decolonization that unfolded between the 1950s and 1970s was a case in point.

Margaret Thatcher's Chief Press Secretary, Bernard Ingham, described the relationship between communication strategists and journalists as one of symbiotic tension: 'The relationship is essentially cannibalistic. They feed off each other but no one knows who is next on the menu' (Franklin 1994: 14). However, on balance, the spin industry probably has the edge over journalists because spin doctors and communication strategists are well paid and so their industry attracts very talented people who know exactly how to steer journalists. Many are skilled ex-journalists lured by higher salaries. Ultimately, whoever dominates the journalist–communication strategist relationship, one thing is clear: spin doctors and communication strategists are now an integral part of the political processes of liberal democracies.

Spin tactics

A core feature of spinning is understanding how the media works, and exploiting one's knowledge of journalistic practices and discourses to provide newsrooms with what they need. Tactics of good communication strategists include:

- Supplying journalists with the sorts of stories and images they need to please their bosses.
- Doing background research for time-pressed journalists to supply the information needed to produce stories. This allows journalists to believe they have control and ownership over their stories.
- Leaking stories to journalists who are not experienced enough to know they are being used.
- Leaking stories to experienced journalists with whom one needs to develop and maintain a symbiotic relationship – for instance, by providing them with an exclusive story. This can create a debt that communication strategists can use to negotiate future favours. Developing such relationships requires great care, tact and mutual trust in order that journalists do not get the impression they are being used or 'spun a line'. Journalists must be handled in a way that allows them to maintain their professional ideology.
- Scripting speeches to provide sound bites and leads, making the journalistic task easier.
- Arranging photo opportunities guaranteeing good, cost-effective images. This often involves arranging staged pseudo-events geared to the needs of time-pressed newsrooms. Pseudo-events are often used as bait to catch journalists. They are designed to attract media attention. Once attracted, other information can be supplied.
- Arranging news conferences to make the collection of quotes as easy as possible. Well-arranged news conferences supply good sound bites, good visuals and a good information package of background research for journalists. This makes it as easy as possible for journalists to construct the news with what is supplied. In some instances, news conferences become pseudo-events. News conferences can also be constructed to make it difficult for journalists to ask questions.
- Running smear campaigns against opponents. This involves running an effective research department that gathers information about the opposition. This information is leaked to journalists to undermine opponents. The Republicans used information about Clinton's sexual exploits in this way. Although smear campaigns are more commonly deployed against those in opposition political parties, they are also used inside political parties during struggles to select or undermine rivals. This works the other way too. Communication strategists prepare contingency plans to deal with problems they anticipate with their team or candidate. This allows for a rapid response to crises. Communication strategists can immediately spin a new line to journalists to minimize damage, create 'plausible deniability', or if possible to deflect attention elsewhere.
- Staged or planted questions when politicians meet the public in shopping malls or during question time in televised parliamentary sessions.

Managing journalists

Communication strategists must ensure that journalists feel like they retain their independence. Tactics that communication strategists use to craft legitimacy for their ideas include:

- Organizing teams to write letters to the press. Even if not published, the impression can be created within newsrooms of a groundswell of public opinion. Nixon called this 'the silent majority' that the elite media ignore.
- Organizing teams who monitor and phone radio talkback programmes.
- Lobbying key columnists and editorial writers.
- Providing journalists with discreet off-the-record backgrounders. This can involve politicians rather than their staffers having personal meetings with 'negative' journalists, to try to charm them and given them off-the-record information.
- Communication strategists can influence journalists' career-paths by providing stories to those deemed friendly while squeezing out the hostile. If journalists assigned to cover stories about politics are frozen out and denied access they will face career problems.
- Providing ostensibly objective information or evidence for journalists to report.

Sometimes, the best strategy is 'jumping over' the heads of journalists deemed problematic. Both Nixon's and Clinton's teams used this approach to communicate with the public via local and niche media, cable TV, direct mail and advertisements, as a substitute for dealing with a negative White House media corps. Communication strategists call this 'going public', 'disintermediation' or 'end-running' journalists (Maltese 1994: 216). This tactic must be used with great care to avoid overly alienating the elite media.

Political communication strategists do more than engage with journalists. They are also in the business of creating celebrities. This involves being able to spot and recruit latent talent: those who are telegenic, can speak in sound bites, sound sincere, and have the discipline and theatrical abilities to follow a script. It also involves training politicians to be televisual performers, to use autoprompts and to give only appropriate answers to journalists. Communication strategists teach them to dress appropriately and possibly improve their appearance through dentistry, contact lenses, hair styling or implants, diet and exercise. Some politicians need to be accompanied by handlers and minders to help them manage their micro-relationships with the media.

Contemporary political communication strategists also use marketing, branding and advertising techniques because politicians have become products to be sold to audiences (see Newman 1994). This involves scripting celebrity performances to position the politician as a brand matching a particular voter profile. 'Candidate positioning' often involves mobilizing the icons and symbols of popular culture and linking politicians to these to make them more credible and appealing. Communication strategists obviously prefer to gain free access to mass or niche audiences by getting journalists to use media releases, cover their pseudo-events and pick up their scripted sound bites. But communication strategists cannot afford to rely exclusively upon free media coverage. Sometimes they must pay to ensure access is gained to the audiences they want to reach. Political communication strategists also engage in the business of paid marketing and advertising, and this involves them in audience and public opinion research. This dimension of selling politicians has seen the growth of a strategic political communication industry that is increasingly expensive to run.

Finally, political communication strategists are also involved in internal communication within political parties. Such internal communication can take many forms, including internal lobbying, rumours, direct mail or scripting party congresses. Further, stories placed in the media (such as leaks) are sometimes actually designed to influence people inside one's own political party.

CHANGES TO THE POLITICAL PROCESS

How has strategic communication changed the political process of liberal democracies? To some extent, each country has been impacted differently because of the different political cultures in each, and because strategic communication became central to politics at different stages in each country. The changes wrought by strategic communication on the political process are most pronounced in the US. Many of the developments in the US soon flow onto other liberal democracies. For this reason, we will focus on developments in the US in mapping how strategic communication has changed the political process.

Strategic communication changes political parties

Strategic communication has changed political parties, as power shifted away from party bosses and hacks towards consultants and spin doctors (Newman 1994: 15). Party machines once fulfilled the role of delivering voters. Party bosses cajoled the grassroots party faithful to ensure voters turned up on election day. Party bosses acquired power by being able to deliver and organize functioning election machines. Strategic communication professionalized the whole process, reducing the importance of party hacks. The new power brokers are no longer faithful party members. Rather, brokers now need to possess media and research skills in order to analyse and steer public opinion. People with these skills expect to be paid as professionals. These professionals are also increasingly involved in selecting political leaders, based not on party faithfulness, but upon how well they can perform in televisual formats.

Strategic communication changes political leaders

Political leaders now require different attributes to be selected as candidates. They need to be credible and convincing performers in image-based media, be visually appealing and be able to speak in sound bites. They must also be able to follow scripts designed by spin doctors. Leaders possessing these skills can, with the help of spin doctors, jump over the heads of party hierarchies to appeal directly to voters. Hence, aspiring leaders with televisual charisma, backed by good spin doctors, can force the hand of party-nominating processes. This has also altered party power relationships in favour of those who best understand the mechanics of strategic communication, television and the internet.

Strategic communication makes politics more resource intensive

Strategic communication has made politics a very expensive business because of the cost of the spin industry and opinion pollsters, and associated media production like direct mail, TV spots, web content and databases. This has placed an enormous burden on political parties to raise money. The result, in the USA, is a professionalized fundraising industry of PACs (see Sabato 1989: 145–151), Super PACs and 501(c)(4) organizations. PACs are political action committees that raise funds for campaigns. Super PACS raise funds but rather than give them directly to campaigns, spend them on promoting a political cause or viewpoint. Super PACs have unlimited funding. 501(c)(4) groups are non-profit organizations that promote social welfare; these organizational structures can also be used to fund political communication. The cost of running this fundraising industry is also high. There has been considerable concern in the USA that the resultant drive for funds has distorted the political process by forcing politicians to sell themselves to large campaign donors. Attempts to regulate PACs have not altered these underlying financial pressures – pressures evident in all liberal democracies that have been remodelled on strategic communication logic.

Strategic communication makes popular culture central to political communication

Strategic communicators have learned to systematically mobilize popular culture to reach voters (see Street 1997). This has generated a new genre of scripted politics, requiring politicians to step outside the normal genre of political performance and adopt a new range of popular and populist faces. For instance, Bill Clinton playing saxophone on *The Arsenio Hall Show* (Newman 1994: 135), Barack Obama appearing on *The Daily Show*, and politicians appearing on morning breakfast television and radio, game shows and variety formats.

Strategic communication amplifies the affective and emotional dimension of political communication

Television reaches mass publics and stirs emotions by presenting audiences with simplified and idealized presentations. As such, it is well suited to deflecting voter attention away from policy problems by:

- mobilizing support for a person or position
- demonizing people
- creating pariah groups
- building selective outrage, indignation and hostility.

Television provides the perfect vehicle for politics-as-hype. Hence, it has become a valued spin industry tool. This has driven political spinning into an ever more visual art. Televisual performances have become the preferred tool for reaching and steering voters. With the growth of the internet, those driving this visualized hype-politics have also learned to use platforms like YouTube and Facebook. Those unable or unwilling to play the game of visual politics will find it difficult to achieve political success in today's democracies.

Strategic communication undermines deliberative modes of political communication

The combination of strategic communication and televisual politics has undermined local political meetings where voters were addressed face-to-face. The arts of oratory, making policy speeches, and question and answer formats of discussion and debate do not mesh easily with the techniques of spinning sound bites and slick images designed for passive mass audiences. Politicians skilled in working a meeting are no longer required and have been replaced by politicians skilled in working mass television audiences. Television has pushed politicians away from engaging in debate, discussion and selling policies, and towards reciting and performing lines scripted by others (Selnow 1994: 142). This televisual politics has also migrated to the internet.

Strategic communication undermines the power of the press within the political process

The power of the press within the political process has declined. Strategic political communication now reaches voters either via television and the internet or by deploying marketing techniques using individualized media like direct mail. The latter is becoming especially important and, as Selnow (1994: 147) notes, falls beneath journalists' radar. Print journalists, who used to be extremely influential within the political process, are increasingly bypassed. Essentially, the press can no longer monitor the multitude of political messages generated because of the complexity of the spin industry's communication activities.

Strategic communication turns politics into a permanent campaign

Strategic communication produces a 'politics of avoidance' (Selnow 1994: 178) because the news process is governed by ongoing opinion polls. Strategic political communication involves running a permanent campaign (Selnow 1994: 177). Building legitimacy requires not just manufacturing consent, but maintaining popularity too. This translates into trying to avoid any issue that might destabilize consent. The spin industry not only constantly tests and monitors public opinion shifts, but also runs focus groups to test the acceptability of issues before publicly discussing them. Issues that look too contentious, or which focus groups reveal may cause problems with important sections of the electorate, are avoided. The result is that politics becomes a bland repetition of comfortable, non-controversial, middle-of-the-road ideas. Real debate is stymied in favour of fluff and distraction. This produces political machines effectively geared towards avoiding the emergence of real controversy. Pseudo-controversy, manufactured by sensationalized images and messages or hyped-up pseudo-adversarial journalism, is acceptable. The result is politics as a poll-driven spectacle geared towards permanently entertaining and distracting the masses within an environment where television and internet imagery is ubiquitous.

DARK MONEY

Dark money is a term that describes money that flows from powerful interests into the political process but is not open to public scrutiny. This money is often not direct donations to political parties, but rather funnelled through secretive foundations and organizations that invest it in advocating for particular causes.

A core feature of mass democracies is elections within which spin doctors compete for millions of votes. For politicians their careers are at stake, and for political parties the outcome of these competitions determine whether or not they will have power. Not surprisingly, given what is at stake, persuasive communication campaigns (run by spin doctors) have become a core feature of the political process. And because these communication campaigns have become enormously expensive, raising huge sums of money becomes central to political success. This has created a fear that large donors (who pay for these communication campaigns) could acquire undue influence over their political benefactors. In places like the USA this has led to legislation geared to regulating the funding of political campaigns. But the emergence of the phenomenon of dark money has only served to demonstrate the naïvety of believing that regulation can either reign in funders or bring about funding transparency. Essentially the 2010 US Supreme Court's ruling on a lobby group, Citizens United, created an opportunity that spin doctors were quick to exploit. This ruling has led to the growth of a whole new industry of non-profit and limited-liability companies who operate independently of political candidates and political parties, but who pay for communication campaigns that help them win voters. Although this expenditure is supposed to be disclosed, the dark money industry has creatively found ways to only disclose support long after the elections are over. The result is that huge amounts of money are made available to run focus groups, develop advertising, run public education campaigns or reach out to voters. American conservatives have been especially creative in building a network of groups such as Freedom Partners Chamber of Commerce, Center to Protect Patient Rights, Americans for Responsible Leadership, Freedom Path, RightChange.com II and A Better America Now. The result is that hundreds of millions of dollars have been made available (effectively anonymously) for the purchase of election advertisements that praise some candidates and some issues, while criticizing others. This has impacted on political outcomes at the national, state and local levels.

What the dark money phenomenon shows is that well-designed communication campaigns do sway election outcomes. Political parties and politicians understand this and so they invest considerable energy into finding ways to fund political communication campaigns.

What are the consequences of dark money for the democratic process?

Identify some organizations that attempt to influence the political process. How are they funded? What communication techniques do they use?

For links to resources on dark money see the *Media and Society* website study.sagepub.com/carahandlouw

BARACK OBAMA'S PUBLICITY MACHINE

The Obama 2008 and 2012 Presidential election campaigns demonstrated how sophisticated American strategic political communication has become (Sabato 2013). Obama's team used a mix of communication forms to target their various audiences. These included:

- visual media: television, web content, posters, photographs
- mass rallies
- celebrity endorsements
- interactive websites
- viral web content
- peer-to-peer web content
- direct mail and email
- on-the-ground canvassing of voters (organized using sophisticated databases)
- traditional news management.

This range of communication forms was used to target multiple audiences with differently nuanced messages at key moments in the campaign. Obama's senior strategist, David Axelrod, constructed a large team comprising a diversified array of communication specialists who made Obama's popularity appear to be the result of natural grassroots support, when in fact Obama's legitimacy was the product of a magnificently planned and orchestrated communication operation. Axelrod's spin was extremely professional. Axelrod built his career specializing in getting black mayoral candidates elected. He became expert in getting his candidates elected by simultaneously mobilizing white voters to vote for a black candidate, plus getting black voters who were often apathetic and demobilized to register and turn out on election day. Axelrod is skilled in researching and targeting his audiences, and in using a range of mass to niche media to reach the audiences he is after with specific messages. Axelrod himself appears somewhat conflicted about the profession he left journalism to enter:

> I believe there is nobility in politics. I believe there is great good that can be done. I know my business and the technology of politics and polling and focus groups, all of what we do, in some way contributes to an atmosphere of cynicism. I try to fight that. I can't say I'm totally blameless. I think everyone in this business has a hand on that bloody dagger. (Montgomery 2007)

A campaign begins by crafting an overall political brand and identity for a candidate that is recognizable, coherent and likeable. Voters need to be able to recognize a future leader, understand what they stand for and feel good about them. Obama's team did this using carefully chosen and compelling visuals; slogans like 'hope', 'change' and 'forward'; mass public rallies that generated excitement and positioned him as a legitimate leader; celebrity endorsements; and well-written, emotive speeches.

Visual communication

Visual content is highly valuable because it is more likely to generate affective resonance with an audience, and is therefore more likely to be engaged with, circulated and shared. Obama's July 2008 Berlin rally was a magnificent piece of televisual show business used by Obama's spin team to address an American audience all the way from Berlin. Even though Obama's team did not manage to get the Brandenburg gate as a backdrop as was originally scripted, they still managed to construct visuals that reminded audiences of Kennedy's Berlin Wall speech. By mobilizing a cheering crowd of two hundred thousand Berliners, Obama's team successfully built a sense of liberalism's victory over communism and of a benign Pax Americana that Americans could be proud of. Specifically, Obama was constructed as someone fit to lead this Pax Americana into a glorious new post-Bush future of globalized liberalism, where the world would be filled with happy cheering crowds instead of Bush's wars. It was a highly skilled piece of spin doctoring.

Obama's team continuously created images that presented Obama, his family and his supporters as typical middle Americans who were the proud product of multiculturalism. To announce the 2012 victory his team posted to Twitter an image of Barack and Michelle Obama embracing. The beautifully shot and carefully crafted image is the most shared item of content in the history of Twitter. Obama's official photographer Pete Souza is widely credited with crafting the visual image of Obama. Obama is the first President to recognize that the official photographer not only plays an important historical archiving role, but also is central to constructing a credible and appealing visual narrative about the President. The images that the Obama team circulate via social media are a combination of serious 'Commander in Chief' images and warm and playful behindthescenes

Figure 7.1   Obama 'fistbumps' a janitor

Source: www.singleblackmale.org/2012/01/30/presidential-fist-bumps-through-the-years/.

moments where the public get to see the 'real' Obama. This stream of images crafts Obama's personality, building up a strong resonance with the public that makes it easier for the campaign to attract the attention of voters and get them to listen. In Figure 7.1 Obama 'fist bumps' with a janitor. The image visually depicts how Obama's respect for working-class and multicultural America is naturally embedded in his everyday life. The image makes Obama's values appear natural and unscripted.

In addition to creating a visual narrative about Obama, his team also position him within niche communities. Often, the campaign would use celebrities or public figures strongly identified with those communities as a conduit. Jennifer Lopez was used to appeal to Latin American voters, Ricky Martin to progressive, gay and Latin American voters, and Bruce Springsteen to appeal to the white working class and the progressive professional class alike. The celebrities created an affective link between Obama and these niche identity groups. They could also use their sense of humour, life stories and identities to create and convey other facets to Obama's personality that he himself could not coherently deploy within a tightly managed campaign. For instance, Obama could not make the jokes Will Ferrell could or express the sentiments that Springsteen could without alienating other groups. But using these celebrities he could craft a link to specific niche identities without losing the overall coherence of his political brand.

Axelrod left nothing to chance in his news management planning. Before the 2008 election a study was conducted of Obama's vulnerabilities. Having identified these, Axelrod prepared anti-Obama advertisements and screened these to focus groups. From their responses Obama's spin team designed response advertisements and had these prepared in advance. One such advertisement was an answer to the charge that Obama had long-standing links to radicals like Bill Ayers. When McCain's campaign did in fact attack Obama in this way, Axelrod had a counter-advertisement pre-prepared and ready to roll. Overall Obama's spin team proved to be highly competent news agenda managers who successfully kept the news messages under control and remained in tight control of the media images required to construct the Obama celebrity persona that Axelrod's team had scripted.

Political campaigns need to sell and advertise a political brand. The campaign managers get powerful journalists, media organizations and public figures to adopt their key messages so that the candidate is represented favourably and coherently in the mass media. They make and distribute advertisements and web content that also convey the candidate and the political brand on a mass scale. At this point, if the campaign is going well, they have a candidate who is recognized, coherent and credible.

IMAGES OF OBAMA

Collect and examine iconic images of Barack Obama such as Obama watching the assassination of Bin Laden, Obama and Spiderman, Obama and the janitor fist bump, Obama's 'Four more years' Twitter announcements, and the Obama 'Not bad' meme. You can find links to these images on the *Media and Society* website study.sagepub.com/carahandlouw

(Continued)

(Continued)

You might also search for images the official White House photographer Pete Souza has taken of Obama and his presidency. Souza is widely credited with crafting the visual image of Obama. You can find a link to a feature on Souza on the *Media and Society* website study. sagepub.com/carahandlouw

How do these images construct Obama's identity?

What do the images say about his values and personality?

How do the images make him appear credible, legitimate and powerful?

Managing data, audiences and participation

Having crafted a compelling political brand, the next step is to mobilize voters by convincing them that the candidate understands their lives, communities and the issues that matter to them. To do this they need to connect the candidate to many different issues to target many different groups of people. This is where a highly sophisticated 'ground game' and differentiated media strategy comes into play. The candidate's overall brand provides a framework or umbrella under which many different communication tactics are used. Campaigns need to be able to find ways to speak directly with individuals about specific issues that matter to them and convince them to get out and vote, while at the same time avoiding accidentally triggering issues that will prompt other voters to get out and vote against them. The ground game is a term that strategic political communicators use for the door-to-door and peer-to-peer aspects of campaign communication. Traditionally, the ground game is played door-to-door in local neighbourhoods. Candidates and their local volunteers walk the streets speaking with locals, attend local meetings and public events, and have ongoing conversations. Obama's team used data to both organize the 'real world' ground game and create a new 'online' ground game.

Online ground game

Obama's team greatly refined their publicity machinery between the 2008 and 2012 Presidential campaigns. Perhaps the most notable development was the investment in database technologies, recruitment of data and social media experts, and use of a sophisticated networked ground game. While mass rallies and publicity were central to the Obama brand, where the campaign pushed into a new frontier of campaigning was the use of data to identify, target and mobilize individuals and issues within social networks. The Obama campaign had begun collecting data during the 2008 campaign. In addition to collecting the personal details of supporters who attended rallies, they also built a database of contributors who had donated to the campaign, and volunteers who had signed up to the MyBO site.

MyBO allowed supporters to post their own online profiles so that they could meet other volunteers online. This allowed people to effectively create their own support groups and to plan events like picnics, neighbourhood clean-ups or running phone banks. MyBO also allowed people to download campaign materials and badges to help them organize their own fundraising events or to go out and canvass voters. In this way MyBO bridged the central and local parts of the campaign – enabling local groups to form and campaign in local areas, but making sure they were distributing content and messages from the central campaign. The campaign organized Camp Obama training workshops where MyBO volunteers learned leadership and campaigning skills. The people trained at these workshops became skilled on-the-ground activists who understood how to roll out the campaign in their local neighbourhoods. All this volunteer activity was used to help promote the carefully crafted image of Obama as a 'man of the people' who was not part of a slick Washington-led machine. But, of course, Obama's 'man of the people' campaign was being run by a well-organized professional team who were precisely marshalling the volunteers into a valuable team of voter recruiters.

Obama's team used data to enhance their grassroots effort by identifying which doors to knock on and the specific issues to speak about with the people who answered the door. This data was gleaned from a myriad of databases from market research companies, public and government records, and information accumulated from previous campaigns. The campaign wanted to ensure they knocked on doors likely to vote Democrat, and avoided doors that would be staunchly Republican. Their aim was to mobilize as many likely Democrat voters as possible, while keeping potential Republican voters dormant. They also knew that to mobilize voters they needed to hit the specific issues those voters cared about and even send volunteers that potential voters would identify with. For example, middle-aged women voters would be canvassed by women volunteers who they would identify with. And the volunteers would address issues that the databases had identified voters in that demographic, or even that specific individual, cared about. Sometimes they would talk about healthcare, other times environmental issues, other times tax reform.

This door knocking also fed data back into the campaign machinery. After visiting a house volunteers would use a mobile app to record whether the database analysts' algorithms were correct. For example, if the database had predicted that the targeted voter was a married mother of four who was interested in healthcare the volunteers confirmed whether this was the case. This enabled the data experts to incrementally improve their algorithms and predictions. Furthermore, the data would then shape future communication from the campaign. If a volunteer was told by a voter that they cared about environmental issues, this information was fed back into the database and the campaign would ensure that the next Facebook post or item of direct mail from the campaign would target that specific issue or at a more general level the campaign could learn in real time which issues were important to key demographics, regions or neighbourhoods.

The online ground game was a virtual extension of these practices. Campaign volunteers could connect their social networks to the Obama campaign, enabling their data experts to identify likely voters within their Facebook networks. The campaign would then advise volunteers to target specific friends with highly engaging content about specific issues that mattered to them. A volunteer might receive an email from the campaign encouraging them to post a video from Obama about environmental issues on a specific friend's Facebook page, while forwarding an email about healthcare to another person in their social network.

Using data

This sophisticated use of data meant that the Obama team was working simultaneously at both mass and niche levels. While at the mass level they created a compelling and resonant brand for Obama, at the niche level, volunteers were delivering highly targeted content within their local neighbourhoods and online social networks about a range of issues. For instance, at the same time they were running highly targeted messaging through email, direct mail and social networking sites, they also bought 30 minutes of national network television prime time at the end of the 2008 campaign. No campaign had done this in modern professionalized campaigns because of the huge cost. The prime time media spot was 30 minutes of expertly crafted narrative about Obama's identity, life history and values. This narrative offered a highly resonant background or framework within which niche messages could be organized.

To achieve this highly sophisticated use of data the campaign team worked between 2008 and 2012 to link together all the databases of information they could acquire, and figure out ways to constantly mine those databases for preferences and patterns. Databases were used to integrate communications across all platforms in the campaign – mass media, email, social, face to face, neighbourhoods and outdoor.

Data drives content

Obama's team used data to inform the decisions they made about the creation and circulation of content in three ways:

- *Synchronized*: the campaign could ensure that the messages specific individuals or niche audiences received were synchronized so that over the course of the campaign they heard a coherent and continuous narrative. The campaign could track and control which audiences and individuals received specific messages and at what times of the campaign.
- *Customized*: the campaign customized the messages it sent to individuals and audiences. This meant customizing not only the content but also the delivery, not only what was said but who said it. For instance, the campaign could analyse an online social network and determine which friend an individual would find most credible on a specific issue. As much as possible, they would ensure individuals received messages about issues that mattered to them from friends that they trusted. Or, after knocking on a door and speaking with a potential voter the campaign ensured that the next piece of content the voter received was about the issues they had identified as important to them.
- *Real time and responsive*: the campaign constantly analysed data to drive real-time shifts in the management of messages and circulation of content. For example, during Presidential debates data experts would undertake live analysis of online social networking sites to determine how specific demographics were reacting to parts of the debate, and then respond immediately. Data experts noticed during one of the debates that younger voters had reacted to Romney's 'binders full of women' line. While the campaign strategists didn't recognize the significance of this line at first, the data experts saw the immediate reaction among key demographics. The campaign responded quickly by producing customized content that picked up on the reaction, using the line to frame Romney as out of touch with the concerns about gender widely held by specific demographics. Much of the mediation of the Romney

gaffe was via internet memes – visual images that appropriate 'in jokes' from popular culture. The campaign understood that the best way to generate resonance around this issue was via the jokes young and hip audiences shared online; this would create the impression Romney was out of touch and didn't 'get it'.

Decision making becomes pragmatic, incremental and continuous

Political mythology holds that campaigns are run by highly skilled and experienced political gurus who have the ability to craft compelling narratives and make 'gut feel' decisions about how to frame issues and respond to events. This mythology sits alongside the growth over the past generation of a variety of techniques borrowed from social and behavioural sciences and market research, which attempt to deduce how voters feel about specific issues, images, words or narratives. Focus groups and polling have become central to the decision-making processes of professional campaigns as they test ideas out on voters.

The assembly of massive databases by Obama's campaign illustrates a further evolution in the nature of decision making within political campaigns. Obama's strategists were constantly tracking and mining their vast troves of data to identify issues, trends and niche groups to respond to. Combining databases with interactive customized media they could constantly road-test communication on small test audiences. This meant that messages, web pages and social media techniques could be developed iteratively. This was perhaps most clearly demonstrated in their development of online fundraising appeals. The campaign iteratively developed an easy-to-use donation widget that was incredibly successful. They were stunningly successful in raising tens of millions of dollars in small donations. The widget was gradually developed in hundreds of small steps targeted at different audiences.

They would design a version of the tool – testing out different combinations of words, images, buttons and donation amounts. They would then make that version available to some users, while making another version with a slightly different combination of elements available to another niche audience. They would then see which combination generated the most donations from what kind of demographics. Over time, they developed a range of customized donation widgets that they knew worked effectively for specific targeted individuals. This process was a pragmatic one based on a continuous testing of communicative tools and appeals, and monitoring the responses, to determine what works. The campaign's use of data was not always targeted in finding out or understanding why specific demographics or groups thought specific issues were important or particular messages appealed; rather they were more interested in simply being able to monitor how people act and then make accurate predictions about how they will act in the future.

While the creation of an overall narrative about a candidate is still significant, this is complemented by the increasing use of data to iteratively respond to and manage an array of different niche audiences.

Much of the fundamental actions of Obama's team were not new. They simply deployed a mix of communication platforms known to all professional communicators. However, what Obama's spin

Figure 7.2   Staffers for Obama 2012 in the group's downtown Chicago campaign headquarters

© Ralf-Finn Hestoft/Corbis

team added to this established foundation was the innovative use of a combination of customized and responsive media, databases, online social networks and grassroots participation. They demonstrated how both the internet and databases are another communication tool that professional communicators can use to reach and manage massive audiences. They showed how the internet can be used to simultaneously manage mass audiences, niche interests and even individuals. Their campaign was perhaps the first mass customized political campaign.

Significantly, much of this enhanced targeting appeared natural. When individuals received a Facebook post or a knock on the door it wasn't apparent that the message was specifically crafted and targeted at them. The people being mobilized do not feel that they are being organized, steered or used. This shows the tremendous potential the internet has as a tool to build populism. People who are being steered in a top-down communication operation can actually be made to feel empowered by their involvement in this communication process. This was one of the triumphs of Obama's publicity machine. Millions of voters were led to believe that Obama was not using top-down manipulative communication. Obama was constructed as representing a new kind of politics in which grassroots bottom-up communication empowered the people. The truth was that Obama was the product of a highly scripted and managed campaign that expertly harnessed the participation of many citizens and their social networks.

DATA AND CAMPAIGNING

Watch Obama's campaign strategists Larry Grisolano and Andrew Bleeker speak at the 2013 Kenneth Owler Smith Symposium at Annenberg School of Communication. You can find a link to the talk on the *Media and Society* website study.sagepub.com/carahandlouw

How did Obama's team use data to manage the campaign's communication?

How did the use of data relate to Obama's other communication strategies?

How is data used to change how political campaigns make and manage identities and messages?

CONCLUSION

A wide range of professional communicators are central actors in the political process of networked media-dense societies. These professionals have reshaped the political process both by developing relationships with established media and popular cultural production, and by developing their own publicity, data and participation infrastructure. Strategic political communication is a complex set of techniques involving managing media, branding, marketing and advertising, online social networks, grassroots participation and data.

FURTHER READING

Several of the readings below examine the construction of powerful political identities using media and popular culture. Campus (2010) illustrates how Berlusconi and Sarkozy each leverage and manage a mediatized political process. Part of their success is attributed to their capacity to create attention-grabbing and affective personalities. Pease and Brewer (2008) use data from an experiment to determine how news about celebrity endorsements benefit political campaigns. They examine Oprah's endorsement of Obama's campaign. Kellner (2009) examines how Obama mastered celebrity spectacle. Nielsen and Vaccari (2013) examine the role social media plays in election campaigns. They find that few politicians generate much direct engagement with citizens. Kreiss and Howard (2010) examine the development of a data infrastructure in political campaigns.

Campus, D. (2010) 'Mediatization and personalization of politics in Italy and France: the cases of Berlusconi and Sarkozy', *International Journal of Press/Politics*, 15 (2): 219–235.

Kellner, D. (2009) 'Barack Obama and celebrity spectacle', *International Journal of Communication*, 3: 715–741.

Kreiss, D. and Howard, P. (2010) 'New challenges to political privacy: lessons from the first U.S. Presidential race of the Web 2.0 era', *International Journal of Communication*, 4: 1032–1050.

Nielsen, R. and Vaccari, C. (2013) 'Do people "Like" politicians on Facebook? Not really. Large-scale direct candidate-to-voter online communication as an outlier phenomenon', *International Journal of Communication*, 7: 2333–2356.

Pease, A. and Brewer, P. R. (2008) 'The Oprah factor: the effects of a celebrity endorsement in a presidential primary campaign', *International Journal of Press/Politics*, 13 (4): 386–400.

Any article marked with is available to download at the website **study.sagepub.com/ carahandlouw**

PRODUCING AND NEGOTIATING IDENTITIES

MEDIA REPRESENTATIONS EMPOWER AND DISEMPOWER IDENTITIES.

* What is identity?

* How do media empower and disempower identities?

* How are media used to make collective identities?

* How do marginalized identities use media to make themselves visible?

In this chapter we examine how media:

- Are central to the ongoing process of constructing and negotiating identities
- Offer resources and spaces through which groups seek to develop, resist and reconstruct identities
- Afford certain identities the symbolic resources to articulate their narratives and ways of life
- Produce collective identities that are related to broader political and economic processes.

EMPOWERING AND DISEMPOWERING IDENTITIES

Identities are a means to acquiring and circulating power. The project of constructing and mediating identity is never fully achieved. The mediation of identities is connected with the ongoing formation and maintenance of power relations. Throughout this chapter we develop an account of the struggle between different groups to construct identity and the consequences that struggle has for social, cultural and political life.

WHAT IS IDENTITY?

Identities are living social relationships that we create via our interrelations with the symbolic and material world. Identities are contingent on the symbolic resources they can access. Identity construction is always organized and maintained in relation to political, economic and cultural circuits of power. Below we set out four key characteristics of identities:

- They are embedded within representations and meanings.
- They are social and constructed.
- They are relational and differential.
- They are never fixed, final or accomplished.

Identity is embedded within representation

Identity is the process of locating ourselves within the social world and its power relationships. We do this by drawing on the representations and discourses available to us. Identities are an ongoing process of marking out who we are and who we might become in relation to how we have been represented and what capacities we have to represent ourselves (Hall 1996: 4).

Identity is social and constructed

Identities are social positions that we enact. They are a result of us using representations and making them meaningful within our social lives and worlds. They are the product of us interacting with others to determine what we are and what we are not. We learn to draw on representations that enable us to construct identities that position us in the social world in order to get attention from others and access to material resources and social relations. Whatever identity we create, others will be pressing on it with their own claims and resources. Our identities sit at the intersection between our own individual agency and creativity, and the socially constructed discourses and subject positions available to us. While we are free as humans to imagine ourselves in unexpected and original ways, we are also constrained by the social structures within which we live and the material and symbolic resources that we have access to.

Identity is relational and differential

Identity is dependent on the process of relating and differentiating ourselves from others and their ways of life. Our own identities are a product of our coming to terms with, and never fully reconciling, our difference from others. The performance of our identity is a creative playing out of our differences with others. The assertion of identities is often associated with desires for, anger about and anxiety over other people and their ways of life, experiences and values. Our identity is dependent to some degree on a lack – a sense of what we are not and can never be. This is often felt as a kind of aching or longing feeling in our imagination. What we are imagining often are the affects and feelings we would experience from the different kinds of attention that would come if we occupied a different place in social relations. Identities attempt to fix and naturalize meanings and social relations as part of the play of power relationships. They are interrelated with the broader social and political processes of creating winners and losers.

Identity is never accomplished

Identity is always in process and under construction. Identity is a key building block of human society and history. We use struggles over meaning to organize the social and material world, to decide who gets access to material, social and symbolic resources. Whichever group establishes themselves and their identities as powerful and dominant, other groups will attempt to create identities and subject positions that resist them. People learn when to accommodate their identities to broader social structures and when to resist them. We remake and reconstitute our identities as part of the continual effort to mark out, protect, contest and consolidate our position in social relations.

In the rest of the chapter we unpack these concepts via:

- analysis of the role the media play in constructing and reflecting identity
- examining how the struggles over identities unfold within media-dense societies and are connected to broader configurations of power and access to material and symbolic resources.

MAKING COLLECTIVE IDENTITY

During the twentieth century, media – particularly cinema, radio and television – were used to construct mass national identities (Buck-Morss 2002). Media became the 'cultural mechanism for constructing [the] collective life and culture of the nation' (Morley and Robbins 1995: 10). Media produced nations as 'imagined communities' (Andersen 1983). National systems of media brought into being shared lives across vast populations. Millions of people within an enormous geographical area, who would never meet each other or even see each other, could imagine themselves as a more or less homogenous collective of people with shared visions and values. Nation states are one attempt to contain identities within political, economic and territorial boundaries. Modern media technologies enabled the leaders of mass societies to address the population directly, immediately and over large distances (Buck-Morss 2002: 134). Wherever the dominant ideologies of liberal democracy, socialism and fascism established themselves politically, large culture industries emerged that fashioned corresponding collective identities. Each of these societies attempted to construct and represent a 'mass utopia' (Buck-Morss 2002). The representations produced by media affirmed the dominant ideas and ways of life of those systems.

National media systems established a web of meaning in which to make sense of the material power of the industrial society and its transformation of the natural world. Media invested industrially produced objects like cars and appliances, and built environments like cities and skyscrapers, with meaning. The material processes taking place in the mass society were represented to their populations as expressions of collective values and ways of life (Buck-Morss 2002: viii). In liberal-democratic, socialist and fascist societies broader social, political and economic processes were presented as part of a positive project of creating and shaping the 'good life'. Industrial society promised material happiness for ordinary people within a gleaming and cohesive urban environment.

Cinema and television were critically important in shaping representations of mass society. When individuals all over a nation tuned into a radio station or went to a local cinema – whether they were in a socialist, fascist or liberal-democratic society – they would hear stories about, and see images of, themselves and their way of life (Buck-Morss 2002: 14). The mass media didn't so much tell them what to think, as reflect back at them their own lives – demonstrating to them how they were part of a broader imagined community, how the life they lived was one shared by and no different from millions of other people living over an enormous geographic area. In America Hollywood played an important role in constructing a homogenous national identity out of an enormous melting-pot of immigrants with a variety of cultural backgrounds, values and ways of life (Buck-Morss 2002: 148). Cinema could position a way of life within the common denominator of the American landscape, and the collective effort to civilize and industrialize it. Films articulated a common desire – an 'American Dream' – that individuals throughout the geographical area 'America' could believe in and use to construct their own life. Through cinema people could see how they were a part of something bigger.

The symbolic project of creating a collective national identity is interrelated with the material effort of creating the nation state. For the identities the mass media produced to make sense and to work within the lives of ordinary people, they had to have some real world purchase. Ordinary people had to be able to recognize the reality presented on the screen. They had to both feel the dreams and desires and believe they were possible. If the cinema of Hollywood presented a middle-class suburban dream – a new home, a modern kitchen, an automobile – then reality had to deliver on the promise. For most Americans in the twentieth century they could see some correspondence between the dream presented by the national culture industry and the reality or possibilities of their own lives. For people whose reality didn't correspond they at least had to be able to believe it might be possible for them. Where groups of people felt they were denied the 'good life' presented as intrinsic to the national identity, new identities and resistances emerged. We observe this for instance in the civil rights struggle, where black Americans used political, economic and cultural methods to resist their exclusion from American life and identity. Throughout that struggle, and into contemporary times, we see forms of culture produced by minority identities that point out how they are excluded from the dominant American Dream and over time their place in it. For instance, the history of black American music from blues and jazz to hip-hop is one of both symbolically resisting dominant ways of life and being appropriated into dominant identities. Mass collective identities have given way both because they were increasingly unable to deliver the mass 'good life' they promised and because they were no longer necessary to the political and economic institutions of the nation state. That is, their symbolic power and their material usefulness both faded. In the rest of the chapter we consider largely the emergence of reflexive identities – at macro and individual levels – in a globally connected and networked world.

From the mass to the individual

With the collapse of state socialism and the emergence of global capitalism and neoliberalism these 'dreams of mass collective identity' (Buck-Morss 2002: x) have given way to personal dreams and desires. Rather than imagine ourselves predominantly as members of a collective national identity enacting a collective project of striving for the good life, we now also aspire to more individual and entrepreneurial identities. Rather than form identities that do their duty to the collective nation, media implore us to create identities that seek individual enjoyment, empowerment and satisfaction (Žižek 1999). While we might live within nation states, we are less committed to the nation as a collective project. Instead, we each compete with each other to achieve a sense of the good life attached more to our own individual desires and dreams. These too are often dreams of material happiness, but importantly, they aren't necessarily embedded in a larger homogenous collective national identity.

Just as the large factories of the industrial era are being reformatted as flexible nodes in a networked economy, the large or mass identity projects of the twentieth century are giving way to contingent and reflexive identity processes. Identity is an important resource within a flexible global economy. For nation states, identity is a crucial resource in constructing a brand that enables them to position themselves as a good place for capital to invest, with a stable political system, an educated workforce, an attractive tourist destination and a wealthy middle class. For individuals, identity is an important resource to be cultivated and worked on in presenting themselves as creative, clever and valuable to potential employers, contacts, acquaintances, or even friends and lovers. Identity is valuable because it is the process of articulating ourselves within flows of meaning. In a society and economy that is increasingly informational, positioning ourselves both as individuals and nations within the right flows of information is critically important.

As the media have been reshaped by global network capitalism, national culture industries have been incorporated into global flows of meaning. While local and national identities are still constructed through media, they exist alongside consumer, liberal-democratic and middle-class identities that are constructed from global flows of information. Global media create a kind of virtual territory out of global flows of ideas, identity and capital (Morley and Robbins 1995: 19). Morley and Robbins (1995: 38) argue that as a consequence, for those with access to global flows of media and culture, identity becomes more reflexive. As individuals we mediate between global, national and local culture. Our sense of place is organized within these complex flows. Global media have reconfigured our identities by expanding the flows of meaning we use to position ourselves in the world and the social relationships we consider our lives to be a part of. We are no longer addressed only as members of a collective national public, but also as consumers, global citizens and niche lifestyle groups connected to a global network. We now fashion our identities in a dramatically expanded flow of media content, culture and information.

The reorganization of national culture industries into nodes in a global network has brought to the fore debates about how societies value and construct identities as both profitable audiences or markets and valued ways of life. Where identities are valued as a way of life, but aren't a profitable audience, they are dependent on societies deciding to protect social and cultural space for them. The challenge is that local and national media and identities are embedded within a global network geared to the commercial and political interests of the American culture industries.

Within this global system America is the key node. All significant flows of meaning and identity happen in relation to America. Local and national identities can be articulated:

- alongside and compatible with American values and ways of life
- in distinction from American values as part of an effort to defend particular local or national practices and ways of life
- in opposition to American values: in cases where oppositional identities do not have the power to threaten or gain traction in the global network system they can be ignored or contained; where they threaten to become a powerful node in the global network they are removed from the network using a combination of technical, cultural, political and economic tools.

Most commonly, identities incorporate global flows of meaning within everyday practices. Media plays a crucial role in organizing our domestic space and daily routines and connecting them to larger public spaces and political and social processes. Those spaces and processes are no longer confined to the nation. But we still tune in every day to a media system; we participate in rituals of media consumption that construct shared identities and ways of life. Importantly, we're increasingly consuming a proliferating and fragmenting flow of content. We still feel a part of imagined communities but we see those communities from our vantage point – one of many – in a global network of flows of identity and meaning. Identity is always made within the flow of history, bound up within the political, economic and cultural structures that powerful groups develop.

CULTURAL IMPERIALISM

Global network capitalism has transformed identities and power relationships locally, regionally and globally. Global electronic communication channels are central to both the economy and politics of the Pax Americana. The practices, discourses and power relationships of global network capitalism are unimaginable outside of these communication infrastructures.

Debates about the role of the west and more specifically America in circulating culture date back to the 1960s. Two conceptualizations of cultural imperialism were developed:

- The first argued that cultural imperialism was the result of a deliberate elite conspiracy (Schiller 1969). This account argued that during the 1950s and 1960s the United States had developed a military-industrial complex completely under the control of the federal government in Washington. Schiller believed the 1960s expansion of American television around the world resulted from a planned effort by an American industrial elite to deliberately subject the world to US military control, multinational capitalism and American values. An American elite was seen to be deliberately conspiring to make other nations dependent on the United States, and the world's mass media were being enlisted to promote appropriate capitalist ideology as part of their broader United States military capitalist plan. Schiller's approach required an assumption that the United States' elite was extraordinarily coherent, effective and goal directed. That is, it assumed an elite possessing the competence and capacity to impose its ideological machinery across the globe.

* The second argued that cultural imperialism was a mediatized process involving 'cultural loss' rather than 'cultural imposition' (Tomlinson 1991: 173). This account developed non-conspiratorial understandings of cultural imperialism by focusing on media processes that caused 'authentic local cultures' to be displaced (Boyd-Barrett 1977, Tunstall 1978). Smaller cultures disappeared not because of an elite conspiracy but because they simply could not compete with the dominant global cultural machinery.

The cultural imperialism and media imperialism arguments were developed upon an analysis of the twentieth century's mass culture industry. Where cultural imperialism focuses on simplistic villain/victim dichotomies and conspiratorial explanations, it is not helpful in understanding a networked and fragmented mode of cultural production.

The global media network is used for a number of hegemonic purposes. An emergent hegemonic elite, plus a wider group of second-tier information-rich functionaries and compradors, now use the global media and information network to intermesh with each other. This group is developing similar practices and living environments. Their lifestyles and global cities, from New York to Munich and Sydney to Singapore, are increasingly interchangeable. Although they are not all Americans or westerners, the global information rich appear to be almost universally familiar with western discourses, and are able to use the new global lingua franca of English. The rapid diffusion of western culture is not happening because an American elite is conspiring to culturally dominate others. Rather, it is happening because the global media network is American built; and a globally dispersed Anglophile group exists which wants to immerse itself in western discourse and cultural products. Under these circumstances – English as a coding system – Anglo-discourse and western cultural products necessarily acquire a prestige, status and usefulness derived from their already-existing dominance. This encourages their use by both elite and non-elite non-westerners from Taiwan to Russia. Effectively, the growth of western cultural domination now seems globally unstoppable, not because it is being manipulated or conspired into existence, but because of the perceived centrality of western players within the hubs of global network capitalism. In a sense, western economic and cultural power is so overwhelming in the early twenty-first century that westerners do not have to conspire to be dominant. There are few parts of the world where a functioning elite exist with no connection at all to western global network capitalism. Even in China, the political and industrial elite have created a class of traders who interface with western production, culture and politics.

Western discourses tend to be dominant within global network capitalism's media networks because westerners mostly built the network, and westerners dominate the emergent hegemonic elite of global network capitalism. While western cultural products dominate global media flows, the network has also enabled a flow of content reflecting a plethora of niche identities. Even so, for the most part these niche identities fit within the rubric of global network capitalism's culture industry. Global flows of cultural content generate a number of questions:

- Is global network capitalism simply a form of United States-driven cultural imperialism?
- Does global network capitalism subsume or acculturate other cultures? If it does, what are the consequences?
- Why have some cultures consciously resisted being subsumed – like the French and Afrikaners – whereas others put up little or no resistance or even actively participate in being subsumed via popular culture, production hubs or trade agreements?
- If cultures are seen to naturally absorb outside influences, grow and mutate – as witnessed by western culture itself – why is there concern about preserving cultural formations?
- Which is preferable: having to adapt to western cultural practices and discourses because of inclusion into global network capitalism, or preserving one's culture at the cost of non-inclusion?
- Does the Pax Americana offer no option other than complete exclusion or inclusion?

IDENTITY POLITICS

If the mass utopias and collective identities of the nineteenth and twentieth centuries have become less powerful and useful, identity itself has remained significant and important to contemporary social, political and economic formations. Below we examine several examples that help to demonstrate how identity politics is simultaneously organized from above and below. That is, identity politics is a process instigated and organized by the powerful as a means of maintaining power, and by groups seeking to acquire power by building coalitions and positioning themselves in relation to dominant power structures. We examine the South African Truth and Reconciliation Commission, the Australian Apology to Indigenous People, gay activism and terrorism. While these might appear to be a collection of markedly different identity projects, we argue that they share a common origin in social-democratic politics that emerged in the United States during the twentieth century and spread across the globe.

Throughout the second half of the twentieth century the Democrats in the United States went beyond their working-class support base and effectively constructed a broad-based coalition that cohered around social-democrat goals. In addition to their traditional base of workers, the Democratic Party built a coalition that consists of Jews, Irish Catholics, African-Americans, Chicanos, native Americans, gays, feminists, environmentalists and the emerging middle class of urban knowledge workers. This coalition has effectively adopted a form of negative identity politics based on decon- structing the dominant white Anglo-Saxon Protestant (WASP) identity that dominated American politics, industry and society. WASPs were seen as an exclusive old establishment. The Democrats constructed an alliance of people who perceived themselves as outsiders discriminated against by the WASP establishment. The Democrats engaged in a process of deconstruction that involved demoniz- ing, vilifying and attacking WASPs and seeking ways to dismantle the dominant WASP American culture. To deconstruct the old dominant culture and build a new set of cultural identities and values social democrats had to capture and use media, cultural and educational infrastructure to promote their ideas as universal values.

The United States is at the centre of global flows of culture. The Democrats have had enormous influence with other social-democrat parties around the world. The agendas of this negative identity politics can certainly be found in the UK, Australia and Canada. In the case of the UK the British Labour Party has developed its own version of negative identity politics which takes the form of delegitimizing the old British establishment. Since 1945 Britain's old ruling class have been under prolonged and systematic attack. Their dominance of institutions such as the House of Lords has been slowly dismantled.

In this process British national identity has been reconstructed. In the case of Australia the Australian Labor Party (ALP) has undermined the British colonial establishment associated with the Menzies era. The British and Australian Labour parties and Canadian Liberal Party have consequently played a major role in facilitating the importation of American cultural values in their countries. This process has reconstructed their national identities in ways that have brought American, British, Canadian and Australian cultures closer together.

The power of the United States has also given the Democratic Party, when it has been in power, the capacity to export its progressive social-democrat agenda to countries across the globe. Most significantly, this has seen western interventions to promote agendas of development and human rights. These agendas effectively promote westernization and Americanization by undermining and deconstructing traditional value systems and the identities associated with non-western and traditional ways of life. This progressive westernization is, of course, useful for promoting groups, practices and institutions that support the functioning of America's informal global empire. Media and communication has played a central role in the construction of new identities around the world that align with the interests and values of America and its system of global networked capitalism. Alongside the construction of new identities comes the destruction of old ones. Just as this process has provided opportunities for groups whose interests are aligned with the constructed universal values of America's informal empire to empower their identities, groups marginalized by this system have sought ways to resist. One example of this is the growth of fundamentalist Islam, which in its militant form has adopted terrorism as a tactic for resisting progressive westernization. We have also seen the emergence or re-emergence of conservative, traditionalist or far-right political movements in the United States, Europe, United Kingdom and Australia.

USING APOLOGY TO POSITION NATIONAL IDENTITY WITHIN UNIVERSAL VALUES OF GLOBAL NETWORK CAPITALISM

The process of deconstructing mass collective national identities in colonial societies has involved mediated gestures of reconciliation. Reconciliation and apology are notable post-colonial political gestures in post-imperial societies (Cunningham 2002, Gibney et al. 2008). The purpose of these gestures is to symbolically mark the reordering of power relationships (Thompson 2008: 42). Gestures of apology are part of the process of making and maintaining power. Mediated rituals of apology and reconciliation disempower old dominant identities and empower new western 'universal' identities. The powerful apologize when 'it is in their interests to do so' (Thompson 2008: 45). In some cases a formerly powerful group is made to apologize to a newly empowered group; in other cases a powerful group maintains their power by allowing symbolic space for a formerly disempowered group. Apologies 'order' and 'reorder' relationships between the 'West and the rest of the world' (Gibney et al. 2008: 1). In Australia apology and reconciliation have been used to reorient the nation from an imperial British identity to an identity serving America's informal empire. In South Africa reconciliation was used to legitimize the post-apartheid transfer of power and wealth. Apologies are meaningful to the groups involved, but they also have utility within power relationships (Gibney et al. 2008: 5).

Apologies are an interesting gesture because they mark the transition from one set of identity–power relations to another. In doing so, they demonstrate the role that media play in constructing identities, and how that construction is embedded in power relations. These rituals are less about recuperating or repairing mass collective identity, and instead are aimed at recognizing a multiplicity of possible identities that fit within the universal values of the Pax Americana. Below we consider the South African Truth and Reconciliation Commission and the Australian Apology to Indigenous People. We examine how these processes functioned as media events that construct, empower and resist particular formations of identity.

South Africa's Truth and Reconciliation

South Africa's Truth and Reconciliation Commission (TRC) was an exercise in identity politics. One way of thinking about 'South African-ness' was to be deconstructed so that a new South African identity could be made legitimate. By demonizing and humiliating those who had served apartheid through a carefully constructed televisualized spectacle that ran from 1996 to 1998, the identities constructed by apartheid were effectively made illegitimate. Apartheid had sought to deconstruct the South African state and replace it with smaller states, one for each ethnic group (one for Zulus, one for Xhosas, one for Tswana and so on), and one white Afrikaner dominated state. Under apartheid, Zulus, Xhosas, Tswanas and so on could not have South African identity because they were to become citizens of other countries. Anti-apartheid forces rejected this apartheid vision and insisted on a single unified South African state. By the 1980s a bloody civil war raged between apartheid and anti-apartheid forces. The Truth and Reconciliation Commission built a new South African identity out of constructing this civil war as a struggle between villains (pro-apartheid forces) and victims (anti-apartheid forces). Apartheid had involved the attempt to construct separate national identities for each ethnic group: Zulus, Xhosa, Tswana, Afrikaners and so on. Those who had fought for these separate nationalist identities were paraded before the Truth and Reconciliation Commission as villains. They were accused of using power and violence illegitimately and of human rights abuses.

The Truth and Reconciliation Commission constructed a highly emotive theatre of accusations and confessions based upon a binary of victims and victimizers. Those constructed as victimizers were made to face the accusations of their victims. The Commission presented a quasi-religious form of theatre because they were adjudicated by Archbishop Desmond Tutu. Instead of ending with an execution – as religious inquisitions of the past might have done – the Truth and Reconciliation Commissions ended with a symbolic reconciliation that required the villains to express remorse and beg forgiveness from their victims.

The Truth and Reconciliation Commission was a process of representation within which identities were deconstructed and constructed. The Commission process opened up discourses and subject positions for individuals to articulate themselves within by confessing and asking forgiveness. The Commission closed out other subject positions, and therefore identities. There was no way for those who fought as part of the pro-apartheid struggle to articulate their actions and identity as legitimate. Those watching this theatre on television were left with no doubt that the Afrikaner nationalists who had constructed apartheid were villains and, by extension, that the idea of separate nationalist identities was wrong. Because so many Afrikaners were publically humbled and humiliated by the Truth and Reconciliation process, many Afrikaners reported feeling that their identity was under attack.

The Truth and Reconciliation Commission's theatre dramatized the real transfer of political power – from a South Africa ruled by whites to a South Africa ruled by blacks. The construction of a new configuration of legitimate and illegitimate identities corresponded with a new arrangement of power in South Africa. This was encoded into the way the Commission repeatedly represented 'black victims' being empowered; while former white power-holders were constructed as villains and made to apologize for being 'victimizers'. For many whites the Truth and Reconciliation Commission consequently became a symbol of their disempowerment within a new kind of political system wherein whites were now a permanent minority in a black-dominated polity. On the other hand, for black South Africans, the sight of apartheid functionaries being humbled and humiliated was uplifting and empowering. Essentially, the Truth and Reconciliation Commission served to make black people feel in charge. It was a formal process of media representation that explicitly constructed the legitimate and dominant identity relationships in post-apartheid South Africa. This empowerment of black people, of course, greatly assisted the new ANC government's identity building project. The Commission helped to promote a dominant black South African-ness in replacement of the tribal identities of Zulu-ness, Xhosa-ness, Tswana-ness and so on. One dominant white identity was to be replaced both symbolically and materially by one dominant black identity. The Truth and Reconciliation Commission served both to solidify a feeling of black South African identity, and also to parade across South Africa's television screens the arrival of this group as the new rulers of South Africa. The Truth and Reconciliation Commission served as a vehicle for deconstructing a South African value and identity system that was anathema to progressive social-democrat values. The Truth and Reconciliation Commission had the added bonus of symbolically demonstrating the progressive values of the Pax Americana by empowering 'good' and 'oppressed' black people and defeating 'bad' and 'oppressive' white people.

Apology and branding Australia

In Australia, the politics of guilt and apology emerged around a series of events. In 1992 the High Court ruled on a case brought by indigenous man Eddie Mabo that the doctrine of terra nullius, which held that Australian land belonged to no one at the time of white settlement, was illegitimate. The Court found that native title survived white settlement. In 1997 the 'Bringing Them Home' report detailed how generations of Aboriginal children were removed from their families. The policy was labelled an act of genocide and detailed the continuing effects it had on Aboriginal people and their culture. Throughout the 1990s and 2000s calls for a formal process of reconciliation and apology materialized but were resisted by the conservative liberal-national coalition government. In 2008, the incoming progressive Labor Prime Minister Kevin Rudd issued a formal apology in Parliament to Australia's indigenous peoples.

These processes of legal and political recognition, reconciliation and apology have had profound effects on the Australian identity, and the relationship between white Australian identity and indigenous identity. There are several ways to make sense of these impacts. Some argue that the process of reconciliation erases the achievements of white settlement and makes ordinary white Australians feel guilty about their history and culture. On the other hand, others argue that the process enables white Australians to come to terms with the violent reality of settlement and to go through the process of establishing an Australian identity that acknowledges that history. Some argue that the process of reconciliation and apology is critical to incorporating indigenous people within ordinary Australian life and culture; that it is an important symbolic process in creating indigenous identities and histories that are broadly understood and recognized. Others point out that these symbolic processes are only really meaningful if they are accompanied by changes in the material economic and social circumstances of indigenous people and their communities.

The legal and political events that led to the formal apology have been reflected in media and cultural representations of reconciliation and apology. Since the 1990s apology and reconciliation have been prominent themes in Australian cinema (Collins 2010). Where indigenous people were arguably invisible or passive within the construction of Australian national identity associated with the British Empire period, post-1990 cinema has seen an active engagement with indigenous stories and characters. Baz Luhrmann's film *Australia* (2008) is the most expensive and highest grossing film in Australian history (Connell 2010). The film uses the visual and narrative form of a Hollywood epic to construct a mythological history for the Australian identity. *Australia* attempts to reimagine Australian identity by addressing questions of native title, colonial and frontier relations, the stolen generations and reconciliation.

Using advertising to craft national identity

While cinema has long been recognized for its role in constructing and mediating national identities, *Australia* was also an exercise in branding and promoting the nation. The film was accompanied by a $50 million print and television advertising campaign funded by Tourism Australia that reached an estimated audience of 580 million viewers worldwide (Hogan 2010). The campaign featured *Come*

Walkabout television advertisements produced and directed by Luhrmann using characters and themes from the film. The film and advertising campaign each visualize Australia's empty interior landscapes, presenting them as places of adventure, self-discovery, personal transformation and redemption. In Baz Luhrmann's *Australia* and the *Come Walkabout* advertisements white people are transformed when they recognize the sovereignty of indigenous people and their connection to the land.

Both the film and advertisements work around a gesture where a westerner apologizes by recognizing the sovereignty and connection to land of indigenous people. When they do they are forgiven and transformed, yet retain their wealth, status and power. In the *Come Walkabout* advertisements tourism is not only about pleasure and consumption, it also has a deeper meaning. Connected to the 'Stolen Generations' narrative of the film, it is imbued with a political and ethical content. Tourism is reimagined as an apology. The film invites audiences and travellers to identify their journey as acknowledging indigenous connection to the country and apologizing for colonial exploitation. Westerners implicitly uncomfortable with tourism in a colonial sense – consuming exotic cultures, exploiting the under-developed world, using culture as a resource for individual pleasure and enjoyment – feel more comfortable with tourism in the post-colonial sense as a transformative journey. If apologies are substantially political gestures, here we see how they are also used to connect cultural consumption like tourism to the performance of meaningful political identities.

While the importance of collective national identities has become less important, the importance of nations being able to convey their economic, social and cultural advantages is critically important in a globalized world. National identities may no longer be as important to controlling a domestic population, but they are important for leveraging that population – and its histories, places, cultural products and ways of life – as economic and cultural capital. As nations have shifted their emphasis to competing in a global network they have also developed corresponding communication activities. The crafting of national identity has become explicitly promotional, seeking to position the nation within a global economic and cultural order. National identity then draws both on its history and specific cultural practices, and on the universal values of a global order (such as consumerism, cosmopolitanism and liberalism).

Australia and *Come Walkabout* are both media products that brand the nation by using the identity politics of apology. Where in the past, nations present themselves as mass collectives, in global network capitalism, nations use the logic of branding to position themselves as players in a global networked political and market system. Nation branding is a 'communications strategy and a practical initiative' that 'allows national governments to better manage and control the image they project to the world' (Aronczyk 2008: 42). A nation's brand links it with the 'shared values of a global order' and in doing so necessarily frames the parameters within which the nation imagines and projects itself (Aronczyk 2008). While a nation's brand works to distinguish itself from competitors, it does that by first agreeing to the criteria for a 'good' nation state. Under the logic of branding, national identities become largely indistinguishable. Every nation claims to have beautiful wilderness, wonderful food and nightlife, great cultural institutions, traditional regions and ways of life and so on. Most nations appeal to the world as a place that is open for business, charming and friendly. This is not so much about presenting a distinctive way of life but instead connecting the nation to universal values of beauty, enjoyment and individual fulfilment.

Australia and *Come Walkabout* each stage the recognition of indigenous people that has taken place as the British colonial empire has been replaced with an American informal global empire. Building and maintaining a global empire is a cultural project, which relies on creating identities that share common values and ways of life between people in the empire. Advertisements can appropriate and commodify the nation's ongoing process of identity formation in a canny way. In doing so, they articulate the prevailing political project of the nation with promotional objectives. Mediated gestures of apology demonstrate the importance of identity to making and maintaining power relationships. They produce promotional narratives that the nation's citizens can identify as part of a globalized identity process. They position the nation and its way of life within a networked global political and economic system.

APOLOGY IN CINEMA AND ADVERTISING

In his examination of the politics of apology Cunningham (2002) outlines several arguments against and in favour of apologies. The objections to apology, he suggests, are:

- Apology is absurd if you can't be held responsible for events you apologize for.
- Apology is only a political gesture. It has no consequence and may even be immoral.
- Apology takes the form of *reductio ad absurdum*. If we begin apologizing for historical events, we would never stop because human history is full of winners and losers.
- Apology is associated with an attack on the integrity of the national identity and history.
- Apologies are the product of a 'guilt industry' working in favour of minority groups.

In response, Cunningham (2002) makes two arguments in favour of apology:

- Apologies are symbolically important. They recognize and acknowledge past suffering that lives on in the present. We might not be responsible but we acknowledge how our collective identities and contemporary social relations are a product of the struggles of the past.
- Apologies have utility. Recognition and acknowledgement enables better social relations.

In Australia, all of these arguments have been mobilized for and against an apology to indigenous people since Bringing Them Home put the idea of an apology clearly within the mainstream political debate in 1997. While progressive forces argued for the symbolic and practical importance of the apology, it has also been met with resistance and cynicism. Apologies can be seen as the product of a 'guilt industry' working in favour of those deemed to have been victimized by the old order. Apologizing becomes a mechanism for demonizing former elites and thereby de-legitimizing their discourses.

Prime Minister Kevin Rudd's Apology to Australia's Indigenous People, in part, stated:

> We apologize for the laws and policies of successive Parliaments and governments that have inflicted profound grief, suffering and loss on these, our fellow Australians.
>
> We apologize especially for the removal of Aboriginal and Torres Strait Islander children from their families, their communities and their country.
>
> For the pain, suffering and hurt of these Stolen Generations, their descendants and for their families left behind, we say sorry.
>
> To the mothers and the fathers, the brothers and the sisters, for the breaking up of families and communities, we say sorry.
>
> And for the indignity and degradation thus inflicted on a proud people and a proud culture, we say sorry.

You can find links to the Apology to Australia's Indigenous Peoples and Baz Luhrmann's *Come Walkabout* advertisements on the *Media and Society* website study.sagepub.com/carahandlouw

> How do Luhrmann's advertisements mobilize the politics and gestures of apology?
> How are the apology as a political gesture and the advertisements as a commercial text related? What are their similarities and differences?

Check out some of Australia's post-apology films:

Baz Luhrmann's *Australia* (2008)
Phillip Noyce's *Rabbit-Proof Fence* (2002)
Paul Goldman's *Australian Rules* (2002)
Rolf de Heer's *The Tracker* (2002)
Ivan Sen's *Beneath Clouds* (2002)
Warwick Thornton's *Samson and Delilah* (2009)
Brendan Fletcher's *Mad Bastards* (2011)
The television series *First Australians* (2008) and *Mabo* (2012)
Rolf de Heer's *Ten Canoes* (2006) is significant, as well as being the first feature entirely in an Australian indigenous language.

Adding another distinctive element to post-apology Australian films are the recent ensemble comedies *Brand Nue Dae* (2009, Rachel Perkins) and *The Sapphires* (2012, Wayne Blair). These two films are musicals featuring a cast of indigenous popular musicians.

Many of these post-apology films have acquired critical acclaim and found large audiences in Australia. Critics have argued that these films help to reimagine Australian national identity (Collins 2010, Haag 2010). The narratives and claims of post-apology cinema are contested.

(Continued)

(Continued)

Some praise its engagement with indigenous culture and country and presentation of colonization as illegitimate. Others see it as denying and demonizing the achievements of settler Australia.

Which arguments for and against symbolic apologies do you find plausible?
Compare Kevin Rudd's apology to the way apology is represented in the films and advertisements.
How are apologies a form of identity politics?
How do apologies reflect power relationships between identities?

ACQUIRING VISIBILITY WITHIN THE UNIVERSAL VALUES OF GLOBAL NETWORK CAPITALISM

If so far we have considered how power relationships form, maintain and leverage identity as part of the political, economic and cultural life of nation states, then we also need to consider how identity is deployed within societies by marginalized groups seeking to resist dominant values or assert their own ways of life. Identity-based constituencies have emerged from global network capitalism's facilitation of lifestyle groups, identities and diasporas. The tactics of niche identity politics are used by both the powerful to retain power, and the marginalized seeking to resist or acquire power.

Larry Gross (2001) documents the role media played in the process of gay and lesbian Americans becoming visible in politics and culture. Like other forms of political activism generated by minority identities, gay and lesbian groups recognized and used media as a source of power in a variety of ways. Firstly, they used independent media to construct their identity (Gross 2001). Gay and lesbian identities were invisible in mainstream politics, culture and media. Individuals seized whatever media they could to construct their identity, way of life and values. These publications made identities and structures of oppression visible. They also gave a constructive and positive account of these identities that individuals could relate to themselves. Where mainstream media banned the word 'gay' or use derogatory terms like 'faggot' they made the people and ways of life attached to the term invisible. They blocked the language that might be used to articulate that identity. Independent media responded by deliberately using language that mainstream media ignored. For instance, a private individual might come to see themselves as 'gay' in a positive sense, rather than a 'pervert' or a 'faggot'. In most cases this involved the production of independent newsletters and pamphlets that were passed around local networks. These small-scale publications played the role of providing a 'space' within which gay and lesbian identities could be articulated.

Powerful groups – like government, police and churches – respond to these emerging forms of independent identity making in a range of ways. They can ignore them, monitor and constrain them, or ban them. The degree of response depends on the extent to which these publications threaten to disrupt existing networks of power. Independent publications are a primary building block in constructing a public or counter-public that people can think of themselves as belonging to (Warner 2005: 10). They create ideas, language and identities that people can draw on to articulate their sense of a shared world. Independent publications can facilitate counter-publics that are in 'tension with a larger public' (Warner 2005: 56). They perform the important function of contravening 'what can be said or what goes without saying' and in doing so 'work to elaborate new worlds of culture and social relations in which gender and sexuality can be lived, including forms of intimate association, vocabularies of affect, styles of embodiment, erotic practices, and relations of care and pedagogy' (Warner 2005: 56).

Secondly, gay and lesbian activists used independent media to organize political action (Gross 2001). Independent media were usually embedded within local social networks like activist organizations, clubs or bars. The production of media became a fulcrum for organizing and publicizing other forms of political action. Activists used local publications to organize protests and mobilized targeted forms of action.

Thirdly, gay and lesbian activists sought to challenge mainstream representations (Gross 2001). In addition to producing alternative forms of representation, gay and lesbian people also worked to challenge representations in mainstream media. Gross illustrates, for instance, placing pressure on journalists and news organizations to use the word 'gay' rather than 'pervert' or 'faggot', demanding that television producers and writers create gay characters who weren't presented as victims or villains. Gross (2001: 30) details the history of journalists deferring to official sources – politicians, police and court judgements, medical practitioners, psychologists and religious leaders – to construct homosexuality as problematic. Paradoxically though, in constructing homosexuality as a problem the media were also making it visible. They played a part in creating a discourse around which activists could generate conflict and debate. Mobilizing to challenge the media required gay and lesbian activists to build networks of power that comprised activists groups, while also working to bring other influential actors into their network. As they convinced the American Psychiatric Association to declare that homosexuality was not an illness, or prominent public figures to come out, or journalists to represent their views accurately, they gradually developed a network of power and legitimacy.

Finally, gay and lesbian activists understood and took advantage of mainstream media rituals (Gross 2001). Simply pressuring mainstream media to change their modes of representation would not be effective on its own. Gay and lesbian activists also learned to use – or hijack – media events to make themselves visible. If mainstream media were ignoring gay and lesbian issues, then they would go to events where there were likely to be prominent political and cultural figures and media attention, and stage snap protests.

Challenging mainstream media portrayals of identity

Over several decades gay and lesbian activists and groups developed a variety of ways of using media to make their own identities visible and to challenge mainstream media to recognize them. Identity politics takes place within established networks of power. The culture industry tends towards representing the majority view. Representations of minority identities are mostly produced by the majority for the majority. Gross argues that, 'When previously ignored groups or perspectives do gain visibility, the manner of their representation will reflect the bias and interests of those people who define the public agenda' (Gross 2001: 4–11). As such, they position minorities in relation to their own world-view: as a problem, a victim, an outsider, an oddity, a villain. For minority groups seeking visibility and recognition they often have to proceed by first acknowledging the power of majority groups. For gay and lesbian Americans to be accepted by majority American culture they needed to articulate their common ground as much as their difference with mainstream American culture. They needed to articulate acceptable forms of difference while assimilating themselves to dominant identities and values (Gross 2001: xvi).

In western societies we can see this logic playing out around the gay marriage debate. There is a widely held view that the legalization of gay marriage is inevitable. This view has been constructed not so much by distinguishing gay and lesbian people as a distinct group in need of special provisions, but rather as entirely normal and ordinary people deserving of the same recognition as any other person. For those groups who resist gay marriage this argument is difficult to challenge. They argue that expanding the practice of marriage to homosexual relationships undermines an institution that, although historically constructed, is fundamental to all forms of human society. Those making the case for gay marriage have proceeded by affirming majority power relations. Their claim is not 'Marriage is a hetero-normative institution that should be outlawed'; instead it is 'We're just like you and we want to be included'. Gay marriage is presented as a simple case of correcting a historical anomaly by affording equal rights to all relationships. This closes out the space for debating how gay marriage marks a fundamental change in the organization of human families and reproduction.

Gross (2001) illustrates how over the course of several decades gay and lesbian Americans became visible within everyday cultural and political life. Gay and lesbian people are visible in political and public debate, and issues affecting them are discussed productively by journalists, politicians and other public figures. Thoughtful, funny and well-developed gay and lesbian characters are seen on television and in film. Gay and lesbian people are prominent and proud in sport, music and cultural life. Their identity is a normal and acceptable part of everyday life. This power base gives them a platform for responding to still-existing forms of discrimination and disadvantage they face. But simply being visible and broadly legally equal to all other citizens does not mean their political project is complete.

IT GETS BETTER

Gay and lesbian activists have adapted to online social and identity networks. For instance, technology industry employees made a series of 'It Gets Better' videos assuring young gay and lesbian people that while being young and gay or lesbian can be difficult, especially if you grow up in regional or conservative areas, over time life gets better. The videos presented the stories of successful, well-educated, middle-class gay and lesbian professionals. The videos demonstrated the capacity of activists to adapt their messages to new communication networks and styles by drawing on affective narratives within short videos that could be virally distributed through social networks.

How is It Gets Better an extension of LGBT activism?

How does It Gets Better use identity to make its message powerful?

What makes It Gets Better a creative tactical use of new media and identity?

You can find links to It Gets Better on the *Media and Society* website study.sagepub.com/carahandlouw

RESISTING THE UNIVERSAL VALUES OF GLOBAL NETWORK CAPITALISM

Not all identity coalitions play within liberal-democratic rules. Some identities use global networks and the politics of identity for violence. The beginning of the twenty-first century has been defined by a greater political, social, cultural and economic engagement between the west and Islam. This involves a struggle over power, resources and identity. One way of viewing radical Islam's use of terror is as a form of communicative identity politics. Terrorism is the weapon of the politically weak – those who are so marginalized from the mainstream political process that their identity is one that takes itself to be wholly excluded. This disempowerment comes from feeling that their beliefs and ideas are not heard, and even worse that their world-view is being deliberately marginalized and silenced. The powerful are an enemy who deserve to be attacked. For some people this sense of being silenced by powerful persecutors can generate feeling of helplessness and apathy. For those who become terrorists, the anger and disempowerment does not lead to apathetic victimhood – instead it leads to a drive to do something that breaks the silence.

Terrorists are doers. They act to make their beliefs heard. Terrorism is propaganda of the deed because it involves doing something spectacular in order to draw attention to whatever message the terrorist is trying to advertise. We often think of violent conflict as aimed at acquiring material territory. Terror uses violence for predominantly communicative purposes. The act attracts attention and causes the circulation of meanings and feelings. Terrorism is a form of identity politics that becomes particularly effective in a media-dense networked society. Recent terrorist events in Boston and London have seen terrorists rely on citizens on the street with smartphones to mediate their violent acts. The more people film and circulate images of their violence and its aftermath the more it satisfies their objectives. Terrorists rely on the media to publicize their identities and activities. Like other forms of marginal identity politics, terrorist organizations have been particularly effective at using new forms of interactive and social media to circulate content, ideas and build communities around shared identities and causes. If terrorists are weak politically, they have learnt to exploit the global media's attention to acts of violence as a way of making themselves visible and felt within the everyday life of nations. They have learnt to harness the media system's circuits of attention as a resource for publicizing themselves.

TERRORISTS ON SOCIAL MEDIA

Just like any other politicians, terrorists need to publicize their identities and activities to target audiences. Depending on the audience they can use mass media (like television), social media (like Twitter), non-mediated communication (like executions in a public space), or institutionalized communication (like mosques and churches). Or they can combine these – for example, executing someone in a public space and posting photographs of the executed on Twitter, knowing that journalists will pick these up and distribute them to a wider audience on television.

An example of this was the way Isis terrorists executed Syrian soldiers then posted photos of the mutilated bodies on Twitter. Western mass media then distributed these images globally. Like other forms of marginal identity politics, terrorist organizations have been particularly effective at using new forms of interactive and social media to circulate content and ideas, and build communities around shared identities and causes.

Identify the different audiences with whom Isis must communicate.
Identify which types of messages and which types of media would fit each audience.
Consider other conflicts. How do marginalized groups use a combination of media and violence to be seen and heard?
How do new media technologies change the way terrorists communicate?

You can find links to stories about Isis on Twitter on the *Media and Society* website study. sagepub.com/carahandlouw

THE POWER OF IDENTITY WITHIN A GLOBAL NETWORK

Minority groups that are able to articulate themselves within a broadly liberal, democratic and consumerist mainstream thrive in the relationships of global network capitalism. In an increasingly networked and flexible society, power operates less by enforcing and policing narrow identities and ways of life, and more by enabling and channelling a network of different identities and lifestyles. Minority identities are not a threat to this system; instead they are a crucial and valuable resource. They are both a source of cultural innovation and a potential market. Global network capitalism is characterized by a proliferation of identities that corresponds with expanding media choices and niche markets. Minority groups have found their political projects fit well with a media system that is seeking to package them as valuable audiences. To some extent, political projects around sexuality, gender, ethnicity, religion and race are interrelated with the recognition of those groups by media organizations and advertisers as valuable audiences. Television channels, magazines, films, books and musicians seek out women, gays and lesbians, and ethnic groups as valuable audiences. To gain their attention and allegiance they both represent the identities those groups aspire to, and give credibility and visibility to their political causes. This is not a cynical exercise necessarily, but simply an illustration of the complex nature of power relationships and the way they are informed by the aspirations and goals of different groups of actors.

As much as a proliferation of identity is commercially lucrative, managing identity is now central to the production and maintenance of power. This is evident both within our national life and at a larger global level. At a national level we can observe how mainstream political parties now assemble a coalition of identity-based groups around which they attempt to build coherent narratives. For progressive political parties this is evident in their appeal to a broad range of identities and causes related to sexuality, ethnicity, gender and the environment. For conservatives, a range of traditional cultural and religious values are articulated together. Each coalition of identities – progressive or conservative – is organized within the large neoliberal economic and cultural framework of global network capitalism.

At a larger global level we can observe the United States using an identity rights agenda to build consensus and legitimacy in the developing world. This form of 'soft' diplomacy bypasses traditional or entrenched nodes of power in countries and reaches out to aspirational groups who identify with the values of the United States. As Secretary of State, Hillary Clinton travelled the world conspicuously focusing on talking with women, girls and young people around rights issues. In doing so, Clinton mobilized a global network of activists that shared identity and rights visions. Clinton's diplomacy was matched with State Department investment in youth and identity movements in many countries in the developing world. The State Department provided resources and training to minority groups, young people, and women and girls. In particular, they taught them how to use new media technologies to make themselves and their causes visible, to network with others like them around the globe, and to place pressure on established nodes of power. The Americans explicitly use identity as a conduit for building legitimacy and power within their global network.

We no longer simply construct our identity out of media representations we consume: we are called on to produce and circulate our identity, to position ourselves and make ourselves visible using media technologies, images and resources. This networked system isn't as focused on articulating coherent collective identities, but instead on providing opportunities for individuals to be seen and felt in peer networks. An individual clicks, likes or shares an item of content because of what it says about them. We are able to access media technologies to produce stories about ourselves and our lives. This is visible throughout our popular culture, from the everyday maintenance of our social media profiles using updates and images we create, news stories we like, brands we interact with; through to the rise of influential bloggers and YouTube celebrities who trade on their sense of taste, ethnicity, sexuality and other cultural resources.

The problem with proliferating and flexible performances of identities is that the political power of identity politics loses its purchase. As McRobbie (2004) – writing specifically about post-feminism – argues, an interactive and participatory media and cultural system produces identity politics already 'taken into account'. By this she means that the cultural system acts as if 'equality is achieved' and all that is required for us to be empowered is for us to participate and perform our identities as we desire. This co-optation of identity is demobilizing. Identity becomes less a fulcrum around which we can destabilize and reorganize power relationships, and more a resource that enables and conserves the current communication system and its relations of power. While we may now be empowered to construct and mediate our identities however we like, both relatively free to say what we like and able to access media technologies to publicize our views, those affordances exist largely because – rather than threaten the system – they are its very lifeblood. The continuous performance of individual identity is at the core of interactive media, just as the representation of collective identity underpinned the mass media of the twentieth century.

CONCLUSION

In this chapter we have:

- defined identity as embedded in processes of representation and always under construction
- examined the role of media in manufacturing collective identities
- illustrated how making and managing identity is interrelated with acquiring and maintaining power.

The chapter has traced the arc from the production of mass collective identities in the twentieth century to the contemporary management of networks and coalitions of niche identities. Identity in the twentieth century was more recognizable as an explicit ideological project. Nation states built enormous media and cultural systems that produced largely homogenous collective identities. Minority identities were largely invisible within these systems. Throughout the second half of the twentieth century, the development of a global and networked system of production corresponded with the proliferation of visible and powerful identities. The production and circulation of multiple identities is central to the political and economic functioning of global network capitalism. A networked and interactive media system depends on our constant participation in the production and circulation of identity.

FURTHER READING

Each of the readings listed here takes up themes related to identity that we addressed in the chapter. The reading by Hall (1996) is a foundational reading in understanding the relationship between identity, culture and media. The readings by Aronczyk (2008) and Volcic and Andrejevic (2011) both consider the role that branding plays in the production of national identity. Bratich (2011) examines the role the US State Department plays in promoting identity politics around the globe. McRobbie (2004) considers the possibilities for feminist identity politics in a popular culture that appropriates critique and resistance. Gross (2001) offers a detailed account of gay activism and media in the United States.

Aronczyk, M. (2008) '"Living the brand": nationality, globality and the identity strategies of nation branding consultants', *International Journal of Communication*, 2 (1): 41–65.

Bratich, J. (2011) 'User-generated discontent: convergence, polemology and dissent', *Cultural Studies*, 25 (4–5): 621–640.

Gross, L. (2001) *Up from Invisibility: Lesbians, Gay Men, and the Media in America*. New York: Columbia University Press.

Hall, S. (1996) 'Introduction: who needs "identity"?', in S. Hall and P. Du Gay (eds), *Questions of Cultural Identity*. London: Sage, pp. 1–17.

McRobbie, A. (2004) 'Post-feminism and popular culture', *Feminist Media Studies*, 4 (3): 255–264.

Volcic, Z. and Andrejevic, M. (2011) 'Nation branding in the era of commercial nationalism', *International Journal of Communication*, 5 (1): 598–618.

Any article marked with (symbol) is available to download at the website **study.sagepub.com/ carahandlouw**

CONSUMER CULTURE, BRANDING AND ADVERTISING

BRANDING IS A CRITICAL COMMUNICATIVE PROCESS IN OUR CULTURE, MEDIA AND EVERYDAY LIVES.

* What is branding?

* Who builds brands?

* How are brands embedded in culture?

* How do brands claim to be meaningful and ethical?

In this chapter we:

- Define branding as a social process
- Consider the relationship between brands and culture
- Examine the labour of branding
- Explore the relationships between brands, social spaces and interactive media
- Consider the role of branding in the ethics and practices of everyday life.

WHAT IS A BRAND?

Brands are woven into our everyday life – inscribed on objects that we use, printed on our clothes, visible on buildings, and embedded in nearly every media text we read, watch or interact with. If brands were first found on products, packaging and advertisements, they now roam much further.

They are also much more than just symbols that convey meanings. In this chapter we will examine how branding works as a social process. That is, brands aren't just logos that suggest particular attributes. Brands are continuously created and circulated within culture. They are created out of interactions between cultural producers and consumers.

Brands and mass consumption

Brands and advertisements were crucial to the development of the culture industry. Early brands and advertisements made claims about the specific qualities of products. Typical information in advertisements included the ingredients, quality of the manufacture, the family name and place of the producers, and the applications and uses of the product. These claims all related to specific and tangible qualities in the product. It contained specific ingredients, was from a particular place and had certain uses. The brand was simply a name and logo that enabled consumers to recognize the product as having those particular qualities.

Brands became important when products started moving further and being marketed to wider audiences. Industrialization enabled the production of quantities of goods much larger than local markets required; the development of transport systems like railway enabled those goods to be transported to wider markets; and the development of media enabled messages about those products to be distributed to those larger markets. With the emergence of mass production, markets and media ordinary people began to much more regularly purchase products from producers and places they didn't know first-hand. The brand became a device for enabling relationships of recognition and trust to form over much wider distances. Brands were a way of socially facilitating the market exchanges that technologies like mass production and transport made possible. Brands also played a role in creating and stimulating desires in newly emerging markets. If industrial production and transport enabled a wider circulation of commodities, then mass media enabled the recognition and desire for those commodities. This wider circulation of commodities also brought producers into contact with each other in new ways. Producers of commodities in one area found their products competing with producers from other areas. If you were able to distribute your products nation-wide, then so were your competitors. Your product now sat alongside them in shops and in the minds of consumers. This competition brought forth the need to differentiate products from one another in terms of their qualities.

The interests of manufacturers coincided with the interests of the early mass media entrepreneurs. Manufacturers were looking for ways to make their products known and desired by the larger markets they could now reach. Early mass media entrepreneurs were looking for ways to generate revenue to support their operations. The newspaper business model was built on generating advertising revenue to support their operations. Smythe (1981) asked the question, 'What does the mass media make?' The answer that immediately comes to mind is 'content': the mass media make news stories or television programmes. Smythe though explained that the content is not the product, but rather a part of the process of producing the final product – audiences. The mass media produce and sell audiences to advertisers. More specifically, they sell audience attention. The content is a device that captures our attention, which advertisers will pay for. An important dynamic at work here is that advertisers will pay for certain *kinds* of audiences, namely middle-class consumers with disposable income.

For this reason, many critics have argued that mass media content tends to reflect middle-class life and values. This basic relationship underpinned the development of mass culture in the twentieth century, and that is why brands are so integral to an understanding of media and cultural production. As we shall argue in this chapter, changes in the way brands are made and managed are also integral to the changing functioning of media and cultural production in the twenty-first century. In this chapter then, we examine brands not just as meanings, but as processes that create and exploit audience attention and participation in ways that stimulate desires and facilitate the circulation of products.

Brands are social processes

Brands aren't contained only in their advertisements. While advertising has shifted towards making more associational claims, brands have also moved their production processes directly into the cultural spaces, practices and lifestyles that their advertisements represent. In Australia, for instance, Coca-Cola has screened summer advertisements over a number of years that depict typical Australian summer pastimes like playing beach cricket or going to music festivals. While the advertisements depict these cultural pastimes, the brand also enacts them. In the summer of 2013 they built a large beach – complete with lifeguards, sand, a pool and Coca-Cola – at sports stadiums during summer cricket matches. Images of the beach were part of the television coverage of the cricket match and circulated on social media. Brands don't just represent lifestyles in their advertisements, they also engage directly in those cultural practices. In this chapter we examine how brands stimulate identities and facilitate the circulation of their products as part of those cultural practices.

Brands are social processes. By this we mean that to understand how brands work we need to pay attention not just to texts and their meanings, but also to the social interactions between people of which those texts are a part. To understand how Coca-Cola works as a brand we need to look not just at the television advertisements, but also at the cultural practices it embeds itself within. Importantly, we need to pay attention too to the work that cultural intermediaries – like sports stars, pop musicians and other celebrities – and ordinary people do in making brand value. This can be as simple as using products as part of our everyday life. When we consume a product, wear particular fashions, or use a certain brand of phone or computer, we say something about that brand to our peers. We also say something about brands when we interact with them online, enter competitions, go to branded events, or are visible on our social media profiles consuming or using them. This view of branding draws our attention away from thinking of brands as something that professionals in advertising agencies create, and towards thinking about the work we all do in creating and circulating brands. Brands only create value when they are meaningfully incorporated into our identities and cultural worlds.

The mode of branding we examine in this chapter – one which is interactive, participatory and reflexive – is attuned to the form of global network capitalism we have discussed so far in this book. Global network capitalism thrives on serving proliferating and fragmenting niches. In this system brands need to both position themselves with different appeals to many different markets at once, and be able to rapidly adapt themselves to changing consumer identities and rituals (Harvey 1989, Lash 1990: 41). Brands are also embedded in the production and maintenance of power relationships in global network capitalism. Individuals use brands to communicate their status and social hierarchy.

Fashion, leisure activities, restaurants and holiday destinations are all communicative cultural experiences. By consuming these experiences we construct our identity and communicate it to others.

BRANDS AND CULTURE

Brands began as a device to convey the 'legitimacy, prestige, and stability of the manufacturer; to educate the consumer about the product's basic value proposition; and to instruct on the use of novel products' (Holt 2002: 80). Holt (2002) describes this mid-twentieth-century branding as 'cultural engineering'. By the mid-twentieth century, brands shifted to appeals that were only 'tenuously linked to functional benefits' of products, and spoke instead to people's ideals, aspirations and desires about the 'modern good life'. This mode of branding grew alongside the post-war middle-class boom which for the first time created 'a large non-elite class that had significant disposable income' (Holt 2002: 82), leisure time, and were moving to rapidly developing suburbs. Branding, as we know it today, is a mode of communicating with ordinary middle-class people. Branding is a set of power relationships that manages the desires, identities and practices of ordinary life. In this period brands aimed to facilitate the 'good life' of middle-class suburban homes, leisure time, television and mass consumption. This mode of branding underwent major changes with the rise of the counter-culture in the 1960s. Branding moved from facilitating a mass homogenous suburban middle-class identity to promoting 'the use of consumer goods to pursue individuated identity projects (Holt 2002: 83). The counter-culture posed an opportunity for brands to embed themselves much more directly in the creative identity-making activities of individuals. If branding emerged as part of the effort to engineer collective identities built around the nation, in the second half of the twentieth century, branding became critical to the liberal project of shifting away from collective national identities and towards individual consumer identities. Branding became part of the social, political and cultural process of mediating desire for individual freedoms, forms of expression and ways of life.

Brands have a complex relationship with cultural and social movements. While it is tempting to consider brands as products of mass culture that co-opt organic and grassroots cultural practices, such a view misses a more complex interface between brands and culture. From the 1960s onwards three important changes began to take place in the communicative practices of brands and advertisements. Firstly, brands began to incorporate a critique of the mass consumer society into their claims. This appeared paradoxical at first, that advertisers would promote consumption via a critique of the consumer society. Secondly, advertising began to expose its own artifice. Rather than pretend their claims were sincere and unmotivated by their own interests, brands began to point out to consumers the constructed nature of their appeals. And thirdly, brands began to invoke the popular idea of an empowered and savvy individual consumer.

The popular view of the 1960s counter-culture portrays it as an organic social movement that rose up to challenge the conformity of the mass society and culture industry. Rock music, denim jeans, sexual freedom, drugs and radical politics were all articulated together in a social movement that claimed to press back against the sprawling suburban conformity of post-war America. This symbolic antagonism between the mainstream and the alternative has been a recurring cultural theme for each generation since. The 1990s saw the rise of 'alternative' popular and music culture that was interrelated in various ways with the anti-globalization movement. Cultural scenes of the first decade of this century have celebrated 'indie' and 'DIY' culture often in conjunction with the participatory promise of interactive media.

Each of these movements presented itself as somehow 'real' and 'authentic' against the 'manufactured' and 'oppressive' culture of the mainstream. The counter-culture appeared to threaten the homogenous status quo of middle-American life with its radical cultural and identity politics. The alternative movement at first seemed to rage against the greed of corporate America and the cultural homogenization and labour exploitation of global capitalism (see Klein 2000). The indie and DIY aesthetic of the past decade has been connected with bespoke, handmade, local and environmentally sustainable forms of cultural production and ethical consumption (see Lewis and Potter 2011). Each of these movements positioned themselves against an imagined mainstream by articulating different identities, values and politics. Rather than present a threat to capitalism and consumption, however, each of these movements was in part created and stimulated by corporate cultural production, and proved to be a valuable resource for brands. In many cases their 'counter' and 'alternative' ideas turned out to be conventional and commercially lucrative. We often like to think of ourselves as creative and autonomous individuals rather than passive dupes of the mass society. We need to consider then how ideas and practices like the counter-culture, alternative and indie are embedded within cultural production and inform how brands work. Branding is a significant part of the media machinery that broke down old dominant identities and associated power bases, and reconstructed new ones that aligned with the power relationships, values and ways of life favoured by American global network capitalism.

The creative revolution

The 1960s saw a 'creative revolution' in the kinds of claims advertisements made (Frank 1997). Bill Bernbach at the advertising agency DDB invented 'anti-advertising: a style which harnessed public mistrust of communication' (1997: 55). In his famous campaign for Volkswagen in the 1960s Bernbach's advertisements began to both critique the mass society and call 'attention to themselves as advertisements' (1997: 65). By taking into account the critique of mass society and the public's knowledge of their constructed nature advertisements reflexively said to the audience, 'We know that you know we are trying to persuade you.' Once advertising made this move, it was no longer caught up in trying to construct and protect an idealized artifice. It was no longer hampered by the anxiety of protecting the authenticity and credibility of its claims. It was free to move into ironic, creative, savvy and associational forms of communication.

Anticipating the emergence of networked modes of production organized around creativity and cultural capital, Bernbach was at the forefront of a generation of cultural producers who recognized that organizations and societies were most productive when they encouraged freedom and critique, rather than trying to discipline and control in a hierarchical fashion. Anticipating a form of cultural production that is commonplace today, he reorganized his agency around creative teams. Bernbach propagated a narrative about advertising as a serious creative and artistic endeavour. Bernbach conspicuously constructed a theory of the meaning and value of his work. His public statements, interviews, memoirs, the organization of his agency and the advertisements he produced can all be seen as 'deep texts' (Caldwell 2008) that help us to construct a portrait of how he understood the practices and value of advertising.

Where most advertising agencies worked to standardized processes and scientific formulas and produced advertisements that sincerely represented the mass consumer society, Bernbach and his agency began to deconstruct both how advertisements were produced and the kind of appeals they made. Bernbach was the first advertiser to incorporate a critique of mass society into advertising itself. His advertisements demonstrate how advertising works not only as promotion but also as 'cultural criticism' (Frank 1997: 55). By examining Bernbach's advertisements in relation to the counter-culture, we can see that advertising didn't co-opt the counter-culture as some organic social movement. Instead, the counter-culture was 'triggered as much by developments in mass culture as changes at the grassroots. Its heroes were rock stars and rebel celebrities, millionaire performers and employees of the culture industry; its greatest moments occurred on television, on the radio, at rock concerts and in the movies' (Frank 1997: 8). The same can be said for the alternative culture of the 1990s that couldn't have exploded into a mass movement without MTV, major record labels and corporate sponsors (Klein 2000, Heath and Potter 2005). And again, the indie culture of the past decade is deeply incorporated within corporate production. Brands promote ethical consumption and bespoke products, and interactive media stimulate and profit from more diffuse and fragmented forms of DIY and user-generated production (Andrejevic 2007, Lewis and Potter 2011, Banet-Weiser 2012). Being individual, creative and different is a continuous project. Outmanoeuvring our peers in the game of life and style is hard work. It makes us productive consumers. Advertising constructs and speaks to the savvy consumer. The counter-culture wasn't a threat to consumerism, but instead a productive mechanism for continuously generating ideas and trends. Furthermore, by building self-critique into their claims advertisements could never be caught out not living up to their claims.

Accounts of how brands work need to take stock of the work consumers do in making those associations between the product and the cultural practices in their own lives. Cultural products like films, music, novels and celebrities do the 'ideological heavy lifting. Brands then act as ideological parasites, tagging along on these cultural practices' (Holt 2006: 374). Once brands have established this connection they then expand ideological expression of those myths: they 'proselytise' them (2006: 375). Brands enhance the amplification of certain cultural practices and identities, that might reinforce broader cultural and political ideas, but they are ultimately only made meaningful and valuable from the work of consumers and cultural intermediaries.

BRAND VALUE

Branding is now 'premised upon the idea that brands will be more valuable if they are offered not as cultural blueprints but as cultural resources, as useful ingredients to produce the self as one chooses' (Holt 2002: 83). Based on the idea of offering 'cultural resources', Holt (2002) argues that brands engage in tactics such as:

- Developing ironic and reflexive personas. They distance themselves from being overtly persuasive; they encourage consumers to adapt their claims and imagery; they make fun of themselves, which protects them from critique (critique is taken into account in advance).

- Embedding in cultural spaces and practices. Brands develop relationships with art, fashion, subcultures, sport and music communities. They make themselves an invested part of those practices.
- Brands engage with us as part of everyday cultural practices. Consumers then incorporate brands into their lives, connecting them with their values, practices and identities.
- Brands engage in below-the-line activities that rely on word-of-mouth and everyday interactions between peers.

Holt (2002) suggests that these activities cause contradictions. On the one hand brands present themselves as an authentic and disinterested part of cultural life, but on the other hand we all know their commercial intentions. The result is consumers who are cynical about brands' sincerity. This can manifest itself in forms of consumer activism. When consumers pressured athletics companies like Nike over their sweatshop practices (Klein 2000) they called out the difference between Nike's 'Just Do It' manifestos and its real world exploitation of labourers. Holt (2002) also claims that brands will run out of authentic things to co-opt. Perhaps more important is not whether brands are authentic or not, but whether they attract our attention and whether we engage with them. Brands rely on our creative participation rather than our sincere belief in their claims.

Brands are social processes that rely on the participation of consumers and other cultural actors to create value. They work by 'enabling and empowering the freedom of consumers so that it is likely to evolve in particular directions' rather than impose a 'certain structure of tastes and desires' (Arvidsson 2005: 244). Brands relate to the process of constructing our individual identity. Individual freedom and expression are central to progressive and flexible forms of capitalism that emerged in the past generation. Brands become valuable through the social actions of consumers. Contemporary accounts of branding emphasize the unpredictability of contemporary consumers as they create meaning and take brands in unintended directions (Holt 2002, Arvidsson 2005, Zwick et al. 2008). This unpredictability is both a challenge to brand managers and a source of value. Brands need to cultivate and constrain consumer creativity (Foster 2008: xix).

Brands are at the centre of corporate business strategy. They are assets to be managed (Aaker 1991). Brand loyalty reduces the cost of keeping old customers and attracting new ones. They create value by facilitating a network of meanings that can be realized as economic value. Some of the ways brands facilitate value creation include:

- Brands prompt increasing sales of a product or service. For instance, marketing managers examine how brand activity corresponds with sales growth.
- Value can be accrued in the brand itself where consumers will pay a premium for products they have added value to through their own creative and communicative capacities (Zwick et al. 2008). Consumers may pay a premium for a brand they associate with their identity and values. They may be transferrable from product to product via the brand logo.
- Brand value may be registered in stock market valuations (Arvidsson 2005). In this case, the stock market values both the associations and affects that exist in consumers' minds around the brand, and its enduring capacity to act as a device to realize economic value from a market.

Brands are a device for making value. That value creation process relies on the participation of consumers. In Robert Foster's (2008: 29) formulation, by participating in the production of brands we 'transfer control' over aspects of our own identities 'to corporate owners of the brand, who defend their brands legally as intellectual property'.

Brands do not just promote individual products; they are more broadly involved in the process of assembling markets and contexts for consumption. Brands work over time to accumulate audiences, data and recognition that can be assembled into durable markets. These market structures are stabilized by organizing the economic, political and cultural frameworks that undergird them. Branding involves working to legitimize uses of urban space, the collection and application of data, ways of life and forms of knowledge. In doing so brands have a larger social impact on how we qualify and value ideas, political issues, identities and ways of life (Hawkins 2009).

Brands play a central role in the development of media technologies and products. They invest significant resources into the media industries in order to establish and maintain relationships with audiences. Once, these relationships were facilitated by selling advertising space alongside media content. Television stations sold time in ad breaks. Magazines sold pages between editorial content. Now the production and selling of audiences is much more complex. Media organizations produce content and experiences that construct, maintain and manage the kinds of audiences that advertisers want to buy. Media aren't just responsible for finding audiences out there and attracting their attention; they are responsible for a much more dynamic process of constructing audiences, and shaping and crafting their practices, identities, lifestyles and values. Brands play an important role then in stimulating media organizations, technologies, products and content, because they are always interacting with media organizations and telling them what they want.

If brands rely on our participation, and we incorporate them into our identities and cultural practices, then we need to pay careful attention to the work they do in addition to creating value for their corporate owners. If brands are a part of culture they are part of the way we 'construct our individual lives, our communities, our histories' (Banet-Weiser 2012: 9). Brands that are open to critique, point out their own construction and rely on consumer participation are fit for a mode of production that doesn't try to transmit messages in a linear fashion, but instead negotiates, reappropriates and circulates meaning as part of larger cultural processes. Brands then don't seek to create and control messages, but rather to facilitate affective relationships as part of cultural life. In this cultural context, 'critique and commentary about branding in advanced capitalism do not lessen the value of the brand but rather expand it as something that is ambivalent, a recognisable part of culture, indeed a recognisable part of ourselves' (Banet-Weiser 2012: 92–93).

THE LABOUR OF BRANDING

Branding involves the labour of an array of communicative and creative professionals.

Analysts, researchers and communication professionals

Modern marketing and branding was first institutionalized with the scientific management and economic disciplines of the early twentieth century. Marketing aimed to rationalize supply and distribution processes. From the mid-twentieth century, marketers developed research and analytic techniques for segmenting and targeting markets with particular messages and products. With the relationships between consumption and everyday life that developed in the post-war societies, marketing began to engage with psychological, sociological and cultural approaches. Today, branding requires an array of technical and cultural experts: economists, data experts, distribution and logistics engineers, sociologists, psychologists and anthropologists. All of these professionals design branding as an ongoing system of conceptualizing, stimulating and managing consumer demand. Within this system of branding, advertising creatives and public relations professionals play a critical role in translating brand strategies into symbols and meanings that will attract the attention and resonate with identified target audiences.

Designers

The design of products themselves and spaces of consumption have been incorporated into the process of branding. As brands have become more than just logos that are attached to products, designers have become critical to designing products that embody brand identities and creating social spaces within which brands can be created and performed by service staff, cultural intermediaries and consumers. Think for example of how critical the design of Apple devices is to the meaning, legitimacy and value of the brand. The functionality and appearance of the device communicates the principles and values of the brand.

Designers are also involved in the creation of 'servicescapes' and 'brandscapes' (Sherry 1998, Thompson and Arsel 2004) where the brand is performed by service personnel, cultural intermediaries and consumers. Brands like Starbucks are constructed via the branded space of their chain stores. Designers create stores that not only efficiently manage the production of the product and service, but also create a cultural ambience for the brand. The Starbucks store produces both a cup of coffee and a social context within which the coffee is consumed as the customers sit, chat or use the free WiFi.

Front-line staff

In service-and experience-oriented economies the aesthetic and emotional labour of employees who interact with consumers is also important in performing the brand. In addition to making the basic product or providing the service (like making and serving the cup of coffee), they engage too in emotional, aesthetic and affective forms of labour that mediate the exchange. Retail and customer service staff are front-line embodiments of the brand (Pettinger 2004, Parmentier and Fischer 2011). Fashion chains employ staff who are good looking and have personalities that match the brand, and mandate that they wear clothes in keeping with the brand image. They are required to engage with customers in ways that perform the personality of the brand.

Cultural producers

Brands rely on cultural intermediaries like musicians, actors, celebrity chefs and fashion bloggers to create value. These cultural producers deploy their identity, and the attention they attract, to embed the brand within their lifestyle and social networks. This can be as subtle as wearing certain clothes or using a device in public. Or it can be more detailed like direct endorsements of brands as part of their own cultural production. The celebrity chef Jamie Oliver is a personal brand in his own right; in his sponsorship deals and television programmes he cross-promotes other brands by incorporating them into his narratives about cooking good food at home. Brands increasingly engage with cultural intermediaries to produce branded content. Sainsbury's contracted Jamie Oliver to produce recipes and cooking tips using products from their store. In the fashion industry, brands increasingly cultivate relationships with leading style-bloggers who are highly influential with hipster audiences.

Consumers

Brands engage consumers in the creation and circulation of brand messages. While consumers have always added meaning to products and services by incorporating them into their everyday life, brands invest resources in engaging with consumers in cultural spaces and encouraging them to circulate content on their social media profiles.

BRANDS, SOCIAL SPACE AND PARTICIPATION

Brands engage with consumers by offering cultural resources and experiences that encourage their active participation in meaning making. Everyday life is increasingly characterized by social and cultural spaces where we are invited to interact with brands. Retail spaces like Apple and Starbucks stores are designed as branded experiences; online spaces like Facebook, and public cultural spaces like music festivals and sports events, are all places where we engage with brands within our every-day lives. Branded spaces are designed to anticipate and harness the creativity and innovation of consumers (Moor 2003: 58). Analysing a Guinness-branded music festival in Ireland, Moor (2003) explains how participants create and then embed the brand into the social enjoyment of music.

Where brands use culturally embedded strategies they rely less on telling consumers what to think or believe, and more on creating and managing social spaces where they anticipate and harness the freedom and creativity of consumers. The capacity to channel and cultivate consumer participation is greatly enhanced by a networked and interactive media system that can watch and respond to consumers in real time. While participants in interactive media and branded social spaces are free to create meanings, identities and social relations, they do that within communicative processes con-trolled by media organizations and brands (Andrejevic 2011: 287). The more they participate, the more their communicative and social capacities are rendered visible and appropriable by brands.

Brands at cultural events

At music festivals – like Lollapalooza and Coachella in the United States, Glastonbury and Reading in the United Kingdom, and Splendour in the Grass in Australia – the production of brands is incorpo-rated into the enjoyment of popular music and culture. Music festivals are a productive site for brands because music fans use the festival to circulate and mediate their identity and cultural practices using smartphones and social media. Popular music plays the role of stimulating a circulation of memories, emotions and feelings between people. Popular music is part of our practices of giving and gaining attention (Meier 2011). Festival attendees use their smartphones to create and circulate images that position them within a flow of content related to the festival. The festival offers a set of cultural resources audience members use to portray and position their identity within the network of hundreds of thousands of images, updates, likes, comments and tags generated by the thousands of festival goers. These images are part of the story they tell about themselves and their enjoyment of the festival.

Splendour in the Grass is a music and arts festival held in Australia. The festival features music performances by international acts and an extensive arts programme. Partnering alcohol brands build large themed bars where they attract festival attendees to drink, dance, socialize, take photos and circulate them online. These themed bars are woven into the festival experience. The festival assembles a productive audience, cultural resources and brand activations within a purpose-built social space. In recent years, Smirnoff built a multi-level cocktail bar, Jägermeister a hunting-lodge-themed bar, and Strongbow a bar on the deck of a large antique sailing ship. The themed nature of these spaces weaves the brands into the way fans enjoy and remember the festival. For instance, sitting on the deck of the Strongbow ship, audience members could drink cider, watch the bands and imagine themselves sailing through the festival. The branded spaces contribute to feelings of wonder, fantasy and enjoyment as they drink, relax, dance and socialize. Festival goers engage with these branded spaces as part of their movement through a wonderland experience composed of affective engagement with each other, mood-altering substances, and music and arts performances.

The brand activations are part of the atmospherics and memories of the festival. Festival goers incorporate them into the flow of images they create and circulate online using their smartphones. The brands get caught up in a network of images of festival goers, musicians, artists and performances. In mediating their own identity as part of the cultural schema of the festival, consumers also create value for brands. To create an image using a smartphone, festival goers use their capacities to observe, judge and affect one another. After capturing the image they crop it and add filters that articulate its mood, and they log hashtags that position it within social networks online. They watch the flow of images they contribute to, adding information to them in the form of likes, shares and comments. These practices create valuable attention and data, which begins in the first instance with the festival goer using their creativity to capture images and circulate them through social media.

The music festival and its partnering brands create a material cultural space that brings together cultural experiences and resources that festival goers use to curate and structure as flows of images on social media. Contained within the fences of the music festival are not just performances and brand logos but a productive audience who use their smartphones to position themselves within a flow of images. The circulation of images reproduces the cultural schema of the festival and its sponsoring brands. They link together their own identities, cultural performances and brands. Brands also employ photographers who take photos of audience members and upload them to Facebook. In addition to creating themed spaces with brand logos, they also hand out branded items like sunglasses, bags, beach balls, blow-up couches, t-shirts and so on that also get captured in the thousands of images circulated by the audience at the festival. These images become micro-advertisements that connect the brand to many different identities and their online social networks.

As festival goers participate in branded spaces and use their smartphones to record those experiences on social media they craft a network of shared associations, dispositions and affects that are valuable to brands. The images have a double function:

- As content that connects together the brand, a cultural experience and their identity. The images circulate highly credible brand messages through online peer networks.
- As devices that generate data within the databases of social media. As images circulate, friends view, click, like, tag, share or comment on them. Each of these interactions generates valuable data for social media platforms and brands. Over time, brands develop profiles of the kinds of people that attend music festivals and engage with branded spaces. This enables them to design and target future engagements with cultural spaces and audiences.

Brands that create value by establishing and managing social spaces and processes appear to be able to adapt to the creative meaning-making activities of consumers. Through these spaces and activities brands create value by enabling and managing consumer participation with cultural resources and purpose-built social spaces (Holt 2002, Moor 2003, Thompson and Arsel 2004, Arvidsson 2005, Foster 2008).

Brands and mobile media devices

Within social spaces like music festivals we can see how cultural experiences, smartphones and social media are assembled in the creation of an open-ended form of branding. This mode of branding brings together 'soft', culturally embedded activities with 'hard', calculative and predictive analytics. The brand engages with the cultural experiences of consumers; this prompts them to create media content that is registered online where it generates data that is used to assemble and manage markets. Brands connect together real-world cultural spaces with the technical capacities of interactive media. This enables them to develop brands as 'devices for the reflexive organisation of a set of multi-dimensional relationships' between brands, culture and people (Lury 2009: 69). The brand is not only, or even primarily, a symbol representing a particular meaning; instead, it is a device that assembles ongoing relationships between people, places, experiences and products. The brand becomes coextensive with the social relations it stimulates and manages.

The creative participation of consumers and cultural intermediaries creates value even 'where their experimentation and innovation is "resistive in nature"' (Zwick et al. 2008: 168) because value is made via the capacity of individuals to affect one another, rather than adhere to specific meanings. Brands rely less on particular representations of authentic, cool or counter-cultural values. Instead, authenticity is grounded in the capacity of participants to animate affective connections and circuits of attention and recognition (Taylor 2007, Meier 2011). As far as the creation of brand value is concerned, authenticity is simply the capacity of popular music to establish an affective link between the brand and target market (Meier 2011: 409). The brand doesn't attempt to appropriate some particular meaning, but instead to position itself within cultural practices and circulation of affect and meaning that changes continuously.

THE MERCHANTS OF COOL AND GENERATION LIKE

The media critic and filmmaker Douglas Rushkoff has made two films about branding and promotional culture. The first film, *The Merchants of Cool* (2001), examined the emergence of 'coolhunting' as part of brands' efforts to make themselves a part of constantly-evolving frameworks of meaning. The second film, *Generation Like* (2014), examines how social media have evolved into a platform for harnessing the productive activities of fans in the publicization, promotion and branding of products.

Both films can be watched online at the PBS website (www.pbs.org). You can find links to these films and other resources about brands and culture on the *Media and Society* website study.sagepub.com/carahandlouw

What is coolhunting? What are the limitations of coolhunting?

What does coolhunting tell us about the relationship between brands and culture?

How have brands adapted to social media?

Select brands that you use or are familiar with. How are they embedded within your everyday life, cultural practices and identities?

Imagine you are a brand but you cannot make advertisements or buy advertising space on television, newspapers or magazines. How would you build and manage the brand?

What kinds of information and data would you need about consumers and their lives to manage the brand?

How would you collect and analyse information about consumers to manage the brand?

What kinds of cultural intermediaries would you need to work with to promote the brand?

How do brands make use of social and mobile media to engage us in everyday life?

ETHICAL BRANDS AND EVERYDAY LIFE

In this chapter we've conceptualized brands as social processes. We've claimed that they are embedded in culture, rely on the participation of cultural intermediaries and consumers, draw on critiques of the mass society and draw attention to their own appeals. Once brands are embedded into everyday life and culture, they become part of the way we construct our everyday practices, ethics and politics. They become one of the resources we use to make our lives meaningful. Brands now make claims about their broader role in society and their environmental, ethical and political standpoints. This is just as much a deliberate commercial strategy as it is a consequence of brands' more complex engagements with culture. For brands to engage in cultural and identity-based forms of communication they inevitably end up making claims about the things people care about in their everyday lives. This sets in motion a series of consequences. As much as brands profit from their engagements with culture, they are also accountable to them. Consumers and citizens expect them to match up to the cultural and ethical claims they make (Klein 2000, Lewis and Potter 2011, Banet-Weiser 2012). Banet-Weiser (2012) suggests that one consequence is a more ambivalent relationship between consumers and brands. On the one hand we use and engage with them every day, we find them meaningful, we agree with the ethics of some of the claims they make. On the other hand we are frequently cynical and dismissive of their sincerity, motivations and intentions.

Žižek (2010a: 53) draws our attention to the ethical claims embedded in everyday practices of consumption. He suggests that a traditional way of thinking about philanthropy and charity held that some individuals were wealthy and powerful. They used that wealth and power to donate to causes they believed were important. The powerful were patrons of causes that they either cared about or believed were important. 'In the morning', Žižek (2010b) argues, the wealthy 'grab the money, in the afternoon [they] give half the money back to charity.' In today's capitalism, how-ever, 'When you buy something your anti-consumerist duty to do something for others is already included into it.' He offers the example of Starbucks' claim that: 'It's not just what you are buying, it's what you are buying into ... when you buy Starbucks, whether you realize it or not, you are buying something bigger than a cup of coffee. You are buying into a coffee ethics. Through our Starbucks Shared Planet program we purchase more Fair Trade coffee than any company in the world, ensuring the farmers receive a fair price for their hard work, and we invest in and improve coffee growing practices and communities around the globe'. Žižek describes this as 'cultural capitalism'. Consumption is an ethical, symbolic communicative act: 'You don't just buy a coffee; in the very consumerist act you buy your redemption from being only a consumerist.' This form of branding aligns with the progressive social-democrat values that construct 'capitalism with a human face' and position identity-based forms of consumption as acts that express the values of global network capitalism.

The ethical consumer

Writing about Fairtrade coffee shops where customers choose where the profits will be donated from each cup of coffee, Lewis and Potter (2011: 4) argue that 'Attempts by social justice-oriented businesses to reconfigure the privatized moment of spending as a communal act, thus positioning consumer choice as a site of responsibility, are increasingly commonplace in today's marketplace.' Ordinary everyday life is beset by questions and decisions that seem attached to larger ethical and political concerns. Purchasing goods and services is more than just about satisfying our demands for the necessities of life; it has become a social and political act that constitutes our identities, social worlds and power relationships. We now feel we need to mark out who we are, what we value and what kind of society we want via our consumption practices. Our everyday lives seem connected to larger 'community, national and global concerns' (Lewis and Potter 2011: 10).

The flexible and networked society of global capitalism poses new kinds of ethical questions and political possibilities. Our ethics are no longer moored in traditional communities and moral codes, but in everyday choices we make in a reflexive communicative network. Buying a coffee or a bottle of water becomes an act that says something about the fate of natural resources and labourers in the developing world. As global network capitalism creates new kinds of connectivity, we develop new ways of understanding our place in complex networks. As much as brands make claims about their ethics, those claims make consumers aware that products don't just have particular attributes they desire – those objects themselves are part of a network of social and material relations. Our decision to purchase a coffee isn't just about the taste, but also about the ethics of its production, as well as the ambience, affects or meanings of consuming it in the store, office or as we walk through the city. In a networked consumer society, responsibility devolves to every individual in the network. Consumption becomes a symbolic communicative act marking out not just what we want, but how we understand our place in the social world, what our values are and how we want to be seen by others.

Brands stimulate and manage ethical consumption. Ethical consumption displaces collective action as a means of shaping the kind of society we want to live in in favour of individual and private choices (Potter 2011). Ethical consumption invites consumers to 'work on themselves' at the same time as they monitor corporations' values and practices (2011: 119). When we purchase a bottle of water that claims to donate money to clean water projects in the developing world we both mark out our own values and send a message to the network or market about the kinds of products we desire. We communicate our ethics via our consumption. In doing so though we also add qualities and value to brands by making them ethical and meaningful (Foster 2008, Potter 2011).

On the one hand where a bottle of water or a cup of coffee claims to us that it will contribute to clean water or sustainable production, it works as a sincere ethical claim. On the other hand, Žižek (2010a) provocatively suggests that despite the apparent sincerity of ethical consumption, we are in fact often cynics. That is, we know the bottle of water or cup of coffee won't actually fix the problems in the developing world. We aren't naïve enough to believe that disposable bottles of water and coffee cups could ever be environmentally sustainable. But these acts of consumption make us feel good. They help us build an identity that works for us, positions us in our social networks and makes life enjoyable. So we do them anyway. Regardless of whether our thoughts about ethical consumption are sincere or cynical, by participating in it we validate the idea that we must act. Brands encourage us not to think but to act. Ethical consumption is an important part of the way network capitalism functions. Ethical brands produce 'capitalism with a human face'. Žižek agrees that helping others and protecting the environment are good causes, but in appending these principles to brands we obscure how global network capitalism causes many of these problems in the first place.

The 'ethicalization' of everyday life

In the famous 'chicken' scene in *Portlandia* – a satire of hipster life in Portland, Oregon – contemporary anxieties about ethical consumption are astutely skewered. A couple ask a waiter in a restaurant about the chicken on the menu. The waiter tells them, 'The chicken is heritage breed, woodland raised chicken, that's been fed a diet of sheep's milk, soy and hazelnuts.' The diners continue to enquire about the chicken: Is it local? Is it organic? Are the hazelnuts local? How big is the area where the chickens are able to roam free? Taking their enquiries seriously, the waiter goes away and returns with a biography of the chicken including a photo and life story. She tells them, 'The chicken you will be enjoying tonight … his name was Colin, here are his papers.' The waiter assures them the farm does a lot to ensure the chickens are happy. The couple make further enquiries about the farm and its owners, telling the waiter, 'It tears at the core of my being someone just cashing in on a trend like organic.' The diners then ask if the restaurant will hold their seats while they go to the farm to check on the living conditions of the chicken before placing their order.

The scene is a satire of the 'ethicalization' of everyday life and the 'reflexive doubt' (Dean 2010) that characterizes ethical consumption. As much as we feel compelled to consider the ethical consequences of our everyday life and consumption, we simultaneously are unable to make any firm judgements. We are encouraged to be informed consumers, but the networked society's modes of production and communication are so complex and fragmented that we are unable to get and assess information. Faced with decisions like this we become anxious, static or cynical. This leads us to be increasingly dismissive or anxious about the consequences of our choices. Brands' ethical claims conceal their role in stimulating these anxieties as much as offering solutions to them. As much as brands' ethical claims respond to consumers' demands for more responsible forms of production, they also construct and anticipate them.

In this chapter we've examined how brands facilitate cultural and communicative practices. Branding appears to be part of the communicative logic of global network capitalism. It is a series of symbols, social spaces and processes embedded into our everyday lives, politics and culture. We live in a 'promotional culture' (Wernick 1991) that informs how we think about our lives, politics and societies. We are each engaged in the day-to-day promotional work of positioning ourselves in networks of communication and production.

BRANDS' STORIES ABOUT THEIR ETHICS AND VALUES

Apple is one of the most valuable brands in the world. It was initially built on positioning itself in relation to 'cool outsiders' who identified with progressive political and identity narratives. The Apple brand of the early 1980s positioned itself by drawing on the 'mass society critique'. The famous '1984' advertisement depicted a homogenous mass watching an anonymous figure speak at them. The imagery conjured up the mass society idea of a passive audience consuming content. A woman arrives and throws a sledgehammer through the screen, blowing it up. A voice-over tells us, 'On January 24th Apple Computer will introduce Macintosh. And you'll see why 1984 won't be like "1984".' The advertisement promised that Apple would 'break' the dystopian mass society depicted by Orwell in his famous novel. Apple's brand narrative used the counter-culture mythology to position its

(Continued)

(Continued)

customers as creative, independent and autonomous. While everyone else was watching TV, Apple consumers were creating the future.

Apple relied on its passionate consumers to embed the brand in their cultural narratives and identities. Apple consumers presented themselves as intelligent, savvy, urban hipsters. They worked in cool creative jobs in hip cities and shared progressive cultural and political values. As much as the Apple brand was created with clever product design and advertising, it was also created by strategically managing its hip adopter-elite. Online communities and influential bloggers were part of the development of the Apple brand (see Muniz and O'Guinn 2001). Over the past decade Apple has rapidly risen from a niche brand to a market leader. This has presented Apple challenges as it tries to manage an adopter-elite niche market segment alongside a mass consumer market. The Apple flagship stores have been an important part of this strategy. The stores are a material space that embody the brand for the mass market. Ordinary consumers can go to these stores to speak with Apple experts at the stores' Genius Bars. These stores are important material 'brandscapes' (Thompson and Arsel 2004) where the brand is performed and materialized. Apple also uses stage-managed product launches to generate discussion among technology journalists, bloggers and adopters.

The Apple brand is not just made in its advertising and stores: the use of the products by consumers and cultural intermediaries, and the way those products are organized within an Apple ecosystem, also build the brand. The ecosystem organizes consumer interaction with the product within a network wholly owned and controlled by Apple.

In recent times, Apple has also had to contend with an identity crisis as consumers perceive a gap between the clean, innovative and ethical brand rhetoric and the production conditions in Chinese factories, and the control of innovation through its closed eco-system, application and content stores. In these instances we can see what Banet-Weiser (2012) calls the 'ambivalent' nature of brands. On the one hand Apple connects with things we believe in, on the other hand it embodies the contradictions of the globally networked consumer society. The brand is a device for managing a globally networked information business – a way of articulating production and consumption together in profitable ways.

Consider some of your favourite brands today. How do they both celebrate and critique the mass society?

How is today's mass society different from the one imagined by Orwell, or the mass society of the mid-twentieth century?

What are Apple's brand values?

How does Apple prove or demonstrate those values?

How do their narratives develop over time?

Examine the ethics, responsibility and Fairtrade policies of brands that you use. You can find links to policies and other resources about ethical brands on the *Media and Society* website study.sagepub.com/carahandlouw

What claims do brands make about citizenship?

What forms of citizenship do they offer consumers?

How do brands make purchasing goods and services meaningful?

What does buying an ethical brand communicate about you?

What impact does buying an ethical brand have on our society?

What contributions do ethical brands make to society?

Are contemporary brands that offer us ways to convey the environmental, social and cultural causes that matter to us better than brands that simply offer us qualities within the product and service?

CONCLUSION

In this chapter, we considered how brands work as a social process. Brands only become meaningful and valuable when we interact with them, incorporating them into our identities, cultural practices and social lives. While we can determine their efforts to take advantage, stimulate, amplify and even exploit particular identities and practices, we can also sense their possibilities and limitations. They don't exert control over us, but they do structure the social spaces and processes in which we relate to each other. Cohen (1963) argued that mass media don't tell us what to think, but do tell us what to think about. The interactive and participatory forms of branding we have examined here follow a similar logic: they establish the communication spaces and processes within which we construct our identities. As brands have become more open-ended and participatory processes, and as our media systems have become more interactive, brands have become more embedded in our everyday cultural practices.

Examining the contemporary processes of branding helps us to consider how the identity and communicative work of ordinary individuals is increasingly important to how media functions to create and maintain power relationships. It doesn't work only by telling ordinary people what to think and do, but by constructing their action and participation in particular contexts. Ordinary people and the way they communicate and live their lives are very important to the production of brand value. Their communicative and identity-making capacities need to be incorporated into the social process of branding. Their identities take on the features of brands, and vice versa. Banet-Weiser (2012: 43) argues that brands rely on our labour, and that labour is the capacity to produce affective relationships around brands. This makes brands flexible and ambivalent. They are not monolithic objects, but adaptive social processes.

Brands offer us opportunities and resources to express ourselves and make our identities visible to others. As we become engaged in the process of connecting self-expression to the creation of brand value, we may also become less engaged in forms of communication directed towards encountering others (Chouliaraki 2013). Brands invite us to reflect on the self rather than encounter the experience of others. As brands incorporate ethical duties and claims into the forms of participation they offer us, we use them as devices for expressing our own values. In the process, we make brands meaningful, durable and ethical parts of our cultural world, and we format our identities within the logic of brands. This neuters processes by which we might encounter others and reflect on our role in global processes of consumption (Chouliaraki 2013). In this chapter, by examining brands as a social process, we've considered how promotion and participation are practices central to the functioning of the globally networked media system.

FURTHER READING

The readings by Banet-Weiser (2012) and Holt (2002) are useful in charting the development of brands that are embedded within culture, rely on the participation of consumers, and adopt savvy and ironic dispositions. The reading by Holt (2002) in particular charts the transition from branding as a mode of 'cultural engineering' to a more open-ended and participatory process that draws on cultural life. Meier (2011) explores the connections between branding and popular music. Meier offers critical arguments that consider how authenticity functions within commercial popular culture. The readings by Banet-Weiser (2012), Chouliaraki (2010) and Lewis (2008) each examine the interrelationships between promotion and branding, culture, politics and ethics. They address themes related to ethical consumption, humanitarianism and activism within a commercial popular culture.

Banet-Weiser, S. (2012) *Authentic TM: The Politics and Ambivalence in a Brand Culture.* New York: NYU Press.

Chouliaraki, L. (2010) 'Post-humanitarianism: Humanitarian communication beyond a politics of pity', *International Journal of Cultural Studies,* 13 (2): 107–126.

Holt, D. B. (2002) 'Why do brands cause trouble? A dialectical theory of consumer culture and branding', *Journal of Consumer Research,* 29 (1): 70–90.

Lewis, T. (2008) 'Transforming citizens? Green politics and ethical consumption on lifestyle television', *Continuum: Journal of Media & Cultural Studies,* 22 (2): 227–240.

Meier, L. M. (2011) 'Promotional ubiquitous musics: recording artists, brands, and "rendering authenticity"', *Popular Music and Society*, 34 (4): 399–415.

Any article marked with ⊗ is available to download at the website **study.sagepub.com/ carahandlouw**

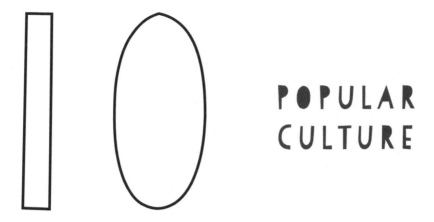

POPULAR CULTURE

POPULAR CULTURE IS INTEGRAL TO THE CREATION OF MEANING AND EXERCISE OF POWER.

* How are power relationships represented in popular culture?

* How does popular culture provide instructions for everyday life?

* How do powerful groups use popular culture?

In this chapter we consider the uses of popular culture:

- Crafting and mediating identities and social life
- Making sense of social reality
- Making value from the mediation of identity
- Mediating political participation
- Managing power relationships.

POPULAR CULTURE AND GOVERNING EVERYDAY LIFE

Popular Culture is a pervasive part of everyday life in western societies. Our identities, leisure activities, cultural practices and political participation are all mediated through popular culture. Our interest in this chapter is examining the role popular culture plays in mediating social reality and managing power relationships.

Popular culture is often used as a term that incorporates mass culture, celebrity culture, commercial culture and amateur cultural production. To begin with we might think of popular culture as the culture of the people or ordinary people. In doing so, however, we must acknowledge that often popular culture shapes our understanding of ordinary everyday life in the first place. Popular culture constructs and shapes everyday life and identities as much as it reflects them. Furthermore, in western societies there is arguably no useful distinction to be made between the popular culture of ordinary people and industrialized, mass-produced and commercial culture. Given our interest in this book, we pay particular attention to the relationship between popular culture and media production. These circuits of production and cultural practices are interrelated with each other. For this very reason, popular culture helps us understand power relationships. In particular, it helps us to consider why the everyday cultural practices and identities of ordinary people are so important to the creation and maintenance of power relationships in contemporary societies.

Popular culture is a symptom of larger social formations

Janice Peck (2008) suggests that we approach popular culture by moving back and forth between texts (like television programmes, music, magazines, even fashion or trends) and context (that is, larger historical, political or social processes and formations). We should aim to understand popular culture's texts as symptomatic of, and conditioned by, social, cultural and political formations. By approaching popular culture in this way we can conduct an analysis that avoids falling into the trap of debunking the claims of popular culture, and instead try to understand how popular culture works to enact identities and power relationships, and how it constructs our understanding of social formations. Our analysis of popular culture, we propose, has to be wise to – astute about – the way we are embedded in popular culture, and often already approach it in a canny and knowing way. As ordinary people, living in a media-dense world, we already participate on a daily basis in practices of critically dissecting and deconstructing the popular culture we live in. One of the central claims of this chapter is that we need to think in a more nuanced fashion rather than simply being savvy know-alls who think to ourselves 'I get it': 'I get that reality TV isn't really real', 'I get that Oprah's invocation to read that best-selling life-changing book is a promotional tactic', 'I get that this home improvement programme is trying to get me to shop at Home Depot or Bunnings on the weekend'. There really isn't any point to this kind of critical – yet apathetic – savvy deconstructing and debunking. We need to think about popular culture in a productively critical way – in a way that enhances how we understand the world we live in.

With this in mind, we argue that we should look carefully at how popular culture is made, how popular culture makes its claims, and how they work despite that fact the we can see how they work. Rather than doing a simple 'ideology critique' that points to the constructed nature of media representations, we instead are trying to think about how ideology functions as something people do, and therefore works despite the fact we can see through how it works. This is different from an ideology critique that stops at simply pointing out the contrivances of popular culture texts. Part of the reason we must approach popular culture like this is that popular culture today rapidly appropriates and recuperates a critique of itself. One way to think about this is as a 'wink'. Popular culture constantly winks at us, to let us know: 'We know you know how things really are. We know that you get it.' Deconstructing popular culture's representations has become a central part of its rituals of entertainment and enjoyment. Think of reality TV programmes like *American Idol* or *Big Brother* that give viewers constant backstage access to contestants' preparations or backstories so that we can judge and critique the authenticity of their performances. Popular culture makes deconstruction an element of the way its representations function. Popular culture constructs a critique of itself as part of its very functioning. This has been described as a strategy of 'protecting artifice by exposing it' (Andrejevic 2004: 16). Audiences are part of these practices too; they are conscious, savvy and cynical about the contrived nature of popular culture (Andrejevic 2004: 19, Teurlings 2010).

The questions we need to ask then are not just about the meaning of texts and the gap between the meanings in the text and the social reality they claim to represent. We know that life isn't really how it appears in fashion magazines, or home renovation shows or television dramas. Following Peck (2008: 7), the questions we might ask about popular culture are instead:

- How are power relationships represented in popular culture?
- Who is presented as powerful?
- Who is powerful and why?
- By what means does one become empowered and to what ends?

By asking these questions we can approach popular culture in terms of the way it facilitates power relationships. This means we think about the meanings it creates differently, less concerned with the content of meanings and their authenticity, and more concerned with how those meanings facilitate social relations.

POPULAR CULTURE IN NEOLIBERAL TIMES

In this chapter we address forms of popular culture that are grounded in the power relationships of global network capitalism. Contemporary popular culture reflects social and political relationships that have been characterized as neoliberal. Where in the managerial era the state took direct responsibility for managing mass populations via institutions, laws, education and media and culture, in the global network era the management of populations changes its character. 'Governing at a distance' is a way of describing the shift away from big government, big labour and mass consumption (Harvey 1989) and towards smaller government, free market and flexible labour relations and niche markets. Ouellette and Hay (2008a) employ Foucault's idea of 'governmentality' to describe how this process works. Governmentality refers to 'how we think about governing others and ourselves' using 'techniques' to 'reflect upon, work on, and organize [our] lives' (2008a: 9). In this approach power functions via the 'knowledge and procedures associated with social institutions' (2008a: 9). Power is facilitated via interactions between institutions and people.

Institutions seek to shape knowledge via the practices, technologies and processes they create and enable individuals to participate in. Those living in liberal societies are free, but that freedom is organized by particular institutions who set rules for what we can and can't do and what we do and don't say. This conception of governing expects individuals to participate in their own governance and exercise personal responsibility. The success of the contemporary liberal state is built upon its capacity to create an assembly of institutions, practices and values through which people govern, discipline and police themselves. This system encourages people to see their life circumstances as the outcome of their own choices and changeable through their own actions. Governing at a distance then involves developing cultural institutions and practices that act as broad frameworks within which people take care of their own lives.

Popular culture and government at a distance

Popular culture plays a role in facilitating 'government at a distance' by creating institutions and practices that fashion responsible individuals who take care of themselves. For instance, television talk shows, fashion magazines, talk radio, breakfast television and reality TV all provide an instruction manual for everyday life. This mode of thinking about government fits well with global liberal-democratic capitalism's belief in a free market that incentivizes individual initiative. Popular culture produces and legitimizes these identities and cultural practices. Critics argue that by celebrating the productive and enterprising individual, popular culture elides the 'vital difference between conceiving empowerment at the level of individual well-being versus understanding it as a socio-political, hence collective, undertaking' (Peck 2008: 7).

Governing at a distance by making individuals responsible for their own lives has two consequences for thinking about power relationships. Firstly, this mode of power is exercised in a participatory rather than authoritarian fashion. Individuals are encouraged to participate in practices that make and maintain social and power relationships. Popular culture might be disciplinary in terms of giving us advice on how to discipline and organize our lives, but it isn't repressive, it doesn't force us to do it; rather it advises us on what we should do if we want to be successful in this society. This leads us to the second point: that popular culture is now much more about managing populations than constructing mass identities. Popular culture helps to produce and manage populations that see themselves as part of the power relationships of a neoliberal society. It offers schemas for making sense of their position in those power relationships, and offers techniques or practices through which people believe they are empowering themselves. Communication professionals effectively steer people into systems and identity which embed them into rituals of self-governance.

Popular culture became important to power relationships with the birth of mass liberal democracies. The mass enfranchisement of ordinary people – from the underclasses, to the working class, to the growing middle class – presented the challenge of making sure they were appropriately incorporated into the power relationships and institutions of society. As far as the emerging mass media was concerned this involved using it to ensure that appropriate forms of citizenship, civil society and democracy were promoted, that people were educated on the right way to think about themselves as citizens. With the rise of neoliberalism and its emphasis on the responsible individual, this role for popular culture becomes arguably even more important to the functioning of power relationships. While popular culture of the twentieth century was characterized as a mass project to create mass national identities, with the emergence of global network capitalism and networked communication technologies – like cable TV and internet – we see a fragmentation of that mass into a diversity of niches who can all be served by popular culture. Popular culture becomes fragmented, not so much organizing a homogenous mass identity, but managing the identities of proliferating niche groups. Popular culture facilitates identities that serve commercial and political ends, but they don't have to adhere to homogenous ideologies, as long as they act within the broad framework of rules and values of society. Ouellette and Hay (2008a: 13) argue that contemporary television diffuses and amplifies governing at a distance, 'utilising the cultural power of television ... to assess and guide the ethics, behaviours, aspirations and routines of ordinary people'.

Popular culture as lived social practices

The power relationships framework of this book encourages us to pay attention to both the cultural content of media *and* the political economic context within which it is produced and consumed. The shape this approach takes in a chapter addressing popular culture is one that moves back and forth between popular culture texts and the context within which they are produced and consumed. It is important to note that we aren't making either a simplistic 'direct effects' or 'ideology critique' argument about popular culture – as if it implants ideas in our minds that we act on. Instead we are paying careful attention to how popular culture produces, and is produced by, power relationships.

Popular culture isn't an inert product made and delivered to us; we as individuals engage in the production of cultural practices and social relationships. In neoliberal times popular culture often involves the work of producing, monitoring, evaluating and improving ourselves using the resources and within the institutions of the society in which we live. This can be as simple as thinking about a cooking show like MasterChef. It instructs us on how to cook better, which will make us better people, healthier and more popular with our friends who will like coming over for dinner. Watching the show is part of developing our ability to cook; we buy cookbooks and better food at the market, and act to improve our skills. But this also makes us actors within a system of popular culture that commodifies food culture, and connects it to big food and home appliance brands, supermarkets, restaurants, celebrity chefs and their cookbooks. We don't just work on ourselves; we also – through our freely chosen actions – give form and validation to the institution of cooking shows and the cultural practices they enact. It isn't just that we sat on the couch and the ideas went into our minds: the popular culture text was one part of framing a whole way of life. Popular culture then becomes a 'cultural technology' that is part of broader institutions of politics and commerce. Popular culture assembles cultural identities and practices within market structures. Whatever popular culture text we look at – in this chapter we mainly look at contemporary genres of television – we need to under-stand those popular culture texts not just as isolated containers of meanings, but as a part of broader cultural and economic systems.

ORDINARY PEOPLE AND POPULAR CULTURE'S PROMISES AND PRACTICES

If popular culture is the culture of ordinary people then this chapter considers how the experience of the ordinary person has become central to the creation and maintenance of power relations. In this section we frame our discussion by considering some of the claims and practices of contemporary popular culture.

Access to reality

Media and popular culture claim to offer unmediated access to reality so that we can see 'how things really are' (Couldry 2003, Andrejevic 2004, Turner 2010, Wood and Skeggs 2011). Nick Couldry describes these claims as the myth of the mediated centre. This refers to the common belief and everyday practices that suggest the media are the centre of the social world and 'that in some sense the media speak from and for that centre' (Couldry 2003: 46). Media establish themselves as speaking on our behalf and in our interests. This centres the media as a 'privileged frame through which we access the reality that matters to us as social beings' (2003: 58). By constructing themselves as a privileged window onto reality the media first and foremost communicate their own power and their own centrality to the production of identities, culture and social relationships.

Participation and surveillance

The production of popular culture is increasingly organized around the participation and surveillance of ordinary people and everyday life. Graeme Turner (2010) argues that ordinary people are much more visible in today's popular culture than they once were. Talk radio, tabloids, reality TV and social media all incorporate ordinary people's practices and everyday life into their media rituals and representations. We are asked to vote, comment, express our opinion, perform and judge as ordinary and aspiring people participating in the production of popular culture. These forms of participation are also increasingly connected to surveillance technologies. Mark Andrejevic (2007) has described these technologies as constituting a 'digital enclosure' within which the media processes that we participate in are watched, tracked and responded to. While we take this issue up at length in Chapter 11, for the purposes of our discussion of popular culture in this chapter what we are interested in is the way that popular culture popularizes surveillance and monitoring as ordinary everyday practices (Andrejevic 2004, Ouellette and Hay 2008a).

By thinking about how participation and surveillance are related we can consider the difference between talk and celebration of participation in popular culture and the actual quality of that participation. Many critics argue that participatory rhetoric tells ordinary people they are empowered, while organizing them within uneven power structures (see, for instance, Andrejevic 2007, Ouellette and Hay 2008a, Hindman 2009, Couldry 2010). As we come to see the media as the platform through which we participate, they gain legitimacy and importance. We can't imagine social, cultural or political processes without the media organizing our participation. This invokes the promise that participation will create media that reflect our way of life, identities and values. This implicitly suggests that if the twentieth century was 'bad' because it produced top-down homogenous content for mass audiences, then the new interactive cultural industry is 'good' because audiences get to participate in shaping its content. This promise obscures the way this participation facilitates commercial and political processes. The emergence of interactive media and popular culture continues the management of cultural production begun by the twentieth-century culture industry. Contemporary popular culture presents itself as an antidote to the mass society, claiming to empower ordinary people, at the same time that surveillance technologies give it increasing control over the construction and management of social life. Popular culture encourages us to carefully monitor, inspect and judge ourselves and our peers; at the same time it in turn carefully monitors and responds to us.

Rules, regulations and personal responsibility

Popular culture enacts rules and rituals for making judgements about ourselves and others (Couldry 2003, Ouellette and Hay 2008a). When we watch reality TV we see the production of frameworks for governing everyday life. *Big Brother* sets the rules within the house; *American Idol* judges act according to the rules of the music business; *Supernanny* tells parents and children what the household rules are; Trinny and Susannah tell us what clothes we should wear. These rules cannot be challenged from within the popular culture formats. Contestants on *Big Brother* play by the rules or leave, *American Idol* judges' advice is gospel, *Supernanny*'s rules cannot be challenged. These rules and regulations are often set out and employed by expert judges on the show. Experts give advice and make final decisions or call on the public to decide, based on their advice. The judgements we are encouraged to make are always about individuals' compliance with the rules, rather than the rules themselves and how they might reflect broader social or political structures. By participating in spectacles of making judgements against pre-set rules we arguably don't see broader social structures.

By engaging us in rituals of making judgements against set rules, popular culture obfuscates how social relations are produced, even as it promises to show 'how things really are'. We might think of reality TV here having a disciplinary function, in so far as it produces a spectacle of teaching us the rules for everyday life, and demonstrating to us how the powerful enact those rules (Andrejevic 2011, Wood and Skeggs 2011, Couldry 2011). The judges on *America's Next Top Model* are fashion industry insiders who know the rules for making it in the business; the police officers on *Cops* and *Highway Patrol* are state officials who enforce the law and so on. Popular culture formats like reality TV do the work of positioning who has power and how to judge people (Woods and Skeggs 2011: 9). Those rules and judgements create and facilitate power relationships. While we all have the power to participate, we have to play in social structures controlled by others. As viewers we can also position ourselves relative to other ordinary people. We are encouraged to judge and place people in a social hierarchy (Couldry 2011). Think of the conceited enjoyment of middle-class audiences judging 'white trash' contestants on reality TV programmes. The book and film *The Hunger Games* can be read as a comment on these practices, where poor and ordinary people have to fight to the death for the enjoyment of a more refined urban middle-class audience. These spectacles of judging people are a visible and enjoyable part of our consumption of popular culture.

Producing commercially valuable and politically useful identities

Popular culture and media don't corrupt or 'spectacularize' some pre-existing mass democracy; rather they enact democracy as it is now, as a product of today's power relationships (Ouellette and Hay 2008a: 206). If neoliberal popular culture envisions democracy as self-government, then forms of popular culture like reality TV can be seen as doing that work of government. The media's commercial imperatives direct them first and foremost to generate audience and participant behaviours which will result in commercially viable popular culture. While these activities are a 'direct and sustained intervention into the construction of people's desires, cultural identities and expectations of the real', they don't necessarily have 'intrinsic content or necessary politics' (Turner 2010: 24). Popular culture reinforces the economic and cultural power of the media, driven in the first instance by commercial imperatives. It operates 'like an ideological system but without an ideological project' (Turner 2010: 25). While we can discern connections between the content of media texts and broader political projects, we can't assume the media have a particular interest in those political projects.

Popular culture enterprises don't reflect dominant values because they are motivated by sincere belief in personal responsibility or because they are in some kind of conspiratorial relationship with other political or corporate elites. Rather, producing content that reflects power relationships makes commercial sense. What we can discern from these different perspectives is that popular culture is the outcome of power relationships between commercial, political and cultural elites, in a messy and fragmented way. They interact with each other to create a cultural hegemony – a system of meaning making – that reflects their commercial and political interests relative to each other. The question we should ask isn't 'Does popular culture succeed or fail in enhancing democracy or the quality of our lives together?', but rather 'How does popular culture conduct liberal democracy and make its processes appear rational and common sense?'

PERSONAL RESPONSIBILITY ON TALK SHOWS AND REALITY TV

Popular culture's narratives of personal responsibility are acted out by people who producers select on the basis that they can emotionally perform their identities. They need to be able to connect their identities and everyday experiences to the broader narrative of the programme and the commercial interests of its sponsors. What participants offer television producers is not their skills, but themselves – their identities and life stories – and often in doing so, what they are selling is their place, their vantage point, in social relations. In doing so, they make sense of those social relations and how they live them. Participants must construct themselves in questionnaires, audition tapes and meetings as the right identities for the production (Mayer 2011b). Initial applications and casting calls require ordinary people to divulge aspects of their life stories, personal circumstances and beliefs. This involves affective and emotional labour, the capacity to exploit your life situation with compelling stories, emotions and imagery.

Performing our identities

These emotional performances by ordinary people arguably first emerged on television talk shows during the 1980s. Oprah Winfrey is perhaps the icon or archetype of this genre. Oprah encourages viewers to see their life circumstances as a consequence of individual choice, rather than larger social, cultural and political structures (Peck 2008: 44). Neoliberalism presents rewarding individual initiative as a common-sense foundation reconstructing the economy, society and culture. These narratives of individual initiative worked hegemonically to serve both liberal political and commercial ends. For Oprah, narratives of personal responsibility and self-improvement can inform the production of an 'enterprising self'. That enterprising self engages in practices of self-improvement by drawing on resources provided by the culture industry: books, media products, fashion, exercise regimes, diets and supplements, information technologies and so on. Oprah succeeded by fashioning deep affective connections with her audience. They participate with her in the practices of self-improvement she advocates. She is able to mobilize these connections as a commercially lucrative set of relationships and as politically powerful identities connected to a liberal account of the American Dream. Her audience works hard for her on themselves, and by extension, this shapes how they think and act as citizens and consumers within a liberal capitalist order.

Popular culture does the work of stimulating and fashioning cultural practices: identities are built not just out of what we think, but how we go about living our lives. Oprah doesn't just tell her audience what to think, she instructs them on what to do and how to live their lives. Oprah doesn't necessarily explicitly promote and celebrate the economic and social changes of neoliberalism. Her programme doesn't explain for instance why massive changes in employment conditions were necessary or how they made America a better society. Instead, what Oprah's programme does is construct identities and practices that shape the way people understand processes that affect them. So, when individuals lose their jobs or find themselves living in communities that no longer have viable industries or social networks, and begin to feel lonely or depressed or struggle financially, they don't see those processes as the outcome of the power relationships – the new rules – that neoliberalism created. Instead they see them as individual problems that they themselves must fix. Oprah becomes a hero because she offers them understanding and empathy, and moreover, a kind of cure – a set of meanings and practices that they can undertake to make their life better (Peck 2008). Popular culture works here in an implicit and indirect way, shaping the cultural resources and practices we engage with in making sense of our world and our lives and our relations with others. This works as both a political and commercial appeal. For instance, Oprah's book club offers books that contain content that serves her narratives of self-improvement and enable the further mediation of her brand, and at the same time it is a powerful marketing tool for the book industry. Publishers report seeking out authors whose narratives fit within the Oprah brand. The Oprah brand becomes a way of life that other products and brands can be inserted into.

OPRAH'S BOOK CLUB

Oprah's book club provides an example of how her show integrates political and commercial processes. Oprah's book club was credited with revitalizing the commercial publishing industry and reading as a public practice. That is, it was said to have both commercial value to the book industry while also making a political contribution to American life. Over time Oprah positioned reading as part of the work of 'building', improving and working on ourselves. For Oprah, books are a resource in a regime of self-improvement and work. The book club positioned these narratives within a sense of public deliberation and discussion, which fits American democratic ideals. By reading the carefully selected books and engaging in discussions facilitated by Oprah, her audience engage in local-level forms of democracy organized around self-improvement. Furthermore, the books Oprah selects are a kind of 'therapeutic toolbox' (Peck 2008: 186) for her readers, books that contain content that serves her narratives of self-improvement and enable the further mediation of her brand. Literature serves as a resource for building, mediating and valorizing the Oprah brand. The Oprah brand becomes a way of life that other products and brands can be inserted into.

Peck (2008) argues that narratives of 'self-care' and personal responsibility go hand in hand with more precarious forms of economic and social life. The more vulnerable we are the more work we need to do to improve ourselves. If neoliberalism celebrates the enterprising individual it also blames the vulnerable and suffering individual for their own circumstances. Oprah mediates, manages – and profits from – these political, social and cultural arrangements. The Oprah brand stimulates and profits from the precariousness and vulnerability ordinary people feel in neoliberalism's power relationships. It isn't just that Oprah's narratives 'naturalize' neoliberalism with their narratives of personal responsibility; it is that Oprah also sells a cure that is highly economically profitable for her and her associated brands. The more vulnerable ordinary people are the more they seek out Oprah – and her brand – as a set of meanings and cultural practices for making sense of and coping with their life circumstances. Oprah's advice can't ever solve their problems; in fact it has an economic interest in sustaining them. Oprah prompts a desire for self-improvement, and then captures and commodifies it as both attention and a set of cultural practices. Oprah profits from the desiring subjects she crafts. Oprah's spirituality stimulates the anxiety that her programme claims to address. Popular culture provides 'imaginary resolutions' to 'manage desires'. Oprah creates self-enterprising neoliberal subjects who do the work of enacting the 'natural' values of a neoliberal economic order (Peck 2008: 222). Those prescriptions have to be repeated because they cannot resolve the real-world social conditions.

What impacts does Oprah's book club have on the book industry, novelists, audiences and reading as a part of cultural life?

How does Oprah's book club change the kinds of stories, characters and identities that the publishing industry produces?

How does the production of these kinds of stories and characters reflect power relationships?

What kinds of 'instructions' do books selected for Oprah's book club offer on how to live a good life?

POPULAR CULTURE'S EXPLANATION OF SOCIAL RELATIONSHIPS

Popular culture shapes how we understand and respond to social problems. While Oprah is a global icon, narratives of self-improvement and entrepreneurialism are more broadly evident within our popular culture. Ouellette and Hay (2008a) describe the genre of 'charity TV' which provides healthcare, home improvement and other forms of assistance to those it deems needy and deserving. The deserving are those who have shown appropriate initiative, and in doing so fit the values of an enterprising society. Television programmes that provide housing or healthcare to the misfortunate demonstrate needs being met, but don't address how those needs are socially situated in wider power relationships. The genre draws attention only to those problems that can be fixed within the schema of popular culture: a house that can be rebuilt, or a surgery that will be successful, or a school meals programme that can be changed. It doesn't consider the power relationships underlying those problems. While these genres appear to have a pedagogical ideological function – to teach ordinary people certain values – that political function is interrelated with a commercial system of production. Charity TV integrates products and brands into this welfare provision and narratives of personal responsibility. In Australia, for instance, *The Block*'s provision of home renovations to needy and deserving families gives opportunities for retailers, homeware and technology brands, and construction companies to provide goods and services. The brands use popular culture to embed themselves within narratives of personal responsibility, social responsibility and community building. Brands aren't just advertising their products, they are part of the liberal social practices and values that popular culture models.

TELEVISION DRAMA AND MAKING SENSE OF THE GLOBAL NETWORK SOCIETY

If above we've argued that genres like talk shows and reality TV reflect but don't critically address larger social and political formations, in this section we consider how television drama attempts to illustrate how the experience of ordinary people is embedded in larger political and economic structures. Popular culture can contribute to larger public understanding of social and political structures. *The Wire* (2002–2008) and *Treme* (2010–) are two dramas produced by David Simon for the HBO network, a cable network that has created a profitable market segment providing quality television to an educated middle-class audience.

The Wire examined the decay of the American city and public institutions through intersecting storylines about police and law enforcement, the drug trade, working-class industry, the school system, local government and the journalistic print media. *Treme* documents and dramatizes the efforts of the people of New Orleans to rebuild their city and culture in the wake of Hurricane Katrina. The programme features New Orleans locals and musicians performing in New Orleans bars and venues, and connects this portrait of everyday life to wider political and economic processes associated with the reconstruction. *The Wire* and *Treme* are each popular culture texts that reflect and work through the social and cultural world produced by global network capitalism. Each series documents the challenges that ordinary people face navigating the processes of government and everyday life in the post-industrial or post-disaster American city.

We might argue that these dramas counteract the 'bad' representations of popular culture with 'good' ones. *The Wire* has been praised for stimulating the 'sociological imagination' (see Penfold-Mounce et al. 2011: 155) and a 'commitment to a complex understanding of the social' (Bramall and Pitcher 2013). Where reality TV ignores social and political structures, these programmes pay attention to them. Where other aspects of popular culture are said to present stereotypical characters and images of gender and race, these programmes offer a different perspective. Producer David Simon makes a sustained argument for the power of popular culture's representations. Simon's many interviews, letters, blog posts about the programmes, show 'bible' and pitch documents offer an account of the meaning, power and value of the programmes. Simon wants to produce reflections of the social world, to talk about it, in ways that might change it. He hopes that his stories about the American city will 'matter somehow'.

Representing 'real' life?

Several characters and storylines on *The Wire* and *Treme* are based on real life characters and events. One example is the character Snoop, played by Felicia 'Snoop' Pearson on *The Wire*. On the show she plays the role of a drug gang member; in real life she was part of the drug trade and had spent time in prison as a teenager for manslaughter. *The Wire* producers sought out characters like Snoop, asking them to act out scenes in their own words and style. After her role on the show ended Snoop was arrested by police in an inner-city estate for drug offences. David Simon (cited in Rastogi 2011) responded to these events in a public statement. We can read the statement as a 'deep text' that explains part of the way Simon understands *The Wire* as a popular culture text that makes a contribution to the understanding of contemporary social life. Simon wrote that the 'war on drugs has devolved into a war on the underclass' who lived in parts of America where the 'drug economy was the only factory still hiring', and that the education system is 'crippled'. He argued that the campaign to imprison this underclass for drug offences was amoral:

> Our constitution and our common law guarantee that we will be judged by our peers. But in truth, there are now two Americas, politically and economically distinct. I, for one, do not qualify as a peer to Felicia Pearson. The opportunities and experiences of her life do not correspond in any way with my own, and her America is different from my own. I am therefore ill-equipped to be her judge in this matter.

The statement demonstrates Simon's efforts to illuminate broader political and economic processes via his dramatization of everyday life and power relationships in America. Simon hopes drama might change how people think and act.

After producing *The Wire*, David Simon moved on to produce *Treme*, a drama about life in New Orleans after Hurricane Katrina. With *Treme* we can see many of the same complex relationships between reality and fiction, between cultural production and the understanding and maintenance of broader social and political structures. Critics have argued that in celebrating the music of New Orleans *Treme* contributes to rebuilding and branding the city as a cultural tourism destination (Thomas 2012: 215). The programme repositions New Orleans within the new flexible economy. In doing so, *Treme*'s depiction of the struggle to protect New Orleans culture simultaneously contributes to its commodification. For critics, *Treme* makes a promotional 'good news' argument for the city that ignores the power relations that inform day-to-day life for residents of New Orleans before, during and after the Katrina crisis.

Critical apathy

The show does pay attention to some of these issues: for instance, one character's search for her brother who went missing after being arrested by police; the efforts of residents working through labyrinthine government bureaucracies in order to get their homes and neighbourhoods rebuilt; the corruption of 'disaster capitalism' in the contractors and corporations that profited from the recovery money; and the investigation of police shootings. But the fact is that none of these issues are seriously connected to a consideration of class, underclass or institutionalized racism (Gray 2012: 271). For Gray (2012: 272), *Treme* elides the exploitation that produces the black identities which the rebranding of New Orleans profits from: 'What the series does not show is that with these "precious" and "real" traditions that are in danger of being sacrificed comes crushing poverty, economic isolation, food injustice, and social inequality among the very people who are the source of these unique gifts to the nation.' And while the attention to life in post-Katrina New Orleans should be 'lauded', we must also pay attention to the way that *Treme* is a cultural commodity that sells 'quality black programming' to a valuable middle-class audience: 'This is all very much in keeping with the entrepreneurial neoliberal project of branding and marketing blackness as quality television.'

Dramas like *Treme* and *The Wire* might satisfy the yearning of an educated, middle-class and predominantly white audience for socially liberal and progressive representations that they see as 'good' (Bramall and Pitcher 2013: 87). The culture industry is capable of serving the desires of many niche audiences with different views of reality. That doesn't necessarily disrupt power relationships, but can in fact serve to maintain them. If an educated middle class can watch content that serves to legitimate their world-view, while other audiences watch different content that legitimates their world-view, then this serves to maintain different positions in the social order.

The view *The Wire* presents of 'the complexities of post-industrial global capitalism offers a seductively intelligent vision of social and cultural complexity' (Bramall and Pitcher 2013: 88). This vision responds to the desires of a middle-class audience and their belief in the myth of the mediated centre (Couldry 2003), that is, their fantasy of knowing how the social world *really* is via popular culture texts. Educated middle-class viewers watching *The Wire* arguably encounter a cathartic vision of the collapse of public institutions, and the futility of individuals struggling against the system. They enjoy identifying with the characters in the show as they struggle against arcane institutions and complex problems. Their continual failures and abjectness are a kind of alibi for our apathy.

Treme and *The Wire* are each complex texts that both press on and facilitate the power relations they critique. In some moments these popular culture texts appear to have the capacity to disrupt social life and draw critical attention to power relationships in productive ways; at other times they simply provide entertainment that reinforces cultural identities and practices. As part of the power relations they critique, we can say that they inevitably help to sustain them. But power relationships – and their cultural form as hegemonies – are always under construction and negotiation. Throughout all of the examples we have considered so far in this chapter we see meaning and power being constantly enacted and performed as a series of social relationships between producers, cultural intermediaries and audiences.

DAVID SIMON'S DEEP TEXTS

THE LETTER TO NEW ORLEANS

On the eve of *Treme*'s debut David Simon wrote an open letter to the city of New Orleans where he responded to the way the show brought drama and reality together. In the letter he explained that *Treme* 'sometimes lies about details to convey thematic truth'. He said to the people of the city that he expected them to hold him 'to certain standards' as the drama takes 'liberties with a profound unforgettable period in [the] city's history'. He finished his letter by asking 'Why? Why not depict a precise truth ...?':

> Well, Pablo Picasso famously said that art is the lie that shows us the truth. Such might be the case of a celebrated artist claiming more for himself and his work than he ought, or perhaps, this Picasso fella was on to something. By referencing what is real, or historical, a fictional narrative can speak in a powerful, full-throated way to the problems and issues of our time. And a wholly imagined tale, set amid the intricate and accurate details of a real place and time, can resonate with readers in profound ways. In short, drama is its own argument. (Simon 2010)

David Simon claimed that *Treme* was an argument for the city. The letter is a deep text in the sense it is an attempt to theorize and explain the real meaning and value of the fictional drama.

How does Simon explain the value of *Treme*?
How do dramatizations of our cities, lives and histories affect us?
Does drama play a role in crafting and changing power relationships?

DAVID SIMON'S STATEMENT ON FELICIA 'SNOOP' PEARSON'S ARREST

When Felicia 'Snoop' Pearson was arrested on drugs-related charges Simon made the following statement:

We believe the war on drugs has devolved into a war on the underclass, that in places like West and East Baltimore, where the drug economy is now the only factory still hiring and where the educational system is so crippled that the vast majority of children are trained only for the corner, a legal campaign to imprison our most vulnerable and damaged citizens is little more than amoral. And we said then that if asked to serve on any jury considering a non-violent drug offense, we would move to nullify that jury's verdict and to vote to acquit. Regardless of the defendant, I still believe such a course of action would be just in any case in which drug offenses – absent proof of violent acts – are alleged. Both our constitution and our common law guarantee that we will be judged by our peers. But in truth, there are now two Americas, politically and economically distinct. I, for one, do not qualify as a peer to Felicia Pearson. The opportunities and experiences of her life do not correspond in any way with my own, and her America is different from my own. I am therefore ill-equipped to be her judge in this matter. (Simon, cited in Rastogi 2011)

What does Simon's statement say about his values?

How does television drama contribute towards public debate about and responses to crime and race?

Can drama prompt conversations that reshape how people think and act?

Can drama reveal power relationships in constructive ways?

You can find links to Simon's letter to New Orleans and statement about Felicia 'Snoop' Pearson on the *Media and Society* website study.sagepub.com/carahandlouw

COMEDY NEWS AND POLITICAL PARTICIPATION

In this section we examine the forms of political participation that popular culture genres like comedy news afford (for an overview of the genre see Baym 2005 or Feldman 2008). Popular culture formats like comedy news ask us to feel empowered and to enjoy participating in a spectacle where we see the real state of things. Jon Stewart, Steven Colbert and John Oliver act as our confidants; we join them in debunking the game of politics and laughing and snickering at our political leaders. A preoccupation of these forms of political communication is debunking or revealing the backstage process, motivations and real beliefs of politicians and their parties. In the United States, political satirists have emerged on comedy news programmes like *The Daily Show*, *The Colbert Report* and *This Week Tonight* as influential commentators on the political process. Audience research demonstrates that audiences take their explanation and exposure of the political process to be highly credible, even more credible than traditional news media (Baym 2005, Feldman 2008).

Comedy news offers a spectacle of meaning making that makes fun of the powerful and their modes of control. One way to read this is to celebrate it as evidence of the openness of our democracy – that we are free to say whatever we like. Some scholars have argued that the integration of the political process with comedy, popular and celebrity culture democratizes politics and enables citizens to understand complex political issues (Scammell 1995, van Zoonen 1998, Temple 2006). These accounts suggest that the satirical debunking of the political process reinvents political coverage by opening up new forms of critical enquiry and engaging an estranged audience of mostly younger citizens in the democratic process (Baym 2005, Feldman 2008). Baym (2005) describes *The Daily Show* as advocating a 'conversational' or 'deliberative' theory of democracy.

Powerful people making fun of themselves

We could though read it another way. Comedy news provides one example of popular culture's capacity to appropriate an ideology critique. By this we mean that popular culture incorporates a critique of itself into its practices and representations. Popular culture has demonstrated a canny ability to expose how power relationships are constructed. This protects artifice by exposing it (Andrejevic 2004). On comedy news, and other forms of snarky political culture like internet memes, we view a packaged version of an ideological critique that promises to show us how things really are. Instead of concealing how power relationships work, popular culture constantly exposes them. Rather than being a productive position that promotes better forms of democracy, this arguably contributes to a kind of cynical inertia.

The game of debunking and exposing power relationships becomes a form of entertainment and enjoyment, rather than a practice which materially changes our democracy or the power relationships in our societies. Popular culture takes critique into account by exposing to us how things really are. The risk is that enjoying the game of politics takes over from its more important purpose of imagining and creating a society. Guy Rundle (2010b) suggests this greatly diminishes 'the wider intellectual framework within which a more imaginative politics might evolve'. Politics becomes a communicative game, rather than being about the real business of acting in the world (Dean 2010). Critics argue that the savvy attitude invoked by decoding, debunking, backstage revelations, confessions and exposing politics is an apathetic and debilitating one (Postman 1987, Marshall 1997, Kerbel 1999, deVreese 2005, Andrejevic 2008, Teurlings 2010).

The powerful use popular culture to make fun of themselves, their institutions and their power. In fact, when westerners see political leaders who use mass media to demonstrate their immense power our immediate reaction is often to find it deluded or self-indulgent or to make fun of it. Think of the way that images of North Korean parades of military power are sniggered at by westerners in YouTube videos or in Hollywood films like *Team America*.

THE WHITE HOUSE CORRESPONDENTS' DINNER

The White House Correspondents' Dinner began in 1920 as an event that recognized the achievements of political reporting each year. Since the 1980s, the dinner has gradually transitioned towards an event that satirized the President and Administration. Sitting Presidents have more regularly participated in this satire, poking fun at themselves, their opponents and their relationships with the press. The dinner has drawn criticism as an event that illustrates how symbiotic the relationships between politicians and journalists are. We might also argue that the dinner offers a forum for powerful political actors to position themselves as part of 'in jokes' that mock their own status. These activities ought to prompt us to consider why the powerful now so routinely expose and mock the workings of power.

The Presidents' performances at the White House Correspondents' Dinner provide one example of the powerful 'winking' and 'nodding' to the public, indicating to them that they know the public can see through their power and their meanings; that they can see how their political interests drive the meanings they make; that they can see how power really works. We might argue that the kind of ideology we see at work here is one that in general celebrates a continuous revelation of the backstage, of power relations and sites of power, by making fun of the powerful and having the powerful make fun of themselves. This political culture maintains power relationships by letting the public feel like they are part of the back-stage action or inner circle of elites. This should prompt us to consider how this disposition works to create and maintain power relationships, and why the powerful would not only sanction it, but also actively participate in it.

At the 2011 White House Correspondents' Dinner President Obama began his speech with a Hollywood-style montage that presented his birth certificate set against other symbols of real Americana like the Stars and Stripes, Uncle Sam, eagles, Rocky, baseball, Michael Jordan and WWF wrestling. The montage poked fun at the 'birther' controversy sparked by the conservative Tea Party movement and right-wing figures like Donald Trump. He began his speech by noting that his birth certificate had been released, but that he was prepared to go a 'step further' and release his 'official birth video'. He then screened the famous 'Circle of Life' scene of Simba's birth from the Disney cartoon *The Lion King*. Obama remarked, 'I want to make clear to the Fox News table, that was a joke. That was not my real birth video, that was a children's cartoon.' His speech featured many more jokes that referenced contemporary political and popular culture, celebrities, comedians and journalists, and poked fun at his opponents and himself.

Obama's 2012 speech began with a spoof recording of Obama backstage before his speech. The gag was that as Jimmy Kimmel was preparing to introduce him, his backstage remarks were broadcast because his microphone had been 'accidentally' left on. Obama was backstage warming up his voice, flushing the toilet, checking out his grey hairs, and complaining that he had to open for Jimmy Kimmel and tell 'knock-knock jokes to Kim Kardashian' and other celebrities. When he was prompted to go on stage by his minder he said, 'OK I'm going, God forbid we keep Chuck Todd and the cast of *Glee* waiting.' He then took to the stage to tell the audience that he 'could not be more thrilled' to be talking at the White House Correspondents' Dinner and went on to say that it was an 'honour' to open for Jimmy Kimmel and he was 'delighted' to see Chuck Todd and the cast of *Glee*. In this opening gag he poked fun at himself, as a political leader. He 'winked' at the public, saying 'I know you know' that you think everything political leaders say is contrived based on what people want to hear.

(Continued)

225

(Continued)

Why would the most powerful person in the world publicly make jokes about himself?

Why in the past ten years have powerful political figures engaged in these comedy formats and made jokes about their own power?

What does the President's performance at the White House Correspondents' Dinner say about his identity, values and the way he exercises his power?

You can find links to Obama's appearances at the White House Correspondents' Dinner on the *Media and Society* website study.sagepub.com/carahandlouw

Cynical participation

The mixing together of politics and popular culture appears to be part of the construction of political identities that participate in the political process in a cynical way. Their stance is a default distrust of elites. Be they progressive or conservative, these political identities double as commercially lucrative audience segments. During the 2010 congressional elections Jon Stewart and Stephen Colbert staged a Rally to Restore Sanity and/or Fear in response to Glenn Beck's Fox-sponsored Restoring America rally. The rally was a media ritual that relied on the participation of 250,000 of Stewart and Colbert's progressive fan base. Fans participated in amplifying and adding to the savvy and snarky critique of the media-political process. This was evident in the signs that they brought to the rally, which both expressed their exasperation at the political process itself and mocked conservative populism. Slogans on the signs included:

- 'I'm mad as hell but mostly in a passive aggressive way'
- 'WTF I thought I voted for a muslim' (with an image of Obama)
- 'The Mad Hatter called, he wants his tea party back'
- 'Don't let Glenn Beck tea bag our children'
- Sikh man holding a sign: 'Am I acting suspicious?'
- 'Real Americans drink coffee, I like mine black'
- 'If your beliefs fit on a sign. Think harder'
- 'Don't be a douche'
- 'I like tea and you're kind of ruining it'.

While we can read these signs as evidence of a healthy democratic process – here we have citizens taking to the street, expressing their views collectively and holding the powerful to ridicule, if not account – we can also detect other processes at work. Stewart and Colbert's audience faithfully reproduced their representative frame, creating a collective, repetitive, exhausting, savvy 'snarkasm'. If Jon Stewart is one very funny and very clever satirist, here we get to see what it looks like when that snarky disposition is taken to the street by a quarter of a million people. While the form of their actions indicates democratic participation (taking to the streets in a mass rally to express their views), the disposition of that participation (to express complete exasperation in the political process) is entirely passive and resigned. As Guy Rundle suggests, there is no idea being presented here, no vision for a different kind of politics. Instead, progressives get off on the failure of their own politics (Dean 2010). Writing about the rally Rundle (2010a: 89) reflected:

> It was exciting, it was wild, it was a mad carnival – and, it has to be said, something of a fizzer. It was all a little bit nothing, a little bit meh, it was something that had to be great to be good, and was just all right. It was odd and underdone and half-assed. It was a perfect expression of American progressivism today.

Furthermore, the rally – in relentlessly mocking the populist conservative right – arguably acts as one part of a larger process of 'fragmentation' in public political discourse in America. Conservative Americans watch Fox News and go to Glenn Beck and Tea Party rallies; progressives watch Stewart and Colbert and go to their comedy rally. Each position is caught up in mocking the other, rather than finding a productive space to examine their differences.

For Rundle, Stewart and Colbert's sketches and the crowd's passive-aggressive, ironic and snarky signs weren't symptomatic of public deliberation – as Baym (2005) might argue – but were an example of an 'exhaustion of ideas and purpose' (Rundle 2010a: 92). The rally was adept at making fun of elites, articulating that progressives knew how the political process worked and how broken it was, and mocking conservative populists like the Tea Party, Glenn Beck and Sarah Palin. But that doesn't necessarily amount to a productive form of political debate. The rally was unique because it removed Stewart from the routines and rituals of *The Daily Show*. By placing himself within the ritual of a public political rally he had to articulate his political vision. He had brought a quarter of a million people out; now he had to tell them what they were marching for. In Rundle's (2010a: 92) view he was left with no option but to demonstrate he didn't have any point:

> After all there's nothing wrong with holding a rally for reason, or more moderation, but when you suggest that the latter is served by accepting everyone's world view as valid, then you betray the former. Some things can't be solved by asking everyone to play nice. At some point if you're going to draw a quarter of a million or so – six billion in Stephen Colbert's estimate – to hear what you have to say, you'd better stand up and say that while there are many ways to look at a thing, some of them are plain wrong, and pernicious in their error.

Rundle's point is that progressive cynicism, in not making a positive argument of its own, leaves the door open to pernicious conservative populist arguments. And it then responds to those arguments by mocking them and making fun of them. This in turn reinforces the politics of their perceived conservative populist enemies like Glenn Beck, Fox News, Sarah Palin and the Tea Party. Each is dependent on the other as something to mock.

Profitable niche audiences

This fragmentation of identities isn't just a political process, it is also a commercial one. As media can serve fragmented audiences, it has contributed to the creation of increasingly fragmented identities. News networks no longer need to speak to mainstream America. While it might appear that Fox News is an ideological project (and in part it is), it is more substantially a commercial project. Murdoch and News Corp identified that a conservative news network would attract a large and loyal following. The political identity that Fox News cultivates is commercially lucrative. It creates a loyal market segment. The business of Fox News is built around the proposition that it makes business sense to have a highly engaged audience. Fox convinces its audience that the American way of life is under threat and that it is the only news network that cares (Farhi 2003).

While we could proceed down the path of critiquing one or both of these positions as problematic for a healthy democracy, perhaps at the first instance we should just simply observe that media have the capacity to cater to, amplify and stimulate an array of political dispositions. And that, even where they then offer those dispositions plenty of space to participate, that participation can be an end in itself, or directed towards primarily commercial rather than political means. There is nothing inherently democratic about participation, and therefore we shouldn't see participatory media rituals as automatically empowering. Instead, they might be conservative in the sense that they enable the functioning of the status quo power relationships. Progressive and conservative media rituals – be it Fox or *The Daily Show*, Glenn Beck or Jon Stewart – are each reflective of the populist participatory ideologies of the interactive era. What they share in common is that they each display symptoms of the decline of symbolic efficiency, a distrust in representations and power elites, and an unending drive to debunk, deconstruct and reveal some truth, which is always just out of reach (Žižek 1999, Andrejevic 2013).

CONCLUSION

By examining TV talk shows, reality TV, television drama and comedy news formats in this chapter we have argued that popular culture plays a role in organizing our understanding of, and participation in, broader social and political processes. Popular culture's texts are symptomatic of, conditioned by, and play a part in producing power relationships. Popular culture is adept at simultaneously exposing its own constructed-ness, organizing audience participation and offering frameworks that govern everyday life.

In this chapter we have:

- considered the pedagogical function of popular culture in creating and structuring rules and frameworks for everyday life, and how we think about ourselves
- considered the role of popular culture in making sense of society and providing access to reality
- examined the forms of political participation that popular culture invokes
- considered popular culture's role in cultivating cultural formations that serve both cultural and political ends.

FURTHER READING

The readings below address a range of issues we explored in the chapter. Ouellette and Hay (2008b) analyse how reality TV offers a framework for governing everyday life. Turner (2006) offers an argument about the participation of ordinary people in popular-culture formats like reality TV. Peck (2010) examines the frameworks of self-improvement offered by Oprah. The readings by Baym (2005) and Feldman (2008) consider the role that comedy news plays in informing the public and enabling deliberative forms of democracy.

Baym, G. (2005) 'The Daily Show: discursive integration and the reinvention of political journalism', Political Communication, 22 (3): 259–276.

Feldman, L. (2008) 'The news about comedy: young audiences, The Daily Show, and evolving notions of journalism', Journalism, 8 (4): 406–427.

Ouellette, L. and Hay, J. (2008b) 'Makeover television, governmentality and the good citizen', Continuum: Journal of Media & Cultural Studies, 22 (4): 471–484.

Peck, J. (2010) 'The secret of her success: Oprah Winfrey and the seductions of self-transformation', Journal of Communication Inquiry, 34 (1): 7–14.

Turner, G. (2006) 'The mass production of celebrity "Celetoids", reality TV and the "demotic turn"', International Journal of Cultural Studies, 9 (2): 153–165.

Any article marked with (⊗) is available to download at the website **study.sagepub.com/carahandlouw**

SOCIAL MEDIA, INTERACTIVITY AND PARTICIPATION

MEDIA MANAGE POWER BY STRUCTURING OUR PARTICIPATION IN THE CREATION AND CIRCULATION OF MEANING.

* How do interactive media technologies organize participation in public life?

* What are some of the differing accounts of interactivity?

* How are power relationships formed and managed in an interactive media system?

We begin this chapter by conceptualizing social and interactive media. We then map out some key claims about interactivity. Interactive media:

- Enable new forms of participation: ordinary people can create and circulate content and express their point of view
- Are responsive and customized
- Facilitate greater transparency and surveillance.

INTERACTIVITY, PARTICIPATION AND POWER

In the Utah desert the US National Security Agency has built one of the largest data centres on earth. Many of the activities taking place at the centre were revealed by Edward Snowden during 2013. The purpose of the facility is to 'intercept, decipher, analyse, and store vast swaths of the world's communications as they zap down from satellites and zip through the underground and undersea cables of international, foreign and domestic networks'. The centre collects the 'complete contents of private emails, cell phone calls, and Google searches, as well as all sorts of personal data trails – parking receipts, travel itineraries, bookstore purchases' in order to paint 'detailed portraits' of our lives (Bamford 2012).

We often think of the power interactive media have granted to ordinary people. Where once we were merely consumers of mass media, now we can actively produce and distribute content. Where once we could only listen, now we can speak back. Although these narratives sound good, they deserve scrutiny. While some celebrate the capacity of interactive media to enable various forms of public expression (Benkler 2006, Jenkins 2006, Hartley 2010, Jarvis 2011, Jenkins et al. 2012), others argue these claims to empowerment are overstated and misleading, that in fact this is a far more controlling system and that our participation is an integral part of established concentrations of power. Interactivity, so the argument goes, does little in its own right to increase the quality of life or economic, political and social power of ordinary people (Andrejevic 2007, Dean 2010, Lanier 2010, 2013 Morozov 2011). While we can blog, upload videos and photos, comment, like and share content with each other, each of those activities takes place within a system that watches, responds, manages and profits from those activities. There is no doubt the audience is active, and we live in a media culture that calls on us to participate every day. What matters though is that we make careful distinctions between being 'active' and being 'powerful' (Morley 1993: 16). What are the qualities of our participation? Who does participation benefit? What kind of political and cultural formations does participating in interactive media produce? How do interactive forms of media change the way meaning is made and circulated? And what role do ordinary people play in making and circulating meaning? How are interactive media implicated in the exercise of power?

The media system being built around us can no longer be understood simply in terms of who says what to whom with what effect. We must also account for how speaking is interrelated with watching and listening. Power is concentrated not just in the capacity to speak, but also in the ability to collect and analyse information and create and manage interactive networks. This involves watching and responding to what others say and do – channelling, amplifying and constraining them. The data centre in the Utah desert offers one illustration of the immense concentrations of power that go hand in hand with the development of interactive media. If we are to have a robust account of the power that interactive media grant ordinary people to speak, we need a corresponding account of the power that interactive media grant often-established actors like states and corporations to watch everyday life. We then need to consider how this watching conditions the social spaces and processes in which we act. We need to carefully examine the capacity to speak in relation to how we are heard in meaningful ways.

WHAT ARE SOCIAL MEDIA?

Social media are embedded within interactive digital networks. Interactive digital networks comprise the whole range of internet technologies that collect, organize and circulate information. Social media refer to the emergence of web and mobile technologies that enable users to create and circulate content within social networks.

Users create and circulate content

Social media are characterized by users who create and circulate content within a network of other users. Those networks are shaped by a combination of user preferences and automated decisions made by those who control the network. On social media we tell a story about ourselves and our everyday lives (Livingstone 2008). Our peers, corporations, media organizations, political parties and governments provide us with content and cultural resources that we incorporate into our identities. We communicate who we are via the news stories we comment on, the brands we like, and the political and popular figures we makes jokes about or express faith in. This story about ourselves is constructed as a mobile and real-time part of our daily life.

Commercialization of the web

Social media are part of the ongoing technical development and commercialization of the web. Google, for example, bought YouTube for $1.6 billion in 2006 as part of their strategy of integrating 'search engines with content, social networking and advertising' (van Dijck 2009: 42). Facebook bought Instagram in 2012 for $1 billion so that they could retain control over the flow of personal photographs through the social web. Social media are increasingly central to how the web and networked economy function. Social media networks are converging with the provision of services and the databases of state and commercial institutions. Web technologies are becoming more responsive and flexible. Algorithms that intuitively read, organize and interpret information for users will be intrinsic to the next generation of the web. Social media users' creation and circulation of information is increasingly integrated with automated algorithms and databases that shape, manage and harness those activities.

Media devices and everyday life

The web that is developing around us is one that not only affords greater opportunities to make and circulate information, it will also be more intuitively integrated into our everyday life. Via devices that we carry around with us it will be able to locate, organize and present information to us in real time based on an array of different variables: where we are, what we're looking at, who we're with, who has come to this location in the past, where we're going, where it predicts we will go next, what we're talking about, what our mood is, what our tastes are, what our past movements or preferences are, what people like us have done or thought or said in the past, and so on. The web is a series of interconnected databases and algorithms that delivers customized information to us, just as much as we contribute and circulate information through it. The fundamental difference between this media system and a broadcast one is two-fold. Firstly, on broadcast media like television every member of the audience saw the same content. That is no longer the case; the interactive media system customizes content to individuals by watching and responding to users. Secondly, on television we saw content produced by professionals within bounded institutions. That is also no longer the case; we now see a mix of content that is produced by individuals and ordinary people. Professionals play the role of producing, editing and managing the flow of content.

Social media and social life

Media are social practices, something humans do (Couldry 2012: 33). Practices are enabled and constrained by power relations. We use media to organize the social world: coordinate societies, interact with each other, build communities, create and maintain trust, and convey and legitimize ideas, people and values. We use media to create and maintain social institutions and our way of life. Couldry (2012) maps out some of the intrinsic practices that form interactive and social media:

- *Searching*: search engines are a hub of online networks (2012: 45). The information we access online about news, politics, health issues, maps, popular culture, finance and so on begins with search engines. Increasingly, those searches are informed by information that Google collects about us. Search engines are key points of organizing information and representations and are therefore key nodes of control in the creation and maintenance of networks (2012: 105).
- *Showing*: everyday life is mediated and shown in online networks (2012: 47–48). Whether it is a large public event like a protest or a disaster, or a personal event like a party, ordinary people use smartphones to record, upload and circulate images and content in real time. Whenever something happens someone will be there to record and circulate it. Much of what we show online isn't so much a product of our own creative and analytic efforts to represent the social world, but rather an immediate live cataloguing of daily life.
- *Presencing and archiving*: individuals and institutions put information about themselves online to sustain a public presence (2012: 50). These activities are key to constructing a social identity. Being present in networks is critical to building social, economic and political capital. If presenting is the live real-time maintenance of being seen and felt in networks, then archiving is the process of managing information traces over time (2012: 51) to create ongoing narratives and histories about our lives, identities and communities (2012: 51).

Social media are part of a series of social practices that we use to create our identities and organize our lives. As we move through everyday life with our smartphone in hand we search for places on maps and recommendations on review sites; we show images of events that unfold around us; and we create digital traces that position us in social networks in ways that are visible publicly to our peers and privately to the databases and algorithms of platforms.

Social media and the active user

Social media platforms need active users who create and circulate content. The active user is a provider of sociality, content and data (van Dijck 2009: 47). Without them the platforms couldn't function or create value. Social media platforms, though, work to channel and contain user activity by 'brokering sociality' and 'engineering connectivity' (van Dijck 2011: 10). Platforms are built around dynamic power relationships. The forms of communication and control that social media enable are the result of an ongoing 'negotiation between owners, users, content producers, law makers, engineers, marketers about the control of data and technology' (2011: 12). The active user is constructed and constrained within the possibilities of the platform (2011). Users can only be active on the terms that are set by the social media platforms they use.

Social media platforms are a combination of material structures and hardware (like server farms and broadband networks) and immaterial processes like databases, software and user interfaces. These platforms, protocols and interfaces set the coordinates and protocols for communication (van Dijck 2011: 3). Just as broadcast media of the twentieth century called into being particular publics and action, and reshaped how commercial and state institutions interacted with those publics, networks of today are transforming public communication and life (2011: 3). Power on a social media platform is not grounded only in relationships of who produces and who consumes content, but more fundamentally in who controls the communicative spaces, processes, networks and flows of content.

INTERACTIVE MEDIA ENABLE NEW FORMS OF PARTICIPATION

Throughout the twentieth century our active meaning making and decoding of media texts was largely confined to our private lives. We could read the newspaper or watch a television programme and come to our own interpretations and views of the representations we encountered. We had little capacity, however, to express our ideas in a wider public context. For most of us, our views were confined to our friends and family, and perhaps to other civic bodies we participated in (like a trade union, a church, a sporting club or a local pub). Interactive media have expanded the capacity for us to publicize ourselves, our everyday lives and our perspectives to a wider audience. Via blogs and social media platforms anyone with access to the internet can create and circulate content. Using the communication conventions of online networks – like hashtags, discussion boards or groups – we can also circulate our views to a network of people who are interested in the same issues or events as us. We can also use those technologies to organize social networks and formations around shared interests and ideas. The fact of this capacity of ordinary people to publish and circulate their views and organize social networks shouldn't automatically lead us to conclude, however, that they are now more powerful, or that mainstream media are less powerful, or that elites are now more accountable. Instead, we need to consider how these technologies organize how power is made and maintained.

Arguments about the active audience have come and gone since the emergence of mass broadcast media in the 1930s. Media and audiences have always been 'interdependent … joint constructors of meaning' (Livingstone 1993: 7). While hegemonic discourses are always under construction and contingent, they weren't ever dependent on a media system that prevented people from thinking or saying what they really thought. In western democracies most people appear to consent with the ideology of the mass media. In this context, the more active the audience is the more they circulate and promote the messages and content of the mainstream media and its commercial and political allies. Morley (1993: 14) argues that while hegemonic discourses are always insecure and incomplete, this doesn't mean they are easily deconstructed in practice. In fact, we need to understand how the active meaning making of audiences – and indeed their resistant decoding and creative modification of meanings – are interlaced with their submission and complicity with hegemonic structures. Our creativity and resistance helps hegemonies function: it helps them to appear legitimate, accommodating and open-ended. If this could be said about television, it becomes even more important when we examine interactive forms of media that are even more dependent on our participation.

Considering the quality of participation

What interactive media bring to the mix perhaps is the mass amplification of the ability of audiences to create and circulate meaning. This participation appears to more readily affirm hegemonies than disrupt them. What we need in the interactive era is not just an understanding of the interaction between audience and text, but also how interactive media manage audience participation – encoding them into the continuous production of texts and meanings. Texts are no longer discrete bundles of meaning produced and distributed to an audience for decoding. Interactive media continuously incorporate the audience into the production of the text. The audience watches itself participating. What we need to pay attention to then is how texts establish and manage the coordinates within which that participation takes place. One reason this matters is that increasingly our participation as audience members is coextensive with our participation as citizens (Livingstone 1998: 197). It is in our everyday practices as audience members that we reproduce larger social structures and communicative processes (Morley 1993: 17).

This raises some important considerations:

- Ordinary people may have more opportunity to speak but this doesn't mean they are circulating new or different meanings. Much audience participation involves recirculating already existing media content without adding new meaning to it.
- Even if ordinary people are free to say whatever they want and circulate truly oppositional or radical ideas online, it doesn't necessarily follow that this will have any material effect on the real world. Where we do see real change, the activities of citizens on interactive media networks is often unfolding within a context where hegemonies are under other material, political and economic pressures.
- We need to pay careful attention to the quality of public dialogue on interactive and social media. The capacity to circulate information is only meaningful if the content we circulate is accurate, credible or constructive.
- Interactive and social media networks are often characterized by emotional or affective forms of communication. These media networks mobilize how we feel as much as what we think. Social media can rapidly amplify and circulate feelings of outrage and anger. These affective responses can be uneven, spontaneous, unpredictable and reactive. They can also spread quickly throughout a network.
- Online networks are often organized around a small group of 'knowing', educated and elite users. These are people who are educated, media-savvy and socially connected. They know how to channel publicity to generate responses from the network, and to use those responses to advance their own political and commercial interests.

- Interactive and social media platforms are increasingly composed of fragmented sectional interests. Users gravitate towards networks composed of people like them. Media organizations and social media platforms encourage and engineer this segmentation. In liberal democracies this segmentation is mostly undertaken for commercial reasons; in other states it can also be undertaken for political reasons. Regardless of the purpose, this segmentation does have effects on the nature of public life and political debate.
- Interactive and social media are characterized by savvy, snarky and ironic forms of communication. On the surface, participants who make clever and informed jokes about the powerful, or convey their cynical distance from the claims of the powerful, appear empowered. They appear informed and knowledgeable. But too often this surface disposition belies a fundamental apathy.

While there is no dispute that we are now more active participants in the creation and circulation of media content, what really matters is careful analysis of the qualities of that participation. We need to distinguish between 'speaking and being heard' (Hindman 2009). It doesn't matter that we can speak if no one is listening, or if our capacity to express ourselves isn't interrelated with material political processes that might change the world. That is, we need to pay attention to how our voices are valued both in terms of the quality and content of what we have to say, and the process of speaking and being heard (Couldry 2010). Nick Couldry encourages us not to fall for the claim that growing incitements to speak and participate are automatically empowering; instead we have to carefully examine how media, cultural and political processes engage us and value our voices. While ordinary people have the capacity to make and distribute meaning within interactive media, it does not appear to give them the ability to shape the way interactive space is organized (Hindman 2009, Turner 2010, Andrejevic 2011). We need to distinguish between the capacity to create content and the capacity to manage the spaces within which meaning is circulated.

INTERACTIVE MEDIA ARE RESPONSIVE AND CUSTOMIZED

During the twentieth century we developed an understanding of media representations appropriate for a broadcast media system. We grew accustomed to thinking of media representations as being publicly distributed and relatively static. Whatever a newspaper printed or a television station broadcast was final at the moment of transmission and available to anyone who accessed that publication or channel. In distinction, an interactive media system is responsive and customized. There are many ways that interactive media respond and adapt to users. The basic conceptual distinction though is that a broadcast media system couldn't make immediate and real-time decisions about the content it served a specific audience member, whereas an interactive media system can. A print publication or television station could conduct market research that informed their content and programming decisions. This research would shape content over a long period of time. And it did have effects on the way that audiences were segmented (see Turow 1997). This was a relatively imprecise activity, however, and viewers could still actively choose to view content that wasn't targeted at them. An interactive media system, however, shapes the content that it serves based on rapidly increasing flows of information it collects about users.

The more that audience members engage with interactive media systems, the more information they collect about them and the more effectively they can control the content served. For the most part, the decisions of organizations like Facebook and Google on the content that is served is guided by their commercial interests to serve content that fits their advertising-driven business models.

Customization

The sorting and customization of content enabled by interactive and networked media systems has benefits for both media organizations and consumers. For consumers, customization arguably offers greater convenience. As the interactive networks we use learn our interests and preferences they can make it easier for us to find the content we are seeking. As Amazon collects your purchase history it can recommend books it predicts you might like. As Google collects your search history and location it can serve you search results appropriate to where you live and what your interests are. These networks can also deliver content on-demand. The rise of businesses like Netflix and Hulu are rapidly moving television towards a post-broadcast business model. Viewers no longer sit down at a specified time to watch a television programme; they log on and stream content at their own convenience, often suggested to them by the platform's algorithms. There are opportunities for organizations that can take advantage of these more networked, asynchronous and fragmented forms of content production and delivery. They are no longer confined to having to create a mass audience that will consume one selection of content. They can continuously serve an array of different combinations of content to individuals based on their interests and demands. This increases the capacity for selling content and targeting advertisements.

A number of critiques (Hindman 2009, Lanier 2010, Morozov 2011, Pariser 2011, Turow 2011) have raised questions about the social and political consequences of a media system built on the routine sorting and customizing of content based on information collected from users. Pariser (2011) coins the term 'filter bubbles' to describe the selections of content we are served based on the information that networks collect about us. He uses the example of Facebook's news feed algorithm to make his point. Facebook makes decisions about the content it shows in a user's news feed based in part on decisions it makes about the closeness or affinity between that user and other users in their network. The algorithm recognizes affinity being performed when users acknowledge each other with likes or comments, share similar interests, express similar ideas or share connections in common. Pariser explains that although he has both progressive and conservative friends on Facebook, he is more inclined to express progressive views himself and share items of content to his own profile from progressive friends. Over time, Facebook learns that he has an affinity with progressive political views and news content, and so gradually removes conservative friends and content from his news feed. It is important to note that Facebook does not do this by deliberately labelling people and content 'progressive' or 'conservative' based on a judgement about the meaning of content being circulated. Its algorithm doesn't understand meaning; it makes a judgement based on the affinity between people based on who and what they interact with. It determines that some people are like others in terms of their interactions and expressions, but it doesn't necessarily know what the specific nature of that affinity is.

Pariser argues that he wants to read the views of his conservative friends, he just doesn't often post those views himself or engage with them. Aside from his personal preference to read conservative content, he makes a broader political point. That is, democracy depends on us encountering the views of people who aren't like us. During the twentieth century we lived in largely broadcast democracies, where the function of the media in part was to construct a public within which different points of view were disseminated, canvassed and debated over periods of time (although this is partly an idealized account of broadcast democracy). In an interactive post-broadcast democracy we risk losing this broad-based public, as we are sorted into smaller bubbles of people who are already like us.

These observations about the filtering of content online raise three important issues:

- Automatic algorithms become *the new gatekeepers*. Media systems have always had gatekeepers who decide what information is shared with the public and how events and ideas are represented. Traditional gatekeepers are journalists, editors and media advisors. They interact with each other to shape the way events are represented. While these gatekeepers still exist, in an interactive media system automatic algorithms also make decisions about the content that you see, and this can shape your view of immediate events or longer term understanding of issues.
- In a networked form of communication *we can only see those parts of the network that we are connected to*. The system learns which connections matter to us, and prompts us to make new connections based on our past or current interests. It predicts the kind of position we would like to have in a network. This means, though, that parts of public life, points of view and people become increasingly invisible to us. We are confined to parts of the network consisting of people like us.
- *Networks are asymmetrical*. Publics are constructed, performed and called into being continuously. Networks create a constantly-shifting set of connections between individuals based on convenience, proximity and affinity. They do not create publics where people with different points of view encounter and negotiate with each other.

Predictions and decisions

The consequences of increasingly customized information don't only extend to what we know about. They arguably also change our orientation to the truthfulness of representations. The ability to customize our media also leads us to choose between interpretations of events and issues. The problem is not only that we don't see the multiple sides of a debate, but also that we increasingly become immersed in a chosen perspective. We choose the facts that match how we feel about an event or issue (Andrejevic 2013: 49). We don't make choices based on our judicious or evidentiary assessment of perspectives. News becomes a customizable commodity. We customize based on our feelings and identity, as much as our assessments of the veracity of representations.

The responsive and customizable nature of interactive media doesn't just impact on the news and views we see in our Facebook news feeds, news sites we visit, and Google or Amazon searches. It has far-reaching and constantly evolving impacts. This is not just a matter of the information used about us as individuals, but also the information collected and used to make predictions about people like you (Andrejevic 2011). Consider the kinds of information an organization like Facebook could collect over the course of your life. It would know not just about your life, but the life course and prospects of the many thousands and even millions of people who share similar demographic characteristics, interests and everyday patterns as you. It can use that information not just to make decisions about what kind of person you are now but what life you are likely to lead in the future.

Algorithmic culture

As we use mobile devices we generate flows of information that algorithms make decisions about. Algorithms are the range of automated or procedural decisions media systems make in assembling flows of content and brokering audience attention. Hallinan and Striphas (2014: 3) define algorithmic culture as the 'use of computational processes to sort, classify, and hierarchize people, places, objects, and ideas, and also the habits of thought, conduct and expression that arise in relationship to those processes'. Algorithms are part of an interactive media system. As they become more important to how content is sorted and displayed to audiences, professional communicators devise ways to tune their activities to the decision-making logic of algorithms. News organizations, film and television producers, brands, politicians and any group seeking publicity need to create content that algorithms will judge to be of interest to audiences.

Hallinan and Striphas (2014) warn that this might create a new kind of cultural conformity. Algorithmic decision making tends to ignore objects that can't be categorized, that polarize opinion or that get an unpredictable reaction. As algorithms play a larger role in deciding what cultural content we see, we may see less culture that is genuinely disruptive, innovative and speculative.

FILTER BUBBLES

Watch Eli Pariser's TED talk 'Beware online "filter bubbles"'. You can find a link on the *Media and Society* website study.sagepub.com/carahandlouw

Pariser argues that algorithms like Facebook's news feed or the Netflix recommendation system tend to show us content that reflects ideas we already agree with, while making the lives and ideas of people who are different to us less visible.

Some argue that these algorithms give audiences what they want, while others say media and cultural producers have an important public role to play in challenging audiences and exposing them to alternative ways of life and points of view.

What are the consequences of algorithms deciding what content we see?

Shaping how we experience space

Responsive and customized forms of media shape the way we see the world around us in the first place. Morozov (2013) takes the example of the map, a media text that for hundreds of years has remained relatively objective. That is, the map of a city was the same for me as it was for you. Google, however, are making maps increasingly responsive and customized. The map of your city might appear differently to you compared to another citizen. The maps we see will give preference to our interests and the places frequented by our friends and people like us. Businesses might be able to pay to make themselves more visible on the maps of individuals they are seeking to target. This makes our choices far more predictable over time. We will go to the places that Google nudges us towards by making them more visible to us, instead of discovering places in our city accidentally over time. These media technologies profoundly change the everyday experience of life in a big city.

Space and our experience of it becomes just another form of information that can be collected, organized and customized as part of an interactive media system. The problem, as Morozov (2013) puts it, is that this system doesn't allow for the 'disorder, chaos and novelty' that have been an essential ingredient in creative and innovative cities and societies. Furthermore, these maps likely privilege commercial spaces with recommendations to us as consumers, and slowly the public spaces on maps become less visible and less important. These interactive maps might play a role in shaping our understanding of our cities and public spaces in the first place. They represent sites of consumption as important, because these will have reviews, recommendations and advertisements, whereas public spaces slip from view. 'In Google's world', Morozov (2013) argues, 'public space is just something that stands between your house and the well-reviewed restaurant that you are dying to get to. Since no one formally reviews public space or mentions it in their emails, it might as well disappear from Google's highly personalised maps.' Morozov's example points to the mobile and locational aspect of the responsiveness of media. Broadcast and print media were largely confined to particular sites of consumption; they didn't follow us around on a device in our pocket all day. The interface between Google search, targeted advertisements, maps and mobile devices prompts us to consider the way increasingly responsive forms of media reshape how that content is embedded in, and structures, our everyday life.

Algorithms organize and shape content you see, which in turn might affect your world-view and your capacity to use the media to participate in public life. This has a collective impact as it fragments public discourses. Profiled and sorted into niches, do we lose the capacity to use media to negotiate important social, cultural and political issues? Importantly, it also calls for a new understanding of control. Rather than shape our identities and lives only with ideological content, media shape our lives with a responsive and predictive mode of control that constantly anticipates our interests, life chances, life course and political viewpoints in ways that don't tell us what to think, as much as they anticipate and shape the information we use to construct our understanding of the world.

INTERACTIVE MEDIA WATCH US

Above we argued that in a broadcast media system we have become accustomed to thinking of media texts as relatively stable. We have also come to think of media production as predominantly the process of creating and distributing meaning. Interactive media though don't just speak, they also watch. On the one hand we need to consider how surveillance is intrinsic to interactive media and the networked economy. On the other hand we need to consider how interactive communication technologies enable greater transparency of social and political institutions and power. At the same time as we are seeing states and corporations rapidly develop enormous surveillance capacities, we are also seeing the emergence of new forms of transparency based on the ability to collect and share information. Broad-based and accessible Freedom of Information systems in many democracies, sites and communities of information sharing and disclosure like WikiLeaks or Reddit, and the use of blogs and micro-blogging networks in many developing and authoritarian countries, all point to ways in which interactive technologies can enable ordinary people to reshape power relations by subjecting the powerful to greater scrutiny and transparency. At the same time though many of these activities are readily incorporated into the power relationships of network societies. The more citizens use social media to organize themselves politically the more easily the powerful can track their opinions and movements. The revelations of WikiLeaks, despite being the largest leak of classified information in history, did not disrupt the US hegemony in any meaningful way. Governments all over the world are developing increasingly savvy ways of circumventing and managing Freedom of Information regimes. As quickly as interactive media afford new opportunities for transparency, the powerful work out ways to both control and benefit from those opportunities.

WHAT IS SURVEILLANCE?

Surveillance is watching with purpose (Lyon 2011: 14–16). Surveillance involves the 'focused, systematic and routine attention to personal details for purposes of influence, management, production or direction'. Surveillance technologies are a routine and normal part of everyday life in industrialized and networked societies. Surveillance was instrumental in the creation of institutions, discourses and mechanisms for producing, disciplining and managing populations (Foucault 1977). Institutions set rules, standards, procedures and norms for governing life in liberal societies. Techniques of observation, examination and judgement are used to ensure individuals comply with the discourses of institutions. Those individuals who internalize the rules monitor and govern themselves. The collection and organization of information underpins the very functioning of modern societies. With the emergence of interactive media, however, surveillance has dramatically expanded, becoming a ubiquitous part of our everyday public, private and work lives.

Surveillance involves relations of power in which 'watchers are privileged' (Lyon 2011: 14). One group watches another in order to manage them as a market, public or population. Importantly though, surveillance usually also relies on the participation and consent of the watched. When we use the internet, travel through public space, open a bank account or take out an insurance policy, make purchases on our credit card, or upload content to our social media profile, we consent in practice to that information being collected, analysed and used to manage further relationships with us and the population of which we are a part.

Surveillance technologies are interwoven with our everyday social lives. We make ourselves and our lives visible to the cameras, databases and algorithms of the networked society. As we move through the city we leave information behind (Lyon 2011: 111). Surveillance is a process of assembling or linking together media technologies, databases, social spaces and practices. Think of your smartphone as a node in an assembly or network of surveillance processes. The camera in the phone, its GPS capabilities, and the internet searches, maps and apps all generate information that is logged in various databases. Surveillance isn't something that just happens 'in the clouds'. It is a material process that requires large amounts of investment in server farms, hardware and labour at one end, and users logging information about their everyday practices and expressions at the other. Surveillance and media technologies are constantly being assembled in relation to each other. We do our part in integrating surveillance into everyday life. We routinely engage in mutual (Trottier 2011) and lateral (Andrejevic 2002b) forms of surveillance as part of our social lives – when we trawl through the photos of acquaintances on Facebook or search the names of work colleagues on Google. Surveillance is not imposed on us by some Big Brother 'out there': it is an ordinary and visible part of our everyday lives.

In a networked society the process of making and managing populations is information intensive, and therefore relies on technologies that collect, manage and organize that information. Surveillance involves a series of commercial and state activities that are entwined with each other. Corporations and states need to track, profile and classify people and populations in order to make decisions about them and to manage them. Interactive societies and economies have developed within a neoliberal context characterized by links between governments and corporations. Corporate innovations in surveillance technologies have been adapted to the state, and corporate and state databases are integrated (or at least share access with each other). As states and corporations interact with each other to build these very large surveillance systems it raises important questions about who 'defines categories' (Lyon 2011: 186): 'When people's life-chances depend upon what category they have been placed in, it is very important to know who designed the categories, who defines their significance and who decides the circumstances under which those categories will be decisive.' The issue is that those who are watched have decisions made about them but the information used to make those decisions is opaque.

Disciplinary and productive forms of surveillance

While we commonly think of surveillance in a disciplinary sense – that is, surveillance systems are used to watch over and identify individuals who are deviant – surveillance more commonly serves productive purposes. It doesn't just identify risks, it also identifies opportunities (Lyon 2011). Databases produce populations that can be used for some purpose: potential consumers, voters or participants. Careful observation of populations generates opportunities by identifying new patterns, practices and innovations (Zwick and Knott 2009). A database is also a tool for producing new network formations that are useful and valuable. Databases can identify 'creative, non-conforming, and unexpected forms of consumer life' that often 'evolve out of the social and cultural innovations generated in uncontrolled and undisciplined spaces of consumer culture' (2009: 225). Databases are part of an interactive media system that doesn't need to control populations with particular ideas and beliefs – that is, in a representational and ideological sense – but rather controls them by watching and responding to them. Used in real time, databases respond to individuals depending on their location, place in a network, mood, activity or demands. Databases organize populations, identify risks, modulate social relationships, anticipate interests and actions, and capture opportunities (Zwick and Knott 2009, Lyon 2011).

Productive forms of surveillance are emergent, convergent and increasingly predictive (Andrejevic 2013). In a networked interactive media system, data is collected continuously and uses for it are constantly emerging. Data collected for one purpose is readily appropriated for other uses as the capacities of databases expand. Increasingly, networked organizations bring data together to create new and useful assemblages. For instance, Facebook collects data about its users' everyday lives, while credit card companies collect information about their purchases. The two organizations might agree to converge their databases to examine patterns that might be mutually beneficial in building their markets and the value of their respective networks. Social and interactive media also offer whole new kinds of data, and new connections between data sets. In addition to who we are, where we are and who we interact with, databases can increasingly collect and use affective data – that is, how we feel about particular things, places, times and people. Tracking the expressions and sentiments of people and populations in real time is useful in predicting and managing consumption, political events and economic transactions.

Just as we often think of surveillance in a disciplinary sense, we also often imagine information in a representational way. That is, data is useful because it contains a particular meaning. Mark Andrejevic (2013: 35) argues that the forms of information management and surveillance enabled by interactive technologies means:

> Two different information cultures will come to exist side by side: on the one hand, the familiar, 'old-fashioned' one in which people attempt to make sense of the world based on the information they can access: news reports, blog posts, the words of others and the evidence of their own experience. On the other hand, computers equipped with algorithms that can 'teach' themselves will advance the instrumental pragmatics of the database: the ability to use tremendous amounts of data without understanding it.

Big data analysis is pushing towards predictive rather than explanatory forms of analysis. That is, we don't need to know why something works, just that it works. For example, Facebook might notice that you often check in at particular places and times of the week and that other people like you do the same thing. It doesn't necessarily need to know why you do it or what it means (for instance, people who like a certain music genre go to a particular bar each Friday night), but this data enables Facebook to predict this pattern of behaviour over time and perhaps connect that data with other content or information it has in useful ways (targeting content or advertisements, or understanding how the social graph intersects with social places and practices).

Surveillance raises many questions about what are personal, private and public goods or resources. While we could think about privacy in terms of secrecy (things we don't want people to know) or intimacy (aspects of our lives that are personal), we should think beyond just our personal privacy to larger questions about control:

- Who owns these networks?
- Who collects, stores, analyses and uses the data?
- What do they do with this information now and in the future?
- How is information used to make decisions about us?
- How do we address the control of information within a democratic society?

In a networked society interactive media assume an importance to the functioning of the economy and politics beyond simply circulating ideas. Power rests with those who build and control the networks of information and communication used to run markets, manage populations and increasingly also organize 'hard' forms of power like warfare.

PARTICIPATION AND PUBLIC LIFE

So far we have argued that rather than take the internet to be inherently democratizing because it enables ordinary people to express their point of view and to bypass traditional information gatekeepers, we need to examine:

- What kinds of participation do the internet and social media enable?
- Who gets to participate?
- What kinds of public social processes and institutions do the internet and social media facilitate?

Blogging

Hindman (2009) canvasses three key claims that have been made about the democratizing nature of the internet:

- The internet broadens debate. Where broadcast media were the preserve of select voices, online anyone can speak.
- The internet enables participation. Where traditional forms of political activity like joining a party are declining, the internet enables the rise of a range of new informal forms of political action that are appealing to citizens traditionally disengaged from politics.
- The internet makes politics more transparent. Information about the political process can be shared and accessed by members of the public more broadly and easily. There are no constraints on the amount of information that can be distributed and who distributes it, and there is less ability for gatekeepers to control what information is distributed.

To these arguments Hindman (2009) offers two responses:

- Firstly, most traffic on the web travels between a small number of powerful nodes. Major search engines, social networks and news organizations control the flow of most content through the web. If you are going to find out some information about a political event or issue you will most likely go to a search engine like Google, a social network like Facebook, or a major news organization's website. These players shape the flow of political information through the web.
- Secondly, blogs are predominantly the media of a new elite, who largely reflect entrenched forms of power and privilege. To produce the content required for a popular and widely read political blog, a blogger needs to be a well-trained professional communicator with the economic and cultural resources to produce compelling content. This includes: the time and money

to fund the production of content; the cultural capital to understand politics; access to political insiders and sources to glean information; and the critical analytical skills to find, read and interpret documents. Furthermore, he finds that the more educated the blogger, the bigger their audience is.

Hindman (2009) argues that there is a difference between speaking and being heard online. Online audiences are just as concentrated as traditional media audiences. Only a few are really heard. To become powerful in this network you need not just to create content, but also to gain the attention of other nodes – who read your content, circulate it further, link to you and so on. To become a powerful node requires technical, economic, social and cultural capital. In recent times, Nate Silver is perhaps emblematic of the highly educated and well-regarded political bloggers. Silver produces a form of content that draws on the resources available in the interactive, networked, big data era. He works for major media organizations, and is highly educated and well connected with the political elite. His blog is widely read because he offers highly skilled analytics of population-level data. Silver doesn't necessarily provide new and alternative understandings of politics, rather he uses data to offer a well-educated audience ways of enjoying the prediction of election outcomes.

NATE SILVER AND DATA-DRIVEN BLOGGING

The popularity of Nate Silver during the 2012 US Presidential race offers one example of the attention and influence a well-resourced and educated blogger can exert on the coverage of politics. Silver uses big data to offer a new kind of meta-coverage of the political process. Where established cable news pundits continually called the Obama–Romney race as very close, Silver predicted a 90 per cent chance that Obama would win. Silver illustrates and extends Hindman's arguments. He is a highly educated, white, middle-class male. After rising to prominence as a blogger, he joined the *New York Times*, and moved into the centre of the media-political process in the US during the 2008 and 2012 Presidential elections. Silver is not just a blogger; he is also symptomatic of another aspect of interactive media – the way big data analysis reshapes how we use information to represent public life. Silver can only do big data analysis of politics in a society where vast sets of data are readily available and where he can get access to those (often private and commercial) sets of data. He is part of a new kind of political elite, reshaping public discussions of politics and upsetting and undermining established elites along the way. His blog doesn't necessarily reshape the way the public participates in the political process, but rather how they understand the way that political preferences are aggregated, predictable and – in his words – designable. Silver, unlike the political bloggers Hindman studied, produces a form of content that draws on the resources available in the interactive, networked, big data era. This reshapes how we understand the political. We shift away from using media to attempt to understand each other, and towards using media to predict each other's actions and views.

(Continued)

(Continued)

Silver's combination of analysing big data sets and blogging about his findings is a new form of meta-coverage; he enables the public to be insiders who have access to how the political events will unfold. This data is used to shape, as much as inform, the public. Silver argues that his meta-coverage of the political process – that is, calling the race – is 'good' whereas pundits' coverage is 'bad', because his is based on empirical data. The issue is that this kind of meta-coverage encourages us to imagine populations as predictable. As we do so, social and political questions become a matter of having enough data to diagnose and solve the problem. Silver's analysis is underpinned by the creation of a particular kind of public – one that willingly submits to surveillance. The more they participate, the more they register their information, the more they can be told about predictions being made about them. Those predictions shape them as a public. Silver illustrates how bloggers aren't just a new elite in the sense that they get to speak about the political process; they also legitimize the networked, informational, predictive form of politics brought about in part by interactive technologies. As our public and political culture celebrates interactivity as politically empowering, it legitimizes an interactive media system that promises democratization, while at the same time engaging in ever more sophisticated modes of control of information and concentrations of power.

How does Nate Silver's coverage contribute to democratic debate and participation?

You can find links to Nate Silver stories and talks on the *Media and Society* website study.sagepub.com/carahandlouw

Social media and political events

If blogging is primarily the media of a well-resourced and educated elite, then it might be argued that social media platforms like Twitter and Facebook facilitate more broad-based participation of ordinary people in public life and political events. The events of the Arab Spring, and other uprisings and protests in authoritarian regimes, have been lauded for demonstrating the role that social media play in facilitating political revolutions. It goes without saying that these claims should be treated cautiously. While social media may have been a tool used to circulate information in these events, it was most likely not the catalyst or a determining factor in any political revolution. The events like the Arab Spring or the 2009 Iranian elections are far more complex than that.

Social media do though change the way information circulates about political events, and that does shape the way people think, feel and act. Papacharissi and Oliveira (2012) offer a helpful study of tweets using #egypt during the Egyptian revolution in 2011. They argue that 'Twitter is frequently used to call networked publics into being and into action during periods of political instability' (2012: 268). Twitter is used to distribute information about events by mainstream media, established actors and ordinary people. The live, repetitive and mobile nature of the platform creates a background ambience for events. Twitter users augment traditional news values with other features (2012: 273–275):

- *Instantaneity*: Twitter users post ongoing and instant updates of events as they unfold.
- *Crowdsourced elites*: elite status is granted via interaction (retweeting and replying) based on how important or useful their content is to the network. The network produces elites by bringing them to the centre of information flows. Some elites are established actors like journalists or political figures central to events who people look to as events unfold. Others have a temporary value to the network given their proximity to events or their live coverage. The networks link them in and out as it requires them.
- *Solidarity*: tweets express solidarity via common identity, cause and values. Twitter functions not only as a site for debate or information, but for the large-scale amplification of sentiments and beliefs. Twitter provides important affective energy for events.
- *Ambience*: the constant feed of tweets sustains an always-on live coverage and anticipation of events. Individuals take events and narrate them via their own emotions and sentiments. This creates an 'ambient information sharing environment'.

The continuous, live, unfolding ambience of Twitter's coverage of events can be described as an 'affective network'. As individuals convey their feelings they anticipate and shape events. How people feel in relation to each other and seek the attention of others shapes public networks like Twitter. Rather than a rational exchange of meaning, ideas or debate, what takes place is a continuous circulation of feelings and affects. In the case of a political revolution, social media doesn't play the role of making the case for the revolution, or mediating between competing demands, but rather in sustaining and mediating the network of actors facilitating political events. News gets caught up in these networks, and takes on an affective dimension. As journalists and individuals report events, others in the network circulate those reports together with their own sentiments. Rather than create content, they circulate and amplify affect. Individuals tweet from their place in the network, blending 'drama with fact' (Papacharissi and Oliveira 2012: 278) and news with emotion and opinion. Individuals use Twitter to find and convey their place in the story. This repetition and mimicry engages participants emotionally rather than cognitively (2012: 278). Participants in a social network re-tweet, share, endorse, disagree, joke and express their feelings about events. They take an aspect of events, their position in relation to it, and circulate it through the network, often with their emotions, sentiments or identities attached. This ongoing process determines the trajectory of messages (or memes) through a social network.

Networks have nodes of power and influence:

- The link structure of networks makes some websites – search engines, social networks, news sites – central hubs of information.
- Economic, institutional and cultural resources make some individuals – bloggers, journalists, political figures, industry leaders – prominent within networks.
- Proximity to events make some individuals temporarily important conduits of information in networks. Proximity can take material and cultural forms. If you are physically at a political

event with a smartphone your content will quickly flow to the centre of networks. Or, if you have a specialist understanding of events because you know the key players or drivers, the network will seek out your expertise for as long as it is useful to narrating and explaining events.

The affective nature of these online networks is significant and important. None of these leaders can autonomously make themselves a centre of power. They always depend on attracting and sustaining the attention and interaction of others in the network to maintain their presence.

Networks can also be used by powerful actors to promote and drive conflicts and disruptions, as much as they are used for collaboration and dialogue (Bratich 2011). Bratich (2011: 621) details how the US State Department funded groups that distributed 'technical knowledge and social media skills' to young protestors in authoritarian regimes. This illustrates how powerful established actors use social media to organize political movements. For Bratich (2011: 622) 'we are witnessing a convergence of sovereign and network powers' where states integrate into networks. The State Department's Alliance of Youth Movements brought together established and new media organizations to train youth in building genetically modified grassroots organizations. This involved a mixture of top-down and bottom-up cultural production. The use of social media in political protests and events does not necessarily 'spring from authentic populist or spontaneous community aspirations' (Bratich 2011: 627).

What each of these perspectives demonstrates is that networks are complex and evolving configurations of attention, influence and power. They are not necessarily more or less empowering for ordinary people than other forms of public communication. They do enact different configurations of power that inform how public and political life unfolds.

THE VISUAL NATURE OF SOCIAL MEDIA

Visual content is critical to the live and affective dynamics of social media. Kraidy (2005, 2006) examines the use of popular culture and new media in political activity in the Arab world. Kraidy (2012) illustrates the connection between videos and social media in circulating sentiments about political events. He argues that videos – often made on smartphones and laptops – adapt old forms of political action like satire, theatre and home-made puppetry with the new digital video and social networks. Videos become especially powerful for several reasons:

Using smartphones and laptops, citizens can easily produce videos.
Using the internet, videos can be widely distributed, bypassing state and media gatekeepers.
Videos can use popular culture codes and images that are easily understood around the globe.
Videos can be resent and recirculated.

To illustrate, Kraidy (2012) examines videos produced by Syrians during the uprising and civil war. Top Goon is a satirical series of videos produced by a group of young Syrians living in Beirut. The videos used finger-puppets, theatre and popular culture formats to satirize Assad and the Syrian regime. One of the videos uses the global format of the *Who Wants to be a Millionaire?* television game show. The video makers adapted the format to 'Who Wants to Kill a Million?', with Assad appearing as the contestant answering questions such as 'If you could commit a massacre in the capital, Damascus, who would you put in charge?' and 'Who's the dumbest person in your regime?'

Kraidy (2012) describes videos like Top Goon as creative insurrection: the use of cultural resources and media technologies under life threatening duress. This below-the-line media circulates online and gets appropriated by mainstream media where it creates alternative perspectives on political events. Kraidy argues that the videos are powerful not because they attempt to facilitate debate and dialogue (they don't), but because they capture attention. Videos circulate across platforms like mobile, television, web and tablet and become the talk of everyday life. They animate ordinary and popular discussions. The videos and their circulation create a performative public as they are replayed and circulated. Aside from their content the practice of sharing jokes about the regime creates social connections.

Public life is performed via the circulation of texts. The repetitive circulation of texts gains attention, brings a public into being and acts as a petition against the powerful. The content of the arguments of the videos is not what matters, the arguments against Assad and the Syrian regime are well known, the role the videos play is in creating content that can be circulated to gain attention. They gain attention because they affect their audiences – with humour, anger and hope. By sharing the videos individuals seek to express how they feel about the situation, and in doing so, affect their family, friends and social networks.

How do insurgents exploit the visual, mobile and networked nature of online media?
What claims about the power of interactive media do you find plausible?
How do interactive media enable marginalized groups to resist dominant groups and represent their identities?
What are the affordances and risks of interactive media to democracy?

You can find links to talks by Marwan Kraidy about the use of insurgent videos in Syria on the Media and Society website study.sagepub.com/carahandlouw

MAPPING OUT POSITIONS ON INTERACTIVITY

Interactive media 'constitute the means to build a different type of social organisation' (Couldry 2012: 109). Our media and popular culture commonly present interactive and participatory media as 'good'. We are constantly encouraged to participate, express our views, comment, like, vote and so on. We are told this activity makes us active and empowered. Interactive media are presented as better – more exciting, more enjoyable and more empowering – than old top-down broadcast forms of media.

Government, corporations and established civil society actors actively resist dramatic reorganizations of power. They see networks as tools to maintain their power. Evidence of networks disrupting global flows of power over the past generation have not materialized. The processes of neoliberalism, globalization and concentration of wealth set in train at the beginning of the network society have continued apace. Networks are incredibly useful and profitable tools to elites that learn how to use them. And the already established elite are in the best position to mobilize the resources required to build and maintain networks. Information abundance and networks offer established actors just as many opportunities as they do ordinary or disempowered people (Couldry 2012: 124).

While there may have been a moment when networks afforded new opportunities for reshaping power relationships, established players are emerging that control and constrain the uses of networks. The commercialization of the web and the large-scale surveillance of the internet by the state are two examples of this. Given this, we ought to ask (Couldry 2012: 115):

- How do networks facilitate and constrain flows of power?
- How do networks sustain political agency?
- How are societies configured by networks?
- How are narratives about interactive media and empowerment constructed?
- How do different groups attempt to make their narrative about interactive media legitimate?

There are a variety of responses to these questions that speak to the affordances and capacities of interactive media (Dahlberg 2011). Interactive media:

- enable the circulation of useful information that informs rational choices
- allow for multiple positions and preferences to be accounted for
- support deliberation, debate and argument that eventually arrive at agreement and consensus
- provide space for marginalized and excluded groups to resist and contest dominant ideas or configurations of power
- offer the technical capacity for new forms of social cooperation and collaboration to emerge
- enable performances that create networks of attention and affect.

Just as we can identify several ways interactive media might support political agency, we can also point to some of their shortcomings. Couldry (2012) questions the capacity of interactive media to sustain long-term, meaningful, positive political projects. He implores us to think of the long-term contexts and structures that sustain political action and the public. He cautions against views that foreshorten the social by celebrating individuals acting in temporary networks around singular issues (2012: 117). Without social institutions that support public life, networks are empty (2012: 118).

While networks might enable new forms of communication and participation in public life, they appear to (Couldry 2012: 125–128):

- Be weighted towards short-term disruptions rather than long-term positive projects; this serves the interests of established actors.
- Enable established actors to amplify their messages and circulate information, without increasing the capacity for ordinary people to be meaningfully heard.
- Increase the opportunities for counter-politics, but displace opportunities for sustained action around explicit goals. Networks encourage transparency, revelation, being a watchdog, veto and feelings of outrage and anger: they destabilize and amplify feelings rather than contribute to ongoing social processes and publics.
- Create forms of participation which serve the interests of corporate media: there is no correlation between internet access and political participation (2012: 127). In an on-demand media system it is actually easier to avoid politics, and if your social network incrementally avoids politics then algorithms and filters will increasingly dis-embed you and your social world from the political
- Saturate everyday life with media in ways that constrain the possibility of political action: as ordinary people and their everyday lives become more publicly visible this places a constraint on positive politics, that is, the hard work of 'persuading others to change how they live' (2012: 128). This is because networks inflate forms of disruptive counter-democracy while at the same time closing out the possibilities and opportunities for ordinary forms of democracy; formal forms of political action disappear, as informal, temporary, disruptive forms of political activity proliferate.

Democratic politics needs trust in networks that do not categorically exclude any group or allow any group to act autonomously from the public (Couldry 2012: 118). Networks saturate everyday life with media, and this reinforces the status quo and decreases trust, which both count against the possibility of meaningful forms of change or dealing with complex social and political problems.

MANAGING PARTICIPATION

The information abundance and short-term insurgent forms of political action characteristic of interactive networks also require new forms of political management. Political elites now need to invest significant resources in managing information, open government and the continuous short-term demands of an always-on information network. The spin and media management that are typical of contemporary democratic government are at least in part interrelated with the continuous, emotive, short-term revelations of social media. This arguably distracts elites from doing their job: they too become oriented to short-term and reactive democracy, rather than guiding populations in the establishment of long-term positive political projects and corresponding social institutions and public spaces. Furthermore, good governance involves taking hard and unpopular decisions. The more that interactive networks orient publics towards continuous exposure, transparency and instantaneous assessment of a population's sentiment towards those decisions, the higher the risks and consequences of those decisions. If all decision making is in the open, subject to the continuous feedback of the network, then taking hard decisions becomes difficult, perhaps impossible. Politics collapses to managing real-time feedback from the public.

The continual and amplified circulation of information arguably distracts attention both from examining the real workings of political power and from developing material and meaningful political projects. The old critique of media focused on its top-down structure and its control of particular meanings and representations. We now need to think beyond control of the production of particular representations and messages, controlling the ideas in our heads. Instead, we need to make sense of a mode of control that manages the spaces in which we interact, modulating the ideas we see and circulate, and predicting who we are, what we want and who we might be. We need to think beyond individual privacy concerns to how an interactive media system profiles, sorts and manages populations, flows of ideas, political processes and cultural practices.

CONCLUSION

In this chapter we've examined the paradox that while on the one hand interactive technologies enable forms of communication that are participatory, empowering and democratic, they simultaneously lead to more intensive forms of surveillance and control. While ordinary people are able to participate in making and circulating meaning, in doing so they contribute to the creation of networks that watch, track and respond to them. Mark Andrejevic (2009: 41) argues that our task is twofold: 'To consider the ways in which the deployment of networked digital media contribute to and reinforce the contemporary exercise of power, and to imagine how it might be otherwise.' To do that he suggests we distinguish between the 'real interactivity' of participating in 'shaping the structures that regulate our social lives, not just in increasing the range of choices available within the horizon of those structures and the social relations they help reproduce' (Andrejevic 2009: 49). Perhaps most importantly, we need to differentiate this form of interactivity from what Žižek describes as 'pseudointeractivity, the urge to "be active", to "participate", to mask the nothingness of what goes on' (Žižek 2008: 183). Such a distinction is crucial to the project of making interactivity live up to its promise, rather than settling for the claim that it already has' (Andrejevic 2009: 49).

To conclude, we can offer some preliminary answers to some of the key questions of this chapter. In an interactive and networked media system:

- *Where is power located?* Power is located in networks that control the flow of information: search engines like Google, social networks like Facebook, database companies like Axciom and DoubleClick, political organizations like Obama's 2012 Presidential campaign, and state bureaucracies like the National Security Agency.
- *How is power structured?* Power is structured around participation and interactivity. If a system can watch and respond to participation, it isn't as dependent on controlling what is said. The more we participate the more the system can adapt and control.

- *What is the dominant form of communication?* The dominant form of communication is participatory.
- *How does interactivity legitimate itself?* With the promise of giving voice to ordinary people and by neutering opportunities to reflect critical points of view. For instance, Facebook only has a 'like' button. Critical and challenging views by their very nature don't generate affinity or engagement and so are filtered out of feeds and networks.
- *Who benefits from this system?* Organizations and people who can collect, access, organize, and manipulate information; organizations and people who can build and manage networks; and organizations and people who can harness and modulate participation.

Celebrations of interactivity that focus only on the ability of publics to access information and speak avoid a thorough account of the qualities of participation and good government. In these accounts, participation becomes an end in itself, rather than a means to an end. This scuppers the possibility of careful deliberation about the quality of participation (Couldry 2010), the difference between speaking and being heard (Hindman 2009), and critique of a system that relies on participation in general but pays no attention to particular ideas and expressions (Dean 2010). The problem remains distinguishing between active and empowered, and deliberating over what kinds of participation are desirable (Andrejevic 2007). In the interactive era new divisions of power emerge within access to and control over flows of information (Andrejevic 2013: 59).

FURTHER READING

The readings below offer a variety of critical perspectives and arguments about interactivity and participation relating to personal privacy (boyd 2008, Fuchs 2012), the way social media structures relationships (van Dijck 2011), political participation (Dahlberg 2011), and the exploitation of audiences (Andrejevic 2011).

Andrejevic, M. (2011) 'Surveillance and alienation in the online economy', *Surveillance & Society*, 8 (3): 278–287.

boyd, d. (2008) 'Facebook's privacy trainwreck', *Convergence: The International Journal of Research into New Media Technologies*, 14 (1): 13–20.

Dahlberg, L. (2011) Re-constructing digital democracy: an outline of four "positions"', *New Media & Society*, 13 (6): 855–872.

Fuchs, C. (2012) 'The political economy of privacy on Facebook', *Television & New Media*, 13 (2): 139–159.

van Dijck, J. (2012) 'Facebook as a tool for producing sociality and connectivity', *Television & New Media*, 13 (2): 160–176.

Any article marked with (⊗) is available to download at the website **study.sagepub.com/carahandlouw**

12 MOBILE MEDIA, URBAN SPACE AND EVERYDAY LIFE

* How have the global networked economy and interactive media changed urban life?

* How have mobile devices like smartphones changed urban life?

* How have mobile devices changed our intimate, personal and public lives?

In this chapter we:

- Examine how media represent urban space
- Consider how media organize our movement in and experience of urban space
- Explore how we use media to make ourselves visible in urban space
- Consider how media are used to monitor urban space.

MEDIA AND URBAN SPACE

Media are central to organizing the symbolic structure of cities. Throughout the twentieth century, broadcast forms of media like radio and television cultivated mass publics and organized life in mass industrial cities. As media become more mobile, pervasive and interactive they become part of the architecture of our cities (McQuire 2008). Public space, workplaces and homes incorporate media technologies. Digital networks enable decentralized and heterogeneous social structures. Our lives are no longer confined to our immediate position in space: our family, our home or neighbourhood or even our city. Via broadcast and networked media technologies we can embed ourselves within social relations and flows of culture that are organized in a relational sense across large and disparate geographical areas. The city becomes a 'relational space' (McQuire 2008), one where our experience is grounded in the social relations we construct using media.

In this chapter we examine how media organize life in urban space:

- Media play a critical role in *representing urban space and life*. We use media to imagine ourselves living together. It is through media that we come to construct images in our minds of our city and its patterns of life.
- *Media facilitate power relationships* within urban space: they make clear who has power and how that power is exercised. They also mediate our participation in political and community processes. Over time media play an important role in making urban life cohesive. They fashion collective identities and values that we adhere to. Without media playing these roles our urban spaces would be chaotic, violent and dysfunctional.
- *Media organize space in a material sense*. Public spaces and buildings are organized around large screens. Large stadiums are built as sites of media production. The living areas in our homes are organized around television screens. Our trains and coffee shops have WiFi. Fast broadband networks are built through our neighbourhoods.
- *Media organize interaction in everyday life*. Media tell us what is happening, where to go to get things and how to get there. Media are central to getting things done in the city. When events unfold, media are critical to directing populations, preventing chaos and asserting control.
- Media are *central to being seen and felt* in urban space. We use media to make ourselves visible to our peer networks and the broader public. We use media technologies to stay present in large and dispersed social networks. We are more likely to obliquely watch and be watched by a large range of acquaintances in our online social network than we are to have ongoing relationships with a range of people in our immediate neighbourhood.
- Media technologies are used by corporations, governments and individuals to *monitor life in the city*. Aside from the examples of corporate and state surveillance we have already discussed, mobile devices are increasingly used by individuals to monitor themselves and their lives. Take for instance biometric and social fitness apps on mobile devices. These apps monitor our physical activity together with biometric data like heart rates and sleep patterns. This charts our own life rhythms and progress against that of our peers. The smartphone is a 'complex device for listening' (Crawford 2012: 217). It listens to us and we use it to listen to others. This monitoring extends the rationality of modern capitalism and bureaucracy into our everyday lives and the way we monitor and manage ourselves, our bodies and our relations with others (2012: 222).

Media do more than just produce and circulate meaning. They organize social life. As media technologies are incorporated into the infrastructure of our public and private spaces their importance to social life becomes more central. Each of the roles of media in urban space set out here is dramatically intensified by mobile media. Mobile media are a key ingredient in creating lifestyles characterized by constant flows of information, visibility and monitoring.

In addition to critical and celebratory accounts of mobile media and urban space, we should also give consideration to the kinds of communication urban space ought to enable. Hamelink (2008: 298) argues for cities where architecture and urban space 'invite people to impart, seek, receive and exchange information, ideas and opinions, to listen to each other and learn from each other in an ambience where their autonomy, security and freedom is optimally guaranteed'. Recognizing the reality that human life is predominantly urban, and that conflict in cities needs to be managed, Hamelink presses against the increasingly rationalized forms of control characteristic of mobile media and urban space. In place of cameras and databases, Hamelink argues for urban designs that enable richer forms of human communication. He proposes a number of provocative questions:

- Does the city – despite the processes of privatization – have enough public space left for people to meet?
- Does the city have places that, although privately owned, function as public meeting places (e.g. your favourite pub)?
- Do meeting places provide for free speech? Can people express opinions and ideas without the risk of intervention?
- Can people communicate without being under 24/7 surveillance?
- Does the city offer views that inspire people to converse with others?
- Are there lots of small markets and myriad cultural events?
- Are there places where people can withdraw for inner conversation with themselves?
- Does the city have a good balance between large, open spaces and small, intimate spaces?
- Do city dwellers feel that their urban space has human proportions?
- Are there a variety of architectural structures and socio-economic functions, like in the world's great streets?

As urban space is organized by economic and technological forces, Hamelink prompts us to consider how media can be used to create a communicative city. He argues for a city where urban space facilitates an array of distinctively human forms of communication.

Media networks both disperse economic activity around the world while also concentrating power in media cities that act as 'command and control centres for the global economy' (McQuire 2008: 20). For the affluent in these global cities this means greater interconnectedness through media, travel, cultural consumption and flows of consumer goods. For the poor it means a life increasingly lived in contained local spaces. New forms of connectedness are accompanied by new forms of exclusion. These modes of control choose how nodes are connected to the network. They can exclude and contain as much as they connect. The spaces we live in, and the possibilities that exist within those spaces, are shaped by flows of information and the way we are connected to and embedded in the networks of global capitalism.

A NEW GEOGRAPHY OF POWER

As global network capitalism has taken shape a new geography of power has emerged. Power is built on being connected to the electronic information network. There are, of course, many different levels and qualities of connectivity, such as:

- a super-elite who control networks and connectivity in general, setting the terms on which others connect and interact
- an information-rich elite who are connected to information networks and are able to use them to acquire cultural, commercial and political capital, but who ultimately do not control the network
- a disconnected underclass with little or no meaningful access to the network; not being connected or having only minimal connection is equivalent to being disempowered.

Some examples of forms of disconnection and disempowerment include:

- living in a society where information technologies are available, but you lack the skills, education, cultural capital or economic resources to access them
- living in a society where you cannot access the communication infrastructure required to use information technologies – for instance, living in a rural or regional area with no broadband or mobile reception, or living in a country where there is no functioning infrastructure
- living in a society where the state limits your access to the internet, or prevents you from connecting altogether.

In theory, satellites make geography irrelevant by creating the possibility for anyone, anywhere to be connected to the communication network. The reality is quite different. Certain locations are clearly privileged because communication networks are simply denser in places like New York, while virtually non-existent in other places (like large parts of Africa).

Global cities

Global cities in particular have acquired an advantage that is now cumulative because they have become the most wired locations on earth. The office towers that make up the New York skyline are filled with information technologies. They have become the telecommunication nodal points of the global economy (Lash and Urry 1994: 26). Within cities like New York, London, Berlin and Tokyo exist 'smart' wired buildings that become the logical sites for global networking capitalists to locate the hubs of their networked empires. Global cities are communication-rich sites because they are densely wired and possess large airports, both required to facilitate rapid global communication. These cities are also the places that information-rich and highly skilled people reside, because they are exciting places to live, have good career opportunities, and are the best services and facilities for cultural consumption. Many university students plan to head to cities like London, Berlin, New York or San Francisco when they graduate, precisely because they offer career and lifestyle opportunities. All these factors have tended to turn certain cities into controlling hubs of the global economy. It is cost effective to locate coordinating hubs where communicatively skilled people already live, and where one can take advantage of already existing communication infrastructures. Many cities around the world invest in rebranding and repositioning themselves competitively within this network. Locations that are communications poor or have poorly educated populations will necessarily be at the receiving end of the Pax Americana's power relationships. These cities find themselves on the periphery and endpoints, rather than nodes, of the global economic networks.

Power and wealth are aggregating where the communication networks are thickest. The United States' urban areas, where the information rich live and work, are emerging as the pre-eminent power centres of global network capitalism. Considerable power is also accruing to the information rich living in the urban areas of eastern Japan, Shanghai, trading centres like Hong Kong and Singapore, north-west Europe, northern Italy and south-east England. A power network is shaping up around the United States, European Union and Japan. The network depends on cities that coordinate production and trade. These cities – for instance, Shanghai, Singapore, Sydney and Sao Paulo – also have dense communications infrastructures and skilled populations. The networker elite coordinate global network capitalism from these global cities. They are increasingly clean cities with dominant service economies specializing in financial, cultural and informational, and high-end industrial production. These cities are the communication hubs from which global network capitalism's hegemonic dominance is coordinated. It is a hegemonic dominance that is pre-eminently an exercise in networking. Power derives from coordinating communicative complexity on a global scale.

Relocating industrial areas

Increasingly, industrial production involving dirty and monotonous labour practices is relocated to places where there is:

- cheap labour possessing a well-developed work ethic
- lenient regulatory requirements concerning pollution and work practices
- an effective legal and policing system to create a stable and predictable operating environment
- infrastructure like electricity, transport and telecommunications to facilitate production – these cities need to be able to receive instructions from the global hubs.

This process has led to the deindustrialization of many cities in the United States, Europe and Australia as production has been shipped off shore to South-East Asia, coastal mainland China and parts of Latin America. The global elite coordinate production facilitates from the urban nodes of the global network. They use information technology to keep in touch with their comprador allies.

Alternatively, they conduct short-term inspection, education, marketing or familiarization tours of the 'margins', as and when required. A middle class of multilingual financial, engineering and cultural professionals travel the globe on behalf of the elite, managing relationships throughout the network. The deindustrialization process has been traumatic for many populations as cities and regions reshuffle their economic bases. Whole populations have relocated to new wired growth points such as Denver, Houston, Seattle, and Phoenix in the USA, Munich and Grenoble in Europe, and Sydney and Melbourne in Australia. Some cities deindustrialized successfully, such as London, New York, Sydney, Pittsburgh and Düsseldorf. These successfully transformed and now-wired cities have developed a mix of high-end industry, service and information economy sectors. But other cities and regions have failed to successfully transform, such as Detroit. Others went through periods of rapid transformation, like Dublin in Ireland, but found the new economy to be so flexible that it just as quickly dissolved. These cities either became high-unemployment ghettos or lost their populations through migration, or are characterized by high-welfare dependency and slow growth. Other areas are still in the midst of traumatic transformation, including most of the deindustrializing Eastern Europe. Significant migration pressures have emerged as people try to relocate away from 'losing' areas of socio-economic decline towards growing or 'winning' areas. As a consequence the international policing of migration has become a major policy issue in the United States, Canada, European Union and Australia as they try to simultaneously encourage the 'right' skilled migrants and deter the 'wrong' unskilled migrants. Other areas have experienced outflows of the most skilled parts of their populations since the 1990s. These include the old Soviet empire, the former Yugoslavia, South Africa and the Middle East.

Some new losing areas are located within the very heart of global network capitalism. The inner-city ghettos of the United States and those deindustrialized 'rust-belt' cities that have not successfully made the transition to informational capitalism offer very material evidence of how global network capitalism has reshaped societies. The United States' African American and Latin American underclasses are heavily concentrated in these ghettos. The point is that this process is uneven not only at a global level, but also within nation states, cities and even neighbourhoods. Many poor inner-city neighbourhoods have gentrified pockets of information-rich workers. Lash and Urry (1994: 146) suggested in the early 1990s that approximately two-thirds of the population of OECD countries have been integrated into the informational economy. They work in information or service industries and are immersed in the consumer lifestyles and identities of the global economy. The other third of the population in OECD countries have not been successfully integrated. This third are often unemployed industrial workers, who lost their jobs when industrial plants moved offshore. They appear to have drifted into the status of a permanent unemployed underclass, living in high-unemployment rust-belt cities like Buffalo in the USA, Roubaix in France and Wollongong in Australia. Where industrial jobs have re-emerged they have not brought the forms of social organization they did in the twentieth century. In Australia for instance the mining boom of the last decade has mostly employed a large flyinflyout workforce. Rather than rebuilding

Figure 12.1   The abandoned Book Tower, one of Downtown Detroit's most noted buildings

© Robert Wallace/Corbis

Figure 12.2   Abandoned factory near the city centre, Detroit

© Barry Lewis/In Pictures/Corbis

or establishing new industrial towns and cities, workers are flown in to remote temporary communities where they live in mobile accommodation like 'dongas'. Where once industrialization stimulated the development of communities and cities, global network capitalism has found ways to build a labour force without building corresponding viable communities. Lash and Urry (1994: 111) have noted that these problematic deindustrializing areas in OECD societies share something in common with non-OECD countries. From the point of view of the informational economy they are 'dead spaces'.

Dead zones

Much of Africa is also such a 'dead area'. Except for South Africa, the continent is not well plugged into the infrastructure of global information capitalism, and few Africans have the cultural capital required to plug in. In fact, Africa currently looks set to be the main loser of globalization because Africans simply cannot compete in the global market. Many of the dead areas are at risk of socio-economic collapse because global network capitalists are avoiding investing in those areas perceived to be unruly and ungoverned (like large parts of sub-Saharan Africa and the Middle East); seen to have legal practices that are unhelpful to global network capitalists (like Russia and Iran); or seen to have populations that are unproductive (like Africa). It seems likely that the networker elite will respond differentially to these dead areas, adopting one of three approaches:

- Efforts will be made to integrate those areas perceived to be important for the expanding hegemony of global network capitalism because of strategic location, resources or potential markets (like Russia). This will involve expanding the communications network to such areas; encouraging the emergence of network hubs and a local networker elite in these areas; and tying these hubs into the wider network of global informational capitalism.
- Areas perceived to be problematic but strategically important to global network capitalism's existing hubs (like Bosnia, areas off the coast of Somalia where pirates operate, and underclass areas of the developed countries) will be policed and contained.
- Dead areas where the costs of integration and/or policing are not seen as warranted (like Congo) will be cordoned off or abandoned.

Each of these strategies is contingent. Russia's political elites and oligarchs for instance have an uneasy relationship with the hegemonic American elites. While the west has been content to cordon off and abandon much of Africa, the Chinese have undertaken massive economic and political investment in recent times, attempting to bring African countries and resources into a Chinese node in the global network. There is a constant adjustment regarding the areas that are integrated, cordoned off or abandoned as the Pax Americana's hegemonic alliance adjusts itself to ever-changing conditions.

PORTRAIT OF A CITY

Consider the city or region you live in.

How does it fit in this network? Is it a global city, a regional hub, a post-industrial city?
How has it responded to the changes brought about by global network capitalism?
What economic and cultural activities happen in your city?
Who lives there and why do they come?

Compare your city to the nearest global city (like New York or London).

How are they connected?
How are they different?

At the beginning of this chapter we examined some of Hamelink's (2008) questions about communication and urban space. Use these questions as a guide for considering the urban spaces you live in.

You can find links to resources about emerging and abandoned cities on the *Media and Society* website study.sagepub.com/carahandlouw

PUBLIC AND PRIVATE LIFE IN MEDIA CITIES

Media order and reorder the spaces in which we live our lives. Broadcast media like television create relationships between public and private life. They position our private everyday lives within larger public spaces via a constant stream of representations. Interactive media reorder the relationship between intimacy and publicity. The home is a key node within broadcast and interactive media networks. With television, newspapers and radio we watch public life unfold from our vantage point in private and intimate space. The walls of our homes are 'electronic screens' or 'strange windows' through which we 'see the world from where we are not' (McQuire 2008: 140). Via television we view the world from our home; with our smartphone we represent our private lives to each other in a constantly unfolding circulation of media. If television made our homes receptor nodes in the media city, then smartphones are two-way interactive nodes connected to our bodies. With smartphones we publicize our private and intimate selves in social networks. We now use smartphones and social media to add another layer to the real-time mediation of everyday life that television has beamed into our homes since the twentieth century. Social media knit together private, public and intimate aspects of our lives.

Smartphones

We carry smartphones wherever we go. We use them to organize life in the city: to call and text people; to find information about transport, events and places to go; and to create content about our experience in the city with photos and updates. If you collected together all the information on your phone for six months you would have a comprehensive record of where you have been, who you have interacted with, what you have seen and done, what you were thinking and feeling, and perhaps even how your body is functioning. Our phone traces our movement through urban space; most of our communication with other people happens via its screen; it contains all our calendar appointments and photos; we use it to interact with our social network; we even install apps on it that monitor our heart rate, fitness and sleep patterns. Your phone is a device that watches and mediates your life in the city. The integration of mobile devices into our everyday life adds another important dimension to the role media play in organizing urban life. Beyond providing information, mediating power relationships and fashioning collective identities – media now play a critical role in generating information that is central to managing urban populations. Our phones make us visible to each other; they link us together in new ways; they enable information to flow in far more reflexive and instantaneous patterns. The phone dramatically compresses our sense of space and time in the city. When we are waiting for a friend on a corner we can scan our phone for news, send them a message to find out where they are, and scroll through photos our friends have uploaded of their daily life in the city.

The smartphone is the most significant media technology since television primarily because it brings together a range of media functions: interpersonal communication technologies like telephone, text messaging and email; mass media technologies like text, audio and video content; media-making technologies like a camera and sound recorders and applications to process and edit images and video; locative technologies like GPS; body-monitoring technologies; and access to information and social networks. It is not just that the smartphone brings these technologies together in one device, but that in doing so it creates new relations between them. For example, the smartphone fundamentally changes how images work within our popular culture. Not only does the camera enable us to create limitless digital images; the web connection enables us to immediately share those images online. Photographs are no longer confined by the availability and cost of camera and film, or delayed or controlled by processing, or limited to display in photo albums. Images are now made and circulated endlessly through social networks (Chesher 2012: 104). We communicate with each other online largely via images we create with our phones. Images don't just convey representations; they also assemble social networks and register them in databases.

Smartphones and images

Images are particularly important to the development of the social web (Palmer 2012: 86). When Facebook bought Instagram for $1 billion they were strategically investing in controlling one of the key networks through which images flowed through mobile devices. They couldn't afford to lose control and access over the flows of personal imagery through the web. On the social and mobile web, images are more than just representations of people, events and places. We are accustomed to thinking of images as being rich in representational meaning – they are said to paint a thousand words. On the mobile and social web they also generate information and networks (Palmer 2012: 90). We use images to affect one another. We follow images to feel connected to our friends and the world around us. We want to be seen and to see others. These images might be meaningful to us, but more fundamentally they capture our attention. That attention is valuable because it generates information about us and our social world. An image is a device that holds in place a network of associations and affects that can be tracked and responded to. Images are embedded in social networks (Chesher 2012). Our taking and circulating of images creates information about where, who and what is in them, who circulates them, and who views them. This registers information in databases about who and what we pay attention to, and increasingly also, the sentiments or dispositions attached to that attention.

Smartphones and communicative enclosure

The assembly of media technologies in smartphones enables a range of public and personal communicative applications. We use our smartphone:

- to create and circulate a public record of our lives and identities using text, images and videos
- to be seen and felt in our peer networks via updates, likes and comments
- to access public news and information
- to watch television and listen to music
- to organize our personal lives
- for intimate communication with friends and loved ones
- to bear witness to and participate in public events
- to monitor our bodies and movements
- to shop and pay bills
- to decipher and source information in the material world: we point it at signs on the street and ask it to translate to another language, and we use it to direct our movements through our city.

No other communicative device in history brings together this array of activities, and is so interwoven into our public and private lives.

The smartphone is a key device in a media system where the control and production of content is secondary to establishing spatial coordinates within which communication takes place. Mark Andrejevic (2007) describes these spaces as 'digital enclosures' that are 'filled in' with digital technologies that watch and respond to us. A digital enclosure is a social space where each action generates information that can be gathered. The information is used to shape social and communicative processes. This mode of media production relies less on telling participants what to think or believe and more on facilitating the social spaces in which we interact. In this system, ideological modes of control – controlling what is said – give way to more open-ended, spatial and responsive modes of control. What is said matters less than the capacity to harness and respond to communicative activity in general (Dean 2010). Where the television was a media device that embodied one-way, mass, ideological forms of power, the smartphone is emblematic of more reflexive and participatory modes of managing participation. The smartphone is an object that connects us to vast networks composed of urban spaces, material hardware and immaterial social relationships. Social and mobile forms of media can only function because we interact with them. We provide the sociality and circuits of attention and information. The digital enclosures of interactive media rely on us physically taking our mobiles out into our everyday lives and using them to make, access, record and circulate content, information and data. At the same time, the digital enclosure relies on the construction of urban spaces that are wired into information networks. Think of how irritating or disconcerting it is to be in a place without mobile reception when you need to find something out or send someone a message. We are used to being in space that is connected to communication networks.

Berlin resident Malte Spitz (2012) creatively drew attention to the data the smartphone captures when he demanded that his mobile phone company provide him with all the data it had collected about him over a six month period. After much negotiation the company provided him with 35,830 lines of raw data. He used that data to construct a live visualization of his movement throughout urban space over many months. Those movements were tagged with his phone calls, texts, emails, social media updates and calendar appointments. As he moved about on the map, items of information would appear attached to those movements. As whole populations move through a city every day, CCTV, public transport systems, financial transactions, mobile phones and social media generate information about their activity.

Spitz referenced his experiment to the history of surveillance in Berlin. Throughout the Cold War daily life in East Berlin was undergirded by the pervasive information collection of the Stasi – the state secret police who established a vast bureaucracy and intelligence network that reached into the personal lives and relationships of residents. Spitz used his experiment to ask, 'Imagine [if] all the people on the streets in Berlin in 1989 had a mobile phone in their pocket? The Stasi would have known who took part in these protests and if the Stasi would have known who were the leaders behind it, this [the collapse of East Germany and the Berlin Wall] would never have happened' (Spitz 2012). In making this connection, Spitz illustrates the role that information plays in organizing populations within urban space.

Wearable and responsive media devices

Mobile media make urban space increasingly sentient and responsive. The can be used to both manage populations in real time and offer us new ways of experiencing everyday life. Spitz raises a critical view of the way mobile devices make our life within urban space much more visible to corporate and state databases. In contrast, technology companies offer more utopian visions of mobile devices and urban space. In April 2012 Google posted on YouTube a concept video for Google Glass. Glass is an augmented reality technology that integrates media and information into our experience of urban space in real time. The first-person-perspective video showed a man walking through a city wearing a pair of glasses with a computer screen in the top right-hand corner. The glasses manage his communication and information needs as he moves through the city. Eating breakfast he sees a message pop up from a friend asking him to meet up. They agree to meet at a bookstore. As he walks to the subway a message pops up in his Glass to advise him the subway is suspended. Without being prompted Glass plots a walking route, displays it on a map, and gives him walking directions through town. On the way he sees a poster for a gig he wants to attend. Glass views the image, deciphers it and records the date and time that tickets go on sale in his calendar. Arriving at the bookstore, Glass directs him to the book he is looking for and then tells him how far away his friend is. Meeting up with his friend, Glass checks him in at a food truck on his social media network. He takes a photo of street art on a city wall and posts it on his social media profile. His girlfriend calls him and he shows her his view across the city while playing her a song on a ukulele.

Some of the activities and interactions depicted in the video are now an ordinary part of life in the city. We text our friends when we're out and about to see if they want to meet up. We used to have to make plans in advance, face to face, by phone, or even by mail. If public transport is suspended, or there is a traffic jam, we reach for our phone, load a map and ask it to plot the shortest alternative route. We also log on to Twitter or a news site to find out what the cause of the delay is or how long it will last. We check in at cool bars and restaurants. We take photos of our everyday lives in the city and post them to social media. Malls and shops now have interactive maps and apps to make it easy for us to locate products. We even encounter images and objects in the city that have QR and RFID chips that our mobile devices recognize, enabling us to access content, make entries in our calendar or directly purchase goods and services. Brands put QR codes on advertisements on city walls or shop windows that enable passers-by to immediately purchase the goods in the image. Nothing in the Google Glass video is that far-fetched. Whereas our use of smartphones as we move through the city is increasingly ordinary and mundane to us, the glasses in the video present a seamless integration of media technologies into our experience of city life.

Google Glass naturalistically augments our reality. Speaking about Glass in February 2013 Google founder Sergey Brin (2013) said that when he started Google his vision was that eventually you 'wouldn't need to have a search query at all you'd just have information come to you as you needed it'. Responsive media technologies like Google Glass depend on the larger development of media-dense urban spaces. These devices can only augment our experience of urban life if they can access information via high speed mobile internet. The device is connected to a network of material communication infrastructure and databases. It requires other users entering and circulating information that it can find and use. Urban spaces are adapting to mobile devices and information networks. When you check in or buy tickets at a sports stadium, the stadium might use a database to tell you which of your friends are seated nearby. When you pass by an advertisement or poster on a city wall your mobile device will recognize a QR code that will take you to an online store or media content. When you enter a bar or restaurant an RFID chip might prompt your device to check you in on social media. When you get the bill your friends might use a social app to transfer money to each other and pay. All of these uses of mobile devices only work because the device is embedded within a technical and social network of information and activity.

Google Glass is one manifestation of the fantasy of the 'sentient city' (Crang and Graham 2007: 790). A sentient city remembers who we are and anticipates our actions. Using mobile devices our experience of urban space is overlaid with 'dynamically changing information' (2007: 792). We are becoming used to the web customizing its responses to us. As mobile media and material spaces become integrated, real locations will also be able to remember and anticipate our actions and interests. Using a combination of mobile devices, information and databases, buildings, retail and public spaces will begin to recognize and respond to us.

ALTERNATIVE VISIONS OF MOBILE DEVICES AND URBAN SPACE

Above we examined arguments about mobile devices from Malte Spitz and Sergey Brin. Brin is the co-founder of Google and behind the development of Google Glass. Below we offer some further visions of mobiles in everyday life.

APPLE iPHONE 5: PHOTOS EVERY DAY

In 2013, as part of the launch of iPhone 5, Apple released as series of television commercials depicting the use of the iPhone in our everyday lives – taking photos, playing and listening to music, creating and circulating videos.

In the Photos Every Day advertisement individuals use their iPhone to capture everyday moments of their lives in the city. Two young skateboarders photograph each other doing tricks; a jogger photographs a mountain as he jogs along a road; a man photographs some street art; a person films a favourite song at a live music gig. These individuals are depicted cropping, filtering and uploading the images to social networking sites. Technology companies present mobile devices as integral to people experiencing, enjoying and making themselves present in the life of the city.

In distinction to Google's and Apple's celebratory and promotional accounts of these devices, we can also consider alternative visions of the role these devices play in constructing and managing our experience of urban space.

(Continued)

(Continued)

'ADMENTED REALITY'

Technology companies imagine that mobile devices will be background and ambient technologies pre-empting and organizing our informational needs. In his remix of the Google Glass concept popular culture hacker Jonathan McIntosh (2012) offered an 'ADmented Reality' video as a rejoinder to Google's 'augmented reality' fantasy. If Brin's vision for Google Glass was one where real-time information of the mobile web makes life in the city friction-free, seamless and easy, then McIntosh's remix was one where the objects and spaces we encounter in urban space prompt targeted advertising. In the remix video, as he pours a coffee an advertisement for Starbucks pops up; as he eats breakfast an advertisement for McDonalds is displayed; and the suspended subway service prompts an ad for rental cars. The remix points to the commercial interests that drive the development of technologies that knit together urban space and mobile media. The development of mobile media is propelled by organizations seeking out ways to capitalize on denser and faster flows of information to identify, target and respond to us as we move through the city. Mobile devices both position us within flows of media content and subject our everyday lives to continuous surveillance.

'I FORGOT MY PHONE'

'I Forgot My Phone' is a short film by Miles Crawford released in 2013. The film depicts a woman spending the day with her partner, going to lunch with her friends, watching children play in a playground, having a drink with a friend, and going to a gig in the evening. In each of the scenes she is the only one without a smartphone. In one scene where she goes bowling with friends, she scores a strike but none of them see because they are all on their phones. At a birthday party everyone is filming the cake as they sing 'Happy Birthday'. In the evening she lies in bed in the dark with her partner while he scrolls on his phone. The film taps a popular sentiment that as we use our phones to capture everyday moments we become disconnected from the human relationships that make those moments important to us.

Our use of smartphones as we move through the city is increasingly ordinary and mundane to us. Google Glass imagines a future characterized by the seamless integration of media technologies into our experience of city life. Apple's iPhone ads characterize the smartphone as enriching our enjoyment of everyday life in the city. 'ADmented Reality' and 'I Forgot My Phone' offer alternative visions of the way these devices structure city life. Compare the visions of mobile media, urban space and everyday life these the two films offer.

How will technologies like Google Glass change the quality of our lives in urban spaces?
What power relationships do technologies like Google Glass facilitate?
What are the political, commercial, cultural and interpersonal implications of a technology like Google Glass?

Consider some of the arguments about the relationships between our smartphones and emerging devices like Google Glass and our experience of urban space.

How do these devices construct, order and manage populations in urban space?

You can find links to the launch video for Google Glass, Sergey Brin's Google Glass talk, Malte Spitz' mobile fine map, Apple iPhone advertisement, the 'ADmented Reality' spoof and 'I Forgot My Phone' video on the *Media and Society* website study.sagepub.com/carahandlouw

PUBLICITY AND INTIMACY

Publicity

Smartphones facilitate new ways of publicizing our identities. They alter the boundaries between public and intimate aspects of our lives. We use smartphones to engage in 'ego-casting' and 'life-casting' as we post streams of content about our actions, thoughts and feelings to social media profiles (Dean 2010). These are seen by ever-widening networks of people (Livingstone 2008). At the same time, mobile media devices enable us to send content to intimate others. Where once our intimate thoughts were confined to our conversations or written letters, with smartphones our intimate relationships are played out via a stream of images and videos. The use of smartphones to craft the public and intimate aspects of our lives is part of the process of fashioning our identities as lived social relations (Livingstone 2008). We use smartphones to tell stories about ourselves and our lives (2008: 399). This involves making judgements about how we position ourselves, and make ourselves visible, in social networks.

We use the images we take with our phones to position our identities within a flow of meanings that construct our social world. When we publicize ourselves as members of a social network we seek attention from others: we want them to see us, feel us and interact with us. Writing about young women's depiction of going out for the night on Facebook, Brown and Gregg (2012) observe posts anticipating the night-out, live mobile updates and images while they are out drinking, and bonding in the days after as they go through photo albums. As Brown and Gregg (2012: 362) illustrate:

> The 'peak' of the night out is also routinely documented by the live post or photo update, as mobile devices allow a narrative thread to be maintained for onlookers. One of the amusements for the Facebook audience is in discerning the moment of intoxication, either during or after the event. Tell tale signs are when words which may have been chosen carefully just hours earlier become careless, provocative or even incoherent. These insider jokes extend to being privy to a friend's suffering the next day, when they are 'dying'. Facebook and drinking are thus a twinned entertainment, in that the experience of each is mutually enhanced in combination.

Social media enhance the enjoyment of excessive alcohol consumption because they enable people to amplify the telling of good stories and the sharing of memories (Brown and Gregg 2012: 361). Participants use Facebook to mediate their anticipation, enjoyment and memorialization of weekend drinking. This mediation positions their identity within the shared rituals and pleasures of drinking culture. Smartphones and social media are used to broadcast live events through social networks and to archive them (Bennett 2012). These practices of witnessing, recording, presencing and archiving (Couldry 2012) publicize our identities, connecting them to the networks of attention our smartphones give us access to.

The flows of images we construct, and position ourselves within, are registered in the databases of social media. Social media use analytics to capitalize on the way we publicize our lives and identities. As we create, upload and interact with images, we link together identities, practices and places. Images of ourselves and our lives enrich other data that social media platforms might have. Our desire to be seen and felt – our 'will to image' (Hearn 2008) – in peer networks produces texts that assemble social networks online. The smartphone connects together our use of our own appearance, bodies and human capacities to communicate within the social world with the networks and databases of social media. The calculative and predictive capacities of big data depend in part on the affective capacities of smartphone users publicizing their lives and registering them on the databases of social media (Clough 2008, Lury 2009).

Intimacy

At the same time as we use smartphones to make ourselves public, we also use them to circulate intimate images between friends and lovers. When we send them via mobile messaging applications like Snapchat – where the images are timed to expire after being viewed for a short amount of time – we aren't so much archiving our relationships as we are using mobile media to perform them in real time. Snapchat is an ephemeral and live performance of our identities and relationships. We use these images to enact and negotiate the intimate, playful, amusing and erotic dimensions of our relationships. Creating and sharing intimate images is part of expressing pleasure, desire and forming relationships of trust (Hasinoff 2013). Even though images might begin as an intimate exchange, the boundaries between the intimate and the public online are socially and technically unstable. It is technically easy to copy and exchange images that were originally shared privately; we have to trust others we share the images with not to circulate them further. The circulation of intimate images depends on trust between people. Even though applications like Snapchat are designed to delete images, recipients can still easily make copies when they view them. If intimate images spill outside of private relationships they can intimidate and harm because we lose control over how our bodies and identities are publicized.

The circulation of intimate images can challenge social and legal frameworks. When two young people send sexually explicit images to each other the law might consider them to be producing and distributing child pornography. In many jurisdictions young people have been placed on sex offender registers as a result of images they made or received. In many cases images that were produced and distributed in intimate relationships get more widely distributed in peer networks, causing harm to the people in them. As the intimate becomes public we lose control over how our identity is made visible and positioned in the social world. The use of mobile media to circulate intimate images is embedded in complex networks of interpersonal and institutional power. Smartphones make the intimate and public aspects of our identities porous. As we register the intimate in images we open our identities up to be seen in new ways.

Participants in Albury et al.'s (2013: 18) research offer a nuanced range of explanations of these images and the way they circulate within social relationships:

- private selfies or self-portraits for self-reflection rather than sharing
- public selfies posted to social media platforms that are intended to be shown to friends and strangers – these might include images of new clothes or hair-styles
- joke images that display nudity in humorous ways
- flirtatious sexual images created and shared consensually between intimate partners
- offensive and unethical sexual pictures that might be produced consensually but shared for revenge, or produced without consent, or distributed outside of a peer or friendship context.

What matters to the young participants in Albury et al.'s (2013) research is the way that the images circulate within relationships of trust. Both parties ought to consent to the sharing of images and trust that the images will not be more widely circulated. The images are important because they express how we feel about our relationships with each other. To share intimate images expresses trust, excitement and intimacy. These are affective and emotive relationships. The creation and sharing of intimate images is part of the meaningful and creative formation of our relations with others within contemporary mobile media culture.

We use smartphones to construct the public and intimate aspects of our identities. Some of these practices raise social, legal, ethical and moral questions. While 'sexting' is one such practice that has attracted attention because of its vexed legal status, there is a proliferation of image practices like the rituals of judgement surrounding 'selfies', 'Am I pretty or ugly?' videos, the fitness culture surrounding 'fitspo', and the more transgressive 'thinspo' hashtags, blogs and networks. This range of practices demonstrates the varying ways in which mobile devices are used to publicize the intimate. The question to be considered is to what extent these practices are creative and empowering representations of ourselves that enable us to live richer and more playful relationships; and to what extent the circulation of these images does harm to their subjects and viewers. To respond to these questions we need to consider not only the images and their content, but also the relationships they circulate within and facilitate. An image only makes sense when we examine the rituals of judgement, meaning making and affecting that it enables.

Social networking platforms attempt to regulate these flows of images in a variety of ways. On Instagram, 'selfies' and 'fitspo' images often stream alongside 'thinspo' and pornographic material. Instagram attempts to police these flows by banning hashtags like #thinspiration. Users respond by reorganizing their identities, and associated flows of images, through new hashtags like #thynspiration or #thynspooo. This demonstrates the fluid and creative nature of these image-making and -sharing practices. One thing all of these representations of the self appear to have in common is their promotional and competitive positioning of our bodies and selves in publicly visible ways. As these modes of media practice open up our private lives and bodies to wider public visibility we become embedded in competitive games of positioning and promoting ourselves and bodies within flows of images. At a personal level we might consider whether this thwarts the construction of reflective and thoughtful identities. At a larger social level we need to examine how publicizing ourselves and monitoring each other via a constant flow of images is implicated in the responsive forms of control characteristic of interactive media. The more we participate in making ourselves and our relationships visible within social networks, the more those relationships can be tracked and responded to by those who control the networks.

CONTROLLING SOCIAL MEDIA

Above we examined how interactive media set the terms and coordinates within which we participate, and how social media platforms attempt to regulate flows of content in the platform.

Instagram bans the use of over 200 hashtags to prevent users from forming communities to share harmful content, sexually explicit content, content that attempts to 'game' the app's popularity algorithms, and content that is considered offensive. When users search for or click on these hashtags no listings are shown. Banned hashtags include:

#17bitch	#deepthroat	#jizz
#adiosbitchachos	#dildo	#kikmeboys
#anal	#foodorgasm	#kikmenow
#arse	#freshasfuck	#loseweight
#balls	#fuck	#milf
#bang	#fuckFriends	#mouthtopenis
#bestfuckingtimeever	#fuckfuelprices	#nopecsnosex
#bigboobs	#fuckmyjob	#photography
#bigbootyhoe	#fuckthelaw	#popular
#bigtits	#fucktherules	#popularpage
#birthdaysex	#getnakedpls	#proanorexia
#bitchcanigetacosmo	#incest	#probulimia
#BitchDontKillMyVibes	#instabitch	#sexyteen
#Blowjob	#instabody	#slut
#classybitch	#instafuck	#thinspiration
#clit	#instagirl	#thinspo
#cock	#instasex	#weed
#cum	#jailbait	#whitepower

The Data Pack provide a banned hashtag search tool: http://thedatapack.com/tools/blocked-hashtag-search/

You can find links to this tool, lists of banned Instagram hashtags, Instagram's terms of service and guidelines against self-harm images, as well as reports on sexting on the *Media and Society* website study.sagepub.com/carahandlouw

Should Instagram ban hashtags? If so, which ones should be banned?

Which hashtags constitute a grey area as to whether they should be banned or not?

Select some of the banned hashtags. What practices or identities are Instagram trying to ban and why?

How do social media platforms control the flow of content online? What content do they prevent from circulating and why?

What kinds of information do we grant social media platforms the rights to collect? What do they use it for? What are the consequences of these uses?

How do our likes or preferences shape relationships on social networking sites?

What are the differences between intimate, private and public content and data on social media?

How do social media organize social relationships? Who controls, manages and profits from these relationships?

What responsibilities do social media platforms have to control the flow of content?

What flows of information should be regulated?

What kinds of control of information exist on social media?

WORK WITH MOBILE DEVICES

The smartphones we carry in our pockets are created by workers in factories from cities on the edge of the global network. Global trading networks connect spaces together and create uneven relationships between them (Harvey 2000: 23). As technologies reshape how human activities are organized, they create and entrench relationships of wealth and power. Mobile media depend on human labour to create the material devices that enable networks to function. Smartphones, routers, modems and servers all need to be produced and maintained. The development of communication networks has underpinned the rapid industrialization of urban space in the developing world. Qiu (2012) documents the experience of workers in Foxconn factories that produce mobile devices for Apple, Nokia, HP, Sony and Dell. The growth of networks involves the growth of networked forms of labour. Since the 1990s the Chinese state has opened up industrial zones around the Pearl and Yangtze River deltas. These zones have attracted enormous inflows of investment in factories to produce products for global brands and an influx of rural people to work in those factories.

Mobile device factories

In China, Foxconn is estimated to employ up to 1 million workers. They work in 'iPod cities' with up to 400,000 workers living in dormitory-style accommodation. These cities rapidly upsize and downsize as demand from the global market rises and falls. Qiu (2012: 175) describes these workers as 'programmable labour' who undertake tasks 'calculated by computer to the precision of certain seconds per movement of the worker's arm, turning workers into nothing but programmed parts of the industrial machine. The daily quota of a female worker, for example, is to put 5800 tiny screws into 2900 devices.' These labourers find themselves on the periphery of mobile media networks. While in their spare time they might connect to the information network in internet cafés, or buy counterfeit smartphones with their meagre wages, for the most part their lives and aspirations are confined to the industrial nodes of the global information economy.

Within these cities on the outskirts of the global networked economy, Qiu (2012: 184) finds workers using mobile technologies to develop tactics for everyday forms of resistance – organizing solidarity activities and distributing subversive poems and information about work practices. These tactics though take place from below, while above, the strategies of global capital and the state structure the global information network, and the workers' place in it as labourers. Mayer (2011a) also observes that workers use their creativity and ingenuity to survive in the rationalized factories of the globally networked economy. Mayer (2011a) argues that workers on a television production line in Brazil create the material devices that are central to the immaterial forms of labour and creativity that global media and information networks thrive on. Media device factories thrive in places like China and Brazil where unskilled labour is cheap but dependable and where the state provides stable and favourable political and economic conditions, cheap electricity and functioning infrastructure. This process has been unfolding in the developing world since the emergence of networked economies in the 1970s. These factories both 'exploit and support' the cities they have developed (Mayer 2011a: 40). While the factories generate enormous wealth and growth, very little of it is returned to the workers in the form of public space and infrastructure. While workers are creative and resourceful, they live and labour in precarious circumstances.

If devices are made on the plugged-in edges of the global information economy, once they are disposed of many of them find their way out of the global network altogether. E-waste is an ecological and health catastrophe on the edges of cities completely unplugged from the information economy in Africa and South Asia. Electronic devices are shipped here as part of bogus aid and other forms of corrupt trade. The poorest of the poor, working often in slums or on the edge of city dumps, dismantle, salvage and burn discarded electronic devices for their precious metals. The toxic chemicals released by the burning devices poison people who live and work in the dumps. Some devices are salvaged and sold to organized criminal networks who trawl through the old hard drives looking for information they can use for identify theft and fraud. Our mobile devices travel through a lifecycle from industrial production cities of the global economy, to the middle-class information cities, to the waste dumps in parts of the world disconnected from the information network. Electronic waste overwhelmingly travels from the industrialized countries to the undeveloped world. Greenpeace (2009) have used mobile media technologies to track the movement of e-waste across the globe. They attached GPS devices to track electronic goods as they travelled from industrialized countries to Nigeria and Ghana. They have used the information to ask consumers to put pressure on companies in their home countries. E-waste, however, remains a largely invisible problem in the global information economy.

In the developing world the experience of labouring at the outskirts of the global information economy is undertaken in highly rationalized factories or totally unregulated dumps. In the developed world mobile devices have also dramatically transformed work and home life. For information-rich workers in the global middle class, mobile media technologies afford new forms of flexibility and creativity at the same time they alter the rhythm, boundaries and expectations of professional life.

Mobile professionals

For many professionals web-enabled mobile devices mean that work is no longer confined to the workplace. They work continuously while travelling to and from work and at home in the evenings and on weekends. Mobile media technologies remake our homes into productive parts of the media and information economy. While working from home is sold to workers in technology advertisements and by managers as a creative and autonomous benefit, for many the reality is a dramatic extension of work into private space (Gregg 2011a, 2011b). Technology advertisements, corporate and government policy present mobile media technologies as enabling work–life balance. No longer confined to the workplace we are able to better accommodate work to our other interests and commitments. Often advertisements present us as working in idyllic settings. Rather than the office, we work in a public library, or café, or at the beach. This change to work particularly affects women who are encouraged to use mobile media technologies to balance home and work life. In particular, child-caring responsibilities can be organized around work (Gregg 2011b). They can work when children are asleep, or keep an eye on tasks via their laptop or phone. Rather than have their career interrupted by parenthood, mobile media are presented as empowering to women. Mobile media establish expectations that we are always available to respond to emails, proffer ideas or undertake tasks. The rhetoric of technology advertisements overlaps with the claims of government and industry investment in creative and innovative industry policies. While these policies accelerate economic growth in the developed information economies, they also make work seem enjoyable, empowering and creative.

This examination of several kinds of life and work within the media city demonstrates the differing tiers of experience and control. The experience of this middle class is different from the global working class and majority poor in the informal economies of the developing world. The working class experience power in more direct and disciplinary fashion. Their livelihoods depend on maintaining work in the factories of industrial cities. Their urban experience isn't characterized by the malls and leisure spaces familiar to the middle class because they don't have the income to spend there, but also because they don't have a choice about where they live and work. The global middle class have economic and cultural capital to seek out employment and lifestyles in desirable urban spaces. Industrial cities do not need to make their working-class populations feel empowered, because the population has nowhere else to go. Likewise, the state can effectively ignore or contain the majority poor who live their lives out beneath the formal nodes of the global economy, while the information-rich middle classes find themselves experiencing a greater incursion of mobile media and work into their private lives and spaces. They experience power in a more participatory fashion, recognizing that to get ahead they need to be continuously plugged in to the rhythms of professional life.

CONCLUSION

In this chapter we have examined:

- the role interactive and mobile media play in organizing urban space
- how global network capitalism creates differentiated spaces and modes of control depending on their centrality to the production and management of labour, capital, information and populations
- the increasing importance of mobile life in the mediation of public, private and intimate life.

The modes of production, communication and control examined here illustrate key trajectories in the application of mobile and interactive media in managing flows of media, resources and power.

FURTHER READING

The readings below address a variety of perspectives relating to mobile devices and life in the media city. Hamelink (2008) considers how urban space might foster better forms of communication. Gregg (2011b) examines how mobile devices change our work–life balance. Hasinoff (2013) explores cultural, legal and ethical questions relating to the use of smartphones for sexting. Brown and Gregg (2012) and Livingstone (2008) each examine how we use social media to construct and perform our identities. Nardi and Kow (2010) and Nakamura (2009) each examine labourers on the edges of the digital economy by exploring the case of 'gold-farming' (people who build up characters for sale in networked games like *World of Warcraft*).

Brown, R. and Gregg, M. (2012) 'The pedagogy of regret: Facebook, binge drinking and young women', *Continuum*, 26 (3): 357–369.

Gregg, M. (2011b) 'Do your homework: new media, old problems', *Feminist Media Studies*, 11 (1): 73–81.

Hamelink, C. J. (2008) 'Urban conflict and communication', *International Communication Gazette*, 70 (3–4): 291–301.

Hasinoff, A. A. (2013) 'Sexting as media production: rethinking social media and sexuality', *New Media & Society*, 15 (4): 449–465.

Livingstone, S. (2008) 'Taking risky opportunities in youthful content creation: teenagers' use of social networking sites for intimacy, privacy and self-expression', *New Media & Society*, 10 (3): 393–411.

Nakamura, L. (2009) 'Don't hate the player, hate the game: the racialization of labor in World of Warcraft', *Critical Studies in Media Communication*, 26 (2): 128–144.

Nardi, B. and Kow, Y. M. (2010) 'Digital imaginaries: how we know what we (think we) know about Chinese gold farming', *First Monday*, 15 (6). Retrieved from: http://pear.accc.uic.edu/ojs/index.php/fm/article/view/3035/2566 (last accessed 17 September 2014).

Any article marked ⊛ with is available to download at the website **study.sagepub.com/carahandlouw**

13

CONSTRUCTING AND MANAGING AUDIENCES

MEDIA ORGANIZATIONS MAKE AND MANAGE AUDIENCES.

* How are audiences made?

* What work do audiences do?

* How have interactive media changed the production and management of audiences?

In this chapter we:

- Examine how audiences are produced
- Identify forms of audience work
- Explore how audiences are becoming more fragmented and flexible as media organizations assemble, watch and respond to them in real time.

PRODUCING AUDIENCES

Media institutions are organized around the strategic and rationalized production of audiences. Attracting and sustaining the attention of people is the core activity of professional communicators. Professional communicators cultivate, channel, direct, segment and track audience attention as part of the process of assembling markets and shaping public opinion. Their task is to get audiences to pay attention to media, consume messages and incorporate them into their identities and ways of life, and to manage audience participation in the creation and circulation of ideas. There are four basic questions we can ask about audiences:

- What do media do to audiences?
- What do media mean to audiences?
- How do audiences use media?
- How do media produce audiences?

Asking what media do to audiences involves examining how media effect, shape or cultivate attitudes, behaviours, beliefs and actions. Asking what media mean to audiences or what audiences do with media draws our attention to how audiences take media symbols and texts and use them to make sense of their world, organize their everyday lives and construct their own identities. To understand how media effect, shape or are meaningful and useful to audiences, we need to consider how that is grounded in the rationalized production of audiences. Whatever audiences do with media, they do it within coordinates and systems established and managed by cultural producers.

Audiences do not just exist 'out there'. They do not come into being by accident. Making audiences is resource intensive. Media organizations and professional communicators construct audiences because they are useful and valuable. Resources and creativity are invested in creating particular kinds of audiences. Commercial media produce audiences to sell to advertisers. Public, private, state or community media produce audiences to shape cultural and political life. The content and connectivity that media organizations produce is not the end product: it is a device for attracting the attention of individuals who are then packaged into an audience.

How are media organizations funded?

The media system is assembled from the demands of many groups. Those who invest resources shape the content, formats and platforms that get produced. There are a variety of ways that media production is paid for:

- *Publicly funded*: where a government funds media production often in order to create national identities, legitimate ideas and ways of life, and facilitate social cohesion.
- *Privately funded*: where wealthy patrons fund media production. This can be to serve their sense of the broader public interest or their specific political views and ambitions.
- *Directly audience funded*: where the audience directly pay for the full cost of the content, for instance books and musical recordings.
- *Indirectly audience funded*: media that are funded by advertising revenue. Advertisers recoup their investment when the audience purchase the products and services in the advertisements. The challenge with this model is assuring advertisers of the return on investment. Media organizations and advertisers need to produce evidence that the audience is paying attention and purchasing. Research is conducted to give tangible value to the audience's attention and productivity.

- *Mixed funding:* many media businesses mix together several elements of these models. For instance, newspapers and magazines collect revenue both through direct payment from the audience and advertising. Many privately funded media businesses generate revenue both through their wealthy patrons and advertising.

What all of these models share in common is the purposeful production of an attentive audience that is valuable to some group because it serves their commercial or political interests.

How are audiences made and packaged?

As media organizations grew and became more institutionalized and commercialized they developed methods to quantify, describe and position their audiences for advertisers. Audience and market research techniques and industries developed in collaboration with media organizations. Audience research and ratings provided ways of creating the audience as a reliable and quantifiable product that could be sold to advertisers. Audience research constructs the audience on several variables. The size, location and demographic characteristics of the audience are quantified. Advertisers need to know how many of certain types of people's attention they are buying when they purchase advertising time and space. Qualitative and cultural information about audiences is also important (Hackley 2002, Holt 2002). Media organizations and advertisers seek to qualify the lifestyles, cultural interests, values and practices of their audiences. This informs both the production of media content and advertising. Producers develop ways of understanding how audiences consume media content as part of their everyday lives. They want to understand how media, like television, are incorporated into the rhythms of everyday life. The development of breakfast television for instance responds to the morning routines of middle-class families. Breakfast programmes are light, conversational and repetitive. They are attuned to an audience that has the television on in the background as they get ready for work and school.

The development of media genres and content and their corresponding audiences is embedded in the broader use of media to construct public life. While the primary driver in the creation of audiences is often their commercial value, these processes are also entwined with broader political and social processes. In Chapter 10, for instance, we examined how popular culture genres like reality TV fashioned content that shaped commercially valuable audiences within the framework of a neoliberal and networked society. The commercial interests of media organizations and advertisers correspond, or at least find a balance, with other powerful interests in society. Advertising is a central part of the broader representational and social role of the media. Just like news, films, books and television programmes, advertising plays a role in creating public identities and social formations (Turow 1997: 26). The work of producing audiences as valuable social formations overlaps with the work of creating publics that sustain particular political formations and configurations of power (Livingstone 2005).

How do audiences make value?

Advertisers and media organizations work together to maximize the productivity of audiences. The easiest way to make an audience more productive is to get them to watch more advertisements.

For media organizations, the more advertisements an audience watches, the more revenue that can be generated from advertisers. Audiences will only watch a limited number of advertisements, though, before tuning out. Television stations that only broadcast advertisements would end up with very small audiences. Media organizations need to optimize their audience size and quality with the volume of advertising. As the size and quality of the audience grows, the more valuable it becomes; as the advertising space increases, the more likely the audience size and quality will shrink. This limitation to increasing the productivity of audiences is the basis of continuous innovation in the construction and management of audiences. Media organizations are driven by the need to find ways to make their audiences more productive.

If there is a limit to how many advertisements an audience will watch, then advertisers and media organizations invest in extracting more value from their attention by making their watching time more efficient. They do this in a number of ways:

- *Refining the audience* so that it contains higher concentrations of people that advertisers want to talk to. This means attracting the attention of people with certain levels of income, demographic and lifestyle characteristics.
- *Filtering out people* who advertisers don't want to talk to. Advertisers do not want to pay for wasted viewers, and they also want to be able to discriminate who they appeal to. They don't want to attract people whose use of their product might lessen its value in the estimation of their target market.
- *Integrating advertising* into media content. From the development of MTV in the 1980s through to the reality TV formats of today we have seen a wide array of ways in which advertising and content have been embedded within each other. This both quantitatively increases the available time for advertising, while also making more qualitatively credible advertising where brands are embedded within lifestyles and identities.
- *Expanding the range* of formats and channels so that media and advertising can be more continuously incorporated into everyday life. We now encounter media content throughout our public, private and personal life. Whenever we do, our attention is being packaged and sold as an audience commodity.

Each of these strategies expands and intensifies the reach of media content and therefore the creation of larger, more engaged, more refined and therefore more valuable audiences.

From mass to niche

As media organizations and advertisers sought ways to make audiences more productive, they began to create more and more refined audiences. This fragmentation of audiences for commercial reasons has arguably had larger social ramifications. Turow (1997: 3) argues that a combination of technological and social forces have brought about a 'major shift in the balance between society making media and segment making media. Segment making media are those that encourage small slices of society to talk to themselves, while society making media are those that have the potential to get all those segments to talk to each other.' The broadcast media system of the twentieth century, whether by design or by accident, had 'acted out concerns that people ought to share in a larger national community' (Turow 1997: 3). This was partly historical accident: the available media technologies – newspapers, radio and television – were limited in the array of content they could produce, and media organizations had finite resources to create content. Media organizations didn't have the technologies or resources to serve a proliferation of niche audiences, and advertisers had little use for them even if they could, because the industrial economy could only produce mass 'one size fits all' products. Furthermore, the media were constrained within political formations that pressed in favour of social cohesion. The emerging middle classes sought comfortable homogenous lifestyles. The political class promoted these ideas and values.

Since the 1970s this arrangement of technological capacities, industrial economies and political interests has been changing (Turow 1997, Hesmondhalgh 2007, Napoli 2010):

- Media technologies have developed that enable the creation and delivery of content to multiple niche audiences. From cable television through to the internet we have seen a proliferation of channels, devices and formats that can create content for increasingly refined audiences.
- The broader economy has adapted to more customized goods, services and experiences. Just-in-time, flexible and computerized manufacturing, the emergence of global retail economies, and the growth of online retail have greatly expanded the array of choices available to consumers.
- Consumers identify with a multiplicity of niche lifestyle identities, rather than mass class, cultural or ethnic identities. Politics has become increasingly organized around loose identity formations, rather than broad class structures.

The technical capacity to produce niche audiences has developed as part of broader social and economic changes that have created more flexible economies and more fragmented identities, lifestyles and politics.

Innovation in the production of goods and services drives the demand for new niche audiences, just as the creation of new audiences and their lifestyle and interests drives the growth of goods and services to meet their demands. Markets are assembled out of an interconnected series of relationships that unfold over time. Societies and markets have fragmented alongside one another (Turow 1997). The segmentation strategies of advertisers are interconnected with a broader breaking-apart of western societies along economic, racial, regional and lifestyle characteristics. Advertising industries and lifestyle brands have driven, profited from and responded to these changes. As incomes become more polarized, or new suburban communities are created tailored to specific classes and lifestyles, or as new groups enter the middle class and become a powerful consumer base, marketers respond to them as new commercial opportunities. At the same time, marketers look for ways to use media technologies to create ever more refined audiences. In doing so they play a part in further stimulating and entrenching the change processes they respond to.

From representational to responsive control

In the mass media system the predominant tools for controlling the construction of audiences were content and channels. These amounted to mostly representational forms of control. Representations work within structures of identity and taste. They attract the attention of some, while alienating others. Representations were the primary tool mass media had for building audiences by attracting the attention of specific kinds of people. If an advertiser wanted to speak to young middle-class people, media organizations created content that would attract their attention. In addition to content, media organizations could also use formats and channels to control to some degree where and how their content was distributed. For instance, some magazines and periodicals would only be distributed to middle-class neighbourhoods or sold at quality stores (Turow 1997).

As much as they communicate specific meanings, representations have also always been a key sorting mechanism, attracting the attention of some, and repelling the attention of others. The emergence of interactive media enables representative control to be complemented with responsive modes of control. Intensive surveillance of audiences enables the shaping of content based on many variables (Andrejevic 2011, Turow 2011). Media organizations can use information about their audiences both to shape representations and to discriminate between who sees what content in increasingly sophisticated ways. This enables further segmentation and customization of audiences.

Advertisers don't just produce content; they also contribute to the production of the system of media and cultural production (Turow 1997: 186). Their media planning and buying power influence the development of media channels and formats. Their desire to deliver their messages embedded in particular lifestyles influences the broader formation of the media system as a whole (Jhally 1990). The technologies, content and form of media become coextensive with advertising (Hackley 2002, Bratich 2005, Turow 2011). In addition to influencing the production of particular types of content (like reality TV) they have also influenced the development of technologies and media organizations that can manage and respond to audiences in real time (like Facebook).

The work of producing audiences

In commercial media systems audiences are constructed as consumers. Bratich (2005: 254) argues that 'the rise of the consumer society was dependent upon the ability to activate media subjects' as desiring consumers. Producing and managing audiences involves ongoing collaboration between many actors (Balnaves et al. 2011). Marketers, advertisers, media organizations and other influential social institutions enable and constrain each other in the production of media content, products and audiences. Marketers and media organizations constantly stimulate and adapt to social, economic and technological change. Advertisers seek to understand, shape and respond to society, lifestyles, identities and media use. Their use of information is purposive and pragmatic (Turow 1997: 185). They build audiences that have commercial value, and they adapt their methods based on what creates value. They don't have long-term positive or normative projects about the kind of society they are creating, although their need to interact with other powerful social institutions and elites means that the media system they are a part of might pragmatically reflect certain ways of life and values. And they might pragmatically learn that certain ways of life and values create more valuable audiences.

Advertisers and media organizations need knowledge of how society works in order to do business (Turow 1997: 186). As much as they make particular audiences, advertisers and media organizations increasingly watch and respond to social life in order to continuously assemble the most efficient audience formations they can. They track social change so that they can respond to changing technologies, economic formations, social institutions and lifestyles. Advertisers and media organizations watch, film, record, question and track audiences in an effort to respond to their cultural identities and practices (Hackley 2002, Holt 2002). They 'immerse themselves in consumer life in order to generate intimate knowledge, insights and understanding of consumers and consumption within cultural contexts' (Hackley 2002: 219). Advertising both reflects and shapes cultural identities and practices. The development of audiences is embedded within broader social, cultural and political changes or projects (Hesmondhalgh 2007, Napoli 2010). While companies might work with other powerful actors to respond to and shape audiences, they don't control the processes within which this takes place. They don't entirely govern the factors that create new lifestyles, lead to the emergence of new ethnic groups, or change configurations of economic and political power. But they can work to respond to those changes and channel them to their own advantage. The audiences that media organizations and advertisers create are never entirely their own productions, but the production of audiences is characterized by asymmetrical relationships where consumers are observed by market and media researchers (Hackley 2002: 220). Marketers and media organizations work together to locate and channel the productive capacity of audiences. Audience members are productive subjects where they form desires, communicate them, affect each other and act on them (Bratich 2005: 254).

MEDIA KITS: PACKAGING THE AUDIENCE

Media businesses package their audiences as commodities to sell to advertisers. Print publications like magazines produce media kits that they make available to prospective advertisers. You can often find these media kits on magazine and newspaper websites. Media kits promote the publication's audience. They detail the audience's qualities: size, publication channels they access, their demographics, tastes and interests.

Interactive media businesses like Google and Facebook often don't provide media kits, but rather provide advertising products where advertisers can construct and price audiences with a range of characteristics.

Explore the media kits and advertising products of media that you use. You can find links to media kits and advertising products on the *Media and Society* website study.sagepub.com/carahandlouw

Make an advertisement for yourself or an identity group to which you belong.
What characteristics do you have that advertisers would seek?
What kind of attention do you offer? Where can you be found? What kinds of media attract your attention?
How would an advertiser find you and appeal to you?

AUDIENCES AND WORK

Audiences are a social construction. The active ingredient in the audiences that media industries produce is human attention. Audiences are a valuable commodity because they undertake social activity that is productive (Smythe 1981, Jhally 1990). To understand the value of audiences we need to examine what they do. Audiences undertake two kinds of work: watching and being watched. On the one hand we might say that audiences are compensated for their productive work watching advertisements with the free content that they enjoy consuming, and furthermore, that the individuals who are part of audiences freely choose to consume media content and advertising. On the other hand, we might say that audiences pay twice, once by paying attention to the advertisements and then a second time when they buy the products that include in the cost the price of producing the media content that they received for 'free'.

The work of watching

The work of watching involves the activity of paying attention to representations (Smythe 1981, Jhally and Livant 1986, Jhally 1990). This includes watching advertisements, but also consuming media representations that more broadly construct our identities. When audiences watch advertisements they gain knowledge about, form desires for, and learn to classify brands, products and services. Audience members learn how to incorporate them into their identities and lifestyles; and most importantly, they go and buy them. Watching also has a broader social value. Watching advertisements and other forms of commercial media like lifestyle television, drama or news also teaches us how to desire certain lifestyles and acquire particular tastes. When an audience member watches an advertisement for a luxury good like jewellery, or sees a celebrity wearing designer fashion, or sees an expensive sports car in a Hollywood film, they might never be able to afford those goods, but they learn that they are tasteful and desirable. The audience member plays a part in giving those goods a social value and meaning. Part of what the person who purchases the luxury good seeks is the attention and desire of others. A wealthy person buys an expensive car not just because it is a pleasure to drive, but because it distinguishes them in the eyes of others. Advertising is a social system that relies fundamentally on our participation and communication. Audiences do the work of making it function by watching the advertisements and content and constructing meaning around them. Of course, it goes without saying that this process of making meaning from advertisements is never assured. Many of us will watch advertisements for luxury goods and distance ourselves from them. We'll profess to see through their appeals. From our own values, tastes and vantage points in the social structure we'll dismiss their claims. Nevertheless, despite the fact we see through and attest not to believe advertisements, we still do the work of paying attention to, recognizing and understanding advertisements. Advertising works despite the fact that we see through it and understand how it works (Carah et al. 2012). By watching media and advertisements we craft our identities, our lifestyles and our consumption habits from the cultural resources and ideas provided. The mass media produce productive audiences who make meaning with these cultural resources rather than through fixed ideologies.

The work of being watched

The work of being watched is critical to a flexible interactive economy (Andrejevic 2002a, 2004). The differentiation possible in production (like making customized goods and services) finds its corollary in media technologies that can sort, categorize and flexibly produce audiences. The work of being watched comprises two key elements:

- *User-generated content*: where audiences produce themselves and their lives as media content that others consume. When audiences participate on reality and lifestyle TV, upload photos to social media, comment on news stories and so on, they undertake the productive activity of both producing and circulating media content. Their lives and social world become an integral part of the content they watch.
- *User-generated data*: where audiences submit to forms of monitoring and surveillance. Our use of interactive media technologies involves the pervasive production and collection of information about us. As audiences watch and produce content they also produce data that is used to rationalize their productivity as an audience.

Watching, being watched by producing content, and being watched by producing data are all inter-related. As audiences watch, interact with and produce media they also generate data. Audiences both connect together their own identity and social networks with the resources provided by media and cultural producers; and they register those relationships in databases where they can be tracked and responded to (Andrejevic 2011: 287).

Practices of audience participation and surveillance have existed in the media system for a long time. Market research and audience ratings have monitored audiences, and genres like quiz shows, talk shows and talkback radio have used ordinary people and their lives as content. The contemporary media system though is increasingly premised on the work of being watched. Audiences both submit to monitoring and produce content as a continuous and intrinsic part of everyday media use. This makes them more productive and efficient:

- *More efficient* by responding and adapting the content so that the serving of specific messages and advertisements to particular consumers is optimized. If you know who is viewing at any given moment and location you can make sure they are seeing the right content.
- *More productive* by expanding the usefulness of the audience's attention. No longer is the audience productive only when viewing advertisements targeted at them; they are now productive whenever they are being watched because they are, at a minimum, generating data about their habits, tastes and preferences.

The work of being watched goes hand in hand with a broader popular culture that presents interactivity and surveillance as good, empowering and fun. Confessional talk shows which present self-revelation and self-improvement as core identity-making practices; popular culture genres like 'securitainment', border and home security; and celebrity culture – all call on our participation and use surveillance technologies as forms of entertainment. These various cultural formations turn being watched into an ordinary, and also inescapable, aspect of entertainment and everyday life. As much as we willingly participate in the surveillance of ourselves and our lives, it is increasingly difficult to live in society without participating in being watched. If we want to use the internet, watch content online, be a part of social networks, travel through the city, open a bank account or take out an insurance policy we increasingly have no option other than to participate in interactive media systems that watch us (Andrejevic 2002b).

Rationalizing watching is embedded within the broader development of a flexible economy that sells more customized goods and services to increasingly refined niches. Paying attention to audience participation in watching and being watched illustrates how media are more than just the production of representations that set ideological coordinates within which social life is contained. A system of media that watches also responds to the innovation and open-ended communication of audiences. Their activity becomes a productive resource to be steered and channelled rather than something to be disciplined and contained. In this system, the more active an audience is, the more they participate and the more value they create.

For a media system to be able to watch us, it requires our participation. Surveillance involves deducing patterns, behaviours or qualities by watching the mediation of social life. These analytic surveillance capacities depend in a large part on audiences uploading continuous streams of personal and contextual information about their lives and social world.

Ranking, rating and judging

The work of being watched involves audiences judging and promoting content, products, services and experiences. While the data audiences generate about their preferences is used to optimize marketing appeals, audiences are also continuously drafted into the work of communicating their judgements and tastes to others. This promotional work involves:

- rating and ranking products, places and experiences
- reviewing products, expressing tastes and preferences, and displaying our consumption of goods and services within everyday life
- creating and circulating images that link together our identities with social spaces and brands.

Our identities become integrated with products, brands and consumer experiences in 'one promotional package' (Hearn 2008: 209). We shape the cultural context for consumption where we circulate images of ourselves at branded events, like brands' Facebook pages, or get packaged in social ads on social media platforms.

Much of the content we generate and circulate online expresses sentiments, feelings and preferences. Social media and commerce sites work to capture and harness these expressions. This activity generates information that connects together our preferences for a product, place or experience with other demographic, behavioural and locational data. Furthermore, our ranking and rating also generates media content. Our peers see us promote commodities on our social media profiles when we share experiences of products and places. The value of audience or consumer reviews depends on their credibility in the estimation of others. Ranking, rating and expressing taste is productive because brands can only generate valuable reputations via the approval of other people (Hearn 2010: 423). Rankings and sentiments are particularly valuable when they are expressed by people like us or people that we trust. When social media sites use your identity within social ads to advertise products to your friends, they are assuming that your friends will trust your sense of judgement and taste. When you rate a hotel or review a book your action generates content that those sites use to attract attention and package products for other consumers (Hearn 2010). Even our purchasing history becomes promotional content. For instance, when we log on to Amazon we see books that 'other people like us' bought, or Netflix can predict films and Spotify predict songs based on the preferences of people with similar viewing or listening habits to us.

The work of ranking and rating also extends to the variety of ways we critique, reflect and position ourselves in relation to popular culture. This work is a form of promotional labour where audiences participate in shaping the commodities that are then sold back to them (Martens 2011). Audiences and consumers often pay a premium for the commodities they have added value to or helped to create a context of consumption for (Zwick et al. 2008). When we add content, provide feedback and generate data through our use of products and services, we contribute to their ongoing development. We are part of the social process of innovating their features and uses.

The feedback and innovation of consumers, fans and users is often part of the spectacle of consumption and popular culture itself. Fans feel empowered when their ideas are incorporated into media production. Andrejevic (2008: 27) finds that as fans engage in critiquing and reviewing television programmes they begin to identify with the imperatives of producers. They take up industry discourses about how best to promote the show, which audiences it appeals to, and how the show might be developed in the future and tailored to those audiences. Andrejevic (2008: 27) argues that 'The promise of virtual participation in the production process, in short, invites viewers to adopt the standpoint of producers, and thereby facilitates the conversion of viewer feedback into potentially productive marketing and demographic information.' Audience expressions of taste and criticism are productive and valuable activities that help producers create more valuable commodities. Fans are incorporated in a continuous feedback loop that rationalizes the production of cultural products.

AUDIENCE PARTICIPATION IN THE WORK OF BEING WATCHED

Audiences don't just create content and submit to monitoring, they also undertake the work of constructing and legitimizing relationships of watching. This involves creating relationships of affect and attention, identifying with the promotional logic of the culture industry, and articulating a cynical distance towards their own participation. This cynical distance sustains relationships of watching, making them dependent on audience participation and impervious to their critique.

Creating networks of attention and affect

Audience members' communicative capacities create the social networks through which meanings circulate (Terranova 2000). Their activity is freely given and unpaid, simultaneously enjoyed and exploited. This free labour is imperative to the functioning of networked forms of cultural production that rely on the continuous open-ended communication of users (Terranova 2000). Affecting is the social process of stimulating and channelling the 'living attention of others' (Brennan 2004: 50). Where audiences produce and circulate content on social media or participate in reality TV shows they do the work of channelling social interactions through media platforms and registering networks of attention in databases. This work is affective labour where audiences:

- employ their identity and emotions to attract attention from each other
- make judgements about taste, style, mood and dispositions that tell others how they feel about something or someone.

The creativity of audiences is central to the value production and control mechanisms of networks. The more audiences participate, the more information they generate, the more they strengthen the capacity of networks to stimulate, respond to and predict their interests. While audiences are often free to participate in contributing to, and even creating aspects of, networks, ordinary users rarely have control over how those networks develop or how their participation is directed and appropriated.

The data that interactive media assemble depends in the first instance on audiences' capacity to judge and understand their cultural identities, meanings and milieu. It is audiences that improve the quality of data on the platforms of social media by registering links between cultural content, social spaces and identities. When audiences comment, like or rate each other's bodies, appearances, pastimes, products, brands, services and cultural products, they add important sentiments and affects to the data that interactive media collect and use. Audiences contribute meanings that are grounded in their everyday lives. This is a kind of work only audience members can do because only they can access and modulate social connections, ideas and feelings from their vantage point in the social world. The interactive media system's ability to predict and respond to social life depends on this important work of registering social lives and sentiments online. Rather than specify particular meanings, media organizations and their partnering brands establish coordinates within which they manage and harness audience participation (Moor 2003, Foster 2008, Zwick et al. 2008).

Identifying with the promotional logic of the culture industry

We see audiences identify with the work of being watched where they adopt the logic of branding and promotion into the production of their own lives and identities (Hearn 2008). Just as we evaluate brands and products, we evaluate each other and present ourselves in competitive and promotional ways. This normalizes branding and promotional forms of communication. Not only are we fashioning ourselves using resources provided by commercial popular culture, we are also adopting a promotional form of communication in the way we convey our identities to others. Writing about

YouTube videos young girls create and share, Banet-Weiser (2012: 65–66) observes that they use commercial pop songs, images from popular culture, branded products and gestures from famous celebrities. While the young audience members produce the content, they do so using the resources of commercial popular culture. Not only does the production of their own identity incorporate and promote brands, celebrities and products; they also construct their identity as if it were a brand. Incorporating branding and promotional logic and the commercial products of the culture industry into the production of our own identities arguably legitimizes the work of being watched. It makes branding a general and ordinary mode of communication within everyday life.

Articulating cynical distance

There is another aspect of audience activity that, perhaps counter-intuitively, produces value. As much as they participate in interactive media and popular culture, audience members also cannily distance themselves from that participation, claiming to be cynical about the claims of media representations or the extent of their involvement in shaping media content and systems. Audience members distance themselves from the work of being watched by articulating savvy and cynical attitudes to media representations. Savvy audiences seek to 'be seen in a particular way: as savvy viewers who are not taken in by the transparent forms of manipulation practiced by producers' (Andrejevic 2008: 37). Audiences produce a savvy social disposition that protects commercial forms of media production. By downplaying the value of their own participation in the media system they obfuscate its value. Audience cynicism normalizes the promotional character of media and advertising, rendering it legitimate (Hackley 2002: 221).

While audience members don't sincerely buy into the promise that 'interactive technology will fundamentally alter the power relations between consumers and producers', they still participate nonetheless, using interactive media to 'let others know that he or she has not been taken in by the ruse' (Andrejevic 2008: 39). Audience debunking of the constructed nature and claims of media representations inoculates a system of cultural production that functions despite the fact that it has been exposed. This is a particularly valuable activity because it legitimizes and positions our participation within the current power relationships of the commercial media system. We participate without either believing in the ideological claims of media or seeking to meaningfully resist them. This disposition is active in the sense that it produces valuable attention and affect; at the same time it is docile in the sense that it doesn't threaten to undermine the social relationships encoded into commercial forms of interactive media.

As audience members 'get off' on their failure to make an impression on a debunked symbolic order, they create valuable attention and interaction without the system having to rely on ideological cohesion. The problem, as Andrejevic (2008: 38) argues, is that their participation creates

> a sense of political inertness – only the dupes imagine that things could be otherwise; the nonduped may well crave social change, but they are not so naïve as to be fooled by their desire into believing that it is actually possible. … If the viewers cannot be insiders, at least they can make it clear that they are not being fooled by the insiders, and this is the closest that the interactive technologies bring them to the inner sanctum.

The desire to reveal ourselves as non-dupes doubles as labour that creates networks, content and reputations that are useful in the interactive media system, while at the same time it also insulates that system from its users' critical faculties. Audiences participate, continuously, on the terms of the producers and organizations that control the networks. They create value by participating regardless of the content of that participation.

BUZZFEED AND NATIVE ADVERTISING

For much of the twentieth century the relationship between editorial and content was a relatively clear one. A reader of a newspaper could clearly see the difference between the news and the advertising. This was true in most mass and broadcast media. The audience could discern what was advertising and what was the editorial or entertainment content.

The deal that formed between media organizations, their audiences and advertisers was relatively stable. Media organizations produced content that audiences wanted to see, and to fund the production of that content media organizations sold space to advertisers. The audience had to watch advertising to support the production of the news and entertainment.

As we have discussed in this chapter, this model has changed dramatically with the emergence of interactive and social media. One key change in the production and sale of audiences is native branding and advertising. Native advertising refers to paid promotional content that is presented as part of the editorial content.

One of the innovators in the development of native content is the news site BuzzFeed. Rather than sell advertisements that sit alongside the editorial content, BuzzFeed sells brands opportunities to sponsor and play a role in creating the editorial content.

BuzzFeed is a news service that has developed interdependently with the social web. It depends on getting its audience to share its content through their own online social networks – 75 per cent of views of BuzzFeed stories come from social media feeds, rather than people visiting the site. One of the consequences of this is that there is little opportunity to provide advertising in the traditional sense because the audience don't visit the actual BuzzFeed website.

BuzzFeed therefore needs to 'natively' integrate the advertising content into the editorial and entertainment content. Rather than sell advertising space BuzzFeed sells 'social storytelling'. It has a team of brand content writers who work with brands to write stories that combine brand messages with news and entertainment content.

When the Australian government released its Federal budget in May 2014, the bank ING worked with BuzzFeed to create a story: 'What the budget means for anyone who doesn't have an economics degree'. The story was written in the standard BuzzFeed style: internet memes, images and humour. The story went through a list of categories: people students, mums, drivers, the environment. For each category a red cross or a green tick was added to indicate whether they were a 'winner' or 'loser' from the budget.

At the top of the story it explained it was published by a 'brand publisher' and at the bottom it stated: 'Brought to you by ING Direct. Check out how their Orange Everyday account can help your salary go further.'

BuzzFeed helps brands to get online audiences to share brand stories. It tells brands that this turns them from a 'fan who passively likes you on Facebook to an advocate who tells their friends they love your brand'. The brand offers a news story that enables people in their target markets to tell their friends what they think and how they feel. In this media model there is no distinction between editorial and advertising content. BuzzFeed argues that its model works in part because younger audiences don't care about the separation between editorial and advertising in the way it is presumed older audiences do.

BuzzFeed explains that it doesn't aim to trick people into clicking on a brand post. Rather, audiences say, 'I know this is an ad, but it's too interesting and too funny not to share, I know I'm doing the work for you but I don't care.' What the audience member gets in return for sharing the item of brand content is the opportunity to make themselves visible and present in their social networks.

Rather than sell empty advertising space for brands to fill, BuzzFeed works with brands to integrate them into the storytelling and sharing practices of the site. This is a commercial media model attuned to the way social media sorts and organizes flows of content. Buzzfeed helps brands generate attention within the feeds of content people interact with on Facebook, Twitter, YouTube and Reddit.

How will native advertising change the relationship between news and advertising?

You can find links to BuzzFeed's native advertising on the *Media and Society* website study. sagepub.com/carahandlouw

THE WATCHED AUDIENCE

The development of interactive networks and the growing power and lowering cost of computing go hand in hand. Networks, computers, databases, servers, software and smartphones are parts of a large technological assembly that collects, stores and organizes data about populations. The proliferation and endless innovation in the uses and applications of data are central to the continuing rationalization and optimization of audiences. Data is central to describing a specific audience to a potential buyer. Television stations' ratings and market research are important in defining the size and demographics, and setting the price for audiences. Increasing amounts of data flowing through interactive networks enable advertisers to buy audiences on-demand. They ask media organizations to assemble specific kinds of audiences for them. Advertisers want to buy a customized product that they can adapt and optimize in real time.

To be able to build and categorize these highly specified audiences, media organizations have to engage in the development of a range of technologies for monitoring audiences. Media organizations invested in the development of these technologies throughout the twentieth century. Television for instance relied on a combination of in-home meters, diaries and surveys (Balnaves et al.

2011: 100). Each technology has limitations. Meters monitor what programme is watched whenever the television is on. These provide an accurate count of what is being watched, but they do not enable researchers to specify who in the family is watching. Some research firms added push-button meters that required the members of a family watching to press the button when they were watching. This provided some measure of who was watching. But people wouldn't push the button if they didn't want to disclose what they were watching. Diaries provide more detail on who watches what, but they are hampered by getting participants to accurately complete them. People routinely underestimate how much time they spend consuming media. Surveys are hampered both by people's recall of what they watched, and their willingness to admit to watching certain kinds of content (Balnaves et al. 2011).

The development of research techniques takes place in a social context. Research firms have developed screens with the capacity to recognise viewers and even to discern the extent to which they are actively viewing, together with their biometric responses (Balnaves et al. 2011: 107). Few people though are willing to be recruited as willing participants in these kinds of monitoring. What this all points to is that the process of packaging audiences for sale is a social one – it relies on the participation of audiences, together with the resources, tools and methodologies available. These audience research methods, though, are incredibly important to the commodification of audiences. They are the method through which industries package their audiences for sale. Marketers, advertisers and media organizations are pragmatic about the ways they create information about their audiences, using an array of approaches from anthropology, statistics and neuroscience. They are also inventive in the way they look for links between audience data and other population data sets.

Interactive media add to these methodologies the capacity for continuous and unobtrusive forms of monitoring. These technologies make our viewing habits, social networks and sentiments available as data. We've always expressed ourselves as audience members; we now do so in a digital enclosure where those expressions can be collected and responded to (Andrejevic 2013: 42). These expressions aren't only our conscious judgements and meanings. They also include the patterns and affects we generate by using media. The speed of our keystrokes, the patterns of our searches, and the movement of our eyeballs might all generate information about us that escape our own cognition (Andrejevic 2013: 96). The 'data-driven fantasy of control in the affective economy' is that 'the more emotions are expressed and circulated, the more behaviour is tracked and aggregated, the greater the ability of marketers to attempt to channel and fix affect in ways that translate into increased consumption (Andrejevic 2013: 58). The construction of increasingly valuable, rationalized and customizable audiences depends on both getting audiences to work harder – by paying more attention, generating more content, and interacting more often – and building a comprehensive infrastructure to capture an increasing array of audience attention, expressions, sentiments and movements.

The work of being watched is central to responsive forms of control

Audiences are an integral part of the contemporary market research process. They not only actively collect and upload information to databases as part of their everyday lives; they also continuously stimulate the circulation of information through social networks. Interactive and social media are composed of the continuous interaction between the social networks that users create and the technical apparatus that stimulates, shapes and valorizes those networks. The technical apparatus wouldn't work without the voluntary everyday activities of audiences doing the work of being watched. The content that audiences create animates online networks as others view, like, tag and comment on them. That content is a product of audience members' judgements and capacity to create social connections, it produces data that enables other forms of purposive watching to take place in the databases of social media. A photo an audience member takes and uploads to Facebook isn't just a text that contains meanings; it is also a device that creates data about that person and their social network. Only the audience member – using their position in social networks and capacities to mediate social life – can do this work (Carah 2014a).

This conceptualization of the affective labour involved in the work of being watched is useful when examining modes of interactive media and cultural production that don't rely on symbolic or ideological forms of control as much as they rely on the capacity to track, respond to and modulate social relations (Clough 2009, Dean 2010). This mode of production needs labourers who register social connections in databases as much as they produce particular cultural meanings. Value is not grounded entirely in the particular meanings in images and texts but in the network of social relations that the work of affecting creates. Audiences create value by enhancing the ability of the technical apparatus of social media to respond to the open-ended nature of social life. To some degree the production of the audience commodity doesn't depend only on market researchers, but also on cultural intermediaries and practices that stimulate the circulation of content through interactive platforms. The calculative and predictive capacities of big data depend in part on affective labourers who can assemble connections between social life and databases (Clough 2009, Lury 2009). Affective labour is central to connecting open-ended forms of cultural production with the technical capacities of big data.

Audiences undertake the work of being watched within communicative enclosures that rely less on telling audiences what to think or believe, and more on facilitating social spaces where they continuously watch and respond (Carah 2014b). A communicative enclosure doesn't need to specify that audiences convey particular meanings; what they need is the audience to undertake a general circulation of meaning. The communicative enclosure is composed of two elements: setting the coordinates within which audiences communicate, and providing the cultural resources within those coordinates for audiences to work with. In this system, the information that producers and audiences generate is not necessarily the basis of 'rational-critical' forms of understanding upon which 'ongoing process(es) of deliberation based on an evidentiary, representational view of the world' might develop (Andrejevic 2013: 46). That is, media production doesn't form and manage audiences only in a representational sense by distributing specific meanings to them. In addition to attempting to form audiences using representations, an interactive communicative enclosure can modulate the audiences' continual circulation of meaning. The media environment acts as a 'probe' (Andrejevic 2013: 58), constantly monitoring audiences and responding to their constantly evolving identities, social relationships and cultural practices. The communicative enclosure doesn't need to create the specific representations that attract audience attention if it is able to channel audience members' own capacities to give and gain attention from each other.

Databases determine how identities are continuously assembled in relation to each other, cultural practices and social spaces (Zwick and Knott 2009). The databases of interactive media rely on consumers and cultural labourers who create media texts that link together identities, practices and places. Interactive and social media broker this sociality, channelling social interactions 'via algorithms engineered to produce connections between people on the basis of their articulated opinions' (van Dijck 2011: 165). As we use interactive media we add layers of contextual information to databases about social life, social relationships and sentiments.

If a social media platform like Facebook can identify several thousand consumers with a brand, place or cultural pastime, they can also link that network of relationships to the demographic and other behavioural data they already have on those individuals, or individuals like them. As Facebook's analytic capacities develop, these connections become denser. Our abilities to upload content about our social world, together with interactive media platforms' ability to analyse the information that flows through it, enable the increasingly flexible, customized, responsive and predictive production of audiences and markets. For instance, Facebook's ability to create value from analytic surveillance – watching, sorting and targeting – is amplified by these active and productive forms of watching that produce good, or more valuable, data (Carah 2014b). Interactive media platforms aren't collecting data in order to understand in a meaningful way who people are or why they like things. They just need to be able to track and respond to relationships between individuals, social spaces, practices and commodities. They need to be able to follow patterns of recognition and sentiment. Interactive media relies on our desire to be seen and felt by others. It can capitalize on our communication regardless of the particular sentiments we might express. It can respond to us, whoever we are and whatever we think; its primary interest is in assembling us into audience commodities that can be sold.

TRACKING THE TRACKERS: COLLUSION AND GHOSTERY

As we move about the web many organizations track and collect data about our movements. Some of those organizations are well known to us. We know that Amazon uses our search and purchase history to make recommendations; we know Netflix uses information about our viewing habits to recommend films; and we know Facebook uses all the information we enter into the platform to tailor the content in our news feed. But we don't tend to be as aware that Facebook tracks many of our movements on other websites, and uses that information to tailor the information we receive when we use Facebook. And there are a range of other organizations that collect data about our online lives, package it and sell it.

You can install apps on your internet browser that 'track the trackers'. These can show you what organizations are collecting information about you and potentially who they might be sharing that information with.

Install an app like Ghostery or Collusion on your browser. Track the organizations that collect your data as you browse the web over several days or a week. Draw a map of which sites are linked to which tracking organizations. Note the names of those organizations, see what you can find out about them: What do they do? Who owns them? What other organizations are they connected with? What do they do with your information?

Do you prefer relevant and tailored advertising? Why?

Compare the personal and social implications of the collection and use of personal information by advertisers.

You can find links to Ghostery and Collusion, together with resources about advertising and data collection, on the *Media and Society* website study.sagepub.com/carahandlouw

PREDICTING AND DISCRIMINATING

While we are free to generate content and data, we increasingly do so within communicative systems we do not control. Andrejevic (2011: 286) argues that the forms of surveillance characteristic of interactive media are exploitative because we generate information that is used to 'predict and influence' our behaviour in ways that serve the interests of others. While we might enjoy and derive pleasure from interacting, we nevertheless lose control over our own creations. We place ourselves and our social world into a network we do not control. That network uses information we generate to make decisions about us, and people like us, that affect our lives.

Often debates about the information collected from us and used to package us as audiences are framed in terms of individual privacy. That is, we ought to be assured or concerned based on judgements about whether this use of information will have personal consequences for us. This argument about individual privacy can be misleading because it directs our attention away from the larger social consequences of surveillance. The media system doesn't generate value from monitoring your individual private life, but rather by monitoring the lives and interactions of enormous populations, and sorting them into categories of people who are similar to each other. That sorting process determines how meanings flow through networks. We need to consider how the broad-scale collection of information, in sorting us into audiences, also enacts forms of social control and social discrimination that might have consequences – for both us as individuals and the society we live in – that aren't immediately visible.

Turow (2011) describes the extensive data collection that has accompanied the emergence of the web as 'history's most stealthy effort in social profiling'. The data being collected, assembled and analysed to produce audiences involves social discrimination. The use of this data is 'convergent' (Andrejevic 2013) in the sense that data from hundreds of different points – public records, online search and browsing history, mobile apps, social media networks, email accounts, credit cards, consumer and market research databases – is used to sort and categorize us into 'reputation silos' (Turow 2011). Marketers use data to make decisions about us, but we don't know what data is used and how those decisions are made. What is this data used for?

To make predictions about us and our lives

Predictive analytics are used to determine not just who you are, but also what kind of life you are likely to lead in the future. Marketers are developing databases that track consumers over long periods of time to determine the shape of the life course of populations. Brands can adapt, delivering different messages and offers to different individuals simultaneously. Ford might serve an advertisement and branded content about a luxury model to one person, and a budget model to another, at the same moment on the same website (Turow 2011). A financial brand might target a young middle-class consumer knowing they are likely to be an ideal customer in future years, while at the same time not targeting young people from working-class backgrounds. The aspirations of a middle-class life might become less visible to those not already within that social world. Brands can also differentiate products and service offerings in real time. They can target messages to mobile devices based on where we are or who we are with.

To discriminate between individuals

The predictive aspects of this kind of target marketing are bound up with forms of social discrimination. A system that makes decisions about who you are and the life you are likely to lead can shape the way you see the world.

The primary level of discrimination is sorting individuals as targets or waste (Turow 2011). Targets are individuals that media want to locate and attract the attention of. Waste are individuals who are of little interest to advertisers and therefore not of any value. If you are part of social groups that are routinely classified as waste you are unlikely to have content targeted at you. That means you'll likely increasingly see a random flow of content that doesn't reflect your world or your concerns. It'll be content that is made and aimed at other people. This will disproportionately affect poorer and marginalized groups. They have always been to some degree excluded from media content that has always been targeted at the middle class. This will be exacerbated. On the other hand, those of us identified as targets will be served increasingly customized forms of content that are based on the need to organize and sort us as audiences. When you log on to a news site it will serve you content that matches your demographic interests with advertisers' needs. This has consequences not just for the advertisements and entertainment we see, but our whole world-view. It may shape over time the political, cultural and social perspectives we are exposed to. We may be less likely to see the world of people who are unlike us, whose life circumstance are not like ours. This may make it harder for us to understand the broader society we live in, because we will be clustered into 'silos' of content based on our value to advertisers.

There are also questions to be posed about social mobility. For instance, your social network might indicate that you are part of a certain social class or race, or live in a location that is less likely to be educated and wealthy. The system may be less likely to serve you advertisements or content related to finance products, property markets, home renovation or other aspects of a middle-class lifestyle. Increasingly, you won't know much about ways of life you aren't already embedded within.

Other ways social discrimination works might include (Turow 2011):

- Information about your household profile – like your income, ethnicity, religion – could be used to make decisions about advertisements that are served to your children.
- Information about your diet gathered from your supermarket shopping profile could be used to make decisions about advertising for food, or your health across the course of your life, or the eligibility and cost of health insurance.
- Information about your Facebook friends or other online social network could be used to make decisions about your potential reliability as an employee or borrower.
- Content you access online and searches you conduct could be used to make decisions about your mood, or mental health or physical health conditions you might have.

These decisions affect the advertisements and content you see, which in turn might affect your world-view and your capacity to use the media to participate in public life.

One way of responding to these developments is to empower consumers to take greater control of the information environment they are immersed in. This would require greater transparency of what data is collected and how it is used. And then, consumers would need tools to be able to opt out of data collection and targeting, or to correct data in databases that is erroneous and making incorrect decisions about them. Turow (2011) for instance notes efforts to make the online advertising industry place a button on advertisements that when clicked on reveals any information that was used to inform the targeting on the advertisements and where that information came from. And then, consumers should be able to turn off data sources they don't want advertisers using or to correct information that is incorrect. These kinds of reforms are not so much aimed at the broader questions about social discrimination as they are about giving individual consumers the ability to control their profile. This would favour more empowered and educated consumers who are already being targeted with a wealth of high quality content, and have the aptitude to make decisions about how that content is shaped. Often, consumers are actively engaged in this setting of preferences on news sites, social networking sites and so on anyway. For consumers already marginalized from this system, it wouldn't make much difference. In many ways these kinds of consumer protections would simply draft consumers into additional labour in optimizing and making these systems more efficient. They would basically be fact checking the databases that advertisers are using.

Of more consequence is how the construction of valuable audiences articulates with or is embedded in a broader fragmentation of public discourse and public life. As that intensifies do we lose the ability to use media to negotiate important social, cultural and political issues? Despite whatever impacts these systems might have on us as individual consumers, we need to address the collective impact that they have on our society. It is clear that these predictive and responsive data-driven forms of communication cede control to groups whose primary aim is to anticipate our interests and life chances. And while that might be primarily motivated by their commercial aims, it also has impacts on the way our public life functions.

BUILDING THE FACEBOOK NEWS FEED ALGORITHM

In a blog post on Facebook, user-experience researcher Jane Justice-Leibrock explains her research with Facebook users to determine how best to prioritize content in their news feeds. Facebook aims to keep people engaged with the platform for as long as possible. The longer and more frequently people are engaged the more opportunities Facebook has to target them with advertising and generate revenue from them.

To continue to generate audience attention Facebook iteratively develops its news feed algorithm to be able to make more and more accurate decisions about what content to show users. The algorithm prioritizes content that users will find more engaging (e.g. photos), was generated by people they like (based on similar interests, peer networks, and previous interactions via likes, shares, comments and messages), and is about things users are interested in (based on similarity or affinity between posters).

Justice-Leibrock (2013) explains, 'As a user experience researcher, my job is to uncover the true and often unspoken needs of people using Facebook.' She used open-ended interviews to discover that when users said their feeds were 'cluttered', what they really meant was that there were too many stories in there they weren't interested in. To get to the bottom of this problem she undertook a 'card sort' exercise where she got users to show her how they would prioritize content in their news feeds. Justice-Leibrock gave users a stack of recent stories from their news feeds and asked them to prioritize them on a wall. This helped Facebook to understand people's intuitive decisions about the content they wanted to see. Facebook then incorporated these insights into the decision-making logic of the news feed algorithm.

Facebook constantly conducts experiments to improve its news feed. In 2014, one of Facebook's 'mood experiments' caused significant public debate after being published in a journal. *The Atlantic* explains: 'For one week in January 2012, data scientists skewed what almost 700,000 Facebook users saw when they logged into its service. Some people were shown content with a preponderance of happy and positive words; some were shown content analysed as sadder than average. And when the week was over, these manipulated users were more likely to post either especially positive or negative words themselves' (Meyer 2014).

What are the ethical considerations of the experiments used in the design of algorithms?

You can find links to more about Facebook's research experiments and the debate about them on the *Media and Society* website study.sagepub.com/carahandlouw

CONCLUSION

In this chapter we have focused less on what advertisements do to audiences, and more on how audiences are drafted into the work of watching and being watched. We've taken this approach in order to stimulate thinking about an interactive and responsive media system that doesn't control only with ideas and ideologies, but also by establishing a communicative enclosure. Interactive technologies are used to establish coordinates within which audiences participate. In the enclosure, audiences are free to say whatever they like, so long as they can be monitored and responded to. The communicative enclosure turns all our time into productive watching time. Whereas once audiences were only productive when they sat down to read the newspaper or watch television, today as they move through life with smartphone in hand they are frequently undertaking the productive activity of either watching or being watched.

FURTHER READING

The readings below examine the various kinds of productive activity undertaken by audiences: the work of being watched (Andrejevic 2002a), the work of ranking, rating and expressing opinions (Andrejevic 2008, Hearn 2010), and the work of creating content (Martens 2011). The readings by Turow (2011) and Turow et al. (2009) examine consumer attitudes to surveillance and the role that surveillance technologies play in creating valuable audiences for sale to advertisers.

Andrejevic, M. (2002a) 'The work of being watched: interactive media and the exploitation of self-disclosure', *Critical Studies in Media Communication*, 19 (2): 230–248.

Andrejevic, M. (2008) 'Watching television without pity: the productivity of online fans', *Television & New Media*, 9 (1): 24–46.

Hearn, A. (2010) 'Structuring feeling: Web 2.0, online ranking and rating, and the digital "reputation" economy', *Ephemera: Theory & Politics in Organization*, 10 (3/4): 421–438.

Martens, M. (2011) 'Transmedia teens: affect, immaterial labor, and user-generated content', *Convergence: The International Journal of Research into New Media Technologies*, 17 (1): 49–68.

Turow, J. (2011) *The Daily Me: How the Advertising Industry Is Defining Your Identity and Your Worth*. New Haven, CT: Yale University Press.

Turow, J., King, J., Hoofnagle, C. J., Bleakley, A. and Hennessy, M. (2009) 'Americans reject tailored advertising and three activities that enable it'. Available at SSRN 1478214. Retrieved from: http://papers.ssrn.com/sol3/Papers.cfm?abstract_id=1478214 (last accessed 10 September 2014).

Any article marked with ⊗ is available to download at the website **study.sagepub.com/carahandlouw**

MANAGING PARTICIPATION

EXERCISING POWER INVOLVES MAKING AND MANAGING MEANING.

* What are the various roles that meaning now plays in the exercise of power?

* How does global network capitalism use meaning to exercise power?

* How is participation in the creation and circulation of meaning embedded in the exercise of power?

* What role do our identities play in the circulation of meaning and exercise of power?

In this chapter we examine:

* The difference between speaking and being heard
* The difference between participating and managing participation
* The difference between decoding and managing representations
* The difference between being visible and being understood.

MEANING AND POWER

This book has examined how making and managing the circulation of meaning is related to the exercise of power. We have charted the development of culture industries that industrialized meaning making during the twentieth century. Over the past generation these industries have become more flexible and participatory as they have been embedded within global network capitalism.

DECODING AND DEBUNKING

As we become ever more implicated as participants in the creation and circulation of meaning, we become more intuitively aware of the constructed nature of representations. At first inspection we might think this makes us more savvy and astute consumers of meaning. A public less inclined to believe the representations they encounter, we might argue, will be more likely to critically analyse meanings and deduce how they are embedded within power relationships. While an informed public that can creatively and critically decode and differentiate between 'true' and 'false' meanings is important, this needs to be distinguished from a public that is engaged in a game or spectacle of debunking the constructed nature of representations. We can't assume that merely debunking representations necessarily 'speaks truth to power' in productive ways.

Our media and popular culture incorporates a continuous revelation of the constructed nature of representations. Celebrity and political confessions on talk shows, reality TV's self-referential exposure of its own means of production and backstage machinations, and corporate brands' references to the instrumental nature of their own appeals are all suggestive of a media culture that reflects on the constructed nature of media representations. Audiences are both invited to participate in these processes of representation and are presented with images of their own participation in social life. Some argue that audience participation in debunking representations reinvigorates public life by opening up new forms of critical enquiry and engaging previously passive audiences in more active forms of participation (Baym 2005, Coleman 2005, Feldman 2008, van Zoonen 1998). Comedy news, social media and reality TV have all been celebrated in this way. In contrast, critics argue that the savvy attitudes invoked by decoding and debunking representations only stimulates a 'critical apathy' that directs the public away from 'imagining alternatives' (Teurlings 2010: 370). The more that we engage in cleverly deconstructing how representations work, the more we withdraw from thinking that public forms of communication and representation are integrated with our actions in the world. This reluctance to believe representations is characteristic of a post-deferential society where we are less likely to trust that powerful elites, media figures, elected representatives or business leaders believe what they say or will act as they promise (Coleman 2005).

The continuous process of deconstruction makes meaning less stable. Andrejevic argues that 'As users shifted from consuming mediated images to creating them, they gained a self-conscious, practice-based awareness about the constructed character of media representations' (2009: 40). As we grow savvy at constructing our identities from the symbolic resources we find in our media and cultural world, we fashion our identities as flexible representative tools (Turkle 1997). We become less concerned with the values that identities and representations express, and more focused on their usefulness in positioning ourselves within power relationships. The active audience grows cynical about the constructed nature of representations. If we are constructing our identity and deploying meanings and representations, in order to position ourselves in social relationships in advantageous ways, then we suspect others must be doing the same. Knowledge of the constructed nature of representations builds a certain distance towards them (Turkle 1997: 78–79). Of course, the ability to recognize our identities as performed is nothing new. For instance, Goffman (1959) described in detail how we mediate between different aspects of ourselves, adopting different masks depending on the social context.

The paradox that arises in our present moment is that the emergence of media practices and technologies that promise audiences new forms of participation (in the process of representation) coincide with growing cynicism about the purchase those representations have on reality. Rather than believe representations, the audience is encouraged to know how they are constructed, to seek the truth behind their claims. The public becomes invested in uncovering secrets and conspiracies, being privy to revelations about how things really are, exposing how power really works, and getting a privileged view of the inner workings of powerful organizations (Dean 2002: 15). While this quest for knowledge about how things really are might appear empowering on the surface, it can be debilitating if it becomes an end in itself. If scepticism about representations becomes a default attitude in our public life, then representations lose their efficiency in: circulating meanings people can depend upon; mediating social relationships that people trust; and explaining how things are different from what they seem, or could be different from how they are, now (Žižek 1999). Representation is a social process that depends on participants who trust and recognize one another. Representation only works efficiently if the meanings circulating between people are integrated with their actions, embodied in material ways of life and can be recognized as meaningful by others (Couldry 2010). Without a social process of representation underwritten by trust, it would be difficult to understand our relationships with each other and be able to imagine, and deliberate over, how they might be different.

Debunking reinforces dominant power relationships

The process of engaging in an active debunking and deconstructing of representations may serve to support power relationships in several ways. By permitting and even performing a critical deconstruction of their own representations, the powerful inhabit, maintain and control the social spaces where more thoughtful and constructive critique might emerge. We see these practices at work when brands make jokes about their own appeals in advertisements or when political strategists go on cable news to explain how political campaigns work. In each of these cases the process of deconstructing representations and enabling audience participation is incorporated into processes of meaning production that maintain power. If a brand makes jokes about itself or a political campaign exposes its own inner machinations, then the revelations critics might make about the how these processes of meaning making really work lose their impact. The public think they already know how representations work, and while they might exempt themselves from believing in them, they still largely go along with them in practice.

Representations continue to work despite the fact that we can see how they work. Representation is not dependent on decoders believing the meanings they contain. Instead, they act as a schema, or some even argue a fantasy, that structures our reality (Žižek 1989). They don't need to be true: they just need to be useful in making everyday life functional and enjoyable. Representations relieve us of the duty to think, from the hard work of examining our place in the world, or imagining how social relationships might be different (Dean 2010). We might know how they work and be sceptical about their claims, but we go along with them because they make everyday life easy enough. If the traditional conception of ideology – that representations worked only because people didn't know how they obscured reality – was captured in the formula 'They know not what they do', then in contemporary times the formula 'They know but they still do' describes how more cynical participation in processes of representation works (Žižek 1989).

While the public contends with the declining purchase of representations on reality, power is arguably amassed around the capacity to bypass representation (Andrejevic 2013). That is, rather than attempt to manage power only by controlling specific meanings, the powerful develop strategies for watching and responding to a continuous circulation of meaning. This is a more permissive and participatory mode of control. The powerful don't need to control what is said if they have developed the technical capacity to watch and respond to the circulation of meaning in real time. Clough (2008: 16) suggests that the ideological function of media based on creating and controlling the circulation of specific ideas has 'become secondary to its continuous modulation, variation and intensification of affective response in real time'. By this she means that power is exercised not only by telling us what to think about, but by continuously watching and channelling our communicative activities. Where once the culture industry might have tended to thwart the participation of ordinary people, it now works furiously to promote participation. The culture industry's modes of control are more dependent than ever on the participation of ordinary people (Dean 2010). Significantly, however, the culture industry doesn't need to understand what we have to say as long as it is able to harness and channel our communicative activities to capture attention and predict the sentiments and actions of individuals and populations.

MEANING AND POWER IN THE INTERACTIVE ERA

There are four important differences we need to consider when examining the relationship between meaning and power in an interactive and networked culture industry:

- the difference between speaking and being heard
- the difference between being a participant and managing participation in general
- the difference between decoding representations and managing representation
- the difference between being understood and being visible.

Difference between speaking and being heard

Interactive technologies democratize the capacity to speak. They enable ordinary people to create a mediated account of their lives and the expressions and ideas that matter to them. Being free to say what we like and having the means to say it do not necessarily empower us. There remains a critical difference between speaking and being heard (Hindman 2009). We need to distinguish between representations of participation and material and meaningful forms of participation (Turner 2010).

Interactive networks are uneven structures with nodes of power that shape flows of content. Networks are structured around gatekeepers who direct flows of meaning through nodes. What matters is not the capacity to participate in the network, but rather the capacity to position yourself or your ideas as a central node. Power is afforded by being able to be a node that others connect to, pay attention to, or channel ideas through. The powerful are those who can make themselves and their ideas heard within the network. Those who are heard overwhelmingly have economic, technical and symbolic resources: media organizations, political elites, the wealthy and well educated. While networks create conditions for participation, that doesn't necessarily mean that this participation will amount to meaningful forms of deliberation. As networks create connections based on proximity and affinity they create clusters of people who agree with each other. This does not always help to create public spaces or processes where different points of view are exchanged. Rather than reinvigorate dialectical forms of communication, networks may further extend and entrench the one-dimensionality of mass communication systems.

Difference between being a participant and managing participation in general

We need to differentiate between having the capacity to participate in the creation and circulation of meaning, and having the power to control the spaces and structures within which that participation is contained (Andrejevic 2011). Controlling the structures within which participation takes place is critical for two reasons. Firstly, those who manage participation in general can shape flows of meaning. They can give some people or ideas more visibility than others. Networks coalesce over time around nodes, ideas and practices. Secondly, those who control interactive spaces can harness the ideas, social networks and data generated by participants. The key distinction here is that users create information but they cannot control how it is used. The data generated through the ideas, images and interactions we register in networks are used to shape our experience of those networks. Databases watch our participation in order to anticipate our actions and position us within flows of meaning. Participants' creations are used to 'predict and influence' their future behaviours as a 'means of fulfilling the imperatives of others' (Andrejevic 2011: 286). The more we participate, the more interactive networks can shape our social connections and experience of the world.

Difference between decoding representations and managing representation

While some might celebrate active audience participation in decoding representations and creating meaning, that communicative activity takes place largely within systems of representation controlled by others. Mark Andrejevic (2013: 95) argues that the 'appeal is for us to become savvy thin-slicers of data' who are reflexively cynical about the claims of representations. We read the body language of politicians to discern their true motives, monitor our peers on social networking sites, and dismiss the claims made by brands or governments. At the same time media and popular culture provides opportunities for us to express our wariness of representations, we increasingly encounter claims that new forms of data analysis enable a direct and objective access to reality that bypasses the need for deliberation and understanding. If we can no longer trust what people say, we can trust what data tells us. Arguments about the legitimacy of big data attempt to reclaim the possibility of dependable and trustworthy objective forms of knowledge. If subjectivist relativism undermined the possibility of objective knowledge, then big data appears to attempt to bypass the subject altogether. Big data is said to offer an unimpeded objective view of reality without the need to engage in debate or attempt to reach mutual agreement with other people about how to see the world.

Celebrants of big data, like former *Wired* magazine editor Chris Anderson, have argued that companies like Google don't need to know anything about culture, or understand meanings, or examine why people do things. Instead they need to collect enough data to be able to predict the movements of populations over time. Google doesn't need to understand human societies, it just needs to have algorithms that anticipate patterns, flows and movements. Anderson argues that we have entered a world where:

> Massive amounts of data and applied mathematics replace every other tool that might be brought to bear. Out with every theory of human behaviour, from linguistics to sociology. Forget taxonomy, ontology, and psychology. Who knows why people do what they do? The point is they do it, and we can track and measure it with unprecedented fidelity. With enough data, the numbers speak for themselves. (Anderson 2008)

If representations have lost their efficiency and trustworthiness then big data analysis promises us the chance to bypass meaning and understanding in favour of predicting, anticipating and simulating. Despite these claims to bypass representation, big data analysis is an important part of the culture industry's processes of making and managing representations. The collection and analysis of data is a process of representation that produces meanings, distributes them and uses them to structure social life and exercise power.

Data analysis is a process of representation that is embedded within power relationships. Collecting and analysing data involves constructing and implementing 'rules about how the world will appear' (Crawford 2013). Some groups have more power to collect, analyse and use data than others. We need to ask 'Who gets access? For what purposes? In what contexts? And with what constraints?' (boyd and Crawford 2012: 673). Data sets, and the technologies and algorithms to exploit them, are increasingly concentrated within powerful organizations in the networked culture industry like social media, search and database companies. We need to distinguish between people and organizations who create data, have the means to collect it and have the expertise to analyse it (Manovich 2011).

The culture industry still manages the representational process of making and disseminating images and narratives to mass audiences as it did for much of the twentieth century. This process is now accompanied by a data-driven representational process of producing information about the audience as they consume, create and interact with cultural content. This process of representation involves watching the audience to produce continuous real-time depictions of its preferences, activities and rhythms of life. These representations are used to shape ways of life and manage populations.

A representation process increasingly informed by big data analytics isn't based on a deliberative understanding of human relationships or an attempt to facilitate ongoing and meaningful public discussion. Instead, it is a process of representation that aims to render visible certain populations and their ways of life. Some data analysis exercises make predominantly privileged middle-class people visible as profitable consumer targets; other processes make predominantly disadvantaged people visible as deviant or criminal suspects; and still others make some groups of people invisible because they are of little commercial or political importance. Power is exercised by rendering some people and their ways of life visible and others invisible through the way data is collected, analysed and represented. Despite the claims in our popular and political culture that big data offers an unimpeded and objective view of reality, it is in fact a dramatic extension of the role that representation, knowledge and information plays in managing populations. Representations are produced as a schema for anticipating and predicting our actions, rather than as a schema for facilitating deliberation and understanding.

While ordinary people participate in games of debunking representations, power is organized by those who can control populations by using the forms of representation enabled by databases, analytics and algorithms. Surveillance informs the production of representations that 'simulate' reality (Bogard 1996). Rather than watch populations to merely represent who they are, what they think and how they act, surveillance is used to pre-empt and anticipate the movement of populations. These predictions are enacted in representations that, by making real what was anticipated, attempt to respond to the limits of communication. Rather than engage in open-ended processes of deliberation, the use of surveillance to create simulations attempts to 'satisfy a wish to know everything in advance' (Bogard 1996: 15) so that populations can be managed effectively and efficiently. Databases enable the powerful to rely less on understanding the public and more on harnessing flows of communication and information to manage populations. In this system ordinary people are left to be savvy about representational processes – sceptical of the way that meaning and power interrelate, but excluded from the systems that really structure the spaces within which they communicate with each other.

Difference between being understood and being visible

In a system of communication where power is located as much in the capacity to watch and respond to communication as it is in controlling the ideas that are circulated, visibility becomes critical. The powerful don't need to understand what we think if our daily actions and expressions are visible to them because we log them on interactive networks. Understanding why we do things or what we think isn't necessary if databases are able to discern and predict our actions and respond to us accordingly. We arguably acculturate ourselves to this logic, using interactive media not to be understood via deliberative discussions with others, but simply to be visible to our peers, to be seen and felt within social networks. A system of communication organized around using the circulation of representations to make individuals and their everyday lives visible grants power to those who have a greater capacity to watch and respond. At the same time, in displacing understanding it arguably erodes the use of public forms of communication through which we might encounter differences and develop shared ways of life. Representations matter to power relations not just because they enable us to be understood, but also because they make us visible either as the subjects of those representations or as participants who interact with them or participate in their creation and circulation. In this system, power resides with those who have both access to the information and analytics to predict and modulate flows of meaning.

Being visible makes us passive participants in a process of representation that doesn't attempt to understand what we mean or think, but rather just watches what we do. As interactive media systems and technologies like smartphones, search engines, social media, interactive TV, CCTV cameras and swipe cards passively collect data about our interactions, movements and relationships, enormous banks of data become proxies for decision making and displace public forms of discussion and understanding. Governments and corporations won't ask us what we think if they can watch what we do. Societies that rely evermore on interactive technologies to monitor and respond to populations, rather than understand the circumstances of their lives via narratives and deliberation, might lose the capacity to come up with solutions to complex problems that draw on intrinsically human values and judgements (Andrejevic 2013, Crawford 2013).

MANAGING PARTICIPATION

The capacity to manage participation is the key power variable in an interactive and networked culture industry. Managing participation involves assembling a configuration of information networks, urban space and analytic capacity to work in tandem with the ability to produce and circulate meanings. In addition to creating and controlling specific meanings, powerful interests seek to make and manage platforms or assemblies of technology that modulate the circulation of meanings. These activities work hand in hand with other established forms of meaning making. For instance, news organizations and political campaigns complement the production of specific content with sophisticated techniques for both monitoring audiences and publics and responding to the way they circulate and adapt meanings.

Participation creates two valuable resources: attention and data. While meanings shape how we understand and act in the world, this process is interrelated with the more general use of meanings to attract attention that can be harnessed and channelled. The circulation of meaning both cultivates valuable attention and creates social networks that harness communicative capacity and data. Algorithms and analytics exploit the open-ended play, creativity and attention generated via the circulation of meaning. The powerful don't rely on controlling what is said, as much as they rely on channelling and harnessing a continuous creation and circulation of meaning. Above all else, information networks need participants who constantly input useful information about their social world. The value of a database is found in its capacity to determine how individuals are connected to each other, cultural practices and social spaces. As we participate in interactive media systems we register these relationships in databases. The analytical capacities of databases to manage participation depend in the first instance on participants who attract each other's attention and register useful information about their lives. The calculative and predictive capacities of big data depend in part on participants who can assemble connections between social life and databases (Clough 2009, Lury 2009).

Managing participation involves the capacity to:

- Design and organize the social spaces within which people communicate with each other: urban spaces (public, private and domestic) are configured to make people visible to each other and to databases that monitor and respond to their activities .
- Develop a network of interactive communication technologies that enable participants to attract attention from each other and register information about their lives.
- Create an interconnected network of devices that both mediate and monitor everyday life – devices like smartphones embed the circulation of meaning and the capture of data within everyday life.
- Assemble databases that can store and organize information.
- Develop analytic techniques and algorithms that respond to the flows of information generated within the networks.
- Shape flows of meaning by predicting and anticipating the activities of participants.

This system relies on watching and responding to a continuous circulation of meaning. This circulation of meaning requires the participation of ordinary people who use interactive technologies to attract attention from each other, position themselves in communication networks, and connect those networks to their everyday lives. Managing participation doesn't depend on understanding the identities and meanings people circulate, but rather observing and predicting the relationships between people, places and actions over time. Managing participation depends in the first instance then on our desire to attract attention from each other – to be seen and felt in the social world.

The problem with a system of communication that makes us visible without listening to us, and relies on algorithms and analytics to bypass representation as a system of shared understanding, is that we risk losing the deliberative character of social life. We turn away from investing in public processes of communication where we go about the difficult work of attempting to understand each other as an ongoing process. Instead, we lean towards developing technologies that analyse and anticipate our actions.

FLEXIBLE IDENTITIES

A networked and interactive culture industry relies on our participation to create meaning and to manage populations. Our identities are central to this process. We participate because it makes ourselves and our lives visible to others. When we participate in networked communication processes we employ our ability to affect others and to be affected (Clough et al. 2007). By creating and positioning our identity within networks, we participate in the process of channelling the 'living attention of others' (Brennan 2004: 50) through the databases and algorithms of the interactive economy.

Our identities are interconnected with the way our voices are valued. They are only meaningful when they are recognized by others, and they are only valuable to us when they position us within social relationships that are empowering to us. Nick Couldry (2010) makes two important claims about voice:

- Voice depends on frameworks for organizing human life and resources that *value* voice. Without those frameworks that *support* the process of voice, it doesn't amount to much.
- Voice is a process through which we give an account of our life and its conditions. It is an ongoing activity through which we narrate ourselves in the world.

Couldry (2010) considers these two claims about voice in relation to the rise of a neoliberal society characterized by:

- the penetration of market logic into everyday life
- the shrinking of public spaces, processes and institutions as they are 'reformatted' as markets
- the emphasis on individuals who take responsibility for themselves and their own lives.

These structures, Couldry argues, undermine the capacity for our voices to be recognized in meaningful ways that shape the world we live in. Following Couldry we might argue that while our voices and identities are critical to the functioning of interactive and networked forms of communication, it doesn't necessarily follow that these systems enable us to make an account of our lives that has any material purchase on the way the world is organized. Responding to forms of interactive culture that demand our participation but don't listen to what we have to say, Couldry (2010) maps out several conditions for voice. These conditions are helpful for us in critically examining the limits of interactivity and the ways we might construct communication structures and processes that value our voices and identities.

Voice is socially grounded. Voice involves both speaking and being heard. Voice is social in the sense that it is only meaningful when we are recognized by others. This involves taking account of how voice is embedded within social relationships that are characterized by an uneven distribution of symbolic resources. Some of us have more capacity to speak and be heard than others, and are therefore more likely to have our lives and concerns recognized by others.

Voice is a form of reflexive agency. Our voice is embedded within the ongoing process of how we make sense of our lives. Our voice is interrelated with our actions. We have to take responsibility for the stories we tell, and others have to recognize our account of ourselves as being grounded in the reality of our lives. The stories we tell are critical to both making sense of where we have been and where we want to go, of how we position ourselves within social relationships.

Voice is an embodied process. Voice comes from someone who is positioned somewhere. Voice comes from our bodies, which are positioned in specific social relations, histories and places. When we listen to others we need to hear their voice as coming from a different vantage point in the world from ours. When we recognize others and listen to them we are not just attempting to understand them, but to recognize how their identity is different from ours because it is located in a different history and speaks from within different social relations.

Voice requires a material form. Voice is inherently social. An individual's capacity to speak is grounded in larger social formations: institutions, organizations or ongoing social processes. We need material social structures where our voice can be registered and recognized: a classroom, a dinner table, an online social network, a community radio programme or a debate in the national press.

GIVING AN ACCOUNT OF OURSELVES AND RECOGNIZING OTHERS

We can use Couldry's formulation as an analytical framework to examine communication processes, and we can use it as a normative tool to argue for how we think voice ought to be organized in our communities and societies. As an analytical tool Couldry's formulation draws our attention to:

- the social relationships within which people speak, are listened to and are watched
- the positions in the social world from which different groups are able to speak, and how those positions are related to the material and symbolic resources they have; this also involves examining how communication processes enable or constrain identities and ways of life
- the institutions that control and manage communication processes
- the social structures and processes within which our voices might be heard in meaningful ways.

Throughout this book we have argued that industrialized cultural production is critical to the exercise of power because it establishes and maintains identities, social relationships and cultural practices that serve the interests of ruling groups. We have examined how the emergence of a global, networked and interactive economy has changed the role that the industrial production of meaning plays in the exercise of power. Making and managing meaning involves controlling:

- the institutions where meaning is made, circulated and controlled; this includes media and cultural organizations, political and legal systems, security and intelligence agencies, and education systems
- the professions that make meaning, including the institutions that train future professionals
- the social and cultural spaces where meaning is made, interpreted and circulated; this includes spaces where ordinary people participate in the circulation of meaning
- the technologies for controlling flows of meaning, and watching and responding to populations.

Our individual identities are bound up with our capacity to give an account of our life and its conditions. We each desire that this account will be recognized by others and contribute towards shaping the world we live in. We have argued in this book that this process of using meaning to shape our lives and societies is embedded within power relationships. Some groups have more material and symbolic resources to create and control the meanings that organize the social world. For much of the twentieth century the nation state provided the symbolic and cultural space within which identities were constructed. Power rested with controlling national structures for organizing the creation and circulation of meaning.

In a networked and interactive system of cultural production the emphasis shifts towards using identity as a valuable resource to position ourselves within networks. Nations, organizations and individuals are engaged in the continuous work of acquiring attention, engagement and investment. As we become involved in the constant work of producing and positioning our identities within flows of communication, are we less engaged in the construction of broader collective structures? We are increasingly active in the production of cultural content that articulates who we are, where we belong and what we do. Does this help us to create processes and structures through which we deliberate with each other, encounter difference, arrive at positions of mutual respect, and make difficult decisions about how to organize our lives, communities and world?

Chouliaraki (2013) argues that the role of media ought to be to engage us imaginatively in the lived experience of others. Too often interactive and participatory media offer us opportunities to engage with social or political causes as a way of expressing and publicizing ourselves, rather than encountering others. Too much participation is weighted towards 'short-term and low-intensity engagement with a cause, over an other-oriented solidarity of deeply felt commitments' (Chouliaraki 2013: 55). Media need to enable us to encounter otherness, engage in deliberative argument, and witness performances that open up our imaginations and creativity.

FROM TELEVISION TO THE SMARTPHONE

Where television was the critical technology of mass identity construction, the smartphone is rapidly emerging as the lynchpin technology for the production of participatory, flexible and networked identities. Television presented us with a flow of images and representations that connected our private lives with broader collective processes, spaces and ideas. The smartphone is a responsive device that presents us with a flow of images similar to television, but at the same time calls on us to constantly interact with that flow. The flow of images doesn't just offer symbolic resources we use to make sense of the world; it constantly stimulates our interaction. The content that flows through our smartphones is provided by the culture industry, or takes place within an assembly of communicative structures, technologies and devices controlled by the culture industry. We can do whatever we like as long as the culture industry is able to monitor and respond to our activity. While the audience is more actively engaged in the process of creating and circulating meaning, the culture industry sets the parameters within which that participation takes place and harnesses most of the resources it produces.

This process of identity construction isn't only about us drawing on symbolic resources provided by the culture industry; it is also about us participating in making ourselves visible within those flows of meaning. We use the smartphone to position ourselves within networks where we are seen and felt by others. This can include our intimate and private lives when we communicate with families and lovers; our personal lives as we interact with networks of friends and peers; and our public lives when we engage with brands, media organizations, celebrities, political parties and other public forms of communication. Each of these aspects of our life and identity is plugged into a system of cultural production that is extensively monitored, tracked and responded to. The representational elements of cultural production that characterized television are now complemented by a vast array of technologies that monitor and weave together private, personal and public life. These technologies inculcate us in the circulation of meanings produced by the culture industry, engage us in the work of articulating those meanings within our lives, and comprehensively monitor and respond to our actions and expressions. The smartphone is a node for circulation of information through a network. It distributes meaning, harnesses participation, and monitors actions and expressions. The smartphone collects information about our identities, bodies and movements through private and public urban spaces that over time shape how we are positioned in flows of meaning.

We need to carefully examine what kinds of voice are enabled by participating in the continuous exercise of making ourselves visible within the communication networks of the culture industry. One critical argument is that these forms of communication do not support the construction of collective ways of life via processes of understanding and deliberation (Couldry 2010, Dean 2010, Andrejevic 2013). If we spend all our time managing flows of information – liking, clicking or commenting – we are active and reflexive, but we aren't reflective. We have no time to think. Our identities are a product of how we as individuals think through our relationship to the world. The quality of that thinking process matters. The process of making identity is tilted towards making ourselves visible and constantly adapting representations of ourselves in response to pulses of information from the network. An identity used as a resource to attract attention that has pay-offs for our private, personal, professional or public lives is a reflexive production. Identities used in these competitive networks are not grounded, lifelong processes moored in established values and ways of life that are deeply shared and understood between people (Hearn 2008). Identity is a resource to be used in competition with other individuals, rather than a stake in a collective structure or ongoing form of deliberation. The smartphone is the device through which the mutual performance and surveillance of identity takes place.

The technologies and networks of the interactive culture industry promise us access to the 'good life'. Using these technologies, so the mythology goes, we can express ourselves, connect with the people we love, be creative, and more fully experience the beauty of everyday life. Apple's iPhone advertisements are emblematic of this promise. Their television advertisement 'Photos Every Day' features several scenes of people going about their lives: skateboarding through a car park, coming across stencil art on a city wall, running past a rugged mountain vista, seeing a band, eating a meal at a restaurant, dancing in a bedroom with a friend, singing karaoke in a bar. The person uses their iPhone to photograph each of these moments and then share them via social media platforms. The rhetorical claim of the advertisement is that the use of the device to mediate these moments and share them enriches our lives. As we turn these moments into images that travel from our smartphone to the smartphones of others in our networks, our life and identity become visible to them. Our life is seen and felt by others. The device is critical to positioning ourselves within social relationships.

Lauren Berlant (2011: 1) illustrates how these promises of the 'good life' can be 'cruel'. She describes a relationship of 'cruel optimism' where 'something you desire is actually an obstacle to your flourishing. It might involve food, or a kind of love; it might be a fantasy of the good life or a political project. … These relationships become cruel when the object that draws your attachment actively impedes the aim that brought you to it initially.' Is the optimistic account of the role the smartphone plays in empowering our identity here a cruel one? The more we photograph, share, click, like and comment, do we drift further away from the 'good life'? Or worse still, does it thwart us from reflecting on the kinds of lives and communities we want to be a part of? As you walk home and see a beautiful sunset, or watch a favourite band play, or lie in a park with your lover, does using your smartphone to mediate the experience enrich the relationships of which that experience is a part? Does it enable you to realize an identity embedded in the 'good life'? Does your smartphone help you connect with forms of political action that change the relationships in which you live your life? Or does it push you away from them? The forms of interaction facilitated by smartphones arguably lead us to circle around and around the values, lives and experiences we think we seek (Dean 2010). We begin to act as though we think: 'If I just click this, like this, express this idea online, or circulate this photo, my life and its circumstances will be recognized by others, and that will improve my life or the society I live in.'

The smartphone relies on our participation. We do the work of attracting the attention of others, and circulating that attention through communication networks. That has some value for us, but it also accrues value in those networks, which those networks use to structure, organize and rationalize our future use of those spaces. Over time, interactive networks adjust to us: they shape our life trajectories as they discriminate what flows of information we will be positioned within, which ideas we will be exposed to, and who we are likely to connect with. We need to examine how our participation in interactive networks enables us to speak in ways that are meaningful and empowering, and that might enrich our relationships.

Our activity in these networks is a form of productive activity. The culture industry depends on our open-ended social capacity to stimulate and channel attention and recognition. The question for complex human societies though is that forms of communication organized in reflexive networks erode deliberative decision making while promoting predictive and analytic decision making. These decisions are based on trends and patterns in data, rather than on an attempt to understand complex ways of life and problems. In doing so, do we erode the capacity to solve complex problems that depend not on getting attention, organizing participation and sorting information, but on specifically human values like the capacity to understand, believe, trust and affect one another within collective structures over long periods of time?

CHARLIE BROOKER'S *BLACK MIRROR*

Black Mirror is a drama series written by Charlie Brooker. Each episode in the series offers a critical reflection on life in a media-dense society. The episodes are forward-looking: they attempt to imagine the trajectory of media technologies and speculate about their impact on our intimate and public lives, society, culture and politics.

Watch season 2 of *Black Mirror*. Each episode offers a critique of interactive and participatory forms of media. The first episode, 'Be Right Back', raises questions about intimacy, surveillance, simulation and sentiment analysis. The episode follows a young couple. When one of them suddenly passes away, media offer a way for their relationship to endure. What

(Continued)

(Continued)

do our smartphones know about us that our intimate others do not? And how might our smartphones be used in the future to create customized forms of media that simulate our intimate relationships?

The second episode, 'White Bear', offers a critique of our participation in media rituals where we are called on to judge others. The episode draws on the culture of smartphone witnessing, reality TV and tabloid media spectacles, and poses questions about race, class, criminality and punishment.

The third episode, 'The Waldo Moment', explores mediatized politics. It follows a local by-election where the candidates include members of the major parties engaging in a highly professionalized and image-conscious form of campaigning. They are joined on the campaign by a satirical animated character intent only on pointing out the broken nature of the media-political process.

Each episode critically reflects on the nature of our participation in an increasingly responsive media system. 'Be Right Back' suggests that the more we participate, the more value we generate, the more data we create, and the more that data can be used to control the customization of media and affect how we see the world and live our lives. It asks us to consider to what extent customized media will be able to perform human relationships. After watching the episode, ask:

What do you imagine are some of the consequences of a media system characterized by a two-way flow of information that watches and responds to us in real time?

What do you imagine are some of the consequences of a world where media technologies simulate humans?

Would you want a simulation of a distant or deceased intimate other?

How do media technologies affect our intimate relationships?

'White Bear' suggests that the more we participate, the more we enact dominant frames of representation, uneven power relationships and rituals of judgement. After watching 'White Bear', examine media formats and practices where we participate in judging others.

How do the rituals associated with these formats and practices enact power relationships?

What role do smartphones play in 'bearing witness' to events in the world?

How does this 'bearing witness' with smartphones affect our public lives, popular culture or journalism?

'The Waldo Moment' suggests that the more we participate, the more we add to an unending loop of cynicism, snark and apathy. After watching the episode consider:

To what extent do contemporary forms of popular culture and media enable meaningful and productive participation in the political process? You might consider one or more of: forms of media that involve satire, comedy and cynicism; popular and entertaining talk and panel shows, talkback and breakfast radio, and comedy news; political activity and discussion on social media platforms.

Black Mirror provocatively suggests that participation doesn't amount to much on its own. What we also need is more thinking. This involves careful deliberation, evidence gathering and argument testing. But it also involves using our imaginations and creativity. Charlie Brooker reminds us of the power of creative and provocative thinking. He may not always get it right, but he does manage in much of this series to unsettle us and prompt us to think. To help us think critically about the media, we need to engage with scholarly debate, political argument, and the worlds of art, popular culture and everyday life.

We need to be able to carefully and critically analyse how things are now. But this then needs to be coupled with the work of imagining how things might be otherwise, and going about the real activity of working together in the world. This demands our creativity and ingenuity. Being a good communicator is about more than attracting attention, using technology or making compelling content. It is about knowing how to orchestrate meaningful and constructive relationships in the world.

We've taken a critical approach to media and society in this book, but that shouldn't be mistaken for a negative position. We don't think media technology is bad. But we do think media technologies are bound up in larger relationships of power. The first impulse of a critical position is to draw attention to how media facilitate power relationships. We've attempted to puncture the fantasy that one day, with the right technologies and tools, we will solve all the problems! Technical problem solving will never be enough. We also need critical thinking: What does it mean to be human? What kind of social world are we making? How will we make space for each other in the world?

CONCLUSION

The end of the twentieth century witnessed the birth of a new form of social and economic organization that is global, informational and flexible. New information technologies are significantly implicated in the emergence of global network capitalism and its modes of production and control. The key critical question to consider is whether communication based on participation, interaction and monitoring will enable creative solutions to emerge for the problems that face any society. Issues like scepticism about the truth of representations or claims about the predictive capacity of algorithms point to the need for us to consider the continuing value of forms of decision making enabled by deliberation, discussion and understanding. Future hegemonic struggles may be increasingly informational and communicative. They will be struggles over controlling information networks and their databases. But additionally, struggles may emerge over what kinds of knowledge are necessary to manage human populations and acquire and maintain power.

Communication is central to the management of populations. We are often told that the interactive and participatory nature of communication is good or empowering (see Durham-Peters 1999,

Andrejevic 2007, Couldry 2010, Turner 2010). Durham-Peters (1999: 6) reminds us that claims about communication are often 'infested with platitudes': we are told that 'Communication is good, mutuality is good, more sharing is better.' We tend to think that our democracies, communities and lives would be better, richer or more just if we had more debate, or dialogue, or participation, or rational exchange of information. Against this mythology, John Durham-Peters (1999: 30) argues that the answer isn't more communication:

> Communication, in the deeper sense of establishing ways to share one's hours meaningfully with others, is sooner a matter of faith and risk than of technique and method. Why others do not use words as I do or do not feel or see the world as I do is a problem not just in adjusting the transmission and reception of messages, but in orchestrating collective being, in making space in the world for each other. Whatever 'communication' might mean, it is more fundamentally a political and ethical problem than a semantic one.

The answer instead, following Durham-Peters (1999), is to carefully reflect on the political and ethical uses of communication in 'orchestrating collective being' and 'making space in the world for each other'. Interactive communication networks depend on our participation. While they promise to give us voice, they also stand to benefit from collecting, accessing, organizing and manipulating information. The central problem then is that the more we express ourselves, the more it enhances our power to watch, respond and shape social relationships.

In a configuration of communication and power that relies on our everyday participation, we need to examine what we think 'good' communication is:

- Would particular kinds of communication – mutual, dialogic or rational – make our lives and societies better?
- What would 'good' communication look like in a world where participating by expressing ourselves is easy, but the complex networks in which we communicate are controlled by elite interests and characterized by uneven flows of resources?
- What does it mean to communicate in a system where our expressions are extensively monitored?
- What role does the mass collection and analysis of flows of meaning play in managing communication and populations?

Before we invest in communication with our hopes and dreams for a better world, we need to ask some fundamental questions:

- Who gets to speak?
- Who gets heard?
- Who gets seen?
- Who gets watched?

- Who are the beneficiaries?
- Who resists these modes of communication and control? How do they resist?
- What does meaningful participation look like in complex and networked mass societies?
- Where is power located?
- How is power structured?
- How are interactive and participatory forms of communication made legitimate?

The struggle between the forces for discursive closure and openness will remain a feature of human society. The question is how those struggles are organized within an assembly of cultural and media production that manages the creation and circulation of meaning, the participation of individuals, and the collection and analysis of information. We need to consider, however, how participatory forms of media change the way we as humans spend our time with each other, make our lives meaningful, and make decisions together about how to live in the world. We can't fall for the mythology that networks enable us all to participate in important decisions about our world. Participating in an endless flow of communication isn't necessarily empowering or meaningful. If everyone must be consulted and must participate, how will difficult decisions be taken?

Participation is not necessarily accompanied by trust or faith in the possibility of being recognized in meaningful ways. Professional communicators are often confronted with the challenge of managing populations who are cynical about the constructed nature of representations. Where building power using media was ostensibly about trust and consent built over time, interactive media shift the emphasis to participation and visibility. Professional communicators are central to creating the communicative structures that control who speaks, who gets heard, who gets seen and who gets watched. Being a skilled professional communicator involves both the capacity to create content that attracts attention and persuades, and the ability to manage complex and continuous forms of participation. Professional communicators are rapidly acquiring the expertise to create social spaces and communication processes where they watch and respond to populations and modulate flows of meaning. But are they retaining or continuing to develop the capacity to understand, manage deliberation, persuade, convince and build trust in leaders, institutions and shared ways of life over long periods of time? Is it possible to manage complex societies and make difficult long-term decisions without building consent in common ways of life, identities and values? The test ultimately of any social system is its capacity to respond to complex problems. It remains to be seen whether a system organized around continuous and predictive analysis and control of flows of information amounts to the capacity to respond to increasingly complex social, cultural, technological and ecological events.

FURTHER READING

In 2014 the international open-access *International Journal of Communication* launched a forum for debate about participation. The forum featured leading international communication scholars in a structured dialogue about the 'participatory promise of contemporary culture and politics'. The contributions to the forum address questions regarding creativity, labour, politics and platforms. The forum is unique because readers can follow leading scholars addressing each other in turn and responding directly to each other's ideas. Below we suggest four exchanges from the forum on creativity, labour, politics and platforms. In addition to the forum, Hallinan and Striphas (2014) and Couldry and Turow (2014) examine the consequences of algorithmic media for our culture and democracy.

Allen, D., Carpentier, N., Bailey, M., Fenton, N., Jenkins, H., Lothian, A., Qiu, J., Schafer, M. and Srinivasan, R. (2014) 'Participations: dialogues on the participatory promise of contemporary culture and politics. Part 3: Politics', *International Journal of Communication*, Forum: 1129–1151.

Andrejevic, M., Banks, J., Campbell, J., Couldry, N., Fish, A., Hearn, A. and Ouellette, L. (2014) 'Participations: dialogues on the participatory promise of contemporary culture and politics. Part 2: Labour', *International Journal of Communication*, Forum: 1089–1106.

Banet-Weiser, S., Baym, N., Coppa, F., Gauntlett, D., Gray, J., Jenkins, H. and Shaw, A. (2014) 'Participations: dialogues on the participatory promise of contemporary culture and politics. Part 1: Creativity', *International Journal of Communication*, Forum: 1069–1088.

Clark, J., Couldry, N., Kosnik, A., Gillespie, T., Jenkins, H., Kelty, C., Papacharissi, Z., Powell, A. and van Dijck, J. (2014) 'Participations: dialogues on the participatory promise of contemporary culture and politics. Part 5: Platforms', *International Journal of Communication*, Forum: 1446–1473.

Couldry, N. and Turow, J. (2014) 'Advertising, big data, and the clearance of the public realm: marketers' new approaches to the content subsidy', *International Journal of Communication*, 8: 1710–1726.

Hallinan, B. and Striphas, T. (2014) 'Recommended for you: the Netflix Prize and the production of algorithmic culture', *New Media & Society*, 1–21.

All of these articles are available to download at the website **study.sagepub.com/carahandlouw**

REFERENCES

Aaker, D. (1991) *Managing Brand Equity: Capitalizing on the Value of a Brand Name.* New York: Maxwell Macmillan.

Abercrombie, N. (1996) *Television and Society.* Cambridge: Polity Press.

Adams, P. (2012) *Grouped: How Small Groups of Friends Are the Key to Influence on the Social Web.* Berkeley, CA: New Riders.

Adorno, T. (2001) *The Culture Industry: Selected Essays on Mass Culture.* Routledge: New York.

Adorno, T. and Horkheimer, M. (2008) *Dialectic of Enlightenment.* London: Verso.

Albury, K., Crawford, K., Byron, P. and Mathews, B. (2013) *Young People and Sexting in Australia: Ethics, Representation and the Law.* ARC Centre for Creative Industries and Innovation / Journalism and Media Research Centre, University of New South Wales, Australia.

Allen, D., Carpentier, N., Bailey, M., Fenton, N., Jenkins, H., Lothian, A., Qiu, J., Schafer, M. and Srinivasan, R. (2014) 'Participations: dialogues on the participatory promise of contemporary culture and politics. Part 3: Politics', *International Journal of Communication*, Forum: 1129–1151.

Alper, M. (2013) 'War on Instagram: framing conflict photojournalism with mobile photography apps', *New Media & Society*, 1–16.

Althusser, L. (1971) *Lenin and Philosophy and Other Essays.* London: New Left Books.

Andén-Papadopoulos, K. (2013) 'Media witnessing and the "crowd-sourced video revolution"', *Visual Communication*, 12 (3): 341–357.

Andersen, B. (1983) *Imagined Communities: Reflections on the Origin and Spread of Nationalism.* London: Verso.

Anderson, C. (2008) 'The end of theory: the data deluge makes the scientific method obsolete', *Wired.* Retrieved from: www.wired.com/science/discoveries/magazine/16-07/pb_theory (last accessed 8 September 2014).

Andrejevic, M. (2002a) 'The work of being watched: interactive media and the exploitation of self-disclosure', *Critical Studies in Media Communication*, 19 (2): 230–248.

Andrejevic, M. (2002b) 'The work of watching one another: lateral surveillance, risk, and governance', *Surveillance & Society*, 2 (4): 479–497.

Andrejevic, M. (2004) *Reality TV: The Work of Being Watched.* Lanham, MD: Rowman and Littlefield.

Andrejevic, M. (2007) *iSpy: Surveillance and Power in the Interactive Era.* Lawrence, KS: University of Kansas Press.

Andrejevic, M. (2008) 'Watching television without pity: the productivity of online fans', *Television & New Media*, 9 (1): 24–46.

Andrejevic, M. (2009) 'Critical media studies 2.0: an interactive upgrade', *Interactions: Studies in Communication & Culture*, 1 (1): 35–51.

Andrejevic, M. (2011) 'Surveillance and alienation in the online economy', *Surveillance & Society*, 8 (3): 278–287.

Andrejevic, M. (2013) *Infoglut: How Too Much Information Is Changing the Way We Think and Know*. New York: Routledge.

Andrejevic, M., Banks, J., Campbell, J., Couldry, N., Fish, A., Hearn, A. and Ouellette, L. (2014) 'Participations: dialogues on the participatory promise of contemporary culture and politics: Part 2: Labour', *International Journal of Communication*, Forum: 1089–1106.

Arnold, M. (1957 [1869]) *Culture and Anarchy*. Cambridge: Cambridge University Press.

Aronczyk, M. (2008) '"Living the brand": nationality, globality and the identity strategies of nation branding consultants', *International Journal of Communication*, 2 (1): 41–65.

Arvidsson, A. (2005) 'Brands: a critical perspective', *Journal of Consumer Culture*, 5 (2): 235–258.

Athique, A. (2008) 'The global dynamics of Indian media piracy: export markets, playback media and the informal economy', *Media, Culture & Society*, 30: 699–717.

Audley, P. (1983) *Canada's Cultural Industries. Toronto:* James Lorimer & Co.

Bahro, R. (1981) *The Alternative in Eastern Europe*. London: Verso.

Balnaves, M., O'Regan, T. and Goldsmith, B. (2011) *Rating the Audience: The Business of Media*. New York: Bloomsbury Academic.

Bamford, J. (2012) 'The NSA is building the country's biggest spy center (watch what you say)', *Wired*. Retrieved from: www.wired.com/threatlevel/2012/03/ff_nsadatacenter/ (last accessed 7 September 2014).

Banet-Weiser, S. (2012) *Authentic TM: The Politics and Ambivalence in a Brand Culture*. New York: NYU Press.

Banet-Weiser, S., Baym, N., Coppa, F., Gauntlett, D., Gray, J., Jenkins, H. and Shaw, A. (2014) 'Participations: dialogues on the participatory promise of contemporary culture and politics: Part 1: Creativity', *International Journal of Communication*, Forum: 1069–1088.

Banks, M. (2010) 'Autonomy guaranteed? Cultural work and the "art–commerce relation"', *Journal for Cultural Research*, 14 (3): 251–269.

Bar, F. and Sandvig, C. (2008) 'US communication policy after convergence', *Media, Culture & Society*, 30: 531–550.

Baran, P. (1964) 'On distributed communications networks', *Communications Systems, IEEE Transactions*, 12 (1): 1–9.

Baym, G. (2005) '*The Daily Show*: discursive integration and the reinvention of political journalism', *Political Communication*, 22 (3): 259–276.

Benkler, Y. (2006) *The Wealth of Networks: How Social Production Transforms Markets and Freedom*. New Haven, CT: Yale University Press.

Bennett, L. (2012) 'Patterns of listening through social media: online fan engagement with the live music experience', *Social Semiotics*, 22 (5): 545–557.

Berger, P. L. (1977) *Pyramids of Sacrifice*. Harmondsworth: Penguin.

Berlant, L. (2011) *Cruel Optimism*. Durham, NC: Duke University Press.

Blood, W. and Holland, K. (2004) 'Risky news, madness and public crisis: a case study of the reporting and portrayal of mental health and illness in the Australian press', *Journalism*, 5 (3): 323–342.

Bogard, W. (1996) *The Simulation of Surveillance: Hyper-control in Telematics Societies*. Cambridge: Cambridge University Press.

Boorstin, D. J. (1971) *The Image: A Guide to Pseudo-events in America*. New York: Athenaeum.

boyd, d. (2008) 'Facebook's privacy trainwreck', *Convergence: The International Journal of Research into New Media Technologies*, 14 (1): 13–20.

boyd, d. and Crawford, K. (2012) 'Critical questions for big data: provocations for a cultural, technological, and scholarly phenomenon', *Information, Communication & Society*, 15 (5): 662–679.

Boyd-Barrett, O. (1977) 'Media imperialism: towards an international framework for the analysis of media systems', in J. Curran, M. Gurevitch and J. Woolacott (eds), *Mass Communication and Society*. London: Edward Arnold, pp. 116–141.

Bramall, R. and Pitcher, B. (2013) 'Policing the crisis, or, why we love *The Wire*', *International Journal of Cultural Studies*, 16 (1): 85–98.

Bratich, J. (2005) 'Amassing the multitude: revisiting early audience studies', *Communication Theory*, 15 (3): 242–265.

Bratich, J. (2011) 'User-generated discontent: convergence, polemology and dissent', *Cultural Studies*, 25 (4–5): 621–640.

Brennan, T. (2004) *The Transmission of Affect*. Ithaca, NY: Cornell University Press.

Briggs, A. (1961) *The Birth of Broadcasting in the United Kingdom: Volume 1*. London: Oxford University Press.

Brin, S. (2013) 'Why Google Glass?', *TED 2013*. Retrieved from: www.ted.com/talks/sergey_brin_why_google_glass.html (last accessed 8 September 2014).

Brown, R. and Gregg, M. (2012) 'The pedagogy of regret: Facebook, binge drinking and young women', *Continuum*, 26 (3): 357–369.

Buck-Morss, S. (2002) *Dreamworld and Catastrophe: The Passing of Mass Utopia in East and West*. Cambridge, MA: MIT Press.

Cain, G. (2010) 'South Korean cartoonists cry foul over *The Simpsons*', *Time*. Retrieved from: http://content.time.com/time/world/article/0,8599,2027768,00.html (last accessed 8 September 2014).

Caldwell, J. T. (2008) *Production Culture: Industrial Reflexivity and Critical Practice in Film and Television*. Durham, NC: Duke University Press.

Campus, D. (2010) 'Mediatization and personalization of politics in Italy and France: the cases of Berlusconi and Sarkozy', *International Journal of Press/Politics*, 15 (2): 219–235.

Carah, N. (2014a) 'Watching nightlife: affective labor, social media, and surveillance', *Television & New Media*, 15 (3): 250–265.

Carah, N. (2014b) 'Brand value: how affective labour creates brands', *Consumption, Markets and Culture*, 17 (4): 346–366.

Carah, N., Brodmerkel, S. and Knaggs, A. (2012) 'Gruen nation: dissecting the show, not the business', *Communication, Politics and Culture*, 45 (1): 60–77.

Castells, M. (1996) *The Rise of the Network Society*. Oxford: Blackwell.

Chen, A. (2012) 'Inside Facebook's outsourced anti-porn and gore brigade, where "camel toes" are more offensive than "crushed heads"', *Gawker*. Retrieved from: http://gawker.com/5885714/inside-facebooks-outsourced-anti+porn-and-gore-brigade-where-camel-toes-are-more-offensive-than-crushed-heads (last accessed 8 September 2014).

Chesher, C. (2012) 'Between image and information: the iPhone camera in the history of photography', in L. Hjorth, J. E. Burgess and I. Richardson (eds), *Studying Mobile Media: Cultural Technologies, Mobile Communication, and the iPhone*. New York: Routledge, pp. 98–117.

Chouliaraki, L. (2010) 'Post-humanitarianism: humanitarian communication beyond a politics of pity', *International Journal of Cultural Studies*, 13 (2): 107–126.

Chouliaraki, L. (2013) *The Ironic Spectator: Solidarity in the Age of Post-humanitarianism*. Cambridge: Polity.

Clark, J., Couldry, N., Kosnik, A., Gillespie, T., Jenkins, H., Kelty, C., Papacharissi, Z., Powell, A. and van Dijck, J. (2014) 'Participations: dialogues on the participatory promise of contemporary culture and politics. Part 5: Platforms', *International Journal of Communication*, Forum: 1446–1473.

Clough, P. T. (2008) 'The affective turn: political economy, biomedia and bodies', *Theory, Culture & Society*, 25 (1): 1–22.

Clough, P. T. (2009) 'The new empiricism: affect and sociological method', *European Journal of Social Theory*, 12 (1): 43–61.

Clough, P. T., Goldberg, G., Schiff, R., Weeks, A. and Willse, C. (2007) 'Notes towards a theory of affect-itself', *Ephemera: Theory and Politics in Organization*, 7 (1): 60–77.

Cohen, B. C. (1963) *The Press and Foreign Policy*. Princeton, NJ: Princeton University Press.

Coleman, S. (2005) 'New mediation and direct representation: reconceptualizing representation in the digital age', *New Media & Society*, 7 (2): 177–198.

Collins, F. (2010) 'After the apology: reframing violence and suffering in First Australians, Australia, and Samson and Delilah', *Continuum: Journal of Media and Cultural Studies*, 24 (1): 65–77.

Connell, B. (2010) 'Looking back at Australia: a Nullah hypothesis', *Metro Magazine*, 164: 104–109.

Couldry, N. (2002) *The Place of Media Power: Pilgrims and Witnesses of the Media Age*. London: Routledge.

Couldry, N. (2003) *Media Rituals: A Critical Approach*. London: Routledge.

Couldry, N. (2010) *Why Voice Matters: Culture and Politics after Neoliberalism*. London: Sage.

Couldry, N. (2011) 'Class and contemporary forms of "reality" production, or hidden injuries of class', in H. Wood and B. Skeggs (eds), *Reality Television and Class*. London: Palgrave Macmillan, pp. 33–44.

Couldry, N. (2012) *Media, Society, World: Social Theory and Digital Media Practice*. Cambridge: Polity.

Couldry, N. and Hepp, A. (2013) 'Conceptualizing mediatization: contexts, traditions, arguments', *Communication Theory*, 23 (3): 191–202.

Crang, M. and Graham, S. (2007) 'Sentient cities: ambient intelligence and the politics of urban space', *Information, Communication & Society*, 10 (6): 789–817.

Crawford, K. (2012) 'Four ways of listening with an iPhone: from sound and network listening to biometric data and geolocative tracking', in L. Hjorth, J. E. Burgess and I. Richardson (eds), *Studying Mobile Media: Cultural Technologies, Mobile Communication, and the iPhone*. New York: Routledge, pp. 213–228.

Crawford, K. (2013) 'Algorithmic illusions: hidden biases of big data', *O'Reilly Strata Conference 2013: Making Data Work*. Retrieved from: www.youtube.com/watch?v=irP5RCdpilc (last accessed 8 September 2014).

Crook, S., Pakulski, J. and Waters, M. (1992) *Postmodernization: Change in Advanced Society*. London: Sage.

Cunningham, M. (2002) 'Saying sorry: the politics of apology', *The Political Quarterly*, 70 (3): 285–293.

Cunningham, S. and Turner, G. (1997) *The Media in Australia*. Sydney: Allen & Unwin.

Dahl, R. A. (1961) *Who Governs?* New Haven, CT: Yale University Press.

Dahlberg, L. (2011) 'Re-constructing digital democracy: an outline of four "positions"', *New Media & Society*, 13 (6): 855–872.

Dean, J. (2002) *Publicity's Secret: How Technoculture Capitalizes on Democracy*. Ithaca, NY: Cornell University Press.

Dean, J. (2010) *Blog Theory: Feedback and Capture in the Circuits of Drive*. Cambridge: Polity.

Derrida, J. (1976) *Of Grammatology*. Baltimore: Johns Hopkins University Press.

Deuze, M. (2005) 'What is journalism? Professional identity and ideology of journalists reconsidered', *Journalism*, 6 (4): 442–464.

deVreese, C. H. (2005) 'The spiral of cynicism reconsidered', *European Journal of Communication*, 20 (3): 283–301.

Durham-Peters, J. (1999) *Speaking into the Air: A History of the Idea of Communication*. Chicago: University of Chicago Press.

Emery, E. (1972) *The Press and America*. Englewood Cliffs, NJ: Prentice-Hall.

Entman, R. M. (1993) 'Framing: toward clarification of a fractured paradigm', *Journal of Communication*, 43 (4): 51–58.

Ewen, S. (1996) *PR! A Social History of Spin*. New York: Basic Books.

Farhi, P. (2003) 'Everybody wins: Fox News Channel and CNN are often depicted as desperate rivals locked in a death match. In fact, the cable networks aren't even playing the same game. There's no reason they both can't flourish', *American Journalism Review*, 32–37.

Feldman, L. (2008) 'The news about comedy: young audiences, *The Daily Show*, and evolving notions of journalism', *Journalism*, 8 (4): 406–427.

Foster, R. (2008) *Coca-globalisation: Following Soft Drinks from New York to New Guinea*. New York: Palgrave Macmillan.

Foucault, M. (1972) *The Archaeology of Knowledge*. London: Tavistock.

Foucault, M. (1977) *Discipline and Punish.* Harmondsworth: Penguin.

Foucault, M. (1979) 'Governmentality', *Ideology and Consciousness*, 6.

Fox, E. (1988) *Media and Politics in Latin America.* London: Sage.

Frank, T. (1997) *The Conquest of Cool: Business Culture, Counterculture, and the Rise of Hip Consumerism.* Chicago: University of Chicago Press.

Franklin, H. B. (1994) 'From realism to virtual reality: images of America's wars', in S. Jeffords and L. Rabinovitz (eds), *Seeing Through the Media.* New Brunswick, NJ: Rutgers University Press, pp. 25–44.

Fuchs, C. (2012) 'The political economy of privacy on Facebook', *Television & New Media*, 13 (2): 139–159.

Gamson, W. A., Croteau, D., Hoynes, W. and Sasson, T. (1992) 'Media images and the social construction of reality', *Annual Review of Sociology*, 373–393.

Gibney, M., Howard-Hassmann, R., Coicaud, J. and Steiner, N. (2008) *The Age of Apology.* Philadelphia: University of Pennsylvania Press.

Goffman, E. (1959) *The Presentation of the Self in Everyday Life.* New York: Anchor Books.

Graber, D. (2001) 'Adapting political news to the needs of twenty-first century Americans', in W. L. Bennett and R. L. Entman (eds), *Mediated Politics: Communication in the Future of Democracy.* Cambridge: Cambridge University Press, pp. 433–452.

Gramsci, A. (1971) *Selections from the Prison Notebooks.* London: Lawrence & Wishart.

Gray, H. (2012) 'Recovered, reinvented, reimagined: *Treme*, television studies and writing New Orleans', *Television & New Media*, 13 (3): 268–278.

Greenpeace (2009) 'Undercover operation exposes illegal dumping of e-waste in Nigeria'. Retrieved from: www.greenpeace.org/international/en/news/features/e-waste-nigeria180209 (last accessed 8 September 2014).

Gregg, M. (2011a) *Work's Intimacy.* Cambridge: Polity.

Gregg, M. (2011b) 'Do your homework: new media, old problems', *Feminist Media Studies*, 11 (1): 73–81.

Gross, L. (2001) *Up from Invisibility: Lesbians, Gay Men, and the Media in America.* New York: Columbia University Press.

Guimaraes, C. and Amaral, R. (1988) 'Brazilian television: a rapid conversion to the new order', in E. Fox (ed.), *Media and Politics in Latin America.* London: Sage, pp. 125–138.

Haag, O. (2010) 'Tasteless, romantic and full of history: the German reception of *Australia* and *Rabbit-Proof Fence*', *Studies in Australasian Cinema*, 4 (2): 115–129.

Habermas, J. (1976) *Legitimation Crisis.* London: Heinemann.

Hackley, C. (2002) 'The panoptic role of advertising agencies in the production of consumer culture', *Consumption, Markets and Culture*, 5 (3): 211–229.

Hall, S. (1980) 'Encoding/decoding', in S. Hall, , D. Hobson, A. Lowe and P. Willis (eds), *Culture, Media, Language.* London: Hutchinson, pp. 129–138.

Hall, S. (1981) 'The determinations of news photographs' recurrence', in S. Cohen and J. Young (eds), *The Manufacture of News.* London: Constable, pp. 147–156.

Hall, S. (1983) 'The problem with ideology: Marxism without guarantees', in B. Mathews (ed.), *Marx: A Hundred Years On*. London: Lawrence & Wishart, pp. 57–86.

Hall, S. (1996) 'Introduction: who needs "identity"?', in S. Hall and P. Du Gay (eds), *Questions of Cultural Identity*. London: Sage, pp. 1–17.

Hall, S. (1997) *Representation: Cultural Representations and Signifying Practices*. London: Sage.

Hall, S., Evans, J. and Nixon, S. (eds) (2013) *Representation: Cultural Representations and Signifying Practices*. London: Sage.

Hall, S. and Jacques, M. (1990) *New Times*. London: Verso.

Hallinan, B. and Striphas, T. (2014) 'Recommended for you: the Netflix Prize and the production of algorithmic culture', *New Media & Society*, 1–21.

Hamelink, C. J. (2008) 'Urban conflict and communication', *International Communication Gazette*, 70 (3–4): 291–301.

Hardt, M. (1999) 'Affective labor', *Boundary 2*, 26 (2): 89–100.

Hartley, J. (2010) *The Uses of Digital Literacy*. New Brunswick, NJ: Transaction Publishers.

Harvey, D. (1989) *The Condition of Postmodernity*. Oxford: Blackwell.

Harvey, D. (2000) *Spaces of Hope*. Edinburgh: Edinburgh University Press.

Hasinoff, A. A. (2013) 'Sexting as media production: rethinking social media and sexuality', *New Media & Society*, 15 (4): 449–465.

Hassan, R. (2003) 'The MIT Media Lab: techno dream factory or alienation as a way of life?', *Media, Culture & Society*, 25: 87–106.

Hawkins, G. (2009) 'The politics of bottled water', *Journal of Cultural Economy*, 2 (1–2): 183–195.

Hearn, A. (2008) 'Meat, mask, burden: probing the contours of the branded self', *Journal of Consumer Culture*, 8 (2): 197–217.

Hearn, A. (2010) 'Structuring feeling: Web 2.0, online ranking and rating, and the digital "reputation" economy', *Ephemera: Theory & Politics in Organisation*, 10 (3/4): 421–438.

Heath, J. and Potter, A. (2005) *The Rebel Sell: Why the Culture Can't Be Jammed*. Chichester: Capstone.

Hesmondhalgh, D. (2013) *The Cultural Industries*, 2nd edn. London: Sage.

Hesmondhalgh, D. and Baker, S. (2008) 'Creative work and emotional labour in the television industry', *Theory, Culture & Society*, 25 (7–8): 97–118.

Hesmondhalgh, D. and Baker, S. (2011) *Creative Labor: Media Work in Three Cultural Industries*. London: Routledge.

Hindman, M. (2009) *The Myth of Digital Democracy*. Princeton, NJ: Princeton University Press.

Hogan, J. (2010) 'Gendered and racialised discourses of national identity in Baz Luhrmann's *Australia*', *Journal of Australian Studies*, 34 (1): 63–77.

Holt, D. (2002) 'Why do brands cause trouble? A dialectical theory of consumer culture and branding', *Journal of Consumer Research*, 29 (1): 70–90.

Holt, D. (2006) 'Jack Daniel's America: iconic brands as ideological parasites and proselytizers', *Journal of Consumer Culture*, 6 (3): 355–377.

Jamieson, K. H. (1984) *Packaging the Presidency: A History and Criticism of Presidential Campaign Advertising*. Oxford: Oxford University Press.

Jamieson, K. H. (1992) *Dirty Politics: Deception, Distraction and Democracy*. Oxford: Oxford University Press.

Jarvis, J. (2011) *Public Parts: How Sharing in the Digital Age Improves the Way We Work and Live*. New York: Simon and Schuster.

Jay, M. (1973) *The Dialectical Imagination*. London: Heinemann.

Jenkins, H. (2006) *Convergence Culture: Where Old and New Media Collide*. New York: NYU Press.

Jenkins, H., Ford, S., Green, J. and Green, J. B. (2012) *Spreadable Media: Creating Value and Meaning in a Networked Culture*. New York: NYU Press.

Jhally, S. (1990) *The Codes of Advertising: Fetishism and the Political Economy of Meaning in the Consumer Society*. New York: Routledge.

Jhally, S. and Livant, B. (1986) 'Watching as working: the valorization of audience consciousness', *Journal of Communication*, 36 (3): 124–143.

Justice-Leibrock, J. (2013) 'User experience lab: how we designed a new news feed using your feedback', Facebook. Retrieved from: www.facebook.com/note.php?note_id=10151359587673920 (last accessed 24 September 2014).

Kellner, D. (2009) 'Barack Obama and celebrity spectacle', *International Journal of Communication*, 3: 715–741.

Kerbel, M. R. (1999) *Remote & Controlled: Media Politics in a Cynical Age*, 2nd edn. Boulder, CO: Westview Press.

Kitzinger, J. (2000) 'Media templates: patterns of association and the (re)construction of meaning over time', *Media, Culture & Society*, 22 (1): 61–84.

Klein, N. (2000) *No Logo: Taking Aim at the Brand Bullies*. London: Flamingo.

Kraidy, M. (2005) *Hybridity, or the Cultural Logic of Globalization*. Philadelphia: Temple University Press.

Kraidy, M. (2006) 'Reality television and politics in the Arab world', *Transnational Broadcasting Studies*, 2 (1): 7–28.

Kraidy, M. (2012) 'Wit under fire: political humour in the Arab uprisings'. Lecture at Engaging Minds, University of Pennsylvania. Retrieved from: www.youtube.com/watch?v=s6g3CO-7aHmQ (last accessed 8 September 2014).

Kreiss, D. and Howard, P. (2010) 'New challenges to political privacy: lessons from the first U.S. Presidential race of the Web 2.0 era', *International Journal of Communication*, 4: 1032–1050.

Laclau, E. and Mouffe, C. (1985) *Hegemony and Socialist Strategy*. London: Verso.

Lanier, J. (2010) *You Are Not a Gadget*. New York: Random House Digital.

Lanier, J. (2013) *Who Owns the Future?* New York: Simon and Schuster.

Lash, S. (1990) *Sociology of Postmodernism*. London: Routledge.

Lash, S. and Urry, J. (1994) *Economies of Signs and Space*. London: Sage.

Lasswell, H. D. (1948) 'The structure and function of communication in society', *The Communication of Ideas*, 37.

Lazzarato, M. (1996) 'Immaterial labour', in M. Hardt and P. Virno (eds), *Radical Thought in Italy: A Potential Politics*. Minneapolis: University of Minnesota Press, pp. 133–147.

Lee, T. (2012) 'Staffer axed by Republican group over retracted copyright-reform memo', *Ars Technica*. Retrieved from: http://arstechnica.com/tech-policy/2012/12/staffer-axed-by-republican-group-over-retracted-copyright-reform-memo/ (last accessed 18 September 2014).

Lenin, V. (1929) 'Where to begin', in *Collected Works: Volume5*. London: Lawrence & Wishart. Retrieved from: http://www.marx2mao.com/PDFs/LeninCW-Vol.5-TC.pdf (last accessed 17 September 2014).

Lewis, T. (2008) 'Transforming citizens? Green politics and ethical consumption on lifestyle television', *Continuum: Journal of Media & Cultural Studies*, 22 (2): 227–240.

Lewis, T. and Potter, E. (2011) *Ethical Consumption: A Critical Introduction*. London: Routledge.

Lipnack, J. and Stamps, J. (1994) *The Age of the Network: Organizing Principles for the 21st Century*. Essex Junction, VT: Omneo.

Lippmann, W. (1965) *Public Opinion*. New York: Free Press.

Livingstone, S. M. (1993) 'The rise and fall of audience research: an old story with a new ending', *Journal of Communication*, 43 (4): 5–12.

Livingstone, S. (1998) 'Audience research at the crossroads: the "implied audience" in media and cultural theory', *European Journal of Cultural Studies*, 1 (2): 193–217.

Livingstone, S. (2005) 'On the relationships between audiences and publics', in S. Livingstone (ed.), *Audiences and Publics: When Cultural Engagement Matters for the Public Sphere*. Bristol: Intellect Books, pp. 17–42.

Livingstone, S. (2008) 'Taking risky opportunities in youthful content creation: teenagers' use of social networking sites for intimacy, privacy and self-expression', *New Media & Society*, 10 (3): 393–411.

Louw, P. E. (2010a) *Roots of the Pax Americana: Decolonization, Development, Democratization and Trade*. Manchester: Manchester University Press.

Louw, P. E. (2010b) *The Media and Political Process*. London: Sage.

Louw, P. E. and Milton, V. (2012) *New Voices: The Transformation of the South African Broadcasting Corporation in a Changing South Africa*. New York: Hampton Press.

Lukes, S. (1974) *Power: A Radical View*. London: Macmillan.

Lury, C. (2009) 'Brand as assemblage: assembling culture', *Journal of Cultural Economy*, 2 (1–2): 67–82.

Lyon, D. (2011) *Surveillance Studies: An Overview*. Polity Press: Cambridge.

Maltese, J. A. (1994) *Spin Control: The White House Office of Communications and the Management of Presidential News*. Chapel Hill: UNC Press.

Manovich, L. (2011) 'Trending: the promises and the challenges of big social data', in M. K. Gold (ed.), *Debates in the Digital Humanities*. Minneapolis: University of Minnesota Press, pp. 460–475.

Marcuse, H. (1964) *One-Dimensional Man*. London: Routledge and Kegan Paul.

Markens, S. and Conrad, P. (2001) 'Constructing the "gay gene" in the news: optimism and skepticism in the US and British press', *Health*, 5 (3): 373–400.

Marshall, P. (1997) *Celebrity and Power: Fame in Contemporary Culture*. Minneapolis: University of Minnesota Press.

Martens, M. (2011) 'Transmedia teens: affect, immaterial labor, and user-generated content', *Convergence: The International Journal of Research into New Media Technologies*, 17 (1): 49–68.

Masmoudi, M. (1979) 'The new world information order', *Journal of Communication*, 29 (2): 172–185.

Mayer, V. (2011a) *Below the Line: Producers and Production Studies in the New Television Economy.* Durham, NC: Duke University Press.

Mayer, V. (2011b) 'Reality television's "classrooms": knowing, showing, and telling about social class in reality casting and the college classroom', in H. Wood and B. Skeggs (eds), *Reality Television and Class.* London: Palgrave Macmillan, pp. 185–196.

McCombs, M. and Shaw, D. (1972) 'Agenda setting function of mass media', *Public Opinion Quarterly*, 36 (2): 176–187.

McIntosh, J. (2012) 'ADmented reality: Google Glasses remixed with ads'. Retrieved from: www.rebelliouspixels.com/2012/admented-reality-google-glasses-remixed-with-google-ads (last accessed 8 September 2014).

McKnight, D. (2010) 'A change in the climate? The journalism of opinion at News Corporation', *Journalism*, 11 (6): 693–706.

McKnight, D. and Hobbs, M. (2011) '"You're all a bunch of pinkos": Rupert Murdoch and the politics of HarperCollins', *Media, Culture & Society*, 33: 835–850.

McNair, B. (1999) *An Introduction to Political Communication.* London: Routledge.

McNair, B. (2012) 'WikiLeaks, journalism and the consequences of chaos', *Media International Australia*, 144: 77–86.

McQuire, S. (2008) *The Media City: Media, Architecture and Urban Space.* London: Sage.

McRobbie, A. (2002) 'Clubs to companies: notes on the decline of political culture in speeded-up creative worlds', *Cultural Studies*, 16 (4): 516–531.

McRobbie, A. (2004) 'Post-feminism and popular culture', *Feminist Media Studies*, 4 (3): 255–264.

Meier, L. M. (2011) 'Promotional ubiquitous musics: recording artists, brands, and "rendering authenticity"', *Popular Music and Society*, 34 (4): 399–415.

Meyer, R. (2014) 'Everything we know about Facebook's secret mood manipulation experiment', *The Atlantic*. Retrieved from: www.theatlantic.com/technology/archive/2014/06/everything-we-know-about-facebooks-secret-mood-manipulation-experiment/373648/ (last accessed 24 September 2014).

Mills, C. W. (1959) *The Power Elite.* Oxford: Oxford University Press.

Montgomery, D. (2007) 'Barack Obama's on-point message man', *Washington Post.* Retrieved from: www.washingtonpost.com/wp-dyn/content/article/2007/02/14/AR2007021401812.html (last accessed 8 September 2014).

Moor, E. (2003) 'Branded spaces: the scope of new marketing', *Journal of Consumer Culture*, 39 (3): 41–60.

Morley, D. (1993) 'Active audience theory: pendulums and pitfalls', *Journal of Communication*, 43 (3): 13–18.

Morley, D. and Robins, K. (1995) *Spaces of Identity: Global Media, Electronic Landscapes and Cultural Boundaries*. London: Routledge.

Morozov, E. (2011) *The Net Delusion: The Dark Side of Internet Freedom*. New York: Public Affairs.

Morozov, E. (2013) 'My map or yours?', *Slate*. Retrieved from: www.slate.com/articles/technology/future_tense/2013/05/google_maps_personalization_will_hurt_public_space_and_engagement.html (last accessed 8 September 2014).

Muller, D. and Gawenda, M. (2010) 'Ethical free-for-all over media access to the fire zone', *Media International Australia*, 137: 71.

Muniz Jr, A. M. and O'Guinn, T. C. (2001) 'Brand community', *Journal of Consumer Research*, 27 (4): 412–432.

Nakamura, L. (2009) 'Don't hate the player, hate the game: the racialization of labor in World of Warcraft', *Critical Studies in Media Communication*, 26 (2): 128–144.

Napoli, P. M. (2010) *Audience Evolution: New Technologies and the Transformation of Media Audiences*. New York: Columbia University Press.

Napoli, P. (2014) 'On automation in media industries: integrating algorithmic media production into media industries scholarship', *Media Industries*, 1 (1): 33–38.

Nardi, B. and Kow, Y. M. (2010) 'Digital imaginaries: how we know what we (think we) know about Chinese gold farming', *First Monday*, 15 (6). Retrieved from: http://pear.accc.uic.edu/ojs/index.php/fm/article/view/3035/2566 (last accessed 17 September 2014).

Newman, B. (1994) *The Marketing of the President*. Thousand Oaks, CA: Sage.

Nielsen, R. and Vaccari, C. (2013) 'Do people "Like" politicians on Facebook? Not really. Large-scale direct candidate-to-voter online communication as an outlier phenomenon', *International Journal of Communication*, 7: 2333–2356.

Noelle-Neumann, E. (1973) 'Return to the concept of powerful mass media', in H. Eguchi and K. Sata (eds), *Studies in Broadcasting*. Tokyo: Nippon Hosa Kyokai, pp. 67–112.

Noelle-Neumann, E. (1991) 'The theory of public opinion: the concept of the spiral of silence', in J. A. Anderson (ed.), *Communication Yearbook 14*. Newbury Park, CA: Sage.

North, L. (2009) 'Rejecting the "F-word": how "feminism" and "feminists" are understood in the newsroom', *Journalism*, 10 (6): 739–757.

O'Connor, J. and Xin, G. (2006) 'A new modernity? The arrival of "creative industries" in China', *International Journal of Cultural Studies*, 9 (September): 271–283.

Ouellette, L. and Hay, J. (2008a) *Better Living through Reality TV: Television and Post-welfare Citizenship*. Malden: Blackwell Publishing.

Ouellette, L. and Hay, J. (2008b) 'Makeover television, governmentality and the good citizen', *Continuum: Journal of Media & Cultural Studies*, 22 (4): 471–484.

Palmer, D. (2012) 'iPhone photography: mediating visions of social space', in L. Hjorth, J. E. Burgess and I. Richardson (eds), *Studying Mobile Media: Cultural Technologies, Mobile Communication, and the iPhone*. New York: Routledge, pp. 85–97.

Papacharissi, Z. and de Fatima Oliveira, M. (2012) 'Affective news and networked publics: the rhythms of news storytelling on #Egypt', *Journal of Communication*, 62 (2): 266–282.

Pariser, E. (2011) *The Filter Bubble: What the Internet Is Hiding from You*. London: Penguin.

Parmentier, M. and Fischer, E. (2011) 'You can't always get what you want: unsustainable identity projects in the fashion system', *Consumption, Markets and Culture*, 14 (1): 7–27.

Pease, A. and Brewer, P. R. (2008) 'The Oprah factor: the effects of a celebrity endorsement in a presidential primary campaign', *International Journal of Press/Politics*, 13 (4): 386–400.

Peck, J. (2008) *The Age of Oprah: Cultural Icon for the Neoliberal Era*. Boulder, CO: Paradigm Publishers.

Peck, J. (2010) 'The secret of her success: Oprah Winfrey and the seductions of self-transformation', *Journal of Communication Inquiry*, 34 (1): 7–14.

Penfold-Mounce, R., Beer, D. and Burrows, R. (2011) 'The wire as social science-fiction?', *Sociology*, 45 (1): 152–167.

Perlin, R. (2012) *Intern Nation: How to Earn Nothing and Learn Little in the Brave New Economy*. London: Verso Books.

Pettinger, L. (2004) 'Brand culture and branded workers: service work and aesthetic labour in fashion retail', *Consumption, Markets and Culture*, 7 (2): 165–184.

Postman, N. (1987): *Amusing Ourselves to Death*. London: Methuen.

Potter, E. (2011) 'Drinking to live: the work of ethically branded bottled water', in T. Lewis and E. Potter (eds), *Ethical Consumption: A Critical Introduction*. London: Routledge, pp. 116–130.

Qiu, J. (2012) 'Network labor: beyond the shadow of Foxconn', in L. Hjorth, J. E. Burgess and I. Richardson (eds), *Studying Mobile Media: Cultural Technologies, Mobile Communication, and the iPhone*. New York: Routledge, pp. 173–189.

Rastogi, N. (2011) 'David Simon, creator of *The Wire*, speaks on Felicia "Snoop" Pearson's arrest', *Slate*. Retrieved from: www.slate.com/blogs/browbeat/2011/03/10/david_simon_creator_of_the_wire_speaks_on_felicia_snoop_pearson_s_arrest.html (last accessed 7 September 2014).

Rock, P. (1981) 'News as eternal recurrence', in S. Cohen and J. Young (eds), *The Manufacture of News*. London: Constable, pp. 64–70.

Rundle, G. (2010a) *The Shellacking: The Obama Presidency, the Tea Party, and the 2010 Midterm Elections*. London: K-ist books.

Rundle, G. (2010b) 'The topic is cancer: the 2010 election and the collapse of legitimacy', *Crikey*. Retrieved from: www.crikey.com.au/2010/08/10/rundle-the-topic-is-cancer-the-2010-election-and-the-collapse-of-political-legitimacy/ (last accessed 24 September 2014).

Sabato, L. J. (1981) *The Rise of Political Consultants: New Ways of Winning Elections*. New York: Basic Books.

Sabato, L. J. (1989) *Campaigns and Elections: A Reader in Modern Politics*. Glenview, IL: Scott, Foresman & Co.

Sabato, L. J (2013) *Barack Obama and the New America: The 2012 Election and the Changing Face of Politics*. Lanham, MD: Rowman & Littlefield.

Saussure, F. de (1974) *Course in General Linguistics*. London: Fontana.

Scammell, M. (1995) *Designer Politics: How Elections Are Won*. London: Palgrave Macmillan.

Schiller, H. (1969) *Mass Communication and the American Empire.* New York: Kelly.

Schlesinger, P. (2009) 'Creativity and the experts: New Labour, think tanks, and the policy process', *International Journal of Press/Politics*, 14: 3–20.

Seel, P. (2012) *Digital Universe: The Global Telecommunication Revolution.* Chichester: Blackwell-Wiley.

Selnow, G. W. (1994) *High-tech Campaigns: Computer Technology in Political Communication.* Westport, CT: Praeger.

Sherry, J. (1998) *Servicescapes: The Concept of Place in Contemporary Markets.* Lincolnwood, IL: NTC Business Books.

Simon, D. (2010) 'HBO's "Treme" creator David Simon explains it all for you', *The Times-Picayune*, 11 April. Retrieved from: www.nola.com/treme-hbo/index.ssf/2010/04/hbos_treme_creator_david_simon.html (last accessed 24 September 2014).

Smith, A. (1979) *The Newspaper: An International History.* London: Thames & Hudson.

Smith, H. (1989) *The Power Game: How Washington Works.* Glasgow: Fontana/Collins.

Smythe, D. (1981) *Dependency Road: Communications, Capitalism, Consciousness and Canada.* Norwood, NJ: Ablex.

Soley, L. C. (1992) *The News Shapers: The Sources Who Explain the News.* Westport, CT: Praeger.

Spitz, M. (2012) 'Your phone company is watching you', *TED*. Retrieved from: www.ted.com/talks/malte_spitz_your_phone_company_is_watching.html (last accessed 8 September 2014).

Steemers, J. (2014) 'Selling television: addressing transformations in the international distribution of television content', *Media Industries*, 1 (1): 44–49.

Street, J. (1997) *Politics and Popular Culture.* Cambridge: Polity Press.

Taylor, T. D. (2007) 'The changing shape of the culture industry; or, how did electronica music get into television commercials?', *Television & New Media*, 8 (3): 235–258.

Temple, M. (2006) 'Dumbing down is good for you', *British Politics*, 1 (2): 257–273.

Terranova, T. (2000) 'Free labor: producing culture for a digital economy', *Social Text*, 18 (2): 33–58.

Teurlings, J. (2010) 'Media literacy and the challenges of contemporary media culture: on savvy viewers and critical apathy', *European Journal of Cultural Studies*, 13 (3): 359–373.

Thomas, L. L. (2012) '"People want to see what happened": *Treme*, televisual tourism, and the racial remapping of post-Katrina New Orleans', *Television & New Media*, 13 (3): 213–224.

Thompson, C. J. and Arsel, Z. (2004) 'The Starbucks brandscape and consumers' (anticorporate) experiences of glocalization', *Journal of Consumer Research*, 31 (3): 631–642.

Thompson, J. B. (1995) *The Media and Modernity: A Social Theory of the Media.* Redwood City, CA: Stanford University Press.

Thompson, J. (2008) 'Apology, justice and respect: a critical defense of political apology', in M. Gibney, R. Howard-Hassmann, J. Coicaud and N. Steiner (eds), *The Age of Apology*. Philadelphia: University of Pennsylvania Press, pp. 31–44.

Tomlinson, J. (1991) *Cultural Imperialism: A Critical Introduction.* London: Pinter.

Tremblay, G. (2011) 'Creative statistics to support creative economy politics', *Media, Culture & Society*, 33: 289–298.

Trottier, D. (2011) 'Mutual transparency or mundane transgressions? Institutional creeping on Facebook', *Surveillance & Society*, 9 (1/2): 17–30.

Tuchman, G. (1978) *Making News*. New York: The Free Press.

Tunstall, J. (1978) *The Media Are American*. London: Constable.

Turkle, S. (1997) 'Multiple subjectivity and virtual community at the end of the Freudian century', *Sociological Inquiry*, 67 (1): 72–84.

Turner, G. (2006) 'The mass production of celebrity "Celetoids", reality TV and the "demotic turn"', *International Journal of Cultural Studies*, 9 (2): 153–165.

Turner, G. (2010) *Ordinary People and the Media*. London: Sage.

Turow, J. (1997) *Breaking Up America: Advertisers and the New Media World*. Chicago: University of Chicago Press.

Turow, J. (2011) *The Daily Me: How the Advertising Industry Is Defining Your Identity and Your Worth*. New Haven, CT: Yale University Press.

Turow, J., King, J., Hoofnagle, C. J., Bleakley, A. and Hennessy, M. (2009) 'Americans reject tailored advertising and three activities that enable it'. Available at SSRN 1478214. Retrieved from: http://papers.ssrn.com/sol3/Papers.cfm?abstract_id=1478214 (last accessed 10 September 2014).

Urry, J. (1990) 'The end of organised capitalism', in S. Hall and M. Jacques (eds), *New Times*. London: Verso, pp. 94–102.

Ursell, G. (2000) 'Television production: issues of exploitation, commodification and subjectivity in UK television labour markets', *Media, Culture & Society*, 22 (6): 805–825.

van Dijck, J. (2009) 'Users like you? Theorizing agency in user-generated content', *Media, Culture & Society*, 31 (1): 41–58.

van Dijck, J. (2011) 'Facebook as a tool for producing sociality and connectivity', *Television & New Media*, 13 (2): 160–176.

van Zoonen, L. (1998) 'A day at the zoo: political communication, pigs and popular culture', *Media, Culture & Society*, 20 (2): 183–200.

Volcic, Z. and Andrejevic, M. (2011) 'Nation branding in the era of commercial nationalism', *International Journal of Communication*, 5 (1): 598–618.

Volosinov, V. N. (1973) *Marxism and the Philosophy of Language*. New York: Seminar Press.

Von Klarwill, V. (1924) *The Fugger News-Letters*. London: The Bodley Head Ltd.

Warner, M. (2005) *Publics and Counterpublics*. New York: Zone Books.

Weber, M. (1978) *Economy and Society: An Outline of Interpretive Sociology*. Berkeley, CA: University of California Press.

Wernick, A. (1991) *Promotional Culture: Advertising, Ideology and Symbolic Expression*. London: Sage.

White, D. (1950) 'The "gatekeeper": a case study in the selection of news', *Journalism Quarterly*, 41: 383–370.

Wilken, R. (2014) 'Places nearby: Facebook as a location-based social media platform', *New Media & Society*, 1–17.

Williams, G. (1960) 'Gramsci's concept of "Egemonia"', *Journal of the History of Ideas*, 4: 586–599.

Wood, H. and Skeggs, B. (eds) (2011) *Reality Television and Class.* London: Palgrave Macmillan.

Zhang, L. (2006) 'Behind the "Great Firewall": decoding China's internet media policies from the inside', *Convergence*, 12: 271–291.

Žižek, S. (1989) *The Sublime Object of Ideology*. New York: Verso.

Žižek, S. (1999) *The Ticklish Subject.* New York: Verso

Žižek, S. (2008) *In Defense of Lost Causes*. New York: Verso Books.

Žižek, S. (2010a) *First as Tragedy, Then as Farce*. New York: Verso Books.

Žižek, S. (2010b) 'First as tragedy, then as farce', RSA Animate. Retrieved from: www.youtube.com/watch?v=hpAMbpQ8J7g (23 September 2014).

Zwick, D., Bonsu, S. and Darmody, A. (2008) 'Putting consumers to work: "co-creation" and new marketing govern-mentality', *Journal of Consumer Culture*, 8 (2): 163–197.

Zwick, D. and Knott, J. (2009) 'Manufacturing customers: the database as a new means of production', *Journal of Consumer Culture*, 9 (2): 221–247.

INDEX

Castells, M. (1996) *The Rise of the Network Society*. Oxford: Blackwell.

Chen, A. (2012) 'Inside Facebook's outsourced anti-porn and gore brigade, where 'camel toes' are more offensive than 'crushed heads' (that surfaced 16 September 2014)'.

Cheney-G. (2011b) 'Between image and information, the iPhone camera in the history of photography' in L. Pierson [...] and J. Richardson (eds), *Studying Mobile Media: Cultural Technologies, Mobile Communication and the iPhone*. New York: Routledge, pp. [...].

Chouliaraki, L. (2010) '[...] post-humanitarian communication beyond a politics of pity'. *International [...]* [...] 13(2): 107–126.

Chouliaraki, L. (2013) [...] *in the Age of Post-humanitarianism*. Cambridge: Polity.

Clark, J., Couldry, N., [...] and van Dijck, [...] (2014) [...]. *[...]*, [...] pp. 1446–1473.

Clough, P.T. [...].

Cohen, S. [...] *Social Theory* [...].

Couch, S.R. [...].

Cohen, S. [...].

Coleman [...].

[...] F. [...].

[...] B. (2010) [...].

[...] N. (2003) [...].

[...] (2003) [...].

[...] (2006) [...].

[...] (2015) 'Class [...] and P. [...].

Castells, M. (1996) *The Rise of the Network Society*. Oxford: Blackwell.

Chen, A. (2012) 'Inside Facebook's outsourced anti-porn and gore brigade, where "camel toes" are more offensive than "crushed heads"', *Gawker*. Retrieved from: http://gawker.com/5885714/inside-facebooks-outsourced-anti-porn-and-gore-brigade-where-camel-toes-are-more-offensive-than-crushed-heads (last accessed 8 September 2016).

Cheshers, C. (2012) 'Between image and information: the iPhone camera in the history of photography', in L. Hjorth, J. E. Burgess and I. Richardson (eds), *Studying Mobile Media: Cultural Technologies, Mobile Communication, and the iPhone*. New York: Routledge. pp. 98–117.

Chouliaraki, L. (2010) 'Post-humanitarism: humanitarian communication beyond a politics of pity', *International Journal of Cultural Studies*, 13 (2): 107–126.

Chouliaraki, L. (2013) *The Ironic Spectator: Solidarity in the Age of Post-Humanitarianism*. Cambridge: Polity.

Clark, J., Couldry, N., Kosnik, A., Gillespie, T., Jenkins, H., Kelty, C., Papacharissi, Z., Powers, A. and van Dijck, J. (eds) (2014) 'Participations: dialogues on the participatory promise of contemporary culture and politics, Part 5: Platforms', *International Journal of Communication*, (Forum): 1446–1473.

Clough, P. T. (2008) 'The affective turn: political economy, biomedia and bodies', *Theory, Culture & Society*, 25 (1): 1–22.

Clough, P. T. (2009) 'The new empiricism: affect and sociological method', *European Journal of Social Theory*, 12 (1): 43–61.

Clough, P. T., Goldberg, G., Schiff, R., Weeks, A. and Willse, C. (2007) 'Notes towards a theory of affect-itself', *Ephemera: Theory and Politics in Organization*, 7 (1): 60–77.

Cohen, B. C. (1963) *The Press and Foreign Policy*. Princeton, NJ: Princeton University Press.

Coleman, S. (2005) 'New mediation and direct representation: reconceptualizing representation in the digital age', *New Media & Society*, 7 (2): 177–198.

Collins, F. L. (2009) 'Connecting "home" with "here": personal homepages in everyday transnational lives', *Journal of Ethnic and Migration Studies*, 35 (6): 839–859.

Connell, R. (2007) *Reading back at American Multiculturalism*. New York: Routledge.

Couldry, N. (2000) *The Place of Media Power: Pilgrims and Witnesses of the Media Age*. London: Routledge.

Couldry, N. (2008a) *Media Rituals: A Critical Approach*. London: Routledge.

Couldry, N. (2008b) '… mediatization or mediation? alternative understandings ...'

Couldry, N. (2012) *Media, Society, World: Social Theory and Digital Media Practice*. Cambridge: Polity.

Couldry, N. and Hepp, A. (2013) 'Conceptualizing mediatization: contexts, traditions, arguments', *Communication Theory*, 23 (3): 191–202.